An Arrow in the Earth

AN ARROW
IN THE
EARTH

General Joel Palmer and the Indians of Oregon

TERENCE O'DONNELL

Oregon Historical Society Press

FRONTIS: Joel Palmer, 1810–1881 (*Illustration by Karen Beyers*)

Support for the research, writing, editing, design, and production of this volume was generously provided in part by Omar C. Palmer, William J. Lang, the William Bowerman Fund of the Oregon Community Foundation, and the Oregon Historical Society's Thomas Vaughan Fund for publication in Oregon Country history.

Second printing, paperback, 1992

LIBRARY OF CONGRESS CATALOGING-IN-PUBLICATION DATA

O'Donnell, Terence.
  An Arrow in the earth : General Joel Palmer and the Indians of
  Oregon / Terence O'Donnell.
    p.   cm.
  Includes bibliographical references and index.
  ISBN 0-87595-156-2
    1. Palmer, Joel, 1810-1881. 2. Indians of North America—Oregon—
  Wars. 3. Pacific Coast Indians, Wars with, 1847-1865. 4. Indian
  agents—Oregon—Biography. 5. Generals—United States—Biography.
  6. Oregon—History—To 1859. I. Title.
  E83.84.P35O36 1991
  973.6'092—dc20
  [B]   90-28778
                                                                   CIP

Designed and produced by the Oregon Historical Society Press.

The paper used in this publication meets the minimum requirements of American National Standard for Information Sciences—Permanence of Paper for Printed Library Materials, ANSI Z39.48-1984.

Printed in the United States of America.

Where the arrow falls, let those who died come to life.
FROM A WILLAMETTE VALLEY INDIAN LEGEND

Contents

Acknowledgments

THOMAS VAUGHAN and Slug Palmer in their interest and support were the progenitors as well as the patient sustainers of this study of General Palmer.

In researching the General's life I was much aided by the staff of the Oregon Historical Society, in particular Layne Woolschlager, Priscilla Knuth, Margaret Haines, Johnyne Wascavage, Steven Hallberg, Elizabeth Winroth, and the late Gordon Manning. Hillary Cummings of the library of the University of Oregon was most helpful, as was Dr. Gordon Dodds of Portland State University. Stanley Sheldon Spaid's 1950 University of Oregon Ph.D. thesis on General Palmer was an invaluable guide. Ruth Stoller of Lafayette, Oregon, was an important source of Yamhill County history, the county in which the General resided, while Dilly and Martha Krake kindly permitted me to tour their house, built by and formerly the home of General Palmer in Dayton, Oregon. Much of the manuscript was typed under difficult circumstances by Edna Nitz, and I am most grateful to her. I wish to express thanks as well to Sheila Henry of Dayton, Oregon, for her kind gift of transcriptions of Palmer diaries. Priscilla Knuth, Bruce Taylor Hamilton, Rick Harmon, Robert Boyd, and the late Malcolm Clark, Jr., read the manuscript and made useful suggestions for its improvement. Likewise, the study has much benefited from the work of the editors, Lori McEldowney and Bruce Taylor Hamilton, and the designer, George T. Resch. Their patience is to be commended as well.

Finally, this study could not have been published without the generosity of Slug Palmer, William Bowerman, and William L. Lang.

An Arrow in the Earth

Prologue

THE HOUSE STILL STANDS, rectangular, white, pitch-roofed, set back from Ferry Street, on the outskirts of town. The proportions are those of the Classic Revival style, serene and simple, the style much favored in the 1850s when he built the house.

Ferry Street takes its name from the fact that it ends at the banks of the Yamhill River where, many years ago, there was a ferry slip. Between the riverbank and the house lies the town, Ferry Street bisecting it. To one side is the public square he gave to the town, hoping the county would put a courthouse there. Today, unkempt, it looks like a little prairie, clumped here and there with fir and oak. On its far side a blockhouse stands, beyond the blockhouse the spire of a church. Across the street, fronting the square, is the town's "business block," turn-of-the-century buildings, two and three stories high, plain but staunch.

It is an exact chronology. The little prairie with its clumps of fir and oak, much as it was when he and the other whites arrived, then the blockhouse, next the church, finally post office, general store, lodge hall, bank, and—coming right down to now—a video store.

Beyond the square and the business block, east across the river, is French Prairie where, in the 1830s, French-Canadian trappers settled down, seeding wheat and children. West lies a little valley called the Grand Ronde, where he gathered the valley Indians and where some still live. Rising to the north are the red hills of Dundee, planted to orchards, prunes, and nuts. Finally, stretching south, the Willamette's long and lovely valley. This is the town of Dayton, Oregon, which he founded, and this the world in which it lies.

On its way to the river, beyond the business block, Ferry Street intersects Highway 221. A few hundred feet along the highway, a road—really no more than a track, so seldom is it used—leads off to the right, soon petering out at a broken gate. Beyond the gate lies a slope of land ending at a creek. This is the Dayton graveyard which, like the square, he gave to the town as well.

One day in the spring of 1881, they brought his body from the house, down Ferry Street, and buried him here. The mourners, coming from near and far, came not so much to mourn him—for he was old—as to honor him for having embodied their best ideals. "Few men, in this or any other country, have labored harder or more disinterestedly for the public good," said Judge Matthew Deady, the state's—and one of the nation's—most eminent nineteenth-century jurists.[1] What was this public good and who the man who fostered it?

With one tragic exception, ours has been a tranquil past. Unlike some states, we never knew the tumult of revolution. Unlike many more, we did not pass through the bitterness of civil war. Race and labor conflicts happened in other places. The Great Depression only grazed us. In general, Oregon history has been a summer's afternoon spent on the banks of a pretty river; but for that one, grievous exception, that five-act tragedy called the Indian wars of Oregon, those thirty years of butchery that bloodied, and stained for good, our beginnings.

The man they now lowered into his grave had passed redemptively through that carnage, for he had believed—and many did not—that the public good of justice and peace must embrace Indian as well as white. That was what Judge Deady meant, and that was the reason the mourners had come from near and far to honor him.

After the mourners left, a granite shaft was raised above his grave. Now, more than a century later, it is a trifle aslant, like an arrow in the earth, and its epitaph dim, like a memory fading. Still, the words are not quite worn away and, when the light is right, can still be read: "General Joel Palmer, born October 4, 1810..."

ONE

From the Blackwater
to the Whitewater

A T A PLACE called Elizabethtown in Canada, across the border from Niagara Falls, the man beneath the stone was born. His parents, Ephraim and Anna, his brother, Fenner, his sister, Polly, had come there seven years before from New York state. They were ninth-generation Americans, descendants of Walter Palmer and William Phelps, both of whom had docked at Plymouth in the 1630s.

Ephraim, like most men of the time, could turn his hand to many things—in his case farming, basketry, preaching, carpentry, and making potash. It was the latter that took him to Canada where, on the banks of the St. Lawrence, he boiled wood ash to leach from it the potash used in making glass and gunpowder. But Joel Palmer could not have remembered any of this, for when he was two, the family fled—probably the only time in his life he had anything to do with flight.

The cause was the War of 1812. The Palmers crossed the St. Lawrence to the safety of the American naval base at Sackets Harbor on Lake Ontario and from there traveled to Lowville, a village in the Blackwater Valley of northern New York. The region was still unsettled, and from the beginning, Palmer experienced the conditions of frontier life.

Then, one day when he was twelve, he left. Ephraim, a Quaker, often traveled the country establishing meetings and engaging in other Quaker works. On this occasion, Joel went along. Near the village of Jefferson in the Catskills, they spent the night with the Haworths, a Quaker couple who took a fancy to Joel. By now, Ephraim had nine children whom he may have found

3

a burden to support in view of his roving ways. Whatever the reason, Joel was bound out, a form of indentured service, to the Haworths for the customary four years.

According to Timothy Dwight, the peripatetic president of Yale at the time, the region of Joel's new home was "singularly shaggy, wild and horrid."[1] How Palmer found it is unknown, but in any event, it was there in those deep, stream-bottomed glens of the Catskills that he spent the formative years of twelve to sixteen.

Barring one significant fact, little can be said of these important years except by supposition. Like most boys, bound or free, he must have done the routine chores—carted apples to the mill, plucked the geese, hived the bees, gone hunting for the wildcats after which the mountains had been named. He may also have scraped hides, for by now a number of tanneries had sprung up at the edges of the Catskills' hemlock forests. It was foul work, and perhaps that was another reason why he left.

The principal reason, however, was probably something else. When he was an old man, Palmer told historian Hubert Howe Bancroft that, during his stay with the Haworths, he attended school for three months—the only schooling he ever had—and that his classmates taunted him for being a bound boy. "I could not bear [it]. I had asperations above my prospects."[2] When he was sixteen years old, he left the Catskills, and for good.

When Palmer arrived in Philadelphia in 1826, it was no longer Penn's "greene country towne" but a red-brick city of one hundred thousand. Here, Palmer took work on a canal project and remained, he told Bancroft, "until I was grown to manhood and married a wife."[3] That marriage was in 1830 to Catherine Caffee who, after the birth of a daughter, died. In 1836 Palmer married again, this time to fifteen-year-old Sarah Ann Derbyshire. Sarah Ann came from an old Bucks County Quaker family of comfortable means (perhaps the kind of alliance Palmer had in mind when he said that he had aspirations above his prospects).

It may have been aspiration as well that led Palmer and his bride to leave Philadelphia in the year of their marriage for the Whitewater Valley of Indiana—west again. Their route took them from Philadelphia to Pittsburgh by canal and rail and then down the Ohio River by riverboat to Cincinnati. From there they traveled north some forty miles to the village of Laurel in Indiana's Whitewater Valley. Named for its river, the valley runs south near that state's eastern border with Ohio. When the Palmers arrived, the slopes and crests of the valley walls were still thick with oak and black gum, walnut, ash,

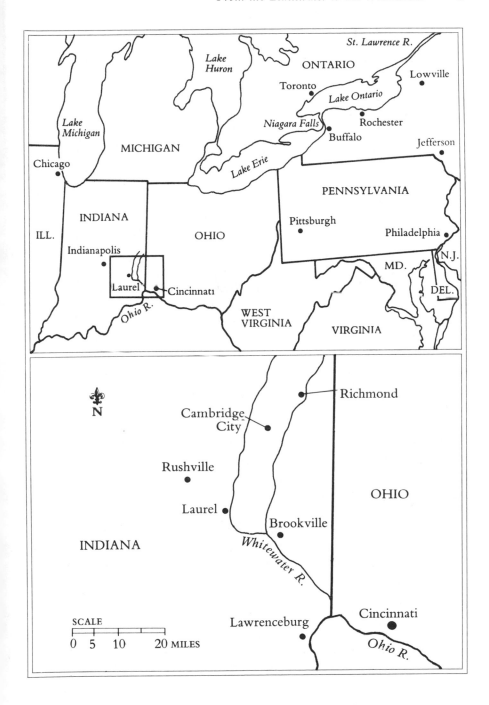

and hickory. But the bottomlands had been partially cleared and grew fine crops of wheat and corn and a tobacco that could not be matched. Down through the center of the valley, between banks of tiger lilies, wild roses, and pennyroyal, swept the shallow, tumbling river. It was as pretty a place as they could have hoped.

The valley had drawn emigrants since the beginning of the century, but they were men who liked to hunt instead of till and who, along with the Indians, left the land much as they found it. The Indians remained in semipossession, and blockhouses were erected in 1812 out of fear of them. It was in those years that Indians killed a man and a boy who were boiling sap in the woods near Laurel. Finally, in 1818, the Indians ceded the last of their land.

In time, a people very different from the Indians and the vagrant hunters came into the valley: sober, industrious, gentle, and—for the times—well off. These were Quakers, from the South mainly, searching for better land and places not fouled by slavery. By 1816, there were ten thousand in the valley, and they had established at Richmond, their principal town, what came to be called "the Quakers' Jerusalem." Though their righteous ways by no means extinguished the boisterous frontier spirit, they were a sobering influence. An aspirant for governorship in 1825 was much condemned on the grounds of ostentation for having put a Palladian window in his house.

That Palladian window signifies as well as anything that the frontier was passing, and by 1836, when the Palmers arrived, it was almost gone. Bear and deer were scarce, coonskin caps were few. There were a fair number of women around who cooked on stoves and men who wore silk stocks. When the Palmers arrived in Laurel, they found an academy where Greek and Latin—along with the flute—were taught. Downstream a few miles, at Brookville, lived a group of men—senators, governors, judges—who formed a galaxy of some brilliance in the empyrean of the West.

It was, then, a diverse society to which the Palmers came: the proper Quaker farmers, the rowdy squatters and their ilk, the silk-stocked lawyers and politicians. Diverse, yet not stratified, for the valley was still a social democracy in which every man thought himself as good as another, whatever he might wear around his neck, homespun wool or silk. This made for social contacts between different kinds of men, loitering at the courthouse, the store, the grogshop. And Palmer, no recluse, was certainly there among them, learning about these different kinds of men and how to judge them. And it was a knowledge to which much would be added by the two very different careers he followed in his years in the Whitewater Valley.

IN THE FIRST HALF of the nineteenth century, canal building was much promoted. There were good reasons for this. In many cases, canals provided transport where none had existed, and in almost all cases, it was cheaper than cartage rates. In the Whitewater, for example, there was no way of getting the valley's produce to market except during the spring freshets, when flour, lard, pork, wheat, and whiskey were loaded onto flatboats and sent downriver to New Orleans. But the spring freshets were brief.

Thus, in the Whitewater desire for a canal was strong. "With it," a Richmond newspaper wrote, "our course will be upward and without it our city will become a deserted village . . . . With it our streets will be the avenues of traffic, without grass will grow upon its sidewalks."

In June 1836, the Indiana legislature finally acted—disastrously as it turned out—by authorizing the state to borrow ten million dollars for internal improvements. One of these improvements was to be the Whitewater Canal, from Cambridge City, where the National Road crossed the Whitewater, through Laurel and Brookville to Lawrenceburg on the Ohio. And it was Joel Palmer who was given the contract to oversee a long section of the canal's construction.

All told, a thousand men were hired to build the canal, to clear the land and dig the channel, to rock the banks and construct the locks. By June 1839, the canal reached from the Ohio to Brookville. The next section to be built lay between Brookville and Laurel, but work had hardly begun when the governor announced that the interest on the state debt now amounted to two hundred thousand dollars, whereas state revenues were less than fifty thousand dollars. Work on the canal stopped, "which left me with a large force of men and materials,"[4] Palmer told historian Hubert Howe Bancroft. And indeed, he and the other contractors must have been in a most difficult position, having purchased materials for which there was now no use and recruited workers to whom, in many cases, back wages were due.

How Palmer handled the crisis we do not know. He himself simply says that he "took to farming." But it must have been in an equitable fashion, or else his neighbors had very short memories, for three years later, in 1843, "the people took a notion into their heads to send me to the legislature."[5]

Indiana politics had long been dominated by the Whigs. With the disastrous failure of the internal improvement program, however, power began to pass to the Democrats. And it was as a Democrat that Palmer represented Franklin County. In his first term, he served on a committee for which he was decidedly qualified: the Canals and Internal Improvements Committee. It was this committee no doubt that was responsible for the resumption of work on the Whitewater Canal in 1842. Returned for a second term in 1844-45, Palmer served on the State Bank Committee, an indication of his stature, for no legislative committee was of greater importance.

By 1845, Palmer was a substantial man in a substantial place. Laurel, through which the canal now passed, had doubled in population and was a prosperous and pleasing town. Nearby quarries, which produced the best blue limestone in Indiana, had supplied the stone for the canal basin as well as several of the town's principal buildings. There was the Laurel Academy, for example, and the Whitehall Tavern, the latter a snug little building on a hill with turfed limestone terraces descending to the towpath. There was, too, "the great stone barn" built at the canal basin and commodious enough to stable seventy horses—this for the use of the farmers bringing their produce to ship by canal to market. At the north end of the town an Indian mound rose some 150 feet, and here, a bandstand was erected. From this eminence, the view was said to be the loveliest in Indiana—the stone town at the bend of the river, the rolling farmlands beyond.

Like most canal towns, Laurel could be a rowdy place, the rowdiness drawn both from the locals and from the Irish and German immigrants brought in to work on the canal. But the town had its cultivated side as well. There was the academy, a lyceum, perhaps a library, certainly a debating club. At the debating club the eloquence of a Lincoln or a Douglas could be approached and, on occasion, equaled by men like Palmer who, though they may have had little formal education, had read much in the classics and the King James Bible and, thus, had a command of the language now gone from American public life.

This, then, was Palmer only a decade or so removed from the bound boy in the hollows of the Catskills, now in a long-tailed, brass-buttoned coat, brocaded vest, polished boots, moving back and forth between his fertile valley with its handsome, prosperous town, the assembly rooms of Cincinnati, the halls of the legislature. A good life in a good place, one would have thought. But he left.

A DESIRE TO SEE the Oregon Country may have been in the back of Palmer's mind for some time, as it was in the minds of many men after they had heard of it. Robert Gray, the American privateer turned merchant adventurer, brought the first news of Oregon following his discovery of the Columbia

River in 1792. Later came the official reports of Meriwether Lewis and William Clark, colorfully supplemented by trappers' tales told in the grogshops of Missouri.

By the 1830s and 1840s, there were a number of published accounts. Missionaries had established a colony of sorts in Oregon and had reported on it in their national journals. Also, Washington Irving's book on Astoria and Benjamin Bonneville's reports had been published.

After reading the journals of Lewis and Clark, Hall Kelley determined to found a new republic in the Northwest. To this end, he published considerable promotional material on Oregon, founded the American Society for the Settlement of Oregon in the 1830s, and sent several memorials to Congress urging United States sovereignty over Oregon.

In 1836, President Jackson sent Lt. William Slacum to Oregon to report on the nature of the country and its settlement. Slacum's extensive report was later used to support United States claims to the Oregon Country. In 1838, Lt. Charles Wilkes took command of the United States Exploring Expedition, which reached Oregon in 1841. The expedition's reports, as well as the memorials from the settlers that Wilkes brought back to Congress, also played a part in the U.S. claim to the Oregon Country.

And finally, in 1843, Thomas Farnham's engaging and widely circulated *Travels in the Great Western Prairies* was published. Farnham came to Oregon with the Peoria party in 1839. He, too, brought petitions to Congress from American settlers in Oregon asking for a U.S. presence.

All told, it was a large body of work for a place so remote. The accounts were of a mixed nature, however: a compound of some truth, much fancy, and many contradictions. Nonetheless, the general message was that this far corner of the continent was a place of milk and honey waiting for settlers.

The notion was rejected for a time. People were not so sure. There was plenty of land at home, no need for more. The crossing would be a hardship, if not fatal to women and children. Finally, how could troops, if required, be moved with dispatch to a place so distant?

One newspaper called the Rocky Mountains "the half-way house between civilization and despair." Horace Greeley deemed emigration "an aspect of insanity" and prophesied that nine-tenths of the 1843 migration would not reach the Columbia River alive.

But they did. As Senator Lewis Linn of Missouri had insisted some years before, even "delicate females" could cross the Rockies. After all, the ascent of South Pass was no more arduous, John Frémont claimed, than a carriage ride from Massachusetts Avenue up to Capitol Hill! Letters from the emigrants of 1843 and 1844 did not suggest that the trek was without travail, but they did indicate that it could be done without significant losses. In short, the accessibility of the Oregon Country was finally established.

The next question was whether getting there was worth it. Although accounts differed, most agreed that there was an abundance of good soil in prairies that required no clearing; unlimited stands of timber; plentiful water in river and spring for transport, power, and irrigation; a long seaboard for trade; a climate both gentle and salubrious; and finally, a landscape remarkable for its beauty. In other words, Oregon was Eden. Some, in parodying these high claims, declared that a tack planted in Oregon would come up a spike and that the Oregon pig was born cooked and already equipped with knife and fork.

Other considerations also beckoned the potential settler. In 1843, a provisional government was formed, which meant there was now a civil code of sorts in Oregon. One particularly inviting provision guaranteed free land to any who might settle there. It was noted, too, that many members of the provisional government were missionaries, or in other words, it was a respectable place—unlike riffraffish California. Finally, in February 1845, the U.S. House of Representatives by a large majority passed a bill calling for territorial status for Oregon. It was true, of course, that since 1818, the region had been subject to the joint occupancy of Great Britain and the United States. But this was a temporary expediency until such time as the conflicting claims of the two nations might be resolved. It was an expediency most galling to the typically Anglophobic American, and thus this legislation that looked toward the eventual expulsion of the detested British and United States sovereignty encouraged emigration.

These, then, were some of the reasons for going. But there were also reasons for leaving the States. Perhaps the most compelling of these was health. The river valleys of the border states, where most of the emigrants lived, were thoroughly pestiferous. In the early 1840s, ravaging epidemics of erysipelas and cholera had occurred, while malaria, tuberculosis, ague, and the "puking fever" were endemic. Much of the disease was due to the frequent flooding of the rivers, particularly the flood of 1844. And the flooding destroyed not only bodies but also buildings, bridges, dikes, and fields.

Then, too, many men, though not many women, yearned for the adventures of a virgin land. Indiana historian John Dillon, writing in 1843, observed that those who now wished to share in the excitement and danger of a frontier life would have to travel far toward the setting sun.

Finally, there were the odd personal reasons. Some were fleeing debt, a few perhaps from a harpy wife, and certainly there were those who feared the sheriff. One old man said he had heard the fishing was good in Oregon; another said that his purpose was to burn down the British Fort Vancouver.

But of all the reasons for going or leaving, the most pervasive was the old American restlessness. A.B. Guthrie, in his superb fictional account of the 1845 crossing, speaks of "the onwardness of its people, their yondering," and one of his characters puts it most succinctly, "just to git where I ain't."[6]

Restlessness no doubt played a part in Palmer's departure as well. Like many emigrants, he had been moving since childhood—to the Catskills, Philadelphia, the Whitewater—roughly every ten years, about the same as the average American today. And surely most of the other reasons common to the migration were also his. In addition, there were reasons peculiar to his own circumstances. He may very well have reached the conclusion that the frequent flooding of the Whitewater would in time destroy the canal and with it Laurel's prosperity—two events that in fact did occur within a few years. There was also the circumstance that never before—or since—were Indiana's finances in worse shape. And indeed, what was true for the state was more or less true for the entire region, which the 1840 census had shown to be the poorest in the United States. In other words, the prospects were poor.

There were, as well, several incidental factors that may have teased Palmer on. The Cincinnati *Chronicle*, the major newspaper available to him, strongly favored emigration. A few miles upstream from Laurel, the National Road passed westward, and there, in the spring, Palmer would have seen wagon after wagon on its way. And like many men of the time, Palmer had debts, and to him—as to others—migration with free land at the end of it may have seemed the best possibility of repaying them. But there was something else that could be even more lucrative on the frontier—political office—and Palmer was, after all, a politician, ready and willing. All in all, then, there were plenty of reasons for Palmer to leave the Whitewater and go to Oregon.

But to do so with prudence. He was not the kind of man to believe all he heard or read, knowing that more than the characteristics of Oregon pigs had been exaggerated. Accordingly, and unlike most, he left his wife and children home while he investigated, when, as he laconically put it to Bancroft, "I took a notion to go to Oregon just to see the country."[7] A few years later, this most offhanded statement of purpose resulted in his *Journal of Travels over the Rocky Mountains*, a book that many judge to be the best description of the Trail ever written, and of its destination, the Willamette Valley of the mid-1840s.

T W O

To Oregon

I STARTED . . . on the morning of the 16th of April, 1845," Palmer's journal begins. But it was with sorrow and uncertainty that he began his journey, sorrow in leaving his family, uncertainty about the journey's result. Both questions, however, were soon settled by his perennial high spirits and optimism, for he decided, "I was right, hoped for the best and pressed onward."[1]

Accompanied by a friend, Spencer Buckley, Palmer set out with a wagon and team of horses, "favored with a pleasant day."[2] And it may have been now that Palmer began taking notes for his projected book. At the nearby town of Rushville, they had expected to be joined by several other men, but the men had grown faint of heart, as had others in Indianapolis who had promised to join Palmer. Finally, Palmer and Buckley went on alone, crossing in three weeks the breadth of Illinois and Missouri to arrive on 6 May at Independence, Missouri, and the United States border.

Independence* was the primary outfitting town for the emigrants, and they usually remained there for several days. Palmer, learning that the main body of emigrants had already departed, hurriedly laid in supplies and left almost immediately. His first night on the trail was at a camp occupied by four other Oregon-bound wagons. The men of these wagons were so loudly drunk, Palmer reported, that it was not until midnight that "I wrapped myself in my blanket, laid down under an oak tree, and began to realize that I was on my journey to Oregon."[3]

* *Independence often was called that "great Babel upon the border of the wilder-ness" and is said to have been named for Andrew Jackson's principal trait.*

It took four days for Palmer and his companions—he and Buckley had been joined by a "clever backwoodsman" named Dodson—to reach the main body of emigrants. En route through what was now Indian country, only one incident of note occurred. A band of Indian ponies cantered through their camp and so excited the party's own horses and mules that many broke loose to follow the ponies. Palmer and Dodson pursued in a chase that Palmer jocularly described as a contest between "the rights of *property* on the one side, and the rights of *liberty* on the other." In the end, property lost, and the party was obliged "to suffer the mules freely and forever to enjoy the enlarged liberty which they had so nobly won."[4] Palmer's telling of this incident suggests a man who could accept adversity with humor and good grace.

On 11 May, just as night was falling, Palmer and his companions saw in the rolling prairie distance a scattering of fires. It was the main body of emigrants, 232 wagons in all and called the St. Louis Division.

Palmer's first night with the division was a lively one and suggests something of the character of these early Oregonians. Shortly after his arrival, guards were posted who, "becoming tired of their monotonous round of duty, amused themselves by shooting several dogs, and by so doing excited no small tumult in the company."[5]

There was turmoil the following night as well, though of a different kind. The heavens opened to loose on the emigrants a maelstrom of thunder, lightning, hail, and rain. The division's three thousand head of cattle bolted in terror and were gathered with difficulty. On the next day, however, the emigrants engaged in the most tumultuous activity of all: giving the division a government of officers and laws.* The creation of ad hoc governments was the practice of all the Oregon Trail migrations. In part this was done for reasons of defense, in part to forestall anarchy, since no civil authority existed in the region through which they were to pass. The character of these governments was determined by the persuasions of the emigrants making up each group. Some constitutions forbade travel on the Sabbath; others did not. Some required that every man carry a Bible, while others laid down the quantity of whiskey each wagon might be allowed. Common to almost all the governments, however, including that created by Palmer's division, were penalties for specific crimes. Murder earned a hanging; rapists suffered thirty-nine lashes on their backs for three days in succession; fornicators the same but for one day only; thieves also drew thirty-nine lashes, plus a fine. There were, in

* *Divisions usually delayed the election of officers until they had been on the trail for several days, perhaps because the emigrants needed time to size each other up.*

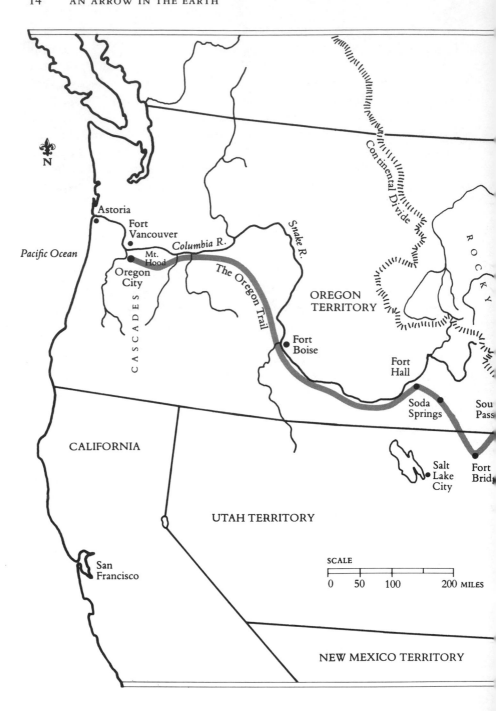

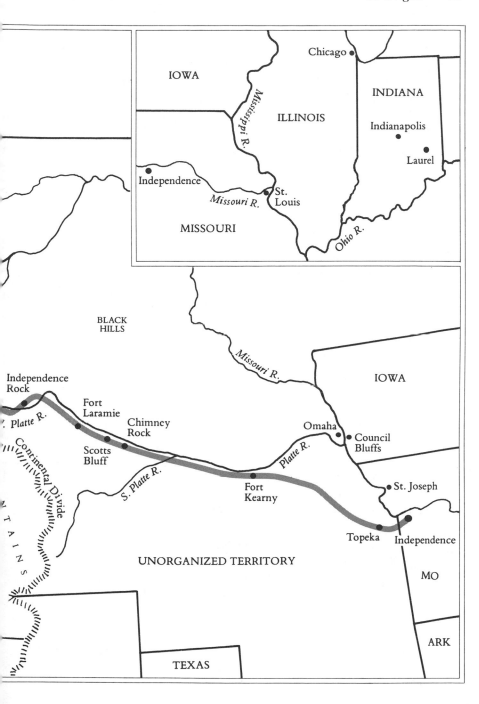

addition, a number of minor offenses—sleeping while on guard duty, for example, and obscene conversation. In general, there was concern that, as one pioneer put it, "we not degenerate into a state of barbarians."[6]

The St. Louis Division stopped for its deliberations at Big Soldier Creek in present-day Topeka. William H. Rector, who joined the division a day after Palmer, provides an interesting gloss on these legislative activities:

> It was my thoughts at the start that we would all bee like one great and good family of brothers and sisters relying on each other for asistance in times of nedd and as a common defence against the Indians should we be atacted by them. but in all this I was sorely disapointed. when we overtook the main company they were quarleing holding meetings, makeing new laws and regulations which ware not respected for one day, many of them would transgress just to show their independance or perverse cusedness.

Rector also provides an explanation for this independence:

> I noticed that most of the troubles originated with those that had lived in retired places they ware apt to think their wrights ware intruded upon or that sombody had got in their way whilest those from towns or more dencely populated places ware acustomed to being jostled in a crowd without complaining.[7]

Palmer in commenting on these organizing activities of his division concentrated on the election of officers. This was a matter of more importance than regulations, for it was the force of individual men rather than abstract directives that influenced the emigrants—when they were influenced at all. The officers elected consisted of a captain, four lieutenants, four judges, three inspectors, and a pilot. It was the choice of the last official that occasioned the most controversy and, indeed, confusion.

The contest for this office was between a Mr. Adams and Stephen Meek, a former trapper. In the midst of deliberations Meek, according to Palmer, ran into the camp to warn that Indians were driving off the division's cattle. According to Palmer, this intelligence caused the utmost confusion:

> motions and propositions, candidates and their special friends, were alike disregarded; *rifles* were grasped and *horses* were hastily mounted, and away we all galloped in pursuit.[8]

The pursuit led to a Kansa village where the Indians, seeing this array of armed whites galloping down in fury upon them, fled in all directions. The chiefs, however, retained their composure and "came forward, greeted our party kindly, and by signs offered to smoke the pipe of peace." They also protested their innocence. This the majority of the whites accepted, and it would have been the end of the affair but for the arrival of a lone Indian who, for some reason, aroused the whites' suspicion. Accordingly, he was hauled off to the division camp and there

> arraigned at the bar for trial, and the solemn interrogatory, "Are you guilty or not guilty," was propounded to him: but to this, his only answer was—a grunt, the import of which the honorable court not being able clearly to comprehend, his trial was formerly commenced and duly carried through.

The Indian was found innocent, and after the whites apologized to him for any inconvenience caused him and offered him some food and a smoke, of which he partook, he departed.[9]

Palmer concludes the telling of this incident with the reflection that "after . . . the affair was calmly considered, it was believed by most of us that the false alarm in regard to the Indians had been raised with the design of breaking up or postponing the election."[10] It was not the last time that Palmer was to see whites use Indians for their own purposes.

Whatever the machinations behind the election of the pilot, Meek in the end was chosen, and now, with all offices and laws in place—however temporarily—the emigration was ready to make its official departure.

Who were the emigrants of the St. Louis Division? All told, there were about a thousand—half adults, half children—and of the adults, twice as many men as women. The preponderance of men was due to the fact that many families employed single men as drovers and to the presence of men like Palmer and his friends traveling on their own.

Most of the men were farmers and thus in contrast to their predecessors, the mountain men. "They didn't talk beaver and whisky and squaws . . . they talked crops and water power and business," writes Guthrie in *The Way West*.[11] And indeed, most were men of at least some means—a few even brought along their slaves—for it took money to buy the gear to get to Oregon. Almost all were from the border states—old Americans—not foreign immigrants, and almost all were Protestants. One of their number, however, Andrew Rodgers, believed the division lacked religious zeal. This may have been the case, for out of the division's twenty-six Sabbaths on the trail, only one was observed with rest.

In general, the division appears to have been a fairly homogeneous group, these American border state, Protestant farmers—yet there were differences. "Almost every variety of men are to be met with," wrote Jacob Snyder in his memoirs of the division. And A. F. Davidson found that to one who could enjoy the scenery of Nature, there was always much to interest and amuse. There were some, however, that neither the works of God, nor man, would interest. They would lie in their wagons, sleeping half the day, neglect to keep their wagons in repair, indulge in sawmill appetites, and grumble. There were differences among the women, too, Sarah Jane Walden, for example, complaining that from some women she heard "rude phrases . . . humiliating to refined ears."[12]

But no one gives a better picture of the division's variety than does Palmer himself.

> An unoccupied spectator, who could have beheld our camp to-day, would think it a singular spectacle . . . . At two of the tents the fiddle was employed in uttering its unaccustomed voice among the solitudes . . . . at one tent I heard singing; at others the occupants were engaged in reading, some the Bible, others poring over novels. While all this was going on, that nothing might be wanting to complete the harmony of the scene, a Campbellite preacher . . . was reading a hymn, preparatory to religious worship. The fiddles were silenced, and those who had been occupied with that amusement, betook themselves to cards. Such is but a miniature of the great world we left behind us, when we crossed the line that separates civilized man from the wilderness. But even here the variety of occupation, the active exercise of body and mind, either in labor or pleasure, the commingling of evil and good, show that the likeness is a true one.[13]

ON THE MORNING OF 14 MAY, the emigrants struck camp at Big Soldier Creek and started out for the six-month, two-thousand-mile journey, ready as they could be. Most had brought along at least two changes of clothing, for in Oregon there was neither flax nor cotton and little wool. The men favored red or blue flannel shirts, denim trousers stuffed into cowhide boots, broad-brimmed black-glazed hats, wide belts with bullet pouches and powder horns together with knives and firearms. When the rains came, a few cut a figure in India rubber capes. The women wore the usual sunbonnets and dresses of calico or gingham, with a bodice that would unbutton for nursing, and an overlay of shawl and apron. Like the men, their feet were in heavy cowhide boots, and some split their skirts and tied them at the ankle to make a bloomer and thus give themselves more freedom. An aggravation of the trek for the women was the difficulty of keeping this apparel clean and in repair when it was torn, worn, caked with dust, stained and rank with sweat.

Palmer in his journal laid down what he considered the proper amount and kind of food required per person—about the amount carried by the wagons of the St. Louis Division: two hundred pounds flour, thirty pounds hardtack, seventy-five pounds bacon, ten pounds rice, five pounds coffee, two pounds tea, twenty-five pounds sugar, ten pounds salt, as well as dried beans and fruit, cornmeal and vinegar. Although Palmer does not mention it, whiskey was usually carried, too.

Then there were the household items: candles, soap, sewing supplies, cooking utensils, a churn, a feather tick, and a cradle. Though Palmer urged that "no useless trumpery should be taken," some was—a piece of good china buried in the flour barrel, a harmonium, a chiming clock, a silver candlestick.[14] It was not that Palmer was a Puritan in these matters—in later years, his own establishment in Oregon would be appointed with fine pieces brought around the Horn—but rather that the exigencies of the journey called for only the necessities. Tools, for example: the usual, plus, if possible, an anvil, a grinding stone and plow molds, and enormously important, much rope. Then there were those items without which life, at least the emigrants' kind of life, could not go on, such as seed and guns, schoolbooks and medicine. After all, the emigrants were bound for a place where there was little but the land and the animals that lived on it—no paper, let alone books; no looms, let alone cloth; no metal, let alone guns. And so the indispensables: flour, medicine, soap, guns, cloth, seed, the plain stuff of their lives—though sometimes woven into it a lighter thread, a pattern with no purpose but to decorate, divert, that silver candlestick, the chiming clock, the demijohn of whiskey.

Finally, there was the transport for all of this, the wagons. Typically, these were about ten feet long with two-foot sides and hooped at either end and at the center to support the white canvas hoods. Inside, they were fitted out with storage chests, space left for the feather ticks between. Some wagons were appointed with considerable elegance. A reporter for the *Western Expositor* described one as a "perfect prairie boudoir" complete with carpet, mirror, chairs, and hung about with ornaments. Some emigrants decorated their wagon-hoods with slogans such as "Westward the Tide of Immigration Rolls" or with gaudy paintings of lions, eagles, elephants.[15] Thus emblazoned did they confront the wilderness.

Last, though in a sense first, came the oxen, without which the emigrants could not have made the trip. They were beasts of prodigious strength and endurance, a team pulling an average load of twenty-five hundred pounds two thousand miles. The West is filled with memorials to the pioneers. There might well be one to the beasts that brought them there.

SO, ON THE MORNING of 14 May the bugles sounded and the St. Louis Division struck camp, the captain and the pilot leading, followed by the wagons, the loose horses and mules, last the cattle herds circled by outriders. It was a noisy procession: the creaking wagons and jingling harnesses, cows bawling, mules braying, the tinkling cattle bells and popping whips—with such cacophony did the emigrants enter into the silence of the wilderness.

It was a good beginning. The early spring sun lay lightly on them, and all around the prairie lapped in gentle, soothing swells of green. Wood, water, grass—those essentials of the journey—were abundant. And of course there was the excitement of the journey's beginning.

Their destination on this first leg of the crossing was the Platte River in central Nebraska, a distance of about three hundred miles. Starting out each morning at eight, resting for an hour or two at noon, making camp at five, they hoped to see the Platte in two weeks or less.

Those two weeks were not without event for Palmer. Three days out, the company camped near a Kansa village. "Although these Indians may be a set of beggerly thieves," wrote Palmer, "they conducted themselves honorably in their dealings with us; in view of which we raised for their benefit a contribution of tobacco, powder, lead, &c., and received in return many good wishes for a pleasant and successful journey."[16]

The next evening there was an instance of the "pleasant," a wedding. After three days of courtship, the pilot, Stephen Meek, had prevailed upon a Miss Schoonover to share his bed and life. A Baptist preacher was brought in, the ladies of the company made a cake with turtle eggs, and following the ceremony, all went dancing on the grass.

But not all was frolicking by any means. As Palmer noted the next day:

> A growing spirit of dissatisfaction had prevailed since the election; there were a great number of disappointed candidates, who were unwilling to submit to the will of the majority; and to such a degree had a disorderly spirit been manifested, that it was deemed expedient to divide the company.[17]

Three separate companies were organized, with the agreement that each would take a one-week turn as the vanguard.

One company of thirty wagons chose Palmer as their captain, "and with some reluctance I consented." His reluctance is understandable. As one emigrant wrote, "if you think it's any snap to run a wagon train . . . with every man in the train having a different idea of what is the best thing to do, all I can say is that some day you ought to try it."[18]

How Palmer dealt with these problems may be seen in two of his early measures. Immediately upon being chosen captain, he dispensed with various offices and formalities that he judged superfluous. On the other hand, and according to John Howell, a week later Palmer "held a court to try some offenders for deserting post and officers for misdemeanor in their official capacity."[19] The message was clear: regulations were to be reduced to a few, but those few were to be kept. Even this fair, firm hand, however, would not entirely succeed in staying the self-willed emigrants.

In this mood of chafing cooperation, the train moved on—now by late May—through the hill country of northeast Kansas. Again the emigrants were struck by drenching rains, and again the cattle bolted. Now, too, the emigrants were told that this was their last chance to get wood to replace any axle-trees or wagon tongues that might break before they reached Fort Laramie, hundreds of miles ahead. Slowly, the sense of the migration as a spring lark, a dancing on the grass, began to pass as the heat of the sun intensified, the dust became more dense, and the long prairie stretched out endlessly before them. Some, particularly the women, began to wonder if going to Oregon had been a wise idea.

How heartened they must have been on 25 May when they sighted Col. Stephen Watts Kearny and 250 dragoons of the Second Infantry. The troops were the first official United States military presence in the West, and the u.s. Army had sent them to escort the emigrants and impress the Indians. The dragoons impressed the emigrants, too. Wearing visored caps and yellow-piped blue uniforms, they rode two abreast, each company of fifty distinguished by the color of their mounts—the long file led by fifty blacks, then grays, bays, chestnuts, with another fifty blacks ending the cavalcade. James Field described them as "hardy looking fellows . . . nearly as dark as natives and some of them with their mustashios, a good deal savager."[20] For the emigrants, who believed that the dragoons would be patrolling the trail as far as South Pass in the Rocky Mountains, the dragoons were reassurance.

Palmer's group reached the Platte River a few days later. The river presented a curious sight. In a valley formed by high bluffs of sand, the Platte ran in a spreading, shallow, muddy smear across the valley floor, gray and black with sandbars and mud flats, smudged green here and there with wooded islands. The emigrants could not get over the shallowness of the river relative to its width—a foot or two by several miles; it struck them as a deformity of nature. Like Francis Parkman after them, they found the water so charged with sand that "it grates on the teeth in drinking."[21] But the south bank of the Platte was to be their path for the next hundred miles. As it turned out, they would be miles of dissension and hardship.

On the evening of 2 June, six miles up the Platte, tired and sore from jolting across the wide furrows left by buffalo herds, Palmer's party held a meeting. Dr. Presley Welch, who had been elected captain of the St. Louis Division before its subdivision into three groups, had spent the week with Palmer's group. According to Palmer, "some dissatisfaction was felt, by our company, at the degree of authority he seemed disposed to exercise."[22] Who was captain of this group, Welch or Palmer? The group evidently believed Palmer to be, for on that same evening he was reelected captain, his first term—like that of the other division captains—having been for only two weeks.

There was another subject of dispute as well. After one of the three groups had served its week-long term as vanguard, was it obliged to wait for the other groups to catch up? Palmer opposed the practice because "our supply of provision was barely sufficient for the journey, and it behooved us [to] make the best use of our time." The other groups did not agree. The disagreement festered. On 5 June, when Palmer's wagons passed the Thomas Stevens group, which was delayed by a broken axle, Stevens took great offense. That evening, according to John Howell, the groups "held a confused meeting . . . which resulted in greater confusion." Palmer had had enough. "They refused to accede to our terms, and we determined to act on our own responsibility. We therefore dissolved our connection with the other companies, and thenceforward acted independently of them." (To so act—independently, that is—was Palmer's way throughout his life.) But the acrimony continued. Howell reported that on 12 June they "held a meeting, resulted in confusion. 2 members expelled"; on the following day, there was "more quarreling and expelled members left and 2 others with them."[23]

Palmer did not dwell on these disagreements in his *Journal*, perhaps believing that to do so would serve no purpose. After all, his book was meant as a guide, not an indictment, and thus it was enough, without going into details, to cite disagreements and thus prepare the would-be emigrant. Anyway, there were more serious matters than these spats that, in the end, had no serious consequences.

The emigrants' three thousand cattle needed grass, and there was a scarcity of grass along the Platte caused by the vast herds of buffalo that fed on the river's bank. This presented another problem as well: the dry, sharp stubs of the remaining grass irritated and would finally crack the cattle's hooves, laming them. More than one emigrant later reported that stray cattle could be tracked by the blood they left behind. The remedy, effective only if it was applied early, was to daub the festering hoof with boiling pitch or tar.

The weather brought other hardships. Not only were there frequent thunderstorms of drenching rain, but there were also daily storms of sand mixing with the choking fogs of dust raised by the forward parties. Now, too, late spring, the heat was intense and in this parched and gritty terrain seldom relieved by the shade of trees.

These conditions were particularly hard on the women, many of whom had not been eager from the start to embark upon the trail—trying now in the heat and rain and dust to keep house and care for children in a jolting ten-foot box. Nor did the evening camp spell much relief. In addition to unpacking gear and preparing food, the women had to haul water for long distances; for camping too close to the river meant mosquitoes in tormenting clouds. Finally, the camps had often been used only a night or two before by other parties and so still stank with animal and human feces. It was now, too, that shortages of wood obliged the women to gather buffalo turds for fuel, initially, at least, a task repugnant to some of them.

These irritations naturally led to quarrels, such as the one reported by Samuel Parker, captain of the Iowa Division.

> A small puling of hair this nite By 2 women . . . the difficulty was left to me to decide and I told them it appared as one pint of beans and a little flower wase all and ordered my wife to git the beans and flower fore them and told them fore each man to give his wife a good licking that nite not over the back But not far from the ass and all wod be well . . . . so it ended.

Another distress from which everyone suffered to some degree was boredom. On the Platte, William Rector observed

> such a sameness of scenery. Each day, the same ridge on our left, bounded the valley, and continued without intermission, making travel dull, tiresome and monotonous . . . . Soon it was the greatest exertion that we could keep awake while traveling.[24]

There was also sickness, particularly measles and whooping cough, and accidents. On several occasions, children fell or jumped from moving wagons and were run over by the wheels. "A child died . . . last evening," James Field recorded,

> sadening indeed to hear the mournful lamentations of its friends in that lonely and desolate part of creation . . . . in the afternoon . . . was buried about a mile above our camp, and as I saw the little procession moving out from their camp on foot, two men with the coffin leading the way, I thought that heavy indeed

must be the heart of the parents who is compelled to deposit it in such a place as this baren region is.[25]

A far more common cause of injury was the accidental discharge of fire-arms. On 8 June, at the end of their first week on the Platte, Palmer recorded that a young man named Forester had been wounded. Someone, in pulling a tent cover from a wagon, dislodged a gun that went off, sending a ball through the spoke of a wagon wheel and into Forester's back. Two nights later, fire-arms again nearly caused a man's death, though under very different circum-stances. A Mr. Risley, pursuing his strayed mule, was mistaken by a guard for an Indian stealing horses. The guard fired, but his gun failed to go off. Another guard fired, but his gun also refused to discharge. The first guard fired again, and yet again, it was to no effect. By now, Palmer observed, "the camp was roused, and nearly all seized their fire-arms, when we discovered that the sup-posed Indian was one of our own party."[26]

Accidents, disease, boredom, quarrels, weather, lame and straying cattle, buffalo turds, broken axles. And although it was rarely mentioned, there was fear—fear of the distance, fear of the future. "Nothing ahead of them was known," Guthrie wrote of the emigrants on the Trail, "none of it was warmed by memories."[27]

Yet for all the hardships, the diaries and accounts of the 1845 migration, and in particular Palmer's, do not suggest that the emigrants were on a trail of misery.

In the matter of health, for example, James Taylor, one of the three cap-tains of the St. Louis Division, wrote his father that one-third of his group had been sickly at the journey's outset but that now many of the ailing were much improved. Sarah Cummins later remembered that "for the first time in my life I began to enjoy fairly good health," and Anna Marie King, reporting on an epidemic of whooping cough and measles, wrote that "for myself I was never heartier in my life since I left Missouri . . . . The rest of our party are getting well and hardy now."[28]

Some recent commentators have suggested that despite the fatalities from firearms and drownings (the most common causes of death), mortality might have been greater had the emigrants stayed at home in the pestiferous river val-leys in which so many of them had lived.

Health was not the only aspect of the trek that had another face to it. Hard-ship also had its obverse side. For the men, hunting was a frequent source of pleasure. "Plenty of buffalo ciled [killed] and one antelope high living in the camp tonight," wrote Samuel Parker. The men also favored swapping, both among themselves and with the Indians. The young particularly appeared to enjoy themselves on the trail. W. W. Walter wrote: "we had dancing every night, buffalo hunting every day," and Jacob Harlan remembered that "every night we young folks had a dance on the green prairie." Seventeen-year-old Susan Parish was delighted that "there was plenty of frolic and where there are young people together there is always love making."[29]

In some cases, these dalliances led to more serious exchanges; pilot Meek was not the only member of the party to ensnare himself in the bonds of holy matrimony. Early on in the trek, for example, thirteen-year-old Miss Packwood went to the bed of her father's driver. And one of the most striking images of the journey comes from W. W. Walter's description of a marriage that occurred at night, the bride and groom standing before the coals of a dying fire. A moment before the preacher's pronouncement of their new state, Walter's father threw an armful of sagebrush on the coals so that in this first instant of their union, there in the darkness, they stood in a great blaze of light.

Another pleasure—and one of the most mentioned subjects in the Oregon Trail diaries—was the landscape. It could, of course, be intimidating—those vast plains ending only at the sky—especially to a people who had lived, as so many had, in the small, sheltered valleys of the border states. But in general, the emigrants relished the grand vistas of what they called "God's creation." There were also those two freaks of nature on the trail: Courthouse Rock, "a stupendous pile of sand and clay," as Palmer described it, and Chimney Rock, which he found to have the "unpoetical appearance of a hay-stack."[30]

Nor was this landscape an entirely empty stage. The emigrants had seen the dragoons, dashing in their blue and yellow, the occasional band of painted Indians, and then, on 18 June, they encountered at a bend in the river a group of trappers in their basket boats—skins on rounded willow frames—heaped with furs. "A jolly set of fellows," Palmer called them. Parkman would encounter a similar group of trappers. He described them as "attired in gayly painted buffalo robes, like Indian dandies; some with hair saturated with red paint, and plastered with glue to the temples; and one bedaubed with vermilion upon the forehead and each cheek."[31]

Perhaps the greatest pleasure of all was the occasional good camp, such as the one Palmer described fourteen days up the Platte: "Our camp, last night, was in a cedar and ash grove, with a high, frowning bluff overhanging us; but a wide bottom, with fine grass around us, and near at hand an excellent spring." Surely at such a camp the fiddles would come out and there would be dancing "on the green prairie," some singing, too, at certain wagons whiskey passed around, preaching at others, and perhaps it was here that the women, finding wild currants and gooseberries, made a slew of pies. Dr. Elijah White, who encountered the St. Joseph Division of the migration, was struck at least in one instance by what a lark the journey appeared to be. When he asked the group how they had fared, an "elderly maiden" replied:

> O, Sir . . . our company are very philosophical; they are not disposed to let
> little drawbacks trouble them; neither do they wish to wear themselves out by
> extraordinary exertions, such as rising too early in the morning, and dashing
> away over the plains, like eager seekers after filthy lucre.[32]

PRECEDED BY HALF A DOZEN other parties, Palmer and his group reached Fort Laramie on 24 June, now more than six hundred miles into the journey. The fort, built by fur trader Bill Sublette in 1834 and rebuilt by the American Fur Company in 1841, was an adobe structure with two towers and a courtyard and stood on the banks of the Platte near its confluence with the Laramie River. The earthen fort was a somber place, there among the barren hills, by the muddy waters of the Platte. In the nearby Sioux villages, scalps on high poles streamed in the wind. Nonetheless, and however somber, the fort was a place to buy provisions and make repairs, and the emigrants were happy to reach it.

While his party bargained for staples and shoed their oxen and horses, Palmer prepared a feast for the local Indians. Parkman wrote that this became an "established" custom at Fort Laramie, and it may have been Palmer who started it. What is certain is that his purpose was to cross the carrot with the stick, not only to feast the Indians but also to caution them.

After each emigrant family had provided a share of food and spread place settings of buffalo skins on the ground, hosts and guests assembled in a circle, half the circle red, half white. All shook hands. Then, each side addressed the other. The chief informed the whites that by their coming they had frightened the game away and thus "the children of the red man cry for food."[33] Still, his people had profited from trade with the whites, and they were pleased to accept the presents, particularly powder and lead, which were customary for the whites to give the Indians. In general, the chief and his people were happy to see the whites and to look on them as friends.

Palmer, as the whites' chief, replied that his people were "compelled to pass" through Indian lands, since their destination was "the great waters of the west," but that they "traveled as friends." But "friendly as we felt," Palmer told them, "we were ready for enemies; and if molested, we should punish the offenders." He added that his party had no powder or lead to give their Indian friends; they had nothing but this feast. Palmer concluded: "We told them to eat what was before them, and be satisfied; and that we had nothing more to say." This brusqueness would always be typical of Palmer's discussions with Indians. The feast commenced. "All was order. No one touched the food before him until all were served, when at a signal from the chief the eating began."[34]

IT WAS AN EXTRAORDINARY SCENE, the white emigrants and the Indians seated together on buffalo skins—the bearded whites in their broad-brimmed black hats and bundled into flannel and denim, the painted Sioux, naked except for breechclouts and earrings of colored glass—to see them breaking bread together. Besides the bread they shared that day on the buffalo skins there was, however, one other thing they shared, and that was a profound distrust of one another.

That distrust had a long history, beginning two centuries before when whites had first encountered Indians. More recently, almost all of the emigrants had had family in an Indian war or fracas. Also, many remembered the War of 1812 and had not forgotten the alliance of the border Indians with the detested British. Finally, and most important, there was the common nineteenth-century belief that Indians were irredeemably inferior to whites and an impediment to progress and so must give way to the whites. Francis Parkman, no nineteenth-century redneck but a polished, Harvard-educated, Boston Brahmin, expressed these sentiments most vividly:

> Unstable as water, capricious as the winds, they seem in some of their moods like ungoverned children fired with the instincts of devils . . . this irreclaimable son of the wilderness, the child who will not be weaned from the breast of his rugged mother . . . . Their intractable, unchanging character leaves no other alternative than their gradual extinction or the abandonment of the western world to eternal barbarism.[35]

It was, then, with such ideas and with old and bitter memories that the emigrants approached the Indians they encountered on the trek. It began badly.

The Indians of the Missouri River frontier had frequent opportunity to mix with whites, and some tended to take on the whites' worst habits, in particular their fondness for alcohol. These were the Indians who also demanded that whites pay tribute before passing through their lands. "Found the Indians troublesome," wrote Jacob Snyder, who would later join Palmer's group. "Came in the morning and demanded pay for passing through their country, which they did not get."[36] What irked the emigrants was not so much the tribute—the calf, for example, that Snyder was eventually obliged to pay—but rather that the demand implied a jurisdiction on the part of the Indians that the emigrants were loath to recognize. What the Indians were demanding, however, was not so much tribute as compensation for the game they were losing to the whites.

To add insult to what the emigrants considered the injury of "tribute," there was the Indians' incessant thievery. With parties too small to defend themselves, the Indians would rifle the emigrants' pockets or valuables. An emigrant hunting on his own, for example, might be stripped and sent naked back to his camp. A group of Pawnees, who were "much the sauciest of Indians," according to one emigrant, sauced away eleven horses from Samuel Parker's group, a serious loss. Andrew Hackleman's party of Yankees was particularly troubled by Indians, perhaps because the travelers' frequent picnicking and observance of the Sabbath had put them well behind the main body of emigrants. On one occasion, Indians rained arrows into their cattle, causing a stampede that smashed six wagons to pieces. On another occasion, Indians stole all their wagon whips. The most humiliating encounter occurred when the emigrants traded with the Crow for some particularly fine Spanish horses; three days later, the Crow stole the horses back.

Of all the 1845 parties, Samuel Hancock's had the most reason to detest the Indians. At one crossing of the Snake River, two of their group, George Hinshaw and Zachariah Hawkins, went off to hunt and did not return. Hawkins was never seen again; Hinslow was found, scalped, his fingertips burned off, and dying. Hinslow was one of the four whites killed by Indians in the crossing of 1845.

In addition to these outrages, there were also little things, grains of salt in the open wounds, small irritants that added up to real vexation. "Some of the Indians go stark," Betsy Bayley complained, a shocking exhibition to people who believed that any exposure of the limbs, let alone the torso, was a wantonness.[37] Nor did it help that the Indians rarely bathed and their skin could be marked by a disfiguring disease. Also, to people whose idea of ornament was a simple tiepin or a brooch, the Indians' penchant for wearing bear teeth, claws, and other animals' parts was certainly upsetting.

All told, then, provocations from the trivial to the heinous, together with the attitude that Indians were little better than animals, did not suggest that the whites gathered that day on the buffalo skins at Fort Laramie would be well disposed toward their Indian guests. Nor was there reason to suppose that the

Indians held their hosts in particular esteem. The Crow chief was right: whites had shot or scared away large quantities of game, they had wantonly killed the buffalo for sport, and they had rifled the graves of his ancestors. In short, there was plenty of reason for enmity on both sides. The extraordinary fact is that, based upon the contemporary accounts of the 1845 migration, this hostility had its reverse side, and it was the side of understanding and consideration, if not affection.

First of all, there was what scholars of the Oregon Trail have called "trade and aid." Along with hunting, whiskey, and praying, the emigrants, as noted earlier, loved to swap, and they had many opportunities to do so with the Indians. Also, aid came from the Indians in various forms, from advice on routes to the location of good pasturage to help in river crossing. At one crossing of the Snake, "Indians, acquainted with the current, rendered valuable assistance to a number of emigrants, some of whom expressed their gratitude in different ways."[38]

There were also instances of simple, gratuitous good feeling. One was the encounter between the St. Louis Division and the Indians, which ended in the whites apologizing to an Indian they had wrongly accused. Another group of the division enjoyed amicable relations with the Kansa Indians, exchanging gifts with them and accepting their wishes for good fortune on their journey. One evening on the North Platte, a band of two hundred Sioux encamped near one of the smaller emigrant parties, much to the whites' apprehension, even though the Sioux chief had pledged no harm. The following morning, grateful that the Indians had kept their word, the whites prepared a feast for them. Farther along the trail, two Indians—a father and son—found young Timothy Lamberson, who had strayed from his group. The son wanted to kill the boy, but the father intervened, giving Lamberson food and setting him on the trail for Fort Hall. In the same region, a man named Smith had his horse stolen. Later, he found the horse with an Indian, whom he assumed to be the thief and whom he set about to kill. His companions intervened, however, arguing that Smith had no proof of how the Indian had acquired the horse. In the meantime, the accused Indian appeared to be so distraught with fear that the emigrants gave him a shirt to compensate him. On another occasion, James Field's camp was visited by a large band of Indians who brought with them a mare that belonged to a person in one of the forward companies.

There was much more acceptance of the Indians along the trail than is commonly realized. W.A. Goulder, the leader of a group in the St. Joseph Division, wrote: "We daily met groups of traveling Indians, who gave us no serious trouble and generally behaved toward us in a friendly manner." William Rector of the St. Louis Division had an even more favorable impression:

> We ware not molisted by indians in fact we did not see but few of the savages until we got to fort laramey from thare on to fort bridger we met with them frequently but they ware sivel and never molisted us in any way whatever the same may be said of the Indians throughout the intire journey. I am inclined to believe that much of the trouble emigrants have had since 1845 have growen out of indiscreat conduct on the part of our own race.

Rector also told the story of how a yoke of his oxen were stolen on the Umatilla River, supposedly by Indians. But

> it afterword come to light that they ware stolen by a little partie of very pias people that seperated from the company on account of the wickedness of the ungodly . . . . Since that time I have allways had more confidence in an Indian thern a pias hypocrate.[39]

In Palmer's party, goodwill toward the Indians prevailed. One of the party's outstanding members was Samuel Barlow, who talked with any Indians he encountered and offered them tobacco, which he had bought in the States for that purpose. It was Barlow as well who called together the young men of the group to dissuade them from the wanton killing of buffalo, "for it was robbing the Indians of their natural food and might arouse the wrath of the great Sioux nation, whose country we were now crossing."[40]

As for Palmer, his attitude was one of goodwill combined with firmness. He never idealized nor deprecated the Indians as a race but differentiated among them, sometimes to the Indians' credit and sometimes not. For example, he wrote of the Sioux at the feast: "They are a healthy, athletic, good-looking set of men, and have according to the Indian code, a respectable sense of honor." On the other hand, he stigmatized a band he encountered near the Columbia River as "a greasy, filthy, dirty set of miscreants as ever might be met."[41] In short, he recognized that Indians, like whites, were not cast from a single mold.

That distrust prevailed that afternoon at the feast on the banks of the Platte there is no doubt, and further, there was good reason for it. Putting aside the past and the depredations suffered by each race, forgetting even white notions of superiority, to expect two peoples so alien in their histories, beliefs, and practices to meet in trust is to expect rather much of human nature. It is, then, all the more remarkable that on occasion their hands touched and they saw in each other a common humanity.

PALMER AND HIS PARTY departed Fort Laramie on 26 June, bound for the Rockies. Soon they were in the Black Hills of what would become South Dakota, the most difficult terrain they had so far traversed. "We no longer find the smooth level prairie on which the wagons roll for miles without pulling," wrote James Field.[42] The grazing was miserable, and in early July it was necessary to divide the group into small parties. Palmer now traveled with only eleven wagons.

It was now, too, that the trains again met up with Colonel Kearny's dragoons, who were returning on their patrol from South Pass in the Rockies. The officers found many of the women distraught. Lieutenant Turner observed that "the females are heartily tired of the toilsome journey," and Lieutenant Cook found that "the women are generally weeping. The sight of our return, thoughts of home, the friends behind and the wilderness ahead! Heaven help them!"[43]

The women had reason to weep. With the need to lighten loads for the undergrazed and bloody-hoofed oxen, many had been obliged to jettison the "useless trumpery" that Palmer had cautioned against. Useless in the material sense those possessions may have been, but emotionally, they were quintessential symbols of home there in that empty world, above all harbingers of the home-to-be—those fiddleback chairs, for example, seen in the mind's eye, bracketing with elegance a fireplace of daub and twigs. Thus the women's heartbreak when, as they turned away so as not to see, the men went through with it. Following in their track, Parkman reported on the result: "the shattered wrecks of ancient claw-footed tables, well waxed and rubbed, or massive bureaus of carved oak . . . . flung out to scorch and crack upon the hot prairie."[44]

Yet Lieutenant Cook ended his description of the weeping women by writing: "They are unexpectedly thriving."[45] Perhaps not so unexpectedly. The sagebrush through which the wagons were passing is said to be one of the most adaptable of plants, capable of surviving all manner of environments. So, too, were the tough women of the 1845 migration.

BY MID-JULY, Palmer's group had passed Independence Rock and gone through Devil's Gap, the gorge of the Sweetwater River. On 14 July, Palmer spotted the first snow-mantled mountains he had seen since the Catskills of his youth. In the mornings the travelers found their water pails topped with a wafer of ice. They had begun to climb. On 19 July, the group reached South Pass and "passed over the dividing ridge which separates the waters flowing

into the Atlantic from those which find their way into the Pacific Ocean. WE
HAD REACHED THE SUMMIT OF THE ROCKY MOUNTAINS."[46] Palmer announced
their arrival in capital letters because it was a capital event; the great barrier had
been penetrated, the continent now one, and they among the first to have
formed the union.

From South Pass in Wyoming to Fort Hall in Idaho, the next leg of their
journey, would take about three weeks. The terrain was not particularly difficult, but it was monotonous and the grazing poor. By now, both the emigrants and beasts were tired. "A weary sameness," Sarah Cummins complained. "Sometimes the mind is sadening and lonely," wrote William Findley. And Palmer, seldom critical, said of Fort Bridger, a little trading post to
which they had all looked forward, that it was "a shabby concern." And then
there was the distance—the distance they had come from home, the distance
yet to go, for they were not much more than halfway to the Oregon Country.
And what was waiting for them there? It was this, the sheer distance, more
than anything, perhaps, that wore them down, the mere idea of it, which
Guthrie illustrates so well in *The Way West*.

> Distance was the enemy, not Indians or crossings or weather or thirst or plains
> or mountains, but distance, the empty, awesome face of distance . . . . There
> was no end to it . . . . Morning and night it was there unchanged, hill and cloud
> and sky line beyond reach or reckoning.[47]

But there was at least a temporary end to it when, on 8 August, Palmer and
his party sighted the red flag and whitewashed walls of Fort Hall, near present-
day Pocatello. The fort, owned by the Hudson's Bay Company, was under the
command of an Englishman named Captain Grant, who Palmer found to have
"the bearing of a gentleman."[48] Camping a mile away, the party traded cattle
for much-needed flour and in general enjoyed the scenes of habitation afforded
by the fort after what had seemed an eternity of empty space.

While Palmer and his group were camped near the fort, an incident occurred that provoked one of Palmer's rare outbursts of anger on the trip. Caleb
Greenwood, a trapper, and a young man named McDougal came to the camp
to persuade the emigrants to go to California rather than to Oregon. The two
men were apparently in the pay of John Sutter, who wanted to increase the
value of his holdings on the Sacramento River by encouraging emigration.
Greenwood told the emigrants that the rivers on the Oregon Trail were impossible to cross without great losses, that several Indian tribes had combined
to obstruct their passage to Oregon, and that both famine and deep snows
would assail them before their trek was over. But the trail to California, they

promised, was lined—if not carpeted—with flowers. Palmer expended only seven words on Greenwood: "An old mountaineer, well stocked with false-hoods."[49]

Nevertheless, more than thirty wagons defected, and a few miles beyond Fort Hall, they turned off with Greenwood to head for California. B.F. Bonney remembered that when the Barlow party split, those who remained on the trail to Oregon called after the others: "Good-bye, we will never see you again. Your bones will whiten in the desert or be gnawed by wild animals in the mountains." As for Palmer, he had the satisfaction of adding a footnote: "the emigrants alluded to, not finding California equal, in point of soil, to their high wrought anticipations, have made the best of their way to Oregon."[50]

Still, there was some truth in Greenwood's warnings. Others at Fort Hall reported that the trail to the west crossed very rough terrain, that there were shortages of grass, and that the Indians were strongly opposed to whites passing through their lands. But the emigrants, now twelve hundred miles from home, were not about to turn back. On 9 August, Palmer and his group struck the trail again, this time toward the Blue Mountains of eastern Oregon.

The route followed the northwesterly bend of the Snake River, the gut of the earth, as Guthrie called it. Then they crossed the valleys of the Boise, Malheur, and Burnt rivers and finally reached the Blues. In truth, the terrain was far from hospitable, a "wild, rocky, barren wilderness, of wrecked and ruined Nature; a vast field of volcanic desolation," as guidebook writers Johnson and Winter described it. Again and again, Palmer noted the dearth of grass and the "stony and dusty" land. There were many river crossings, with those on the Burnt the most troublesome. Palmer found the trail along the Burnt to be

> the most difficult road we have encountered since we started. The difficulties arise from the frequent crossings of the creek, which is crooked, narrow and stony. We were often compelled to follow the road, in its windings for some distance, over high, sidelong and stony ridges, and frequently through thickets of brush.

A bit farther on, he reported, "this road appeared to us impassable, and so difficult of travel, as almost to deter us from the attempt." As it would so often, his optimism carried him through: "knowing that those who had preceded us had surmounted the difficulties, encouraged us to persevere."[51]

On 3 September, Palmer and his group reached the banks of the Malheur, a few miles northwest of present-day Boise. It was here that, ten days before, Stephen Meek had persuaded a thousand emigrants to follow him on what he believed to be a 150-mile shortcut to The Dalles. Palmer, writing after he learned of the disastrous outcome of this diversion in which an estimated seventy-five lives were lost, passed no judgment on Meek.

> This expedition was unfortunate in the extreme. Although commenced under favorable auspices, its termination assumed a gloomy character . . . . The censure rests, in the origin of the expedition, upon Meek; but I have not the least doubt but he supposed they could get through in safety.

Others were less charitable. Barlow wrote that Meek "proved himself to be a reckless humbug from start to finish. All he had in view was to get the money and a white woman for a wife before he got through."[52] Bancroft, on the other hand, charged that Dr. Elijah White was the culprit for having encouraged Meek to attempt the shortcut.

As it happened, Palmer encountered Dr. White on the banks of the Malheur. White had come to the Oregon Country in 1837 as physician to the Jason Lee mission, but he had been relieved of his duties because of alleged misuse of mission funds and alleged misconduct with Indian women. A gentleman of considerable nimbleness, White soon secured an appointment as "sub Indian Agent" for the region. It was an appointment of some delicacy, not to say irregularity, since the treaty between the United States and Great Britain providing for joint occupancy did not envision the presence of American officials. When Palmer encountered White, the doctor was carrying a memorial from the provisional government of Oregon to Washington, asking Congress to recognize Oregon as an American territory. It was the third such request, and White was hoping to be named governor of the new territory. At the time, Palmer did not know that the day would come when he would be obliged to deal with some of the less fortunate results of White's Indian policy.

On 11 September, Palmer's party made the difficult descent into the Grande Ronde Valley and found it the most pleasing place they had so far encountered.

> The bottoms are of rich friable earth . . . . wild flax and a variety of other plants grow in luxuriance . . . . The streams are generally lined with timber, and abound in salmon and other varieties of fish. Upon the sides of the mountains and extending down into the valley are found beautiful groves of yellow pine timber. These mountains are places of resort for bear, deer, and elk.[53]

There was good soil, water, timber, and game—an ideal location for settling.

It was in this paradisiacal setting that Palmer had a curious encounter with the local Indians. He was in the middle of a card game when a chief approached him, shaking an admonitory stick and discoursing on the evils of gaming.

"You may guess my astonishment, at being thus lectured by a 'wild and untu-
tored savage,' twenty five hundred miles from a civilized land." Yet Palmer
"inwardly resolved to abandon card playing forever."[54]

The chief was a Cayuse named Tiloukaikt, who some years before had
come under the influence of missionary Marcus Whitman. Palmer would encounter Tiloukaikt again, but in very different circumstances—far from the
beauties of the Grande Ronde Valley and very far, indeed, from the influences
of Marcus Whitman.

If the trail into the Grande Ronde was difficult and hazardous, the trail out
was doubly so, for between the Grande Ronde and the Columbia lay the Blue
Mountains, the most dreaded of all the obstacles along the trail. The grades
were steep, early snows were a threat, and by now, both emigrants and animals were exhausted from the long months of the trek. Yet Palmer seemed to
take the ascent as a matter of course. The road "is quite steep and precipitous,"
he conceded, but the "scenery is grand and beautiful."[55] Here, too, he first saw
the Cascades, final barrier, and Mount Hood, whose slopes he would be the
first white to climb.

During the next few days, having now descended from the Blues, Palmer
encountered two more persons who, like Dr. White and Chief Tiloukaikt,
would figure significantly in his future, actors waiting in the wings, as it were,
for the drama to begin. On 16 September, he met the Cayuse chief Five Crows
at his camp on the Umatilla River. On the following day, Palmer met Marcus
and Narcissa Whitman. The Whitmans had journeyed from their mission station near Walla Walla to meet the emigrants and trade with them and also to
ensure that they would not be harassed by the Cayuse. Palmer was impressed
by the Whitmans and their activities: "if any class of people deserve well of
their country and are entitled to the thanks of a christian community, it is the
missionaries," he wrote.[56] At the time, of course, Palmer had no reason even to
imagine the tragedy in which Five Crows, Whitman, Narcissa, and himself
were to play such leading parts.

Four days later, Palmer and his party reached the Columbia River near
present-day Biggs, "a beautiful stream; its waters are clear and course gently
over a pebbly bottom," Palmer reported. From here on, the wagons followed
or kept near the river to arrive at The Dalles on 29 September, "the end of our
road, as no wagons had ever gone below this place."[57] From The Dalles on,
there was no road, only the river. And the river, with its rapids, squalls, and
rushing current, was not especially inviting, for the log rafts the emigrants
used to transport their wagons were as matchsticks in its force. Furthermore,

Palmer discovered that no rafts would be available for ten days, and then only at great expense.

Several other circumstances dissuaded Palmer from traveling on the river. Whitman had encouraged Palmer to use the Indian trails that crossed the Cascades to reach the Willamette Valley. Also, he was apparently not traveling by wagon himself and thus was prepared to proceed by horse or foot. Finally, Palmer learned that, six days earlier, Samuel Barlow and a party of seven wagons had struck out overland, determined to hack out a wagon road across the mountains to Oregon City. On leaving, Barlow had declared, "God never made a mountain that He had not made a place for a man to go over it or under it."[58] Palmer apparently agreed.

ON 1 OCTOBER, Palmer and the twenty-three wagons that chose to follow him set out across the high prairies south of The Dalles, passing present-day Dufur and reaching Barlow's camp in Tygh Valley two days later. They found everyone engaged in the hard work of building a road, hacking through the undergrowth with axes, in some cases finding it almost impossible, particularly the tough mountain laurel. After a week of slow progress, Palmer, Barlow, and a Mr. Lock were sent out to find a pass through the mountains.

Following various creeks and forks, the men suddenly came onto a wide plain of sand at the end of which towered Mount Hood. They had seen the peak of the mountain before: now they saw all of it, from base to summit. "I had never before looked upon a sight so nobly grand," Palmer wrote. The men reached the timberline after several miles, the snow now falling, and they camped for the night on the mountain's south face. They started up again the next morning, hoping with the higher altitude to spy a pass through the southern ridges. By now, Barlow and Lock were suffering from fatigue, so Palmer went on alone. It was not an easy climb. Of one stretch he wrote:

> I . . . found that by climbing up a cliff of snow and ice, for about forty feet, but not so steep but that by getting upon one cliff, and cutting holes to stand in and hold on by, it could be ascended . . . . I had cut and carved my way up the cliff, and when up to the top was forced to admit that it was something of an undertaking.[59]

And perhaps especially so because, by now, his moccasins had given out, and he was climbing barefoot.

Palmer continued to climb until he reached a point that gave him an extensive view of the southern ridges and the three gaps that might serve as passes. But the day was ending, and it was twenty-five miles back to the wagon camp, so Palmer descended the mountain to meet Barlow and Lock. The three reached camp at eleven that evening, Palmer confessing that "although not often tired, I was willing to acknowledge that I was near being so."[60]

It is certain that Palmer was the first white to climb high on Mount Hood, but it is less certain just how high he went. "I . . . did not arrive at the highest peak," he reported, "but went sufficiently near to prove its practicability"; that is, an ascent to the summit.[61] Most believe that he probably reached the glacier that, recognizing his accomplishment, was later named for him and which lies on the south side, just below Crater Rock at an elevation of nine thousand feet.

The day following his return to camp, Palmer again struck out to find a pass, this time with Spencer Buckley, his companion since leaving Indiana. All three of the defiles Palmer had seen from Mount Hood proved to be impractical. A more serious problem was the sudden change in weather. Observing the behavior of the birds and squirrels, Palmer knew that a storm approached; this was not unexpected, for it was mid-October and the beginning of the rainy season. This spelled danger. The rains would so swell the streams, particularly the Deschutes, that the emigrants would be caught between them, unable to go forward and unable to go back. "I began for the first time to falter, and was at a stand to know what course to pursue."[62] Should he return to The Dalles or hack on to Oregon City?

Typically, Palmer came to a quick decision and started back to camp to implement it. He and Buckley covered fifty miles that day, much of it without benefit of trail, and it was not until two the following afternoon that they reached their camp. Palmer announced his plan. The road building should be abandoned. Instead, a suitable place would be chosen for the wagons, a cabin built in which to store the emigrants' effects, and some persons selected to guard the wagons and cabin through the winter. Then, the emigrants would pack out, returning in the spring to build the road and repossess their wagons and belongings. The families who had no horses or were short of provisions remained at the camp, while Palmer, Mr. and Mrs. William G. Buffum, and Mrs. Miriam A. Thompson started out on horseback for Oregon City, where Palmer intended to assemble horses and provisions for those who remained behind.

Their journey began with a certain awkwardness, for Mrs. Thompson, who had crossed the plains in a wagon fitted out like a rather grand boudoir, had never ridden horseback before, and so, for the first few hours, the gentlemen were obliged to take turns holding her in place. Then the rains began—by the second day in drenching torrents. At night, the men used branches and blankets to fashion a tent for the women while they themselves submitted to the downpour. The next day, by now on the mountain, so dense a fog descended that they lost the trail. Palmer finally picked it up again, and they struggled on. A few hours later, to their surprise and delight, the group met a relief party. Word of the emigrants in the mountains, short of supplies and with the winter snows about to fall, had reached Oregon City, prompting the citizens to donate more than a thousand pounds of flour, a hundred pounds of sugar, and quantities of coffee and tea. The supplies were now handed over to Palmer who, with a member of the relief party and an Indian, started back to the wagon camp.

Again, the rains were drenching, and as the men moved higher into the mountains, snow began to fall, obliterating the trail. Knowing the danger, the Indian wanted to turn back, but "we showed him the whip," Palmer wrote. * They reached the east side of the mountains where, at the edge of a deep ravine, two packs of supplies slipped their fastenings and tumbled down the slope. The three men found a place free of snow at a lower altitude and set up camp. Pouring water into a sack of flour, they

* Use of the lash on Indians as well as whites was common practice and, in many cases, was prescribed by law. Indians found it particularly degrading.

> wrapped the dough around sticks and baked it before the fire, heated water in our tin cups and made a good dish of tea, and passed a very comfortable night. It had ceased raining before sunset, and the morning was clear and pleasant; we forgot the past, and looked forward to a bright future.[63]

No travail could dampen Palmer's spirits for long.

They reached the camp the following afternoon and found the families there near starvation. Now with supplies and packhorses, the emigrants took heart and departed for the valley, leaving Palmer and several other men behind to build the storehouse cabin. "Tight as a jug," wrote William Barlow of the finished cabin and which they named Fort Deposit. Barlow and two others had volunteered to stay at the cabin to guard its contents until spring. There was "a good store of food and mountains of good dry wood. We had a few books, which would serve to while away the time. In fact, enough of everything to make any lazy man feel happy."[64]

On 25 October, Palmer and the other men departed for the Willamette Valley. Although he later made little of it, this final stretch of Palmer's trek was probably the most difficult he had experienced since leaving Independence six months and nineteen hundred miles before. The first day of heavy rains was followed by a four-inch fall of snow that disguised ice crusts and the pitfalls beneath them. At lower altitudes, these hazards were replaced by huckleberry swamps, into which men and animals sank to their knees. Now, too, the horses began to die from lack of grazing and from the poisonous mountain laurel. When all eleven of the horses from Oregon City had died, the men shouldered the packs, which were twice their normal weight in the soaking rain. So burdened, they were obliged again and again to wade the Sandy River, "cold, and the bottom very stoney."[65] By now, too, their food was finished.

They reached the Clackamas River and the beginnings of settlement on 30 October. On 1 November, "passing through the timber that lies to the east of the city, we beheld Oregon and the Falls of the Willamette."[66] The trek was over.

THREE

Trail's End

THE VALLEY that Palmer finally reached was in essentials much as it is today: one hundred miles long, twenty to thirty miles wide, and walled to the west and east by the Coast and Cascade mountains—a long, fertile, sheltered grassland between the desert and the sea. The grasslands were particularly extensive in the upper valley, south of the Santiam River, though here and there conical buttes rose a few hundred feet above the valley floor. In the lower valley, north of the Santiam, hills encroached on the prairies, the Waldo Hills to the east of present-day Salem and the Eola Hills to the west. In the far northwest corner, an almost separate valley was formed by the Chehalem, Tualatin, and Coast mountains, and when Palmer arrived, it was called the Tualatin Plains.

The river that watered this valley had its source in the Calapooya Mountains, the valley's southern wall. Flowing north in a meander of braided channels, the river was fed by a dozen major streams pouring down from the Coast and Cascade mountains through slopes of hemlock, spruce, fir, and cedar. In the valley, there were savannas of oak and here and there—recent migrants from the mountain slopes—groves of pointy firs, while willow, cottonwood, and alder in an undergrowth of sword fern, snowberry, blackberry, and hazelnut crowded the stream banks.

A huge population of creatures flourished in these tangled woodlands and grass-rich prairies, though by Palmer's time big game—deer, elk, and bear—had largely been hunted out. There remained a vast array of birdlife: meadowlark, pigeon, bluebird, wren, quail, snipe, sparrow, finch, crane, and eagle.

The quadrupeds were in great variety as well: beaver, otter, coyote, wolf, muskrat, porcupine, bobcat, and raccoon. The valley seemingly so still, except for the rushing streams, was, in fact, quick with life.

This, then, was the land and its creatures, all bathed in a temperate air, the heat of the south, the cold of the north meeting here midway between pole and equator in moderation. To Palmer and his fellow emigrants, accustomed to extremes of climate, it was most welcome, indeed, but even more welcome was the absence of the thunder and lightning storms so common to the Mississippi Valley. In the Willamette, there were rainbows instead.

For eons this Eden had lain empty of human life. Then, one day, about ten thousand years ago, a band of Asiatics stepped into it, a people who, over the centuries, had been moving from their Siberian homeland and now had come to rest here on the banks of the Willamette River and its tributary streams. They called themselves—or, at any rate, came to be called by others—the Kalapuya.

Not much is known about the Kalapuya, for relatively soon after white contact they declined radically in numbers. Descriptions by some of the first whites to encounter them suggest a people who were small in stature, dressed scantily in skins, wore cedar caps, braided their hair with otter fur, and for additional ornament, favored tattoos and bangles of bone and teeth. To decoy wild game when hunting, they mounted antlers on their heads. The Kalapuya lived in small bands, rather than tribes, each with a headman and a shaman, or spiritual guide. Also, each individual possessed a guardian spirit, acquired at the time of a pubescent "quest," and there was, too, a pantheon of animal spirits—the bear and the blue jay, the crow, raccoon, and fly.

The Kalapuya were a seminomadic people, moving through the valley from spring to fall, gathering berries, nuts, insects, and particularly the wapato and camas roots. They used cedar bows and arrows of pine, padding through the high prairie grass with the antler decoys on their heads. It was the Kalapuya who had maintained the prairies, burning them off to facilitate food gathering. In the fall, when the drenching rains began to blow in from the sea, they left the exposed prairies for the shelter of the forest borders and their winter homes of brush and bark and cedar planks.

In 1814, Alexander Henry of the North West Company was one of the first whites to encounter the Kalapuya. He was not impressed. Of the Yamhill band of the Kalapuya, he wrote: "They seemed to be an ugly, ill-formed race, and four of them had some defect of the eyes . . . . wretchedly clothed . . . . and altogether the most miserable, wild, and rascally looking tribe I had seen on this side of the Rocky mountains." Of all the bands he remarked that they had "sore eyes . . . scabby arms, legs, rumps . . . on account of their filthy manner of living, their bad food, and the incessant rain for at least six months in the year."[1]

Trader Alexander Ross was only a little less derogatory. He found the Kalapuya "well disposed, yet they are an indolent and sluggish race and exceedingly poor in a very rich country." Ross ascribed this to "the productiveness of their country . . . probably the chief cause of their extreme apathy and indolence, for it requires so little exertion to provide for their wants, that even that little is not attended to."[2]

Henry and Ross were astute observers, though to some degree their observations may have been affected by the ethnocentrism of the time—as our observations today may be colored by the ethnocentrism of our time. A century later, Robert Carlton Clark did not have the advantage of first contact, but as a distinguished historian of the Northwest he had studied the Kalapuya and had come to different conclusions.

> Trade and infant manufacturing had begun. Fishing was highly developed, and the Indian had learned to herd the deer with fire and hunt it by means of artifice. An adequate vegetable diet had been discovered; and food preparation and preservation was very skillful. Because of these material accomplishments, agriculture was as yet unnecessary . . . . Nothing so clearly disproves the supposed inferiority of these Indians as their well-built houses, wonderful canoes, and commissary accomplishments.[3]

Whatever the conditions and attainments of the Kalapuya at the time of white contact, they shortly thereafter went into decline. By about 1833, an estimated 70 percent of the population had succumbed to epidemics, mainly of malaria. In 1841, Dr. William Bailey told Charles Wilkes, commander of the United States Exploring Expedition, that the mortality rate was about 25 percent annually. This decline did not concern most of the missionaries and settlers who had come to the valley. Some even considered it a blessing. "The hand of Providence is removing them to give place to a people more worthy of this beautiful and fertile country," the Reverend Gustavus Hines wrote in 1840.[4] And as if disease had not been enough, the Kalapuya were now assailed by missionaries who wished to deprive them of their spirit gods and by settlers who would deprive them of their land. And the Kalapuya were not the only Willamette tribe to suffer decimation. The Clackamas, who lived below the falls of the Willamette, were estimated by Lewis and Clark to number about eighteen hundred. By Palmer's time, there were little more than one hundred.

Not many months after Palmer arrived, Canadian artist Paul Kane came upon several Clackamas Indians sitting on a bluff above the river. His painting of the men is one of the most haunting in the entire genre of Indian portraiture. It shows four men huddled together, bowed down beneath brown cloaks, their heads touching as though to comfort one another, on their faces expressions of stunned sorrow—figures at bay before a world they could no longer comprehend. When Kane first saw them, there above the river, they were singing, a singing, Kane later wrote, "peculiarly sweet and wild, possessing a harmony I never heard before or since."[5]

THE KALAPUYA WERE NOT, of course, the sole occupants of the valley when the 1845 emigrants arrived. Indeed, the diversity of Oregon's population must have come as a shock to the new arrivals, who were from the tightly knit, homogeneous communities of old America; for them, "foreigner" could apply to someone living in the next county. In the Willamette Valley, they found six distinct groups that were, by and large, incompatible with one another.

By 1845, there were more whites in the valley than Indians, about two thousand of the former. Nevertheless, a few communities of Indians still languished on. This was in contrast to the homelands of the emigrants where, for the most part, the Indians had been killed or driven out. The Indians, then, constituted the first of the alien groups among whom the emigrants now found themselves.

Next, and about as foreign to the emigrants as the Indians, were the personnel of the Hudson's Bay Company. In 1825, the company had established its headquarters on the Columbia at a site they named Fort Vancouver. The company, by now three hundred strong, exercised the right of joint occupancy laid down in the 1818 treaty between the United States and Great Britain. Although the treaty stipulated that citizens of both nations might inhabit the Oregon Country until the borders were fixed, in effect, it was the British company that had for some years ruled the Oregon roost. This did not endear them to the emigrants for whom the two wars against the British crown were relatively recent events and whose presence in Oregon, treaty or no treaty, they much resented. Even the extensive aid and comfort they received from the company's chief factor, Dr. John McLoughlin, did not alter their attitude. As one emigrant said of the company, "it is true these are good folks, and treat us kindly, but somehow or other I cannot like them, and moreover do not like those who like them." Galling, too, were what the emigrants considered the company's "airs"—the decanters of port, the latest London journals, the kilted sentries and their braying pipes. "You had to say the British had manners," Guthrie wrote in *The Way West*, "if you liked manners."[6]

And again, almost as foreign to the emigrants as the Indians was the rather large colony of Catholic French Canadians such as Etienne Lucier and Joseph Gervais who, as possibly the first white settlers, retired as trappers in 1829 from the Hudson's Bay Company to settle with their Indian mates near a bend of the Willamette on what they called French Prairie. By 1845, the French Canadian families had established a church and had a priest, Francis Norbert Blanchet; they spoke a language and lived a life very different from that of the Protestant, Anglo-Saxon emigrants.

A fourth group shared the emigrants' nationality but not much else. The "Rocky Mountain boys" were American trappers who, with the collapse of the fur trade, had taken McLoughlin's suggestion that they settle on the Tualatin Plains. McLoughlin also persuaded several Congregational ministers to join them, apparently believing that the boys required the ministrations of the clergymen more than the Indians did. He was probably right. All accounts suggest that the boys were both indolent and boisterous and lacking in sobriety in every sense of the word.* No group could have been more different from or more antagonistic to the Rocky Mountain boys than the American missionaries. The evangelical religious revival of the 1820s and 1830s in the eastern United States, together with a plea by some Nez Perce for a knowledge of the Bible, prompted the Methodists to send the Reverend Jason Lee and his party to Oregon in 1834. By the time of Palmer's arrival, there were Methodist communities at Salem, Oregon City, Clackamas, and The Dalles. The divines had largely abandoned their mission to the Indians, having found it futile, and were now devoting their efforts to saving the souls of the whites.

From the beginning, the missionaries had not been especially tolerant. In their 1838 memorial to Congress requesting United States jurisdiction in Oregon, the missionaries made it clear that "unprincipled adventurers, Botany Bay refugees, renegades from civilization now roaming the Rocky Mountains, deserting seamen from Polynesia, and banditti from Spanish America [California] were not wanted."[7] The Rocky Mountain boys, settling on the Tualatin Plains, found, for example, that the missionaries would not even sell them potatoes. Daniel Waldo, an 1843 emi-

The indolence of the Rocky Mountain boys reportedly led to their repeated requests for credit from Dr. McLoughlin. When, after many extensions, he refused further loans, they asked him what they should do. "Go to work, go to work, go to work," he reportedly bellowed, although apparently to little effect.

grant, recalled Jason Lee telling him that the mission had always ruled the country and if there were any persons in the emigration who did not like it, they might go elsewhere. And when the Meek detachment of Palmer's emigration wandered dying in the desert, the missionaries at The Dalles refused to send aid. In short, relations between the missionaries and the other Oregon groups were not entirely cordial.

The sixth distinct group was small but powerful. These were the East Coast merchants. The majority had come to the Oregon Country by ship and established themselves in the towns where, with what Palmer called "Yankee enterprise," they were achieving positions of importance. In addition to being Yankees, which set them off so distinctly from the border-state emigrants, the majority of the merchants were Whigs; the other American emigrants were mainly Democrats. In a day when regional differences were far more pronounced than now, the Yankees seemed to come from another world, one distant in more ways than miles from the valley of the Mississippi.

The final ingredients in this Mulligan stew were the '45 emigrants themselves and their predecessors—though even here there were divisions. The first large train to Oregon arrived in the fall of 1842. Many of its 112 members, which almost doubled the number of whites in the valley, had been recruited by the ubiquitous Dr. Elijah White, whom Palmer had met on the banks of the Malheur. Many from this group settled at the site of Oregon City where, employed by Dr. McLoughlin, they began the building of the town.

The 1843 emigration, much larger, about nine hundred in all, had been encouraged to go west by Senator Linn's call for free land for settlers. According to Bancroft, these emigrants were a "people of pronounced character, rudely arrogant and aggressive rather than tame and submissive," and who "rather sought than avoided a contest." The migration in 1844 also contained an element of decided independence because the leader of this group of fourteen hundred, Col. Cornelius Gilliam, had it in mind to leave the Republic altogether and set up an autonomous state. To Bancroft's mind, however, they were "better fitted . . . to be loyal to a government than to construct one."[8] With this larger group, the real settlement of the Willamette Valley began.

The best description we have of these wagon-train people on their arrival in Oregon during these years is given by Peter Burnett, who came west in 1843 and remained to become a legislator, supreme court justice, and California's first governor.

> Our friends were arriving each fall, with jaded teams, just about the time the
> long rainy season set in. The community was divided into two classes, old set-

tlers and new, whose views and interests clashed very much . . . . At any public
gathering, it was easy to distinguish the new from the old settlers. They were
lank, lean, hungry, and tough; We were ruddy, ragged, and rough. They were
dressed in broadcloth, and wore linen-bosomed shirts and black cravats, while
we wore very coarse, patched clothes; for the art of patching was understood to
perfection in Oregon. But, while they dressed better than we did, we fed better
than they. They wanted our provisions, while we wanted their material for clothing.[9]

The emigrants' first concern was to find land on which to settle before winter set in. Peter Burnett, again:

There was necessarily . . . a great hurry to select claims; and the new-comers
had to travel over the country, in the rainy season, in search of homes. Their
animals being poor, they found it difficult to get along as fast as they desired.
Many causes combined to make them unhappy for the time being. The long
rainy seasons were new to them and they preferred the snow and frozen ground
to the rain and mud. There were no hotels in the country, as there was nothing
wherewith to pay the bills. The old settlers had necessarily to throw open their
doors to the new immigrants, and entertain them free of charge. Our houses
were small log-cabins and our bedding was scarce. The usual mode of travel
was for each one to carry his blankets with him, and sleep upon the puncheon-
floor. Our families were often overworked in waiting upon others, and our
provisions vanished before the keen appetites of our new guests. They bred a
famine wherever they went.[10]

The most desirable land for settlement was on the prairie margins, close to
both timber and open land. The emigrants needed the timber for fuel and for
their houses and barns, the open land for their animals and wheat—shelter and
food, the basics of their life. By the time Palmer arrived, many of the best sites
in the lower valley had been taken and settlement was beginning south of
present-day Salem.

The Reverend George H. Atkinson, a Congregational minister and a contemporary of Palmer's, gave a good description of what settlement involved:

An immigrant will come in during the autumn, put himself up a log house with
mud & stick chimney, split boards & shingles, break eight or ten or twenty
acres of prarie and sow it with wheat. You call upon him the next year & he will
have a fine field ripe for the sickle. His large field will be well fenced with newly
split fir rails. There will be a patch of corn, another of potatoes, & another of
garden vegetables. Outside a large piece will be broken for the present year's
sowing. His cattle & horses & hogs will be on the prarie, thriving and increas-

ing without care. A few sheep may be around the house. He has a spring near.
One of his children will be sent away 4 or 5 or 10 miles to a private school,
taught by some young man or woman at $3 or 4 a term for each scholar. The
farmer wears buckskin pants. His family are poorly clad. It is hard to get clothing. His wife has few cooking utensils, few chairs.[11]

Indeed, this emigrant wife had little of anything, especially time.

In the 1908 edition of the *Quarterly of the Oregon Historical Society*, Mrs.
S.A. Long wrote with some testiness that "the amount of labor accomplished
by the pioneer mothers is a lasting reproach to their idle and incompetent descendants." She described the work of Cynthia Applegate:

> Mrs. Applegate [the mother of thirteen children] made all the every-day cloth-
> ing for her husband and sons: coats, shirts, pants, underclothing, socks—spin-
> ning the yarn for these last. Made all the clothing of herself and daughters. And
> for many years did the work by hand . . . . Besides the sewing and cooking,
> milking and tending the milk, she found time for some work in the garden.

In 1848, a woman named Mary Walker recorded this day in her diary:

> Saturday. February 5. Have been cleaning tripe, trying [rendering] tallow, dip-
> ping candles, boiling feet, etc., and have Shopshenamal to work two days and
> have felt so tired and sleepy at night I could not write my journal. Yesterday
> dipped 17 dozen candles. In the evening we had preparatory meeting. But I feel
> that I need more than a meeting to prepare me for the communion, or anything
> else. My mind is so cumbered with a deluge of little corroding cares that all I
> can think is what shall we eat and what shall we drink and where with all shall
> we be clothed.[12]

Whether the men labored as hard as the women is not entirely certain. Lt.
Charles Wilkes of the United States Exploring Expedition, traveling in the
valley in 1841, was troubled by how little the men worked to get a livelihood:

> Two-thirds of the time of the settlers is . . . at their own disposal; and unless
> education, with its moral influence, is attended to strictly in this young settle-
> ment, these very advantages [of the Willamette Valley] will prove its curse.[13]

It is interesting that this should be so similar to what Alexander Ross wrote
of the Kalapuya in 1815:

> The productiveness of their country is probably the chief cause of their extreme
> apathy and indolence, for it requires so little exertion to provide for their wants,
> that even that little is not attended to.[14]

Likewise, the British officer Lt. Henry J. Warre, visiting the valley in 1845, a
few months before Palmer's arrival, reported that this "indolence" seemed to
afflict Indians and whites alike. Also, William Strong, territorial supreme

court judge, commenting on the Oregon character as he knew it in 1850, observed that the settlers were "not very fond of work." And finally, historian Robert Carlton Clark concluded that

> the equable climate and the ease with which a livelihood could be wrested from the soil tended to develop a shiftless and leisure loving disposition among many of the early Oregon settlers.[15]

Wilkes and Ross, Strong and Clark, were not the last commentators to report on this penchant for repose in the Willamette Valley. There are those who would argue that it is still the case today. And however frowned upon the theory is today, Clark may have been right in attributing the indolence of the people to the soil and weather—the valley's great fertility requiring so little effort, the clement seasons, the soft rains, and muffling fogs—something soothing and soporific that slowed people down, tempting them to be rather than to act.

Yet very much at odds with this felicity of environment was another characteristic of the emigrants that again and again provoked comment: discontent. Francis Parkman had prophesied it: "certain it is that . . . after they have reached the land of promise, [they] are happy enough to escape from it." Peter Burnett found that

> our new immigrants not only grumbled much about the country and climate in general, but had also much to say against those of us who had written back to our friends, giving them a description of the country . . . . They often declared that the country was so poor they would return to their former homes.

William Barlow, Palmer's companion in crossing the Cascades, wrote that "many" of the men working on his farm were saving their money so they could move on. John Carr, who arrived in Oregon in 1846, concluded that "nothing but the Pacific Ocean broke up the migratory habit." Henry Warre was also struck by the discontent: "Notwithstanding the advantages to be found in this valley, many of the American emigrants become dissatisfied, and remove to California." In the June before Palmer arrived in the valley, forty-three emigrants of the 1844 train left Oregon for California under the leadership of James Clyman.* Clyman may explain this Oregon discontent best:

> Notwithstanding the ease with which the necessaries of life are acquired, I never saw a more discontented community, owing principally to natural disposition. Nearly all, like myself, having been of a roving dis-

*Whom should Clyman's group meet in the Siskiyous but a group of disenchanted Californians on their way to the greener fields of Or-

contented character before leaving their eastern homes.[16]

ONE REASON FOR THIS "ROVING" TENDENCY in the Oregon population was that so much of it was young, male, and single. According to the 1845 census, 93 per cent were under the age of forty-five and 44 percent of the adult males were single. This led not only to a certain restlessness but also a certain rambunctiousness. One form this rambunctiousness often took was jumping other people's claims.

egon. This occasioned changes in the travel plans of both groups, some going on, others turning back.

It was this irregular form of acquisition as much as anything else that led to the formation of a provisional government—provisional until the suzerainty of the region could be determined—for how could land be held if there was no government to legalize its tenure? Also, there was the problem of probating the estate of a deceased person, a problem that had confronted the settlers in 1841 with the death of Ewing Young. It was such considerations that brought together about one hundred settlers at Champoeg in 1843 to see if a government might be formed. They succeeded, though not without considerable confusion and dissension. One of the more candid of those present, Robert Newell, wrote, "after a few days experience I became satisfied that I knew but little about the business of Legislating as the majority of my colleagues."[17] As for the dissension, John McLoughlin and a majority of the French Canadians were understandably chary of this attempt to form a government in a region still jointly occupied by Britain and the United States. The so-called American party prevailed by a narrow margin.

Thus was created a body of law and a government of three branches—legislative, executive (a committee of three), and judicial. Despite the fact that the provisional government did not have the power to tax (and when it did acquire the power it had great difficulty in collecting the tax—even from its own executive committee) and despite the fact that it was not officially recognized by the majority of settlers over whom it presumed to rule, still the laws enacted were by and large observed.

By the time Palmer arrived in Oregon, the government, seated at Oregon City, had suffered certain changes. The executive committee of three had been replaced by a governor—George Abernethy, a former mission employee—and changes had been made to allow local British participation. Still, there were stresses and strains. Some were content with the provisional nature of the government; others wanted immediate.American annexation. There were also those who, like Colonel Gilliam, favored an independent republic that was neither American nor British. The English party and the American party were the two principal factions in these disputes: the English party consisted of the Hudson's Bay Company and the Catholic French Canadians; the American party was an uneasy alliance of the Rocky Mountain boys, the East Coast merchants, the wagon-train emigrants, and the Methodists. It was because of dissension in the American party that the English party usually held the balance, at least until 1846, when the boundary question was finally resolved.

THIS, THEN, WAS THE OREGON—the land, the people, the life of the place—to which Joel Palmer had come, signaled by his arrival at Oregon City on the morning of 1 November 1845. But Oregon City was not the end of his journey, for Palmer intended to survey as much of the country as possible, and indeed, half of his journal is given over to a description of that survey. As noted earlier, it is the best description we have of Oregon in the 1840s.

He began with Oregon City itself. The site of the town was in its origins a two-mile-square land claim belonging to John McLoughlin. In 1842, McLoughlin had the land surveyed, deeded free lots to "responsible persons," and gave the place its name.

The location of Oregon City is special in several ways. Often called "the crack" by the settlers, Oregon City is hemmed in on one side by dark, sheer, 120-foot cliffs and on the other side by the Willamette River and the falls. As the result of these two features, the bluff and the falls, the town tended to be both dark and noisy, the high bluffs obscuring the morning sun, the thirty-foot falls filling the air with the crash of its never-ceasing descent. Another peculiarity of the Oregon City location, though a happy one, was that it was the gate to the valley and into it poured all the valley's riches. Both pictorial and written descriptions of Oregon City at the time portray it as a well-favored place, despite the darkness and the racket. Henry Warre's 1846 painting shows a rather pretty village of gambrel and pitch-roofed buildings strung along the riverbank, with a church at either end of the main street. Palmer found most of the buildings "not only commodious, but neat." "Neat," too, was the Methodist church, and "splendid" the Catholic chapel.[18]

Palmer went on from these general amenities to the more utilitarian features of the place. There were four mills as well as "four stores, two taverns, one hatter, one tannery, three tailor shops, two cabinet-makers, two silversmiths, one cooper, two blacksmiths, one physician, three lawyers . . . one lath machine, and a good brick yard."[19] He estimated the population to be about six hundred.

One Oregon City institution that Palmer did not mention was the Main Street House, a hotel run by the eccentric novelist Sidney Moss. There, a traveler could get a meal of potatoes, boiled salmon, coffee, and for dessert, bread sopped in Hawaiian molasses. There, also, a visitor might encounter the luminaries of the town, such as the members of the Oregon Lyceum, a debating society, most of whose colorful and, in some instances, outrageous members Palmer would come to know well. According to Jesse Quinn Thornton, the Lyceum "met with great regularity, especially during the misty saason."[20]

By Palmer's time, the secretary of the debating society, Charles E. Pickett, may have already removed to California, but almost certainly Palmer was shown the last issue of Pickett's newspaper, the *Flumgudgeon Gazette and Bumble Bee Budget*. The twenty-three-year-old Pickett (of the Virginia "Fighting Picketts") had started his newspaper with the purpose of "studying the follies of the times," particularly the follies of the legislative assembly that had met in Oregon City shortly before Palmer's arrival. Referring to one member of that august assembly as the "Gilded Chamberpot"—Pickett's archrival, Dr. Elijah White—Pickett described the assembly as "having . . . the appearance of having just being caught in the act of robbing a turkey roost." In fact, Pickett's general opinion of the settlers was not particularly flattering: "Vulgar, tinpedding, shaving, picayune upstart Yankee and Cockney canoille."[21] There is reason to believe that Palmer, the rather sober Indiana Quaker, would have agreed with Pickett, at least in the case of some of the representatives.

However, Palmer spent little time in Oregon City, for his purpose was to view the countryside,

> its fertility, its general susceptibility of improvement, and its capability for the support of a large and industrious population . . . . In this work I was an inquirer after facts, in order to decide the question as to the propriety of taking my family there for a permanent home.

He began his journey on the west bank of the Willamette and proceeded south, upriver. Palmer's principal concerns were the navigability of the Willamette and its tributaries, as well as the character of the adjacent land and timber. In the region of the Rickreall and Luckiamute rivers, which was just beginning to be settled, he enumerated the names of the settlers before continuing on to what he called the "Mouse" river, Mary's River at present-day Corvallis. As he traveled south, he found less and less settlement, almost none along the river itself; the emigrants had not forgotten the floods and malaria of the Mis-

sissippi and its tributaries. Approaching the Long Tom River, midway between what are now Corvallis and Eugene—and as far south as Palmer
traveled—settlement had petered out, yet "these beautiful valleys offer great
inducement to those who wish to have claims of good land, with fine grounds
for pasturage and timber close at hand." The streams creating these little valleys, Palmer found, "furnish good mill sites . . . and are well filled with
trout." With regard to the valley beyond the Long Tom, "I was informed by
those who had good opportunities for obtaining correct information, that it
bore off more easterly, and that it was for eighty miles further up as well watered, timbered, and of as luxuriant soil, as that which I have described."[22]

Returning to Oregon City—in 1845 there were still no ferries on the upper
reaches of the Willamette—Palmer set out to visit the east bank of the river.
Passing the mouths of the Molalla and the Pudding rivers, he arrived at French
Prairie. "They have very pretty orchards of apple trees, and some peach
trees," he reported. "Their wives are natives of the country. Many of them are
raising families that, when educated, will be sprightly, as they are naturally active and hardy, and appear very friendly and hospitable." It was also Palmer's
impression that the Catholic missionaries stationed there "have done much for
the improvement of these aboriginies."[23]

Palmer traveled next to the site of present-day Salem and spent some time
at the Methodist Institute, which a few years later would become Willamette
University. "The course of instruction there given is quite respectable," Palmer wrote, "and would compare well with many of those located in the old
and populous settlements of the States."[24] And indeed, it was later to be Palmer's choice for the education of some of his own children.

At the Santiam River, twenty miles above the Salem site, Palmer turned
back, disappointed that, here and there, he had found the soil "gravelly." But
in general, he had nothing but praise for the valley. Excepting corn, it was
highly suitable for all crops, in Palmer's judgment, and for wheat, "it is not
excelled by any portion of the continent."[25] By now, it was the end of the year.
In the early spring, Palmer would travel back across the continent. He had
time for one more trip, this time to the coast.

Palmer's optimism often led him in directions that would have daunted
many men, and his efforts often resulted in significant accomplishment. That
same optimism, however, sometimes led him to error. This was the case with
the Oregon coast and the Columbia River. The former he held to be very
promising for cultivation; this middle-westerner had no experience of sea
winds. As for the Columbia, which Wilkes had quite written off, this lands-

man was convinced that with "light houses, buoys, and skillful pilots . . . the harbor at the mouth of the Columbia would compare well with those on the Atlantic Coast; and I may say that it would be superior to many of them."[26] Subsequent to Palmer's visit, hundreds of ships sank at the Columbia bar.

But Palmer was not pleased by everything that he saw at the coast. He found the Tillamooks to be "a lazy and filthy set of beings," and James Birnie, the Hudson's Bay Company official at Astoria, struck him as "a distant, haughty, sulky fellow." One of only two persons whom Palmer condemns in his journal (the first, it may be remembered, was Caleb Greenwood, who persuaded some emigrants to desert the Oregon Trail for California), Birnie refused to bury a washed-up body because it was thought to be an American. Palmer wrote, "this, to say the least, was carrying national prejudice a little too far."[27]

On his trip up the Columbia from Astoria, Palmer observed few claims—again, probably because of the emigrants' fear of fevers and floods—but he was convinced that both fishing and lumbering held "out great inducements to settlers."[28] He was also struck by the scenery, particularly the stretch between Oak Point and Fort Vancouver, reminding him of the Catskills of his youth.

Palmer stopped at Fort Vancouver on this trip, but his description of it in his journal is from an earlier visit with John McClure, a fellow Hoosier. They had had an amusing time.

> This was holyday with the servants of the Hudson's Bay Company, and such *ranting* and frolicking has perhaps seldom been seen among the sons of men. Some were engaged in gambling, some singing, some running horses, many promenading on the river shore, and others on the large green prairie above the fort. H.B. Majesty's ship of war Modesté was lying at anchor about fifty yards from the shore. The sailors also seemed to be enjoying the holydays—many of them were on shore promenading, and casting *sheep's eyes* at the fair native damsels as they strolled from wigwam to hut, and from hut to wigwam, intent upon seeking for themselves the greatest amount of enjoyment. At night a party was given on board the ship, and judging from the noise kept up until ten at night, they were a jolly set of fellows. About this time a boat came ashore from the ship, with a few land lubbers most gloriously drunk. One of them fell out of the boat, and his comrades were barely able to pull him ashore. They passed our shop, cursing their stars for this ill luck.[29]

Palmer and his party had had some ill luck of their own:

> In the after part of the night, several of us were aroused by a strange noise . . . .
> In the darkness we discovered some objects near us, which we supposed to be

hogs. We hissed and hallooed at them, to scare them away. They commenced grunting, and waddled off, and all was again quiet, and remained so until daylight; but when we arose in the morning, we found ourselves minus one wagon sheet, which we had brought along for a sail, our tin kettle, eighteen or twenty pounds of meat, a butcher knife and scabbard, one fur cap, and several other articles, all of which had been stolen by the Indians, who had so exactly imitated the manoeuvres of a gang of hogs, as entirely to deceive us.[30]

It is revealing that in this account there is nothing of the righteous and condemnatory tone so characteristic of most of Palmer's contemporaries when confronted with Indian misbehavior.

It was on the earlier trip that Palmer had first met John McLoughlin, whom he found to be "much of a gentleman."[31] Palmer did not believe, however, McLoughlin's claim that the country north of the Columbia was largely unfit for cultivation. This he considered a ploy of the British to discourage the American claim to the northern region. In fact, McLoughlin's assertion was generally accurate.

PALMER'S TIME IN OREGON had now come to an end. On 5 March 1846, he left Oregon and set out on the return journey to Indiana. "Although anxious to be on the way back, yet I left the place with considerable reluctance," he wrote. "I had found the people of Oregon kind and hospitable, and my acquaintance with them had been of the most friendly character."[32] Traveling with Spencer Buckley, the friend with whom he had begun the journey, Palmer soon joined a party of sixteen other men and apparently became the captain of the group for the remainder of the journey. It was typical of Palmer's modesty that the fact is not stated in his book.

Except for a few difficulties with Indians, it was an uneventful crossing. Reaching St. Joseph, Missouri, on 7 July, Palmer paused long enough to write a letter of "correction" to the St. Joseph *Gazette*. The newspaper had reported that employees of the Hudson's Bay Company were responsible for persuading a portion of the previous year's emigrants to take the disastrous Meek cutoff. In his letter to the editor on 17 July, Palmer admitted that he did not have "very good feelings" toward the Hudson's Bay Company, but "justice requires that facts should be stated"—that is, the person responsible for misleading the emigrants was Stephen Meek, not members of the Hudson's Bay Company.[33]

"Justice requires that facts should be stated" might have served as the epigraph of Palmer's book. Surely his determination to state the facts, however they might fall, and to present them lucidly, explains why his description of the Oregon Trail and the Willamette Valley is so important.

Arriving in Laurel, Indiana, on 23 July, after being gone for one year, three months, and one week, Palmer may well have congratulated himself on the successful outcome of his journey—the materials for a book as well as the sheer adventure of the trip—but it is doubtful that he did so, for he seems not to have been the kind of man to plume himself vaingloriously.

FOUR

The Cayuse War

B Y THE AUTUMN of 1847, Palmer was back in Oregon, this time to stay. At home in Indiana, he had decided that Oregon was the place for his family, and he had spent the year preparing for departure. This meant settling his business affairs and equipping for the trip. He also used the time to work up into book form the notes he had made on the 1845 crossing and on Oregon. The book was published by the distinguished Cincinnati house of J.A. and U.P. James, "the Harper's of the West." Palmer's *Journal of Travels over the Rocky Mountains* was distributed too late to serve the author's purpose, however, for he had hoped by its sale to defray some of the expenses of the second crossing and also to pay some of his outstanding Indiana debts. The publishers did provide a few copies, but most did not reach St. Joseph, Missouri, until after Palmer and his family had left for Oregon. At the time of this permanent remove to Oregon, Palmer was thirty-six, Sarah twenty-six, and the children, eleven, nine, seven, four, and two.

Palmer appears to have been elected captain of the 1847 emigration, for Bancroft and others have referred to the group as "Palmer's Train." According to Bancroft, most of these emigrants were people of "comfortable means," and they carried to the Willamette Valley important additions of livestock and plantings, particularly fruit-tree cuttings.[1]

There were, however, some problems with the emigration. In April 1846, the border dispute with Great Britain had finally been resolved, and now, the Oregon Country was indisputably American. This, of course, encouraged emigration, with the result that Palmer was captain of a train of some four to five thousand persons, one of the largest emigrations ever made.

The sheer numbers of emigrants made for many difficulties on the crossing, the most serious of which was a shortage of grass. The route simply could not provide sufficient forage for the thousands of animals accompanying the emigration.

There were also problems with the Indians, particularly in the region between the Blue Mountains and The Dalles. In many cases, these were Cayuse who "attacked several small companies . . . in some instances tearing the clothing from the persons of the women, leaving them naked in the wilderness."*[2]

★ *If any of these women suffered from the black measles, as some may have, they had a terrible revenge. It was contact between measle-bearing whites and the Cayuse that led, within a few months, to the death of nearly half the tribe.*

The emigration, as was usual, reached the valley in the autumn. Palmer and his family had fared well except at the Deschutes River, where in the crossing a quantity of valuable nursery stock was lost to the river. One bonus of the journey was Palmer's companionship with a young Ohioan, Cris Taylor, a man who would become his most trusted friend and associate.★ In the year since Palmer had seen Oregon City, the forest had been pushed back and new buildings had gone up. Principal among the new structures was Dr. John McLoughlin's house, which he built for himself in the Georgian Colonial style.★ Another sign of the town's growing sophistication was that it now boasted the first newspaper established in the West, the *Oregon Spectator*.

★ *Taylor was well known in his time, but there is little extant information concerning him. He was born in 1822, apparently traveled as part of the Palmer family in the migration, perhaps as a herdsman, and clerked in Francis Pettygrove's Portland store. Palmer first employed him during the Cayuse War and thereafter gave him work intermittently for the rest of his life. Taylor became a successful merchant in both Dayton and Oregon City, was a Whig, was one of the founders of Freemasonry in the West, and*

★ *Following the boundary settlement, Mc-Loughlin left the Hudson's Bay Company, removed to Oregon City, and applied for United States citizenship. The house he built in Oregon City would have graced any street in the Republic and remains today one of the state's most beautiful buildings.*

None of this, of course, is to suggest that the town had been tamed. A jail had been built during Palmer's absence, but someone had promptly burned it down—not the last jail to be torched in early Oregon. Then there were the bowling alleys. "We are annoyed by the bowling alleys," the Reverend George Atkinson complained. "Two or three are in constant operation . . . . many

was commissioned a major general in the state militia. He was much admired for his handsomeness and humor. Taylor died in 1892. See Oregonian, 27 June 1892.

young men frequent them."[3]

Far more disquieting was the maelstrom of Oregon politics. George Abernethy still carried on as governor and leader of the "mission party." In fact, there was little political party organization but there were any number of factions: laymen versus missionaries, teetotalers versus drinkers (a serious and fierce confrontation), farmers versus merchants, British and French Canadians versus Americans. All this had been brought to a greater boil by the boundary decision. For one thing, many were displeased that the treaty allowed the Hudson's Bay Company to keep its property rights at Fort Vancouver, that haven where so many missionaries and settlers had received succor from the hands of Dr. McLoughlin. It was this displeasure that prompted historian Frances Victor to conclude: "Man is a preposterous pig; probably the greediest animal that crawls upon this planet."[4]

The second consequence following upon the boundary decision was that territorial status was now imminent, a condition both desired and dreaded. As an expression of the desire, a committee was formed in 1846 to write a memorial urging prompt action on a territorial bill, for the southern states, not eager to add a free-soil territory to the Union, were dragging their feet. "Our forefathers," the memorialists wrote, "complained that they were oppressed by the mother country, and they had a just right to complain. We do not complain of oppression, but of neglect. Even the tyrant has his moments of relaxation and kindness, but neglect never wears a smile."[5] At the same time, it stuck in the Oregonians' craw that, as a territory, they would be subject to United States authority. Heretofore, the people had enacted their own laws and elected their own officials. Hereafter, all principal offices could be appointed in Washington and Washington would review and pass on all Oregon legislation. However much Oregonians wanted territorial status so that they could further legalize their land claims and gain other benefits, this loss of independence was a very bitter draught to swallow.

Furthermore, what small action the federal government had already taken was not greatly appreciated. For example, an act had been passed establishing two postal routes, but not much had come of this. For, as Bancroft sarcastically remarked, "the greater portion of both routes lay through an uninhabited country and as the correspondence of the savages was not great, the matter rested."[6]

Then there was the problem of the actual appointments. The first of these, to the consternation of many, had been none other than Charles Pickett of the *Flumgudgeon Gazette*, ubiquitous as his archrival, the "Gilded Chamberpot," Dr. Elijah White. The *Spectator* was aghast: "Who can credit the appointment or believe that the United States government could have made its appearance in such a shape?" Bancroft was puzzled as well: "In what way had the people of Oregon displeased the President that he should afflict them thus?"[7] In this particular case, there was no need to worry; even before the appointment reached Oregon, Pickett had skedaddled off to the Sandwich Islands.

There was so much concern over appointments that a number of settlers, with what has been called "the supreme audacity of squatter sovereigns," called for a convention at the falls of the Yamhill River. Their purpose was to recommend to President Polk whom he should and should not appoint to territorial office.[8] Of course, Oregonians had no authority to determine federal appointments. They would be entitled only to elect a delegate to Congress, who would have no vote but would be authorized to speak for the interests of the territory. Although Oregon was not yet entitled to a delegate—it was still not a territory—a number of people wanted one anyway, *ex officio*, as it were, to go to Washington and speak for Oregon in the 1847-48 congressional session. However, the body politic of Oregon was dismembered to such a degree that it was impossible to reach agreement on a representative. Instead, the Yamhill convention sent a memorial to Congress—one implying that Congress had better step lively or Oregon would set up on its own.

On 19 October 1847, the memorial was placed on the bark *Whiton*, bound for San Francisco and Panama. For the time being, Oregonians thought this completed the matter of their representation to Congress. However, certain persons noted that the bark *Whiton* cast anchor after nightfall and, furthermore, that once well into the river, it was approached by a small craft from which a lone figure leaped on board. Who might this lone figure be and why a departure of such surreptitiousness?

The figure was that of an exceedingly nimble Virginian named J. Quinn Thornton. Thornton had come to Oregon in 1846 and had become a close associate of George Abernethy. Abernethy, it finally came out, had on his own chosen Thornton as *ex officio* delegate to represent Oregon in Washington. In particular, he was to represent missionary interests in Oregon, such as the nullification of British property rights—that property the mission party coveted. The reasons for Mr. Thornton's departure under the cover of night need no explanation.

Not long after Palmer arrived in Oregon City, the cat, in the form of

Thornton himself, was well out of the bag. "We understand," Palmer read in the *Spectator* on 11 November,

> that one of our distinguished functionaries has gone to the states, that another started in the height of desperation in a Chinook canoe to go around along the coast in order to head off the first one, and that one of the members of the late Yamhill convention intends crossing the mountains on snowshoes to be in at the death.

It may very well have been these shenanigans, which Palmer would have found both instructive and amusing, that kept him in Oregon City for several weeks before departing for his claim. The claim, which he had marked out in 1845, lay ten miles west of Corvallis. On reaching it, he found that it had been jumped. However, he succeeded in getting one hundred dollars out of the jumper and then proceeded down the valley to the Yamhill, where he settled on a claim that he had originally marked out for his brother-in-law, James Derbyshire, who had remained in Indiana. Palmer was not unhappy with the Yamhill claim and now found it even more desirable than his first choice. With the help of Cris Taylor and another friend, he began to fell trees and build a house. But his labors were interrupted early in the second week of December. They would not soon be resumed.

IT WAS 8 DECEMBER 1847, the first day of the legislative session of Oregon's provisional government. The place of assembly was the Methodist Church at Oregon City, a small, green-shuttered building girdled by an ornate, white picket fence and located so close to the falls that when the wind blew right it was bathed in spray. On this particular December morning, the church was lashed by a heavy rain, drumming the roof beneath which the gentlemen of government were gathered.

The first order of business was the election of officers, a procedure that editor Charles Pickett had once characterized as "varied evolutions, manuoevering . . . double dealing and tangling up of affairs."[9] However accomplished, the officers were finally agreed upon, following which there was a reading of Governor Abernethy's state-of-Oregon message to the legislators. Abernethy, a Scot by birth, had come to Oregon in 1840 to manage the finances of Jason Lee's mission at Salem. He soon went into business for himself and, at the time of his governorship, was a merchant and a mill owner. Peter Burnett, considered a sound judge of character—though some might say more charitable than sound—called Abernethy the "William Penn" of Oregon. Frances Victor took a rather different view: "by a certain smoothness of face, of manner, and of soft brown hair over a sloping forehead, [he] had created the impression of mild, almost weak amiability."[10]

Whatever the justice of Victor's charge, the governor's message was reasonably firm. A jail was urgently needed, and laws pertaining to land claims must be strengthened. In particular, the legislators—few of whom were teetotalers—should act to prohibit sale of ardent spirits. It was the governor's final words, however, that would be remembered:

> Our relation with the Indians becomes every year more embarrassing. They see the white man occupying their lands, rapidly filling up the country, and they put in a claim for pay. They have been told that a chief would come out from the United States and treat with them for their lands; they have been told this so often that they begin to doubt the truth of it. At all events, they say: "He will not come till we are all dead, and then what good will blankets do us? We want something now." This leads to trouble between the settler and the Indians about him. Some plan should be devised by which a fund can be raised, and presents made to the Indians of sufficient value to keep them quiet, until an agent arrives from the United States.[11]

It was a sensible prescription, but it came too late.

The legislators adjourned for lunch followed very possibly by a game of horse billiards—a form of shuffleboard much favored in Oregon City, though frowned on by the mission party. Then the sky darkened and it began to snow. In any event, it was two o'clock and time to reconvene. Back in the church and in that muffled silence that snow brings, they learned the terrible news. At Waiilatpu, the missionary Marcus Whitman, his wife, Narcissa, and eleven of their associates had been killed by the Cayuse Indians, while the remaining fifty-three persons of the mission community, mainly women and children, had been taken captive.

Looking back from the different circumstances of the present, it is difficult to imagine the thoughts and emotions of those men gathered in the little, lamp-lit church on that darkening, snow-silent December afternoon. Fear there surely was, sickening fear, deep in the gut. The Willamette Valley Indians might be debilitated and few in number, but east of the mountains, where the murders had occurred, there were large tribes of mounted warriors who were anything but debilitated. This is what struck fear—well-founded fear—that these tribes would confederate and pour down through the mountain passes to flood the valley with the settlers' blood.

But greater than the fear was the outrage, almost as difficult for us to fully comprehend. To the settlers, the Indians were an inferior race to be bettered, banished, or butchered—whichever, but in any event, inferior—and thus the outrage that what they considered to be a barbaric horde should wreak offense on a civilized community. Here, perhaps, the outrage centered not so much on the murders, which were over and done with, the victims with their God in heaven, as with the belief that the captive white women were being subjected to what was considered the defilement of the savages' lascivious embrace. This was the horror, the fate far worse than death, as the nineteenth century would have put it. So the rage and fear, as the day darkened into night around the little church.

MARCUS AND NARCISSA WHITMAN, together with their co-religionists, Henry and Eliza Spalding, came from New York to the Oregon Country in 1836 to save the souls of the Indians. Without question, they believed that, lacking baptism, the Indians would die, damned for eternity. It was this terrible fate of a whole people that the missionaries sought to prevent. And the sooner the better, for as the *Missionary Herald* had written: "The natives of this wilderness should hear the gospel before they are prejudiced against it by the fraud, injustice and disolute lives of the inevitable immigrants."[12]

It would appear that the Cayuse, among whom the Whitmans settled near present-day Walla Walla, Washington, genuinely welcomed their arrival. The missionaries were a novelty. They might possibly be the purveyors of a new and more efficacious magic. And surely they would bear gifts. The Bible and "infant Jesus" are absent from this shopping list. True, the Cayuse wished for what they called "a strange new thing," and one of their chiefs, Five Crows, was to remark a few years after Whitman's arrival that "we have much wanted some thing; hardly knew what; been groping and feeling for it in confusion and darkness."[13] In general, however, the Cayuse expectations of the Whitmans were of a highly pragmatic nature.

This inauspicious attitude was matched by the Whitmans' ignorance of the Indians, which Dr. Samuel Johnson expressed well in another context: "They are strangers to the language, and the manners, to the advantages and wants of the people whose life they would model and whose evil they would remedy."[14] In short, there was, below the surface, misapprehension on both sides. In time, it would fester and break out.

The first impression that most missionaries had of the Indians was not favorable. This was particularly the case for those who gained that first impression at the mouth of the Columbia, where the natives were particularly debased by long association with European and American fur-trading ships.

"Their appearance was revolting," Methodist missionary Henry Perkins wrote. "Dirty, oily, almost naked in their squalid deformity, how could one love the savages for their own sake."*[15] It was a good question. How indeed could the missionaries, whose cardinal tenet was to love their brothers, love brothers whose habits they abhorred—gambling, drinking, stealing, sexual irregularities, near-nakedness, and an almost total indifference to cleanliness. It was hard.

* *Perkins later showed a more understanding attitude toward the Indians.*

The matter of cleanliness presented a particular problem once the Whitmans built a house. It was the Indians' practice to enter the house at any hour and without invitation, sometimes in large numbers. Not only was this an intrusion on much-needed privacy, but it also left the rooms dancing with fleas and lice. When the Whitmans finally restricted the Indians' visits to their quarters but continued to allow whites to drop in, the Cayuse were offended.

Trouble also arose over the inviolability of the Whitmans' fields, as well as of their parlor. When some Cayuse pastured their horses in the corn patch, Marcus Whitman remonstrated with Chief Tiloukaikt.

> He [Tiloukaikt] replied that this was his land, that he grew up here & that the horses were only eating up the growth of the soil; & demanded of me what I had ever paid him for the land. I answered him—nothing—& that I never would give him anything . . . . I spoke to him of the original arrangement for us to locate here & that we did not come of ourselves but by invitation from the Indians, & that the land was fully granted us.[16]

Thus, the matter of tenancy was yet another irritant.

Most discouraging of all were the problems the Whitmans encountered in preaching the gospel. The local Indian languages lacked terms to express certain central Christian concepts.* The concept of eternal life presented particular problems, especially the notion of an eternal life spent in flames, an aspect of their belief much dwelt upon by the Whitmans. The Cayuse, Narcissa Whitman wrote her father, "try to persuade him [Marcus] not to talk such bad talk to them, as they say, but talk good talk, or tell some story, or history." On another occasion, the Cayuse pleaded with Whitman to leave off his descriptions of hell and teach them hymns instead. Sometimes, as Narcissa wrote, they did more than plead: "Some threaten to whip him and to destroy our crops, and for a long

* *Robert J. Loewenberg described how Methodist Henry Perkins labored to find appropriate terms for "hallowed" and "sacred." See "The Missionary Idea in Oregon: Illustrations from the Life and Times of Methodist Henry Perkins," in*

time their cattle were turned into our potato field every   *The Western Shore,*
night to see if they could not compel him to change his   Thomas Vaughan, ed.
course of instruction with them."[17] But Marcus would
not desist; hell was dear to him.

The Cayuse found Christianity disappointing in other ways as well. They
had expected a great deal of baptism, yet from their point of view, there were
no tangible results. It had in no way improved their prowess in the hunt, in
war, or in love. As for those material rewards for belief so lavishly distributed
by the missionaries on their arrival, these had dwindled to such an extent that a
Cayuse chief complained that "God is stingy."[18]

As time passed, the Cayuse and other tribes came to doubt the validity of
Christian doctrine in general. "Where are these laws from?" asked Yellow Serpent (Piupiumaksmaks), a Walla Walla chief. "Are they from God, or from the
earth? . . . I think that they are from the earth, because, from what I know of
white men, they did not honor these laws."[19] He may have had in mind the curious form that "brotherly love" had taken in the relations between Protestant
and Catholic missionaries.

All of these obstacles and misunderstandings might have been overcome if
the Cayuse had liked the Whitmans; they did not. No one expressed a better
understanding of the reasons than Henry Perkins. In a letter to Narcissa Whitman's sister following the tragedy, he wrote, "they were not adapted to their
work. They could not possibly interest & gain the affections of the natives
. . . . Though they *feared* the Doctor they did not *love* him. They did not love
your sister." Perkins gave several additional reasons why the Cayuse did not
like the Whitmans. For one thing, Whitman "could never stop to *parley*. It was
always *yes* or *no*." Also, "he had no sense of *etiquette* or personal dignity—
manners, I mean." And finally, "*he was always at work*. Now I need not tell
you that he & an Indian would never agree. How could they? What would
such a man have in common with an Indian?" As for Narcissa, she "was not
adapted to savage but *civilized* life . . . . The natives esteemed her as proud,
haughty, as *far above them* . . . . It was her *misfortune*, not her *fault* . . . . She
longed for society, *refined society* . . . . The self-denial that took her away from
it was suicidal."[20]

These, then, were some of the issues that galled the relations between the
missionaries and their flock. In themselves, however, they would not have led
to the killings, even though they did much to poison the ground in which the
ultimate causes took root.

Beginning in 1842, the Cayuse saw larger and larger groups of whites
moving across their land: by 1847, in the thousands. The Indians had heard

stories of what had happened to Indian lands in the East, and they knew for a fact what had happened in the Willamette Valley. Gradually, they came to believe that the Whitmans supported a similar fate for the Cayuse, as evidenced, for example, by Whitman's welcome of Palmer and his party at the Umatilla. The Indians were not alone in believing that the Whitmans favored the settlement of their land by whites. Whitman, Perkins wrote, "looked upon them as an inferior race & doomed at no distant day to give place to a settlement of enterprising Americans . . . . He wanted to see the country settled . . . . teeming with a busy, bustling white population."[21]

The Cayuse also believed that the missionaries intended to facilitate this transfer of land by poisoning them. The Whitmans had used poisons for certain purposes, and some Indian dogs had died from poison they had put out for the wolves. Also, Dr. William Gray, Whitman's associate, had injected a nonlethal but sickening poison into his melons to discourage the Indians from stealing them. These practices, combined with the fact that the Indians generally died of the ever more prevalent measles while whites generally did not, led to only one conclusion.

Palmer's emigration of 1847 had been rife with measles, and the Cayuse, trading with the Americans—or stealing from them—brought it back to Whitman's mission. By the time of the Whitmans' deaths, and as noted earlier, nearly half the tribe of three hundred had died. This, together with Whitman's use of poisons and his enthusiastic welcome of the whites, finally settled the matter in the minds of the Cayuse.

The end came on a cold, dark Monday in late November. Whitman, exhausted from caring for the sick, both Indians and whites, was tommyhawked from behind. Narcissa was shot and dumped into the mud, where she was repeatedly lashed with a leather quirt. The Indians killed eleven more whites, although they spared the remaining women and most of the children.

THE FEAR AND RAGE of the legislators gathered in the church at Oregon City were quickly translated into action. A call went out for fifty volunteers, who would serve under the command of H.A.G. Lee. Their charge was to protect the property of the missionaries and the emigrants at The Dalles and to establish a military base, there at the gateway to the plateau and the region of the conflict. The following afternoon, 9 December, forty-six volunteers showed up at Moss' Main Street House, where Judge James W. Nesmith* presented Lee with a flag, hastily sewn by the women of Oregon City. Lee, of the "Virginia Lees" and a companion of Charles Pickett, made "an exceedingly

* *James W. Nesmith arrived in the 1843 emigration and thereafter*

happy reply," according to the *Spectator*, and then all proceeded in the rain to the riverbank. Here, the little force boarded a bateau, stuck the flag in the bow, and cast off to the firing of a cannon and the cheers of the assembled crowd. Thus began Act I of that five-part tragedy—the Indian wars of Oregon.

The following day, the legislators moved to form a major volunteer force of five hundred men who would serve ten months. The prospects of gathering such a force were poor. Most of the first forty-six volunteers were single men, newly arrived, and game for the lark of war. Further recruitment would depend on the willingness of settled farmers to leave their families and fields. There was also the problem of equipping such a force, assuming it could be raised, since the treasury of the provisional government contained only $43.72, while its indebtedness was $4,079.74. In other words, the two basic requirements for any war—men and money—might be hard to come by.

There were those who thought it might be just as well. The Hudson's Bay Company did not want an Indian war to disturb the matrix of their trade. Even more opposed, and desperately so, was the Reverend Henry H. Spalding, Whitman's associate on the Clearwater River near present-day Lewiston, Idaho. Spalding had narrowly escaped the Cayuse attack at the mission and was now under the protection of the Nez Perce—on one condition. This Spalding wrote on 10 December to the Catholic bishop of Walla Walla, A.M.A. Blanchet,* pleading with

occupied a prominent and colorful place in Oregon life. He was an officer in all of the early Indian wars and served as provisional government supreme court judge, U.S. marshal, superintendent of Indian affairs, U.S. representative, and U.S. senator. In between these various activities, he farmed and also spent time in the state hospital. According to Malcolm Clark, he was among the most popular of Democrats as well as being "a monumental he-gossip . . . slightly rowdy, a bit irregular in his habits, possessed of a robust wit not always wisely used . . . a genuine and fascinating character." See Clark, Pharisee Among Philistines.

★ *A.M.A. Blanchet, bishop of Walla Walla, was the brother of Archbishop F.N. Blanchet, the first Catholic missionary to the Oregon Country.*

him to communicate the condition to both the Cayuse and the Oregon legislators. The condition was a simple one: "They [the Nez Perce] pledged themselves to protect us from the Cayuses if [we] would prevent the Americans from coming up to avenge the murders. This we have pledged to do, and for this we beg for the sake of our lives."[22] Spalding wrote his letter on the same day the legislators called for a force of five hundred men.

On 11 December, the assembly took further steps to pursue the war. Governor Abernethy dispatched a delegation to James Douglas, who had replaced McLoughlin as the chief factor at Fort Vancouver. Choking on a large platter of crow, the delegates asked the British for a loan. Douglas refused, saying the company was not authorized to make such outlays; he may have added that a public loan for war against the Indians would prejudice the company's standing with the tribes. The chief factor did agree, however, to make a private, personal loan of a thousand dollars to the delegates as individuals, a circumvention entirely acceptable to the delegates.

The assembly's next act on that busy day was to appoint Joseph L. Meek, the sheriff of Oregon, as emissary to Washington City, as the capital was then called. His charge was to ask for United States protection in the current emergency. Meek was chosen partly for his colorful persuasiveness, partly because he was a shirttail relative of President Polk.* The memorial Meek carried had been phrased to melt the government's cold heart:

> Having called on the government of the United States so often in vain we have almost despaired of receiving its protection . . . . We have the right to expect your aid, and you are duty bound to extend it. For though we are separated from our native land by a range of mountains whose lofty altitudes are mantled in eternal snows; although 3,000 miles, nearly 2/3 of which is a howling wild, lie between us and the federal capitol—yet our hearts are unalienated from the land of our birth. Our love for the free and noble institutions under which it was our fortune to be born and nurtured remains unabated.[23]

These stirring words did not have much immediate effect; the first result of the plenipotentiary's mission was the astonishment of all Washington at the figure that he cut. Eventually, however, his petitions would bear fruit in the form of territorial status.

In Oregon City, the assembly ended on 11 December with the appointment of officers for the volunteer forces. The commander chosen was Col. Cornelius Gilliam, veteran of the Black Hawk and Seminole wars, famed tracker of runaway slaves, hardshelled, hellfire

*In Washington City, Meek, a retired trapper, introduced himself as "envoy extraordinary and minister plenipotentiary from the republic of Oregon to the court of the United States," the "court" a sarcastic reference to what the sheriff no doubt considered an effete and decadent capital compared with his own at Oregon City. Several years ago, the author spoke with an elderly gentleman whose grandmother had known Meek well. "What did your grandmother think of Meek?" I asked him. "She said," he replied, "that he was a whoremonger and a drunkard

Baptist preacher, and the man who some said "preferred   *but for all that a very*
the smoke of gun powder to the smoke of peace pipes."   *fine man."* See Corn-
Second in command and commissioned as lieutenant   ing, *Dictionary of Ore-*
colonel was James Waters who, according to Peter Bur-   *gon History,* 164.
nett, was a "most excellent man, possessed of a kind
heart, truthful tongue, and patient disposition."[24]

The final appointment may have been the most crucial. In the office of the
commissary general, Frances Victor wrote,

> the hardest struggle of the war was carried on—not in fighting Indians, but in
> keeping the men in the field . . . . Without arms, without roads, without trans-
> portation, other than small boats and pack horses, without comfortable winter
> clothing and with scanty food, the war was to be carried on at a distance of
> nearly three hundred miles from the settlements.[25]

It is not known why the assembly chose Joel Palmer for this most difficult of
assignments. Certainly, there were others who desired the office, for however
taxing, it could be highly lucrative if the holder were so disposed. But most of
the legislators probably had met Palmer, and he seems always to have made a
striking first impression. Many of them also knew of his reputation as an honest, just, and efficient captain in the 1845 and 1847 emigrations.

Palmer first heard of the massacre while at his claim on the Yamhill where,
as noted earlier, he, Cris Taylor, and another friend were felling logs to build a
house. Palmer was much distressed. He remembered Whitman from their encounter on the Umatilla in 1845 and in his book had gone out of his way to
praise the missionary. He had again encountered Whitman on the Umatilla
only a month or so before, when they had camped together. "He said to me,"
Palmer later told Bancroft, "that four Catholic priests had located on the
Umatilla that season and that there was a marked difference in the conduct of
the Indians toward him since they had been there. They manifested a hostile
disposition and he apprehended trouble." Therefore, Palmer was not entirely
surprised by news of the murder and had an idea of its cause, an idea he was
never to abandon, even in the face of much evidence to the contrary. Palmer
believed that the priests had instigated the massacre.[26]

Apparently, Palmer struck off immediately for Oregon City to offer his
services in the emergency. At Chehalem Gap, near present-day Newberg, he
met a messenger bearing his letter of appointment as commissary general. He
went on to the falls where, through the good offices of John McLoughlin, he
began to arrange with James Douglas at Fort Vancouver for the purchase of
provisions. The most serious shortage, however, was men. The call for additional volunteers had had little response.

IN THE MEANTIME, the first volunteers under H.A.G. Lee were proceeding up the Columbia. "There has been the utmost good feeling in the company," Lee reported on 16 December.[27] There must have been considerable hardiness as well, for rowing against the wind and current in an open boat through the Columbia Gorge in mid-December would have been exhilarating, to say the least. At Wind River Mountain, thirty miles below The Dalles, the boats became windbound, and Lee, hearing of Indian depredations at The Dalles, hurried his troops on by land. Arriving on Christmas night, Lee and his men routed the Indians. But he also heard distressing news: all the captives from the Whitman mission had been killed and the country east of the Deschutes River was in enemy hands. Lee did what he could: he forted up, he wrote Oregon City requesting a cannon and reinforcements, and he waited.

WHILE LEE AND HIS MEN were braving the winds of the Gorge and Palmer was seeking supplies for an army that did not yet exist, Bishop A.M.A. Blanchet was parleying with the Cayuse. On 18 December, Camatspelo, chief of one of the Cayuse bands, called on the bishop to complain that his young men had "stolen his word" when they attacked the Whitmans; that is, they had acted without his permission. In his dejection, Camatspelo told Blanchet that he had decided to kill his horses and leave the country, since the Cayuse believed that to remain in their land meant death. The bishop proposed that in place of such drastic action the chiefs meet and prepare a petition for peace.

Camatspelo agreed, and on the morning of 20 December the Cayuse chiefs assembled at Blanchet's house. According to J.B.A. Brouillet, the bishop's secretary, Camatspelo spoke first, saying that he was blind and ignorant and without hope for his nation but that the bishop's words had encouraged him to believe that there might yet be peace. The next to speak was Tiloukaikt, who said that he was not gifted with eloquence and would be brief. He then went on for two hours to review the history of the whites in the Indians' land. He made particular mention of a Walla Walla and a Nez Perce who had been killed by whites, acts that would be forgiven if the whites forgave the Cayuse the killing of the Whitmans. Young Chief spoke little, saying that he felt weak. Five Crows also said little, but he may have had a different reason. Five Crows had taken one of the captives, Lorinda Bewley, as a wife, and she now resided in his lodge. The rumor that all of the captives had been killed was untrue. A worse fate had befallen some of them, that "fate worse than death."

Finally, Tiloukaikt's son, Edward, rose, holding in his hand a Catholic ladder, a chart that showed pictorially the history of Catholicism and the errant path of Protestantism. The ladder that Edward held before the bishop and the chiefs was smeared with blood. Marcus Whitman had shown it to him only a few weeks before, Edward said, and had warned: "You see this blood! it is to show you that now, because you have the priests among you, the country is going to be covered with blood!! You will have nothing now but blood!"[28] And Whitman had been right, however wrong his reasons.

After further deliberations, the chiefs agreed to a peace proposal, prefaced with what they believed to be the reason for the massacre: their conviction that the Whitmans intended to exterminate them so that the whole of Cayuse lands might fall to the whites. The Indians then proposed that the Americans forgive the murderers and that peace emissaries be sent to receive the prisoners unharmed. Finally, they stipulated that Americans would no longer travel in their country, since their young men might do them harm.

The council ended with the bishop and the other chiefs imploring Five Crows to release Miss Bewley, but he refused. Blanchet then sent the Indians' proposal to Governor Abernethy together with a letter of his own. He made it clear that the Indians wanted to show that they had acted from "an anxious desire of self-preservation," and, he had added, "I feel myself obliged to tell you, that by going to war with the Cayuses, you will likely have all the Indians of this country against you."[29]

Bishop Blanchet was not alone in fearing a coalition of the tribes. On 23 December 1847, the *Spectator* commented: "It is generally believed now that there is a regular combination of the tribes of the upper Columbia; if this should prove to be the fact, we should have serious times indeed."

The same concern may have prompted the legislature to issue a second call for volunteers on 25 December. Each man was to furnish his own horse, arms, clothing, and blankets and to commit himself to six months of service. The men were to assemble at Portland on 8 January. The first call for volunteers apparently had not been successful, and many men were still reluctant to leave their fields and families in the face of possible Indian attacks. A few days before the call went out, the 23 December *Spectator* had observed: "There is much difference of opinion in the public mind as to the propriety of calling out one hundred men or more."

One segment of this opinion was the peace party. On 14 December, the legislature had gone so far as to ask the governor to appoint peace commissioners, the very measure that, unknown to the legislators, both the Nez Perce and the Cayuse had requested. By late December, however, the governor still had not acted on the request. William Rector, representative from Champoeg

County, expressed the concerns of the peace party and hinted at something else as well:

> I was not in favour of trying to punishing the Indians until we ware in a beter condition the sean of action was remote from us beyond the mountains in a coal country with no means of supplying an armey no armes but such as had survived the journey over the plains and mountains no amunition onley such as the setlers had for their own use, with all these facts before me I was unwilling to hazard a contest with the Indians all for glory. besides all this I was in doubts whether the Indians was so much to blame for what they had don and with all that has com to light since I am still of the same belief but there was not a few of the members but what wanted noteriaty as cournals captains, &c.[30]

Two developments began to counter these proclivities for peace, and both deepened the settlers' sense of outrage. One was the rumor that the Indians continued to violate the mission women; the other was the conviction that Bishop Blanchet and his priests had provoked the massacre.

It is difficult from the vantage point of the present, and now that the fires of sectarian differences have almost gone out, to realize and understand the depth of hostility that then existed between Protestant and Catholic.

To the ordinary Oregon settler, Protestant in religion and republican in politics, the Roman church was seen as the repository of all persecution and superstition, the cohort of European despots, the foe of progress. At the same time, Catholicism had become the largest single denomination in the nation, and its members were mainly "foreigners." There was also the conviction that American Catholics gave their allegiance to the triple crown rather than to the Stars and Stripes. Finally, there was, in the general sense, a pride in fervently held belief, an expression of manliness to sound the charge for one's religion, politics, and region.

All of this being the case, the presence of Catholic priests in the Walla Walla country at the time of the massacre was enough evidence for most Protestants of the priests' complicity. In short, now, with both religious and chivalric sensibilities further outraged, recruitment for the volunteer force showed more success.

In the meantime, Palmer's task increased as well. By late December, he was arranging for the construction of storehouses at the Cascades and was appointing commissary agents to purchase supplies, such as pork, beef, wheat, flour, camp kettles, riding saddles, trail ropes, saddlebags, and ammunition. Payments were to be made in bonds drawing 10 percent per annum and running for three years. All of the supplies required were in short supply in the

Willamette Valley, and there were others that did not exist at all. Spyglasses, for example, were impossible to find, and a Lieutenant Crawford claimed that not a bottle of ink was to be had in all of Portland and would Palmer kindly send him some so that he might continue to write his reports.

To Palmer's problems of procurement, the legislature added another problem of a similarly intractable nature. On 28 December, he was appointed superintendent of Indian affairs of the provisional government. At the same time, the lawmakers passed legislation that could only complicate his new duties: henceforth, no firearms or ammunition could be sold to Indians. Prevented from hunting, the Indians would now by necessity steal even more of the settlers' cattle—beef that Palmer urgently needed for the growing army.

The most serious shortage, however, was ammunition—a shortage so severe that there was talk by Colonel Gilliam and among the volunteers, who by now had assembled, of capturing Fort Vancouver and relieving the Hudson's Bay Company of its powder and shot. On 31 December, Chief Factor James Douglas protested to Governor Abernethy, and the threat caused him to mount guns on his bastions. "It was never supposed that our establishment would be exposed to insult or injury from American citizens, while we were braving the fury of the Indians for their protection," he complained.[31]

EXACTLY. For immediately upon hearing of the massacre, the Hudson's Bay Company had dispatched Peter Skene Ogden of its Board of Management to the Walla Walla country to rescue the captives and prevent further atrocities. Ogden reached Fort Walla Walla on 19 December and learned from William McBean, the company's post trader, that the captives were still alive. McBean claimed that this was due to his intervention. He had, he said, sent his interpreter to the mission to dissuade the Cayuse from further vengeance on the captives. The interpreter had found the prison house surrounded by Indian women with knives and clubs waiting for the chief's word to begin the torture and killing. The chief, warned by the interpreter of the company's displeasure, ordered the women away—and go they did, but not without calling the chief a coward.

Ogden ordered a council of the Cayuse for 23 December. The captives could hardly have had a better qualified interceder. The son of a Canadian chief justice, Ogden had served the fur trade for nearly forty years, had dealt with all manner of Indians, and had married two Indian women. He was small, dark, a little rough, and according to Bancroft, given to "fun and frolic." But he could also be severe, as he was on this occasion when he called the assembled chiefs a set of "hermaphrodites" for having lost control of their young braves.[32]

After a further upbraiding, Ogden told the council that the company would not take sides in any future disputes between the Cayuse and the Americans—after all, the company did not want to jeopardize its trade with the tribes—but there was one matter that must be resolved at once. The captives must be released, and in return, Ogden promised a ransom of blankets and shirts, ammunition, guns and flints, tobacco, oxen, and flour.

The Cayuse agreed. After all, many of the company's voyageurs and trappers were married to their women and were considered brothers; they were brothers in death as well, for the company did not prohibit Indians and whites from being buried side by side. But perhaps the principal reason for the Cayuse capitulation was Ogden himself. Tiloukaikt reportedly said:

> Chief! your words are weighty—your hairs are gray. We have known you a
> long time. You have had an unpleasant journey to this place. I cannot, there-
> fore, keep the families back. I make them over to you, which I would not do to
> another younger than yourself.[33]

In reply, Ogden promised the chief that he would attempt to dissuade the Americans from war.

And so the captives were brought in: "the women, particularly the young, were most unwillingly surrendered by the dusky warriors to whose arms they had been consigned." Five Crows certainly was unwilling to release Miss Bewley from his embrace, for he had long desired a white wife. Sir George Simpson, governor of the Hudson's Bay Company, had observed Five Crows in the throes of such passion at Fort Walla Walla in 1841:

> Young, tall, and handsome, he had lately raised his eyes to a beautiful and ami-
> able girl, daughter of one of the Company's officers. After enduring the flames
> of love for some time in silence . . . he presented himself and a band of retain-
> ers, master and men all gay as butterflies, at the gates of the fort, where the fa-
> ther of his "ladye love" resided.[34]

But Five Crows had been rejected. Miss Bewley later testified that on the morning of her release, Five Crows cooked her a good breakfast and placed before her saddle a new blanket and buffalo robe.

By 2 January, fifty-seven captives had been assembled at Fort Walla Walla, including Spalding and his family, who had been escorted in the day before by their Nez Perce protectors. At noon, "tremulous from injuries," the group boarded the Hudson's Bay Company boats and Ogden took them down the river through the winter-brown hills.[35] They left none too soon. A few hours later, a band of Cayuse galloped up to the fort seeking Spalding's scalp; they had heard that troops had reached The Dalles, and to their mind, Spalding's promise to the Nez Perce that he would restrain the whites had been broken.

On the morning of 10 January 1848, the cannon mounted on Portland's waterfront fired a salvo into the winter air. It was a salute to the passing flotilla that carried the survivors of the massacre, with Peter Skene Ogden standing in the bow of the lead boat. Cannons were discharged again at Oregon City, where the survivors disembarked and fell into the arms of the waiting citizens. Frances Victor described the scene:

> Half-crazed widows; young women who had suffered such indignities and brutalities that they wondered to find themselves alive . . . children who had lost the happy innocence of childhood, whom suffering had made old before their time; men who had become craven through fear—an avalanche of such misery poured into the lap of a small community, still struggling with the hardships of pioneer settlement, upheaved it from its very foundations.[36]

Ogden also had brought Spalding's letter, begging for restraint from the whites—though Spalding now was calling for the reverse—as well as the Nez Perce and Cayuse pleas for peace and Bishop Blanchet's letter advising restraint. But it was too late. The *Spectator*'s editorial of 8 January on the survivors' release gives a notion of the temper that prevailed. After judging that the crime that had been perpetrated on the women was so terrible that it could not even be named, the newspaper went on to urge that the Cayuse

> be pursued with unrelenting hatred and hostility, until their life blood has atoned for their infamous deeds; let them be hunted as beasts of prey; let their name and race be blotted from the face of the earth, and the places that once knew them, know them no more forever.

The force dedicated to this pursuit had finally rendezvoused at a Portland tavern on the east bank of the Willamette. They had come together by fits and starts, their numbers already depleted by desertions.*

There were other problems as well. The commander, Colonel Gilliam, wrote:

Some of the desertions were of a temporary nature, however, as in the case of the group of young men who took a few days off in late December to attend a ball in Hillsboro.

> I had a very tedious time at Portland awaiting there in the rain for the Volenteres for I am not enabled to leiv there untill the Eighth of January and wile there I had to be Col. & Major & Adjutant & Capt. & Sirgant and everything else allmost that you could amgin allmost wich come very nere runing mee off my feet I assure you before the companey was formmed wile there we got a long very well with the ecception of one evening there was a canoe loaded with liccor and two of the men got to fiting nere my tent but I soon had them parted and I supposed that it was in consquence of the liccor that was here.[37]

The force, 220 strong, left for Vancouver on 8 January, vowing, according to Frances Victor, that their first shots would be for the bishop and his priests. Such had been the result of Spalding's mendacious tales combined with the settlers' susceptibility to anti-Catholic rhetoric. At Vancouver, Palmer joined Gilliam to bid the latter goodbye and together they drew eight hundred dollars on their personal accounts to purchase supplies. Then Gilliam, entrusting a large bearskin to Palmer for safekeeping until his return, departed. The men rode up the north bank of the Columbia, their supplies accompanying them on flatboats. On the far side of the Cascades, they crossed the river and continued up the south bank, arriving at the campaign's headquarters at The Dalles on 23 January.

WHO WERE THE PLAYERS in this first act of the thirty-year-long tragedy of Oregon Indian wars? First, the Cayuse. "These Indians had decidedly a better appearance than any I have met; tall and athletic in form, and of great symmetry of person; they are generally well clad, and observe pride in personal cleanliness."[38] So wrote Palmer when on the Umatilla in 1845, and he was not alone in his impression. From the first known contact with the Cayuse in 1811, whites had found much that was admirable in these "monarchs" of the Oregon Country.

The heartland of the Cayuse lay in the Grande Ronde and Walla Walla valleys. It was in the green, edenic Grande Ronde, on the banks of its looping river, that they held their annual summer fairs where they would gamble, wrestle, dance, and race—on foot or on their fleet little piebald mounts.

Their appearance was striking. Samuel Black, an early trader, described them as a high-cheekboned, high-shouldered, flat-bodied people who often stood at six feet or more. They were vain of their hair—"part sometimes Borrowed," wrote Black—and wore it in poufs to either side of the head or down their backs almost to the ground, in some cases sparkled with bits of metal, mirror, and glass.[39] Some pierced the septum of their noses and hung a wolf's tooth from it; they also were given to a slash of lampblack upward from the outer corner of the eye, like a scimitar.

The Cayuse were vain of their clothes as well, with shirts of fringed hide falling to their thighs and sashed low on the hips, fringed leggings, moccasins, and all "richly garnished," Alexander Ross wrote in 1811. The women wore ankle-length garments of ornamented skin, little caps of willow twigs, and according to John Townsend in the 1830s, had "a peculiarly sleepy and languishing appearance . . . . as if naturally inclined to lasciviousness," though he added that they were not.[40]

Above all, the Cayuse were a horse people, and the chiefs' herds often numbered in the thousands. In particular they valued white horses, and to these they would attach feathered headpieces, streak their withers with dyes of different hues, and braid their tails with colored ribbons.

> The Indians augmented nature's coloration by painting and otherwise decorating their mounts as they did themselves, creating an illusion of physical unity between man and beast to match what they considered the mystical union between them.[41]

Most commentators agreed that the Cayuse were imperious with pride, hot-tempered, and "very impatient of insult and revengeful in the extreme," as Astorian Robert Stuart wrote. Elijah White called them "boisterous, saucy." In one respect, whites found them unique among other tribes: they did not steal. This may be one reason why the Cayuse disdained trade, except of a minor sort: "petty trade for a pipe, a hare, or a grouse," Townsend wrote of them at Fort Walla Walla. When at the fort, it was pleasure more than trade that occupied their time. "They scalp-danced, horse-raced, gambled, and otherwise idled their time away. They could be seen on every hillock making their toilet, with looking glass in one hand and paintbrush in the other." So the Cayuse, handsome, proud, vain, aloof, and vengeful, this tribe who called themselves by a word that in their own language may have meant "a superior people."[42]

THEN THE VOLUNTEERS. Most were young, unmarried, and from the border states. Few had had any training, though many probably had served in their local state militias. As a rule, however, militia meetings were infrequent, and "drill" more often than not had given place to wrestling—where a man would stand on a stump and crow like a rooster to indicate that he was ready to take on anyone—getting drunk, playing pranks, and competing in games such as "Pull the Goose."* None of the men had come to the Oregon Country to be ordered about by anyone. Jesse Applegate remarked that they

> were probably brave enough, but would never submit to discipline as soldiers. If the President himself had started across the Plains to command a company, the first time he would choose a bad camp or in any way offend them, they would turn him out and elect someone among themselves.[43]

A live goose, its head greased with hog fat, was hung by its feet from a tree branch. The contestants, galloping under the branch, attempted to pull off the goose's head.

As for their attitude toward the foe, it is impossible to generalize, for they probably differed in their feelings as much as armies generally do: hate, indifference, respect, and sometimes, even pity.

THIS, THEN, WAS THE ARMY that arrived at The Dalles on 23 January 1848 to begin the campaign against the Cayuse. Colonel Gilliam found Lee with only thirteen of his original force of forty-six volunteers, the other thirty-one having drifted off for one reason or another. Perhaps it was just as well—it left fewer mouths for the scrapings of flour left in the barrels. While waiting for Gilliam, Lee had written with evident sarcasm to Abernethy on 20 January: "I've been here for one month and no company yet." As a result, the local Indians were beginning to side with the enemy,

> thinking no doubt, that we have spoken falsely to them, that no more are coming . . . . if our friends in the valley are *brave* enough to leave us in our present situation, after getting us into it, we are determined to be *generous* enough to battle with the enemy and defend ourselves as long and as well as we can.

Cornelius H. Defendorff, Lee's commissary officer, had written in a similar vein to Abernethy on 17 January:

> Serious apprehensions were entertained, that the government of Oregon would do little or nothing for our relief . . . . For when we glance at our position, far removed from the arm of protection, at our numbers—infant like in point of power, at our resources, blighted with an empty treasury; at our credit dishonored even by those among us; and then turn and view our enemy—numerous in number, barbarous in principle, transient in their very nature, whose homes are unfettered by civilization, with almost a boundless waste before them to cover their retreats, such conclusions irresistibly force themselves upon the mind.[44]

It was at this disheartened camp that Gilliam's men finally settled in on the banks of Mill Creek on 23 January. It was on that evening as well that the first casualty of the war occurred. Gilliam described it the following day in a letter to his wife:

> One of the Garde shot a Squaw in the thy thinking that she was an Indian man. It appears that she was acrolling [crawling] along on the ground so that she get to plaice of appointment between her and some of our young men which I am sorry to [say] such things to friequentely occurs at this plaice.

Of more concern to the colonel was the serious shortage of supplies. On 25 January, he informed Palmer that the army could not both starve and advance. Palmer meanwhile had been told by his agent in Salem that the town's only cooper had refused to coop another flour barrel until he was paid in cash—not government scrip—and in advance. And it was flour that the army most urgently needed. Nonetheless, Gilliam apparently felt capable of making a small advance without additional supplies, for on the same day, he wrote his wife that he planned an attack on some Deschutes Indian villages "to gete as meney horses and cattle as I can likewise scelpes."[45] And in fact, on the following day, he started out with 120 men for the Deschutes River.

Two days later, having established a camp five miles above the river's mouth, Gilliam called for volunteers to carry out a scouting expedition that, he said, would "lead them to a tea party," a euphemism that, in view of Gilliam's reputation, suggested a sanguinary brew. A squad formed and, under Lee's command, rode off south along the tableland to the east of the river. At three o'clock that afternoon, rounding a ridge "we suddenly came on a band of Indians . . . charging straight for us," wrote William Stillwell, who later in the battle received an arrow in his hip. The volunteers were not altogether prepared. "There were several of the boys who could not get their guns primed or capped." These problems solved, the volunteers charged, and the Indians fled south. One group was overtaken near the Oregon Trail; two women were captured, one brave was killed, and the remainder escaped.[46]

On their return to camp, another large party of Indians attacked, forcing the volunteers into a small canyon, from the heights of which the Indians rolled boulders down on them as well as "annoying us much with their savage yells," according to Lee.[47] Dodging boulders and returning insults, the volunteers fought on for several hours until the Indians again retreated and the volunteers were free to return to camp.

On the following morning, the whole body of volunteers started south to search for the remaining Indians and any provisions they might have. After a night at Stag Hollow—a rock-ribbed widening of the Deschutes Canyon some twenty miles upriver—and a breakfast that consumed the last of their provisions, "we saw some Indians on the opposite side of the Hollow fortifying themselves with rock breastworks on top of the ridge . . . it gave them the best position by far; there were two Indians to our one and the cliff was a hard one to scale." But the volunteers prevailed, though in what fashion is not certain. Palmer was not present, but he concluded from reports that "the yelling of the troops so far exceeded that of the Indians, the latter were demoralized, and fled from the field."[48]

Skirmishes continued for a day or so, the volunteers now reduced to eating horse meat, "and that without salt." Finally, they came upon an Indian village, deserted except for several old people, whom they left undisturbed, and some stolen cattle, which they retrieved. Meanwhile, as Colonel Gilliam put it, the Indians had "fled like wolves and scattered among the hills and canyons."[49] The engagement was over, and the volunteers returned to The Dalles.

This, the first battle of the Cayuse War, was not sufficiently conclusive to presage the final outcome of hostilities. Although the Indians may have lost more men—the volunteers estimated twenty to thirty Indians killed compared to four whites—and although they did occasionally retreat, the volunteer accounts of the Deschutes campaign do not give the impression that the Indians had been vanquished. What the accounts do suggest is that both sides waged the battle with considerable brio. "The Indians fought bravely until we were close enough to blow powder smoke in their faces," wrote William Stillwell. "The men all acted bravely," Gilliam reported, "the only difficulty is in keeping them back."[50] In short, it had been a good scrap.

However, on arriving at The Dalles, the volunteers' exuberance was dashed by the grisly success of an Indian ruse. Seeing what looked like strayed horses in a distant meadow, two of the guard had ridden off to retrieve them. In fact, the horses had been stolen by some Indians who had staked the horses in the meadow and then hidden nearby. When the unsuspecting volunteers approached, the Indians shot them. Another deception also led to death. A young man named McDonald, bringing in fresh provisions, decided to tease the guard by pretending to be an Indian, a performance so convincing that the guard shot the prankster dead.

In general, the morale at the camp on Mill Creek was in decline. It was cold now, in January, there on the banks of the river, in the blast of the bitter gorge winds. Food was still in short supply, aggravated by the Indians' success in drawing off some of the camp's cattle. There was not enough powder and shot. The death of the three volunteers had been disheartening, and the additional troops promised had not arrived. The volunteers began to believe the valley had forsaken them.

BUT THE VALLEY HAD NOT FORGOTTEN the volunteers: rather, it was hamstrung by problems of its own. Recruitment continued to be sluggish, with the men still reluctant to leave their farms and families. And Palmer was having difficulty obtaining supplies. His agent in Salem informed him that only dribs and drabs of pork and wheat were coming in. Furthermore, there was no warehouse to store the few supplies Palmer did acquire until the infrequent boats arrived to transport the provisions downstream to the Columbia.

At the same time, Palmer was receiving urgent pleas from The Dalles for all manner of supplies. The troops badly needed such necessities as bridles, saddles, boots, belts, scabbards, and shot pouches. They also needed shirts and cloth for bandages. And the quartermaster at The Dalles warned that he would be unable to make future requests, since he had no more paper on which to write them.

Of all the shortages, wheat was the most serious. The situation became so critical that the 7 February *Spectator* issued a public appeal. While admitting that the wheat harvest had been unusually small that year and the emigration unusually large, "yet Oregon's heroic volunteers should have bread as long as there is bread in Oregon . . . . They have gone at your bidding . . . to execute the laws of earth and heaven against those who have shed innocent blood. Shall they have bread?" As Palmer well knew, the question was far from rhetorical.

Despite the shortages of men and material, Governor Abernethy urged Gilliam on in pursuit of the enemy. "Let them know the Americans are not *women*," he wrote. By early February, his bellicosity had cooled, and he instructed Gilliam to tell the Indians that "no friendly tribes will be attacked; that all you want is the murderers, and a restitution of stolen property."[51] Most important, he informed Gilliam that he had appointed three peace commissioners and that Gilliam should remain at The Dalles until they arrived. It is puzzling that Abernethy had waited six weeks to make the appointments, but now that he had done so he could not have done better. H.A.G. Lee, Robert Newell, and Joel Palmer were among the most estimable men in early Oregon.

H.A.G. Lee was born into one of Virginia's most distinguished families. In 1843, at the age of twenty-five, he abandoned ministerial studies and with his high-spirited and irreverent friend, Charles Pickett, departed for Oregon. His first winter was spent at Henry Spalding's mission on the Clearwater, teaching in the mission Indian school and studying the Nez Perce language. In the spring, he took on the job of assistant and interpreter to Dr. Elijah White, then roving about the countryside as a quasi-official United States Indian agent. Poor health, from which Lee suffered, obliged him to retire to Oregon City. There he became editor of the *Spectator*, but his direction was short-lived, for, according to Bancroft, he was "dismissed for publishing some articles reflecting with good reason on the course of the American merchants toward the colonists."[52] In general, Lee was a man of humor, cultivation, and spirit, but his patience could be tried.

Robert Newell had a very different background. Born in Ohio in 1807, he was an early trapper in the West and married a Nez Perce woman, who bore the first five of his sixteen children. Following the "last rendezvous" of 1840, he and his family set out for Oregon in what he claimed was the first wagon to cross the Rockies. He settled on the Willamette River near Champoeg. "As there is no law in this country," Newell wrote in 1843, "we do the best we can." It was no doubt this lawlessness that prompted him to participate in forming Oregon's provisional government, even though "I knew but little about the business of Legislating." He learned. In 1845 and again in 1847,

Newell was chosen speaker of the provisional assembly. He also helped found the Oregon Lyceum and was on the board of the *Spectator*—although his fair-handedness was a constant irritation to the newspaper's backers. Peter Burnett, who much admired Newell, described him well: "He was of medium height, stout frame, and fine face . . . full of humanity, good will, genial feeling and frankness."[53]

Finally, there was Joel Palmer, who must have been greatly admired by his colleagues, for he now held three posts: superintendent of Indian affairs, commissary general, and peace commissioner.

These, then, were the members of the Peace Commission; Lee and Newell knew the tribes of the upper Columbia relatively well and had enjoyed peaceful relations with them, and Palmer, though he knew less of these tribes, was not predisposed against them. Abernethy's charge to the commissioners was simple in formulation, if not in execution: prevent a coalition of the tribes and demand the delivery of the murderers as well as those who had "forced the young women."[54] Furthermore, the tribes were to return all stolen property and promise not to harm future emigrants who passed through their lands.

Palmer and Newell began their journey on 3 February in company with Perrin Whitman, Marcus Whitman's nephew, and an Indian named Elijah, camping their first night in Portland. "They carry the pipe of peace," the *Spectator* wrote on 10 February, and expressed its concern "that the wrongs of the guilty should not be visited upon the innocent." This had been Abernethy's concern, as well, and he had expressed it several times in his letters to The Dalles and in his instructions to the commission.

The men spent the following night at Fort Vancouver, where Palmer made various purchases. He also wrote to A.E. Wait, one of two agents he had deputized to look after commissary matters in his absence.

> The troops in the field must be supplied with provisions at all hazards . . . . If a supply cannot be had by purchasing with such funds as are at the disposal of the department, a resort must be had to levying contributions upon the citizens . . . . In doing this you will be particular in not reducing the amount of breadstuffs below the wants of families . . . . Call upon the citizens through the medium of the press, or handbills, or both, to come forward and aid us. Now is the time to show their love of country, their patriotism, who are friends, who are foes. There are but two sides, for and against; there can be no half-way place.[55]

This suggests that there was no unanimity in the valley on the wisdom of the war. Palmer ended his letter to Wait by suggesting sources for much-needed ammunition. "Such was the multiplicity of cares of the chairman of the Peace

Commission," Bancroft wrote, "who, while delegated to negotiate for Peace, was preparing for war."[56]

The commissioners departed Fort Vancouver by canoe on 5 February and camped ten miles up the Columbia at Prairie du The. Here, they were joined by John McLoughlin's stepson, Tom McKay, who was captain of the French-Canadian volunteers from Champoeg, and by Capt. L.N. English of the Marion County volunteers. According to Newell, all spent "a pleasant and joviial night."[57] The next day, the sun shone, the air warmed, and except for the brunt of Cape Horn's perennially gusty winds, the canoes moved swiftly up the river. To their right were the great waterfalls of the gorge, streaking the dark cliffs silver, while all around the timbered ridges towered in a ragged frieze against the sky—these minikins in their bits of bark, awed but undeterred.

By nightfall, they had reached the Cascades, and it may well have been another "pleasant and joviial night," what with boon companions, the day's good weather, and what so far had really been more lark than mission. But the good times ended the following morning. Palmer and his party woke to find that Colonel Gilliam had left a fifteen-hundred-pound cannon for them to portage around the rapids. It was a delay they could not afford.

FOR AT THE DALLES, there were serious problems. Morale had not improved, and what little discipline there had been was breaking down. A sergeant, in despair of having his orders obeyed, demoted himself to private. More ominous, C.R. Shaw, the judge advocate, resigned his commission and went back to the Willamette. On 8 February, Lee wrote Abernethy that he was making his report under the most distracting of circumstances, "in the midst of a crowded room all talking, laughing, calling on me for information, explanation, interpretation, and more than you can think of, nonsensical." Lee had informed the Indians that

> we wished to remain friendly with all except those actually engaged in the murders, but that our hearts would never be good till they were punished . . . .
> That we had been slow to get mad, had borne much from them, because we loved them and wished to make them like us; but when we began to fight, we never quit till our enemies are all dead. That we are very numerous in our own country—like the trees on the mountains—and that we will never be done coming.[58]

Lee had a more specific problem with Seletsa, the chief of a Deschutes band. After Lee had persuaded Seletsa to ally himself to the volunteers, the chief had suffered depredations from other tribes, "stripped of everything,"

Lee wrote. But Gilliam distrusted Seletsa and sought his banishment. Never-theless, Lee argued:

> should we drop him now, he could not long survive; and to see him abandoned to the vengeance of his enraged people would wound me most deeply. At some future time I will give you a schedule of his property he has lost, so that should I leave the army or fall in battle, there may be some hope left for him. His con-duct has been so honorable and manly, that I cannot but regard him as a friend worthy of my esteem.

Lee's major problem, however, was his commander:

> Col. Gilliam, I think intends taking up the line of march for Waiilatpu in two or three days . . . . So fully convinced am I of the impropriety of moving the army above, before the surrounding tribes have been visited by a messenger of peace as they have requested, that, should that course be taken, I shall be com-pelled to retire from the field and seek in some other quarter a quiet home.

Lee concluded that he would endeavor to restrain Gilliam "till Gen. Palmer ar-rives, but if the General is slow, I fear my efforts will be in vain."[59]

WOULD PALMER AND HIS PARTY arrive on time? Palmer was still miles away working to portage the cannon. He finally assembled fifty men who dragged, heaved, and pushed the cannon the five miles to the top of the rapids. Here, they found that the best of the two boats waiting to receive the cannon had sunk due to high winds and what Palmer considered the carelessness of the crew. Also, many of the flour barrels had been pilfered, and both crews and passengers were helping themselves to provisions meant for the army. Report-ing on these matters to his deputy, A.E. Wait, Palmer deplored their incidence but did not seem discouraged by them. As there are gusty winds at Cape Horn, so in human affairs, he seemed to imply, squalls are bound to come as well.

Palmer and his party started out again the following morning, passing a provision boat on the way, "fast upon a rock." Palmer suspected that the boat had gone aground because "all had been captain"; that is, that the boat's sail-ors, like the army's soldiers, had been unwilling to follow orders. "This will not do," Palmer admonished.[60]

By late afternoon, twenty miles upriver from the Cascades, Palmer's party made camp on an island near present-day Mosier. Here, passing through the eastern gates of the gorge, they were in a different world from the one where they had started out. The sloughs and alder groves of the lower river now gave way to bare, black, basalt cliffs, and in place of the valley's green shallows, tilled fields, and chimney smoke, these arid, lava plains that "smoked with dust and dearth" ran on forever, flat and empty to the sky.[61] The air, too, was different—light and dry, sage-scented—while in the valley—moisture-laden, sweet with clover bloom—it was soft and a little heavy. In general, there was in this high world in which Palmer and his party now found themselves a certain brightness of air and light—edges sharp, colors clear—whereas the valley was blurred and muffled as though perpetually enfolded in a gentle mist, not the kind of place to rouse the blood to war. The high country, on the other hand, sent a tingle through the blood to act.

Upon reaching The Dalles on 11 February, Palmer was relieved to find that the tingle had not as yet sent Colonel Gilliam off to war. In the conference that Palmer immediately called, however, Gilliam proved unsympathetic to the commissioners' desire to ride ahead of the army to parley for peace. The issue was not resolved.

The next day the arrival of the cannon further encouraged the itch of the commander and his troops to fight. The cannon and its escorts were "saluted and cheered," wrote Newell, and in response, the cannon was fired six times, "one gun for each Company our flag hoisted and things appear quite milatair."[62] Newell may have used the term "milatair" in jest, if not in scorn, for he well knew of the army's precious supply of powder that was wasted in these vainglorious displays.

Despite the day's offerings to Mars, Gilliam finally agreed to permit the peace commissioners to proceed ahead, provided they were accompanied by a one-hundred-man escort. This was probably too large a force in the commissioners' view, for as Newell said, "more than a small party would frighten them [the Indians] away."[63] But this was the only agreement they could reach. The question was whether it would hold.

The omens were poor. Order continued to break up, like the boat they had seen shattered on the rocks. Captain English, out hunting, shot an Indian, apparently for the fun of it—"a most Shameful thing," Newell judged. There were also crimes against property. The previous autumn, many emigrants had stored their belongings at The Dalles with the intention of returning for them when the clement weather of spring made their transport more feasible. It was these stores that the volunteers now broke into, appropriating for themselves whatever they found useful. This was an irony, for it was because of the same act by the Indians that the volunteers had engaged in the Deschutes campaign. Frances Victor wrote: "They were ready to punish in an Indian what they had no hesitation about doing themselves."[64] On the other hand, and to a degree extenuating, the volunteers were lacking in many essentials, even clothing, and there was no assurance that Congress would recompense them for their services. In addition, they may have heard that some of the settlers whose property they were appropriating had themselves been busy jumping the claims of absent volunteers.

Whether Gilliam believed that action was the only corrective to the troops' increasing demoralization, whether, as Palmer believed, Gilliam thought it unsafe to divide his forces, or whether he was simply eager to get himself some scalps, Gilliam reneged on his agreement with the commissioners the following day. The entire army, he announced, would march with the peace party.

This was certainly a bitter disappointment to the commissioners, the more so since there was a rumor that all tribes above The Dalles had united to fight the Americans. But then, emissaries from the Deschutes and the Yakima arrived at Mill Creek to report that the intentions of their tribes were peaceable. The commissioners presented the emissaries with tobacco and flags for their chiefs and assured the Indians that they looked forward to speaking directly with the chiefs.

In this confusion of rumor and supposition, and with no clear notion of whether the upper tribes were disposed toward war or peace, the more than five hundred volunteers made ready to set off into their midst. "We fitted up some old immigrant wagons," W. W. Walter wrote, "and got some emigrant cattle, and mission cattle, and made up a train of wagons to haul what little supplies we had with us . . . . and in a very broken manner got under way."[65]

They must have made a late start, for they traveled no farther than Five Mile Creek, named for its distance from The Dalles. Palmer, along with Lee and Newell, returned to The Dalles to check on the whereabouts of some provision wagons that had not made their scheduled appearance at the creek. They found the garrison of twenty-seven men in disarray, "in consequence of bad dicipline"; Capt. J. E. Ross had given up entirely and left for the Willamette Valley. Palmer wrote to Abernethy, informing him of the rumors that all Indians of the upper country, excepting the Yakima and some of the Deschutes, had joined with the Cayuse to fight the whites. This depressing news conveyed, Palmer and the others returned to Five Mile Creek late that night, "in very bad wind and rain."[66]

The weather's mood may have reflected Palmer's mood as well. However optimistic by nature, he did not suffer fools gladly, and thus his impatience with Gilliam and many of the volunteers must have been extreme. Also, he could hardly have been sanguine in the face of the dwindling supplies and the long odds of their being replaced. Finally, the frustrating news that the majority of the plateau tribes had combined with the Cayuse most probably meant the failure of the mission. Hardly the kinds of thoughts to distract him from the bitter winds and driving rains.

By the end of the next day, the volunteers had reached the Deschutes, where they camped at one of the emigrant fords about a mile upstream from the river's mouth. It was a pleasant place—a small valley tufted with bunchgrass and set among round hills, the river running through it at a broil. The men, on the move at last, were in better spirits. Maneuvers were held, though possibly in an irregular manner, for Newell remarked that the local Indians looked on with "astonishment."[67]

The next night's camp on the pebbly-bottomed, willow-fringed John Day River was a pleasant one as well, but Newell reported, "much thieving done at this camp. A bread barrel broke open and one third taken also flour barrels disturbed . . . pork also Stolen." Gilliam asked Palmer to take all provisions into his personal charge, hardly a welcome responsibility. In the middle of the night, "a fals alarm of Indians caused much disturbance in camp."[68]

For the next few days, the volunteers lingered along Rock Creek, a tributary of the John Day and about ten miles south of present-day Arlington. The campsites were excellent, the weather sunny and bracing, the Blue Mountains now dramatically in view. But there was little good grazing grass, so runners were sent out to inform whatever Indians they could find that if the Indians wished to parley, they must come immediately because the volunteers would soon be obliged to move on to better grass. Also, there were apparently problems with McKay's French Canadians, "unfit for service both in the way of dissipline and horses," Newell wrote.[69]

On 20 February, now five days from The Dalles, Palmer apparently decided that Gilliam's desire for scalps could no longer be contained. The commissioners had been forbidden to go in advance of the army, so Palmer's only course of action was to attempt to get a message to the tribes in another fashion. Accordingly, he sent off three letters. One was to McBean, the post trader for the Hudson's Bay Company at Fort Walla Walla. Palmer assured McBean—and through him, Palmer hoped, the Nez Perce and Walla Walla—that the army's only purpose was to capture the Cayuse murderers and that it desired peaceful relations with all others.

Palmer had providentially obtained the second letter from Spalding before leaving the Willamette. The letter was addressed to twenty-three Nez Perce chiefs and pleaded with them to meet the Americans "with good heart." It also contained an admonition to the sons of the chiefs: "Keep quiet, ye young men! do not go over to the Cayuses . . . . The Nez Percés and the Americans are one; therefore do you not depart from us."[70] The third letter, addressed to the Cayuse through Father Brouillet, assured the Indians that all that the commission required was the murderers and the return of stolen goods.

The army set out again the following day, its destination Willow Creek, near present-day Cecil, a hard march of some twenty miles through desolate alkali bottoms. This, together with the postdinnertime arrival of the provision wagons, finally provoked the men. They had had enough.

The men were now nearly two hundred miles from home, barely clad in the middle of winter, and hungry nearly all the time. Furthermore, they had, like all armies, succeeded in finding some liquor, distilled, as it turned out, with polluted water; as a result, most of the tipplers came down with dysentery.* It was in all senses a mess, this ill-supplied, untrained, disorderly, drunken, puking, defecating army, "with the enemy retiring before them, and peace commissioners going after them to turn the war into a farce."[71]

* One recipe for "blue ruin," as the local home brew was named, called for one part raw alcohol to three parts water to which might be added, for flavor and coloring, tobacco, tea, red pepper, ginger, and black molasses.

Mutiny seemed imminent. One company threatened to return to the Willamette if the remaining flour was not issued immediately. Four of the beef cattle were killed in disregard of orders. Tea and sugar were stolen from a sick man. "Most shocking was this to witness," Newell remonstrated. In view of the situation, Gilliam decided to remain at Willow Creek an extra day. There was ample grass, and trout swam in the standing pools of the willow-edged creek. After a parade accompanied by much shooting of guns—which seemed to relieve the volunteers' feelings, if seriously depleting the powder store—Gilliam climbed on a wagon to hector the troops on their duties as patriots and warriors; he also reminded them that mutineers would not be forgotten by their compatriots. Nonetheless, there continued "much talk on the subject of mutiny," and again "a general Shooting off of guns took place . . . at the same time amunition scarce," Newell reported. "I shudder for our Scarcity of this article."[72]

"SCARCITY." This indeed was the central problem, but the heart of it lay more in the need for wheat than for ammunition. Wheat served two purposes—as flour and as currency with which to buy other supplies, for at this time in the Oregon Country there was neither silver nor gold. But whether as flour or currency, wheat presented many problems. The first and most intractable of these was the extraction of it from farmers. Then there were the problems of warehousing and transporting the grain and, in the case of flour, of milling it. Whatever form wheat took, it had to be hauled to the riverbank (in a place of few roads), warehoused, loaded onto the infrequent boats, unloaded at the Oregon City falls, portaged around the falls, loaded again, and in the case of currency wheat, taken down the Willamette and up the Columbia to Fort Vancouver, where it was exchanged for powder, shot, blankets, and medicine.

But again, the toughest problem was procuring the wheat in the first place, and at a fair price. On the day after the near mutiny, the *Spectator* for the second time beat the drum over the volunteers' desperate need for bread. And as Gilliam had told the volunteers that mutineers would not be forgotten, so the *Spectator* vowed that profiteers would not be either. The profiteers the *Spectator* had in mind had been described with some sarcasm by C.R. Shaw, the former judge advocate, in a letter to Gilliam:

> Those that have wheat I am told are holding on to it for a high price some asking as high as 1.50 per bu cash so I am afraid that the army will have to suffer. We will have I have no doubt after the war is over great *Patriots* as we now have great chimney corner warriors.[73]

Shaw knew that the farmers' reluctance to sell their wheat, except at a high price, was partly due to greed, but it was also because the commissary department paid with scrip that the government could devalue at any time. Shaw's only solution was to press the wheat, to simply take it by government order, and that is what Palmer's agent in Yamhill County, Absalom Hembree, did.

There still remained the almost impossible task of getting the flour—pilfered, as often as not, or adulterated with shorts—and the wheat-purchased supplies to the volunteers two hundred miles away. The most hazardous stretch of water lay between the Cascade portage and The Dalles. Now, late February, there was only one small boat plying this stretch and only three men to handle the craft and its freight, and one of these "anxious to return to the refreshing shades of private life."[74] As for the problems encountered in transporting the supplies from The Dalles to wherever the volunteers might be camped, the historical record—perhaps mercifully—is silent.

These, then, were the problems of supply that confronted Palmer and about which he could do little, distant as he was from the locale of their origin. In any event, he was well occupied with his duties as peace commissioner and superintendent of Indian affairs. In his capacity as superintendent, he wrote to Abernethy on 24 February that Chief Beardy's band of the Deschutes, after being shot at by the volunteers every time they attempted to approach the camp, had finally succeeded in reaching the commissioners and suing for peace. Palmer also informed the governor that the latest intelligence placed the Cayuse on Sawmill Creek at the base of the Blue Mountains and that they were expected to make a night attack at any time.

On 24 February, a Yakima boy ran into the volunteers' camp with a message from the devil incarnate, Bishop Blanchet, and addressed to "M. Commandant." Written from the camp of the Yakima chief Ciaies, the bishop reported that the commissioners' gifts of tobacco and flags had been received, the commissioners' message counseling peace had been delivered, and the Yakima chiefs were pleased to accept these overtures to peace and would abide by them. This meant that now the Yakima and a majority of the Deschutes had agreed not to join the Cayuse. But what about the Walla Walla and, most important of all, the Nez Perce? Why, Gilliam was most impatient to know, had there been no reply to Palmer's and Spalding's letters to McBean at Fort Walla Walla and to the Nez Perce chiefs? Why, indeed, for sufficient time had passed for messages from both to have reached the camp at Willow Creek. Finally, Gilliam's patience broke. Over the objection of the peace commissioners, he ordered the army to march.

And so they started out, warm for a February day, the desert sprinkled white with the last bloom of the sagebrush, and ahead the Blues, shouldering against the sky. They followed the Oregon Trail, moving in a northeasterly direction toward the Umatilla and Whitman's mission beyond—a column of five hundred men with their cannon mounted on the hind wheels of an old cart, their "borrowed" wagons, and such beef cattle as were left. At the head of the column rode the peace commissioners, their white flags snapping in the wind. It was a curious sight, a little army riding out to war, out to "git me an Indian," led by men carrying the white flags of peace.

By midmorning, the column was well into the land of the Umatilla Cayuse and their chiefs, Five Crows and Gray Eagle. The commissioners saw the tracks of Indian horses and, a little later, two Cayuse in the distance. The commissioners signaled with their flags, but the Indians wheeled their horses and cantered away.

At noon, the column rode down into Sand Hollow, near present-day Alpine. The hollow is formed by a dry streambed and hills that rise up some four or five hundred feet to the east. It was here that the whites and the Cayuse met. There were, it was estimated, some four hundred Cayuse coming down upon them from the hills. The peace commissioners, raising their white flag, galloped out to them, but a chief gestured to them to go back. It was too late. Peace had lost.

And for several reasons. Two months before, on 20 December, the Cayuse had proposed to Governor Abernethy, through Bishop Blanchet, that peace emissaries be sent to them. There is no record that Abernethy replied to these overtures, even though the legislature also called for the appointment of peace emissaries on 14 December. Nor did Abernethy reply even after 1 February, when the commissioners were in fact appointed. On 23 December, Peter Skene Ogden promised the Cayuse that he would counsel the Americans against war and inform the Indians of the outcome of his efforts. For reasons unknown, his promised communication did not reach Fort Walla Walla until after the Sand Hollow engagement.

Then, there had been Spalding's betrayal. On 10 December, Spalding had promised the Cayuse that he would dissuade the Americans from war, "that Americans will no more come in their country unless they wish it."[75] Yet by late December the Cayuse knew that Lee and his troops had arrived at The Dalles, and they may also have known that Spalding was now urging their extermination.

Next, in late January, the Cayuse learned of the arrival at The Dalles of Colonel Gilliam with a large force, of his attack on the Deschutes, and of his destruction of Deschutes villages. Also, without doubt, they were apprised of the subsequent arrival in early February of the peace commission. But peace commissioners to whom, they might well have asked. To them, it appeared that the commissioners' only purpose was to parley with the Deschutes, the Yakima, the Walla Walla, and the Nez Perce—in short, to strip them of their allies and thus make them in their small numbers vulnerable to American attack. If it were otherwise, why had they not heard from the peace commissioners whose offices they had been seeking for so long?

That the commissioners' letter of 20 February from the John Day failed to reach the Cayuse is another incident in the tribe's long tragedy. This letter—addressed to them through Father Brouillet, then thought to be resident among them—together with the letters for McBean and the Nez Perce, had been entrusted to Elijah, the Nez Perce who had accompanied the commissioners from the Willamette Valley. According to most accounts, Elijah was intercepted en route—Elijah in collusion with the Cayuse chief Tawatoy, Palmer suspected. Tawatoy kept the tobacco and flags that had accompanied the letters, but the letters themselves—all addressed in care of McBean—he sent on, apparently fearing the trader's retribution should he not. By the time the letters reached Fort Walla Walla, however, Father Brouillet had already left the Cayuse. Realizing that the tribe was determined on war, Brouillet had removed to the fort on 20 February. In short, by the time the commissioners' letter reached him, it was too late.

The letters to McBean and the Nez Perce fared better. It happened that they arrived at a time when two Nez Perce chiefs, Timothy and Red Wolf, were visiting the fort. Spalding's message was conveyed to them as well as the commissioners' sentiments to McBean—that is, that the army's mission was a peaceful one, desiring only the apprehension of the Cayuse murderers. The chiefs carried these assurances back to their people, assurances that were also reportedly conveyed to Yellow Serpent, chief of the Walla Walla. "To this fortunate occurence," Palmer later wrote, "we owe, perhaps, much of our success in preventing a general combination of the Indian tribes against us."[76]

But in another circumstance connected with these letters the whites were not so fortunate—and certainly not the Cayuse. We do not know the content of McBean's reply to the commissioners, but it may be supposed that he informed them of the Nez Perce decision—and probably Yellow Serpent's as well—not to ally with the Cayuse. If this message had reached the commissioners, they might have prevailed on Gilliam to wait upon their efforts. After all, it was the lack of answers to the 20 February letters that had finally provoked Gilliam to go into Cayuse country.

Commentators, both at the time and since, believed that if the peace commissioners had proceeded alone, the Cayuse—largely bereft of allies—would have accepted peace on the whites' terms; that is, they would have surrendered those responsible for the massacre and returned the stolen goods. However, McBean's reply did not reach the commissioners—intercepted as well by Tawatoy and on this occasion destroyed—and thus it was that the two adversaries marched, to meet on that February noon at Sand Hollow.

The volunteers formed a defensive circle in the hollow, with cattle and provisions at the center. The Cayuse, in turn, formed a circle around the whites, taunting them. They would kill them all, they cried, and then go to the Willamette and take their women and their land. To show their contempt, the Indians began their attack by shooting a dog.

The Cayuse had never before battled with whites and were convinced they were "women," as they called the whites in their taunts. Until Sand Hollow, the only whites they had dealt with had been missionaries, who turned the other cheek, and emigrants, who were "weary with travel and encumbered with families and herds"—thus the Cayuse confidence—indeed, rashness—in attack.[77] Five Crows and a chief called Gray Eagle rode up to Tom and Charles McKay, thinking themselves inviolate. The McKays shot Gray Eagle dead and shattered Five Crows' arm.

This underestimation of the whites was not the only factor that put the Cayuse at a disadvantage. Although there were about four hundred Indians, a hundred of them were women and "spectators." The women, of course, were noncombatants, though the volunteers prayed that, if wounded, they would not fall into their hands. It is difficult to say who the "spectators" were. Newell suggested they were Cayuse who were not sympathetic to the attack, while volunteer W. W. Walter opined that they were non-Cayuse waiting to see the outcome of the battle. Whoever they were, they left the Cayuse force diminished and divided.

The battle continued until sunset. The troublesome cannon, lugged so many miles, was fired "without much effect." According to Frances Victor, the whoops and cries of the volunteers were what the Indians found most dismaying. With sunset, the Cayuse retreated to the hills, having lost eight of their braves, whereas the volunteers had suffered only five wounded. More seriously for the Cayuse, they had lost the confidence of whatever political allies they might have had. They also suffered defections from their ranks; that night, three Cayuse mixed breeds went to the volunteers' camp "and opened the way for negociating," as Palmer later wrote.[78]

The next day was one of confusion and hardship for the volunteers. The men marched without water and were subjected to both harassment and peace feelers from the Cayuse. That night, in bad humor, the men camped on the banks of a creek that emptied into the Umatilla. Perhaps to cheer them and to celebrate the previous day's victory, Palmer opened a keg of butter from the stores so that the volunteers might enjoy some flapjacks. Thus, it is said, did this tributary of the Umatilla become known as Butter Creek.

The volunteers crossed the Umatilla the next morning. This was an act of ascendancy, for the Cayuse had vowed that the whites should never drink of its waters. A few miles after the crossing, Stickus, a principal Cayuse chief, approached the commissioners with proposals of peace, even though other Cayuse continued to harass the troops. The commissioners, for reasons not clear, declined Stickus' proposals—or, at any rate, postponed discussion of them until they could reach the site of the Whitmans' massacre.

MOVING ON ACROSS THE VAST PLAIN that here tips down to the Columbia, the Cayuse circling ominously in the distance, Palmer had a curious encounter. It was one that would be long remembered by those who would later charge him with undue regard for Indians. Several hundred yards from the trail, a group of mounted Indians looked down on the volunteers from a little mound. The commissioners, Gilliam, and a few other officers rode over to determine who they were and what they were about; the Indians came down from the mound to meet them. When they were close enough, they all shook hands, except one Indian who, on seeing Palmer, threw his arms around him in an embrace. Palmer's horse wheeled and Palmer was flung sideways, his head coming to rest on the Indian's shoulder. The Indian who had Palmer in this fraternal embrace was Tamsucky, and it was Tamsucky who, at the beginning of the massacre, had by a show of sympathy lured Narcissa Whitman from the mission house to the yard where she was flogged and shot.

In 1845, when Palmer was on his way to Oregon, he had arranged to leave some of his horses with Whitman to be picked up in the spring when he returned to the States. Whitman had put the horses out to winter pasture under Tamsucky's care. When Palmer came for the horses that spring, he found them in the best of condition and offered to recompense Tamsucky for his good care. The Cayuse had asked for a length of red velvet cloth, and when Palmer returned to Oregon two years later, he brought the red velvet with him, giving it to Whitman to pass on to Tamsucky. Tamsucky had not forgotten this fidelity to word, and when he released Palmer from his embrace he said, "now no more shoot."[79]

TWO DAYS LATER, the troops arrived at the confluence of the Walla Walla and Columbia rivers and the site of Fort Walla Walla, the Hudson's Bay Company post that had been established there in 1818. On their way, and despite Tamsucky's words, the men had seen no evidence that the Cayuse were united for peace. Indeed, both Newell and Gilliam feared they were regrouping for an attack.

At the fort, the commissioners learned about the lost letter in which McBean had counseled them to take a small escort and proceed in advance of the army into Cayuse country to parley. If they had done so, McBean was convinced, the Cayuse would have come to terms and surrendered the murderers. But now, the commissioners had come with a full army and had declined to hold a council as Stickus and others had requested. The Cayuse, in self-defense, were uniting for war.

Although Palmer probably agreed with this analysis, he distrusted McBean and continued to believe that he had encouraged the Indians to think that

Whitman was attempting to poison them. It is also doubtful that Palmer believed the account of the massacre that Father Brouillet gave to him and the others during their stay at the fort. Lt. A.E. Garrison probably best summed up the general attitude of the Americans toward Brouillet: "I saw one of the priests up there . . . and I confess I felt more like shooting him than I did an Indian."[80]

It was at the fort, too, that Palmer first met Yellow Serpent, the chief of the Walla Walla and one of the most powerful and respected of the plateau chiefs. Yellow Serpent was the whites' ally in the matter of the massacre and their campaign against the Cayuse. When a Cayuse participant in the massacre had come to Yellow Serpent's camp to brag of his exploits, Yellow Serpent had promptly hanged him from a tree. There had been no change in his attitude since then, and Palmer found him to be "decidedly friendly and with all prudent and sensible."[81]

Their discussions at Fort Walla Walla concluded, the army and the commissioners moved up the Walla Walla River toward the mission. Their first night out, 29 February, Gilliam wrote Governor Abernethy demanding more supplies and men. He still believed that the Indians were gathering at the mission to take the field against them, and further, he had heard that the Nez Perce had joined the Cayuse cause. It is also possible that Gilliam's force was being depleted by desertions. Such, at any rate, was the case at The Dalles, where Capt. H.J.G. Maxon complained that three troopers had "eloped" without leave.

Abernethy's immediate response to these demands is unknown, but he may well have been confused, for on this same date, Ogden wrote to him to say that it was his "firm conviction when the troops reach Walla Walla, the enemy will soon dwindle away."[82] The knowledgeable Ogden's convictions were not to be disregarded. Then, too, the war remained unpopular in many quarters of the valley. All in all, it was difficult for Abernethy to know how to proceed.

Meanwhile, the army moved toward the mission, though with the despondency of hungry men. At one point, some learned that the French Canadians had killed and butchered a wild horse. Searching, they found the carcass—covered with ravens. After finally driving the ravens off, they saw that, between the ravens and the French, nothing was left. The only other known incident of note on this march reflects the mixed attitudes and behavior of the volunteers toward the Indians. A.E. Garrison reported finding a wounded Indian by the roadside: "we took him up and cared for him but he died when we got up to Dr Whitmans."[83]

The troops reached the massacre site on 2 March. The mission, what was left of it, stood clustered near an elbow of the river, the river running through a broad plain that the Cayuse called Waiilatpu—the place of the ryegrass. It was a landscape of somber, empty distances, which to the missionaries coming from the green and sheltered villages of New England must have seemed the plains of desolation—bare, dark, and menacing, like the savages who inhabited it.

For the volunteers on that winter's day, looking down on the charred skeletons of the burnt-out, little buildings, black and gaunt in the falling snow, listening to the wind soughing in the ryegrass and to the baying of the wolves who had so lately feasted there, it must have seemed a veritable golgotha. "Parts of bodies laying around," W. W. Walter wrote. Father Brouillet, who had arrived at the mission the day after the massacre, had done his best to give the victims a proper burial, but he had not dug deep enough, and so the wolves, pawing at the graves, had dragged the bodies out. Walter found "what was suppose to be Mrs. Whitman skull with a tomahawk wound in it." They found the scalp elsewhere in the yard and snipped a lock of yellow hair from it for Joe Meek to take to President Polk.[84]

As Bancroft wrote, "three months had elapsed since the tragedy of Waiilatpu, and as yet they had not been able to send the intelligence beyond the silver-rimmed mountain ranges which cut off the Oregon colony from the inhabited world."[85] The reason, of course, was winter, but now the snow in the mountain passes was melting and Meek was free to depart. After reburying his half-Indian daughter, Helen, who had been living with the Whitmans, he started out.

Newell, meanwhile, had grown despondent: "the commissioners have no chance to arrange with the Indians as we are short of provis[ions] and time. Our Col is quite hasty." "Hasty" may be an understatement, for Gilliam, incensed by the devastation at the mission, was determined on war, despite the peace overtures by Yellow Serpent, the Cayuse, Stickus, and the Nez Perce. Nor was Gilliam mollified when Yellow Serpent, the Nez Perce, and a mixed breed named Gervais called the next day with proposals for peace. "Colonel Gilliam left the council in a huff," Newell observed, "and declared he had come to fight and fight he will." Nevertheless, Newell and Palmer were encouraged by this latest deputation, and Palmer wrote to McBean (at McKay's

request, he made it clear) that "with yours and his [McKay's] assistance, with
alittle forbearance on the part of the troops, I believe all that could be desired,
will be accomplished without further bloodshed." Not everyone shared Palmer's confidence. Volunteer John T. Cox wrote:

> The Cayuses, whenever in a hard place, were always willing to stop and hold a
> peace conference with the commissioner, Joel Palmer, and talk long enough to
> get their train out of the way, and then steal off—so, it seemed at least to the
> more military spirits.[86]

Newell's and Palmer's optimism was encouraged the following morning
when Gervais and William Craig rode off to persuade a large body of Nez
Perce to come in for a peace council. Craig, a retired mountain man and a
longtime associate of Meek's and Newell's, had lived for some time among the
Nez Perce, and the commission counted on his influence
with the Indians.* Gilliam felt differently. "Col Gilliam   *Craig, Meek, and
is much displeased with the Commissioners," wrote   Newell had married
Newell, "and says for the future he will have his own   three Nez Perce sisters,
way, and also says on tomorrow he will march to battle.   making them brothers-
if so we are in a desperate State of Civilization." Newell   in-law.
had just about had enough:

> This morning I have concluded to return to my family as soon as possible after
> the Council with the Nezperces. The men are daily finding property but of little
> value. no account is taken of it nor can Mr Parmer say or do in his official ca-
> pacity what he wishes and knows to be right for the want of the Commanders
> assistance. This Army is composed of different kinds of men. Some have come
> to act legally others to plunder and others for popularity.

Newell added, however, that Captain McKay and his company—the French
Canadians—and "nearly all the officers appear to wish to do for the best."[87]

The next day, Craig returned with the Nez Perce, who were heartily
cheered by the volunteers as they rode into the camp. The council followed after "the pipe of friendship had passed around till our hearts were all good and
our eyes watery," wrote Palmer.[88] Present were Yellow Serpent, Camatspelo,
the Cayuse war chief, and eleven chiefs of the Nez Perce tribe.

The assembled chiefs were first presented with a message from Governor
Abernethy, who addressed them as "brothers." The Americans, the governor
reminded the Indians, "have born a great deal," including the continual robbing of the emigrants. As for Marcus Whitman, he had come among them at
their request and for their good; the charge that he wished to poison them was
false, for he was in truth their "best friend." Abernethy demanded the surren-

der of the murderers and rapists and all stolen property and concluded: "we know our Great Chief wishes the Americans and Indians to be as brothers. We wish to be so. Will you let us be as brothers, or will you throw us away."[89] Abernethy's sentiments were probably sincere; for, after all, it was he who before news of the massacre had complained earlier to the provisional legislature that the Indians were not being dealt with justly and that provision should be made for them.

Newell's address to the Nez Perce was also temperate and affectionate in tone. "This day I am glad to see you," he began. "I have not come here to make peace with you, we never have been at war, but always friendly . . . . I am not here to fight, but to separate the good from the bad, and to tell you that it is your duty to help make this ground clean." And in the manner of Abernethy, Newell asked at the end: "will you throw my words away?"[90]

In distinct contrast, Palmer's address was severe. His invective may have reflected the fear of being thought soft on the Indians, symbolized by his "kissing" of Tamsucky, or perhaps, exercised by the golgotha at the Whitman mission, his feelings toward the Indians were, in fact, harshly antipathetic. Whatever the reason, he stated his charge immediately and in clear and accusatory terms: "The land of the Cayuses has been stained with the blood of our brothers—the Cayuses have done it. What shall be done? The great God orders that the guilty be punished."[91]

He described the commissioners' arrival at The Dalles, where they found the Cayuse still on their murderous rampage, having killed two of the men stationed there and threatening to kill more. Next, there were the commissioners' futile efforts at Sand Hollow. "We wished peace," Palmer told the council, "and went in advance of our war chief with a flag to hold a talk, but their young men were surrounding us, and made signs of war. We returned to the wagons with sickened hearts, for we could not prevent the fighting." Also, letters had been sent stating that only the guilty would be punished and that "we did not come to make war upon the innocent." But Palmer repudiated this assurance almost immediately: "The Cayuses have forfeited their lands by making war upon the Americans." This statement must have come as a surprise to all, for it had been a cardinal principle of American policy from the beginning, expressed by everyone from Governor Abernethy to the commissioners themselves, and even now by the *Spectator*, that only those directly guilty of the murders and of violating the women should be punished. Now, Palmer was saying that all Cayuse could be punished, irrespective of their innocence or guilt. It is true that he hedged this extraordinary statement by adding "but we do not want the lands." Still, he had asserted a right that had never been claimed before and that would not be forgotten—although in time Palmer himself may have wished it so, may have deeply regretted that he had sowed this seed that was to bear a crimson fruit. Palmer concluded with a stinging rebuke of the Cayuse for their ingratitude to Whitman and their subsequent treachery and delivered a final threat: "Our war chief will hunt these murderers as you hunt the deer, until he drives them from the face of the earth."[92]

Eight chiefs replied to the whites. The first was Camatspelo, war chief of the Cayuse: "My people seem to have two hearts. I have but one . . . . I have had nothing to do with the murderers." He then told how Tamsucky had come to him to gain his consent for the massacre, but that he had refused, partly out of concern for his sick child: "my heart was there, and not on murder."[93] He would not protect the murderers. Camatspelo's statement must have reassured Palmer, but it also may have embarrassed him, for Tamsucky, who had so tenderly greeted him on the Columbia, had now been identified as one of the murderers.

Next, Joseph, the principal Nez Perce at the council, spoke for

> all the Cayuses present, and all my people. I do not wish my children engaged in this war, although my brother is wounded [his half-brother, Five Crows].
> You speak of the murderers. I shall not meddle with them. I bow my head.[94]

The remaining Nez Perce chiefs reported that they had not known of the Cayuse intention to murder the Whitmans and that they had protected Spalding. Finally, they condemned the murders and pledged not to ally themselves with the guilty Cayuse.

Palmer ended the council by announcing that William Craig, who had lived among the Nez Perce for so long, would be their agent in their dealings with the whites. He also promised them a blacksmith and, should they wish it, a teacher. They were assured that whites would not be allowed to settle on their lands without their permission but warned that travelers passing through were not to be harassed. These matters settled, all adjourned until evening when, as Palmer wrote,

> the Nez Perces gave us a *war dance*, which amused and delighted us much; and we do them but bare justice when we say the performance was well timed, the parts well acted, characters represented to the very life, and the whole *first rate*.[95]

IN GENERAL, the peace commissioners were happy with the outcome of the council. "We felt gratified," Palmer later wrote in his report, with our success in our efforts to prevent a general war with the Indians—in saving the Nez Perces which had been a matter of much anxiety with us—in breaking the ranks of the enemy by calling off their allies—and especially in separating the innocent from the guilty.[96]

But where were the guilty? Apparently, they continued to shelter with the disaffected Cayuse now camped on the Touchet River, about twenty-five miles northwest of Lapwai. The Nez Perce agreed to try to persuade the Cayuse to surrender the murderers. In return, Gilliam agreed to delay his planned march on the Indians. The following day, 9 March, the impatient Gilliam—having had no word from the Nez Perce—set out to attack the camp. On the way, he met a group of Nez Perce and Cayuse, Stickus among them, carrying several hundred dollars' worth of goods the Cayuse had stolen from The Dalles and were now surrendering as a show of good faith and as an inducement to hold another council. Gilliam suspected, and perhaps rightly, that this was a ploy to allow the Cayuse and the murderers to make their escape into the mountains at the great bend of the Snake. The commissioners, however, prevailed on Gilliam to return to the mission and give the council a chance. The issue, of course, was the surrender of the murderers.

Based on the confused testimony of the survivors, there were thought to be five killers. Perhaps because these were the wrong five—the five eventually surrendered were not the five charged by Gilliam—Stickus stated that the Cayuse would refuse to yield them up. Then, to the astonishment of all, certainly to the commissioners, Gilliam agreed to drop the request for the charged five in exchange for Joe Lewis. Lewis, a mixed breed who had worked for the Whitmans, was believed by some to have been chiefly responsible for arousing the Cayuse by telling them that they were being poisoned by the Whitmans.

Why Gilliam made this proposal cannot even be supposed. From the beginning, the Americans had had two purposes in the upper country: to prevent the alliance of the Columbia tribes and a general war and to apprehend and punish the murderers, along with the violators of the women. The commissioners had already achieved the first purpose of their mission. That Gilliam should now abandon the second and be prepared to accept an instigator rather than the five killers finally broke the commissioners' patience. "Seeing such a moove I Concluded to be off," wrote Newell. He later told Lee that if the commissioners had stayed, a "bust-up" with Gilliam would have been inevitable.[97]

And so, on 11 March, Palmer and Newell departed, leaving Gilliam to march on the Cayuse, who had refused to surrender Joe Lewis or any of the alleged murderers. Arriving at Fort Walla Walla at sunset, the commissioners "spent a fine evening" with McBean and Yellow Serpent.[98] Reaching The Dalles on 17 March, Palmer was disappointed to hear from Berryman Jennings, an assistant quartermaster, that supplies in the valley were practically unobtainable for the army. The following day, however, he was cheered by a fruitful council with the Deschutes and could reflect with satisfaction that now, at the end of his mission, the Deschutes, Nez Perce, Walla Walla, Yakima, and some of the Cayuse had all been "pacified."

PALMER ARRIVED IN OREGON CITY on 23 March and presented the peace commissioners' report to the governor. The report made certain recommendations. First, the commissioners were especially grateful for the services of two Indians. One had saved the family of Josiah Osborne following the massacre, and the other had brought dispatches to the commissioners from The Dalles to the Umatilla, a "trip of more than 100 miles through a hostile country, entirely alone, and in about 12 hours; a feat that perhaps few men in our Regiment would have undertaken." The commissioners expressed their "regret at not having the means to make them [the Indians] sensible of the estimate we place upon such service . . . . we could only make them such presents as our private resources would allow."[99] In the context of the report, it is clear that the commissioners were requesting the provisional government to further recompense these Indians for their assistance.

The commissioners' second recommendation concerned the disposition of troops. They urged that at least some troops remain at The Dalles and at the mission "to keep in awe the hostile party of the Indians." This was necessary, Palmer believed, even though volunteers were now needed in the valley to deal with Indian troubles there.[100] For indeed, there had been clashes in the valley with the Klamath, Kalapuya, and Tillamook, and the settlers were much exercised. In some cases, this had led the Americans to retaliate against the innocent—action that provoked the *Spectator* to publish on 23 March, the day of Palmer's arrival, the following condemnation:

> The people, and *all* the people of Oregon should recollect, that they are upon soil to which the Indian title has not yet been extinguished, and that as long as they are on Indian soil, and an Indian bears himself friendly and honestly, that Indian is entitled to humane treatment.

It was because of the Indian troubles in the valley, plus the commissioners' assurances that the Cayuse fangs had been drawn, that Governor Abernethy ordered Colonel Gilliam to return to the Willamette with those troops that were not needed at The Dalles and the mission. The order, however, would not reach Gilliam, for another took priority.

UPON THE COMMISSIONERS' DEPARTURE from the mission, Colonel Gilliam had set out in pursuit of the disaffected Cayuse. At present-day Starbuck, where the Tucannon River enters the Snake, the Cayuse eluded him for good by crossing the Snake to the mountains and the safety beyond. It appeared that in their haste they had been obliged to leave their cattle behind, and these now were rounded up by the famished volunteers. The cattle, however, did not belong to the Cayuse but to the local Palouse who, enraged by the theft, attacked the volunteers. Outnumbered two to one and suffering from drastic shortages, the volunteers fled south, releasing the cattle with the hope that this would mollify the Palouse. It did not. Before the Palouse eventually gave up the chase on the banks of the Touchet, ten volunteers had been wounded. The defeated army made its way back to the mission, its 150 men suffering badly from hunger, "having eaten nothing but a small colt for three days." The smell of food cooking as they approached the mission made some of them sick, while others "were so ravenous they had to be restrained or they would have killed themselves eating."[101]

In camp, the officers held a council to determine a course of action to avert the shortages that threatened their extinction. There were shortages of everything: provisions, horses,* ammunition, and—now that the Palouse had joined the ranks of the enemy—men, as well. It is one of the several ironies of the Cayuse War that on this same day, 16 March, when all agreed on the urgent need for more men, a U.S. ship arrived in the Columbia recruiting for the Mexican war.

The decision finally made at the council was that Gilliam, with half the troops, should return to The Dalles, where they hoped to find supplies and where Gilliam could send a message to Governor Abernethy for more men. It was on the morning of 24 March, on the banks of the Umatilla, that Gilliam pulled a rope from a wagon, somehow entangling it with a gun that went off and shot him dead.

*The shortage of horses was due to a number of causes, but none more grisly than what befell nineteen-year-old W.W. Walter's steed. Angry that the pony continued to throw him, he decided to "tie him down until he would be willing to stand up . . . . but in the morning I was minus a horse—the wolves had

THE NEWS OF GILLIAM'S DEATH reached The Dalles a few days later and, on 28 March, was forwarded to Governor Abernethy by Captain Maxon.* After recounting the circumstances of Gilliam's death, Maxon wrote, "something must be done, and done at once, or we must abandon the war and have the Indians in the valley in a month, stealing our property and murdering the frontier families." Who these Indians were is not clear, for the disaffected Cayuse had presumably disappeared across the Snake, and all the other tribes, excepting the Palouse, had been "pacified." Maxon goes on to report on conditions at The Dalles:

* It was Maxon who, while holding the office of judge in Palmer's 1845 emigration, had set free the Indian wrongly charged with cattle stealing and who, to make amends, had then dined with the Indian and joined him in a smoke. Such gallantry seems to have been typical of Maxon, a man of much spirit who loved soldiering, "such a trooper as Sheridan would have delighted in." Snowden, History of Washington, vol. 3, 48.

eaten him up. We had much to learn in those days." See Bennett, We'll All Go Home in the Spring

> What men we have are in a destitute situation. Some almost without clothing, many without horses, as the principal portion of the horses we have taken, have been claimed by friendly Indians and given up to them . . . . The army threatens soon to be disbanded on account of the expiration of the time of many who have made short enlistments.

As for the volunteers at the mission, "in the very heart of the enemy's country, [they are] almost without ammunition—wholly without bread . . . . Their situation is truly a critical one, and there is no ammunition here to take to them." Maxon then made a general plea to the citizens:

> If there is a continuation of operations, I hope there will be more patriotism shown in the Willamette valley. Indeed there must be or we are lost. Fathers! Please evince your patriotism by sending a little bread to him who is fighting through cold and hunger to protect your warm and comfortable hearths. Mothers, evince that pure and noble patriotism characteristic of your sex, by sending up a few warm garments—and daughters, evince your angelic influence for your country's good, by withholding your fair hand, and fairer smiles from any young man who refuses to turn out to defend your honor and your country's rights.[102]

Abernethy was persuaded. On 1 April, he issued a call for three hundred men to serve for six months and to assemble at Portland on 18 April for departure for the front. The rationale is not entirely clear, but it may have been the fear that the defeat of the volunteers on the Touchet River by the Palouse would encourage the pacified tribes to turn on the Americans. Then, of course, there was the matter of Maxon's plea. Evidently, war was to be resumed in the upper country.

But how to feed the warriors. Palmer had resigned his Indian superintendency on 28 March to give all his time to his demanding duties as commissary general. Palmer first turned his attention to the loan commissioners, those gentlemen appointed to provide funds for the war. One of the commissioners, Hugh Burns, a blacksmith, who was active in political affairs, publicly condemned Palmer for purchasing supplies on credit without the commissioners' permission. Palmer answered the charge immediately in a letter to Burns written on 24 March 1848, the day following his return. Since the letter so clearly reflects the temper of the times and of his style as an adversary, as well as his concept of what public service should be, it is here reproduced in its entirety.

Oregon City, March 24/48

M.H. Burns,

Dear Sir,

I have thought it a duty I owe to myself, to you and to the country to address you upon the subject of our differences of opinion as expressed today.

Not that I regard the matter of so much importance in fact but its results, that there should be an honest difference of opinion as to the powers to be exercised by the different officers when their duties are not defined, is reasonable to expect, particularly among those whose duties seem to come in contact. But that we should so far forget ourselves and the public good as to publicky contend about matters of themselves unimportant surprises me.

I do not claim infalability upon the contrariety. I am liable to error, I may be wrong. You may be wrong or we may both be wrong. I think we have but one object in view and that is to do our duty.

I certainly have no desire to encroach upon your duties or throw obstacles in the way. My only desire is to act so that public good may be served. I am not an aspirant to office. I did not ask or expect one but when called upon I must do my duty as I hold every citizen is bound to do but why quarrel. Can we not each attend to our several duties without vilifying or quarreling about it. Public good demands it, respect for those who placed us here demands it, respect for society and ourselves demands it.

Common sense teaches us that without a unity and concert of action among public functionaries in these trying times we must fail. The present is the time when every man should act with an eye to public good. Let us quit this back biting and caviling about minor matters and discharge our duties and if we differ in mode of doing business let us reason like men and not like children. If we do this we can certainly get along. When I find we cannot I must retire from a service to which I have been called and unasked on my part and one which is not likely to support my family and which nothing but a desire to do my duty as a citizen would justify me in remaining.

I am aware there are many who seek political preferrment and in order to carry out their designs would resort to measures calculated to injure those who they unjustly suppose to be obstacles in their way. Let me again repeat I am not an aspirant. I do not wish to stand in any man's way.

Acts of public men can be considered public and of course are subject to the scrutiny of all and I am not one to complain but there are points beyond which none should be allowed to go.

But to the point, if we differ about matters, let us talk it over among ourselves or call a friend and not disgrace ourselves by publicky disputing about matters upon which we differ. This much I say. I could not say less. Let us either have an understanding so as to act in unison or let us quit the service upon the receipt of this. Please honor me with an answer. I have the honor to be Sir, Your humble servant
Joel Palmer[103]

A month later, Jesse Applegate*—after John McLoughlin, perhaps the valley's most distinguished citizen—wrote a letter to Palmer that serves as a gloss on Palmer's letter to Burns. Of those practices of Palmer's to which the loan commissioners objected, and which occasioned Palmer's letter, Applegate wrote:

> You know that a rigid construction of your duties as commissary-general limits you to the bare investment of the means placed in your hands [by the loan commissioners] but our pecuniary embarrassments have been such that you have been forced to supply the army without means, and while your opponents cry out that by seizing provisions, borrowing money, and buying property as commissary-general, your acts were extra official; yet by taking this responsibility *alone*, you have so far been able to furnish the army and keep them in the field;

Born in Kentucky in 1811, Applegate crossed the plains in 1843 as captain of the "cow column," an experience that formed the basis of his famous monograph, "A Day with the Cow Column in 1843." As surveyor, legislator, publicist, and scholar, Applegate became one of Oregon's most distinguished citizens.

and by your great exertions and perseverance in these *unlawful acts* you have
gained that good will of the people they so much envy.

Applegate also referred to Palmer's protestations in his letter to Burns that he
was not an aspirant for office and that he should not be considered an obstacle
to those who were—a possibly disingenuous protestation by a man who had
held public office in the past and would do so many times again. Applegate put
the matter clearly:

> The office-seekers, of course, wish your downfall and will compass it if they
> can; not because they have discovered faults in you, but on the contrary, they
> fear the people may duly appreciate the ability you have displayed, and the great
> personal sacrifices you have made in their service; and if they can, by alarming
> your fears, drive you to abandon a policy which so far has been successful, and
> obtain for you the character of vascillation and uncertainty, they will succeed in
> their object, which is to deprive you of the confidence of the people, and which
> once lost is scarcely ever regained.[104]

And this indeed may have been the nub of Palmer's problems with the loan
commissioners. Politics and public office were of enormous importance in Oregon at this time. After all, they formed the trough in which the slop of spoils
flowed. And it was the crowding at this trough that accounted for the rough
and tumble of Oregon politics then, and for some years to come, and through
which Palmer would be obliged to dodge.

In the present instance, however, Palmer chose not so much to dodge as
not to budge. A few days after his letter to Burns, he wrote Jennings at The
Dalles to say that he intended to continue paying for supplies by issuing drafts
on the loan commissioners, with or without their permission. "I shall . . . act
for the cause regardless of consequences coin or no coin."[105]

The demand for supplies in the field was now desperate. L.H. Goodhue,
the assistant quartermaster at The Dalles, pleaded with Palmer:

> I am confident your soul is almost burned out with urgent solicitations for sup-
> plies for the army. Allow me for our country and our sakes to turn the auger a
> little more on you and you give it a devil of a rench on the people in the Valley
> that have bread and screw it out of them. Give us ammunition . . . when we
> have had a little bread we have had no ammunition and likewise the reverse.[106]

There were also frantic pleas for clothing and blankets. For this purpose, Palmer rode over to Fort Vancouver to see a Major Hardie, who was attempting
to recruit men to fight in the Mexican war, much to the irritation of Oregonians who were attempting to recruit for their own war. Hardie had a fair supply of blankets and clothing for which he had no use, since he had no recruits,
but he stated that he was not "authorized" to sell them. In the end, an irate Pal-

mer was obliged to leave empty-handed except for "a few pairs." This official obstructionism must have distressed Governor Abernethy, who already believed that Washington did not intend to provide assistance. One of his advisers, at wit's end, had suggested that he seek volunteers from Salt Lake City, to which the governor replied: "the Mormons might be as bad as the Indians."[107]

In fact, recruitment was progressing rather well. Clatsop County recruits resolved to abjure "inactivity" on the one hand and "Don Quixotic battles" on the other. Furthermore, they had obtained a promise from their fellow settlers that they would not jump the claims of the volunteers while they were absent in the field. For this was one of the principal deterrents to enlistment. The *Spectator* wrote on 6 April 1848:

> Let it be said of the people of this valley (if it must be so) that they allowed the defenders of their property, their lives and their honor to suffer for the want of the necessaries of life; but do not let a truthful history of the present war record the stealing of a land claim by one whose life and property were being protected by him whose claim was stolen.

Gallant Captain Maxon's pleas to the ladies of the valley had also had their effect. On 12 April, a statement from fifteen women appeared in the *Spectator*:

> We have not forgotten that the soul-sickening massacre and enormities at Waiilatpu were committed in part upon our sex. We know that your hardships and privations are great. But may we not hope, that through you these wrongs shall not only be amply avenged, but also that you inscribe upon the hearts of our savage enemies, a conviction never to be erased, that the virtue and lives of American women will be protected, defended and avenged by American men. The cause which you have espoused is a holy cause. We believe that the God of battles will so direct the destinies of this infant settlement, that she will come out of this contest clothed in honor, and her brave volunteers covered with glory . . . . We are asked to "evince our influence for our country's good, by withholding our hands from any young man, who refuses to turn out in defense of our honor and our country's rights." In reply, we hereby, one and all, of our own free will, solemnly pledge ourselves to comply with that request, and to evince, on all suitable occasions, our detestation and contempt for any and all young men who *can* but *will not* take up arms and march at once to the seat of war, to punish the Indians who have not only murdered our friends, but have grossly insulted our sex. We never can and never will bestow our confidence upon a man who has neither patriotism nor courage enough to defend his country and the girls, such a one would never have sufficient sense of obligation to defend and protect his WIFE. Do not be uneasy about your claims, and your

rights in the valley. While you are defending the rights of your country, she is watching yours. You must not be discouraged, fight on—be brave—obey your officers, and never quit your posts 'till the enemy is conquered, and when you return in triumph to the valley, you shall find us as ready to rejoice with you, as we now are to sympathize with you in your sufferings and dangers.

And indeed, by 17 April, H.A.G. Lee was able to write Abernethy from Portland to say that 250 volunteers were ready to depart for the upper country, even though the Indian troubles in the Willamette Valley had not abated. Whites had clashed with the Klamath earlier that month, and in revenge, several Indians had been killed by settlers near the Pudding River. "We cannot believe that the friendship of, or peace with the Indians is to be secured by submitting to wanton and repeated aggressions," the *Spectator* complained on 6 April. A visitor to this troubled scene, American painter John Mix Stanley—who had barely escaped the massacre at the Whitman mission—was so exercised by "the Klamath butchery" that he wrote to Robert Newell suggesting that a sympathetic agent and troops be sent to deal with the valley Indians in council.[108] However, Abernethy and Lee, the latter now in command in place of the deceased Gilliam, apparently decided the greatest need lay in the upper country, and accordingly, it was for there that the troops departed.

THE DOUBLING OF TROOPS in the upper country only compounded Palmer's problem. On 29 April, Jennings wrote from The Dalles to say that there was no flour left at all. The situation became so critical that on 4 May the *Spectator* published "A Voice From the Army":

Ye Oregon freemen who dwell at Willamette,
Columbia, Umpqua, or pleasant Alsea,
We call on you all from the Sound to the Klamet;
And ask, your attention, wherever you are.

Through your evergreen vallies the warwhoop is sounding;
Among your green mountains the war steed is bounding;
Your peaceful abodes the rude foe is surrounding;
Then, will you assist us; say, shall we have bread?

Your friends have been murdered, their corpses degraded!
Your daughters dishonored, your weapons defied!
Your rights are restricted, your country's invaded;
Your quiet is threatened, your valor belied!

Does your visage turn pale with confusion and wonder?
Does it ring through your soul like a loud peal of thunder?
Whilst ever the page of Waiilatpu you ponder?
Then, will you assist me; say, shall we have bread?
Let the faint hearted quail, neath the veil of the foe;
Or preach non-resistance, or picture its charms,
Your friends in the army will never disgrace you,
Or suffer dishonor to tarnish their arms
A citizen soldier the pride of our nation
With no titled slave would exchange situation,
And never submit to a hostile dictation;
Then, will you assist us; say, shall we have bread?

In addition to the scarcity of flour, there was also great dissatisfaction with the quality of that provided. On 4 May, Goodhue, at the Whitman mission, wrote Jennings at The Dalles to complain that their flour was unpalatable because shorts and bran had been deliberately left in it.

> I think it would be well to acquaint Mr Palmer of the imposition. The army feels quite hurt by the imposition and they send out some bitter curses on the people of the Valley . . . . I hope for respect sake they will not impose upon us more as above, we feel a pleasure in fighting their battles for them although it costs us many suferings. But such conduct grieves us more than all.[109]

By the end of May, Palmer—despite all his efforts to remedy the shortages—was at the end of his tether and, consequently, delivered the following ultimatum to the loan commissioners: "Can there not be some arrangements made to enable the department [the Commissary Department] to meet its obligation; if not all operations must cease and the army now in the field left without subsistence."[110]

THE ARMY MEANWHILE was suffering not only from lack of supplies but also from lack of success. In early May, Lee had held a council with the Walla Walla and some of the Cayuse to demand the surrender of the Whitmans' murderers. But the Indians were in an impossible position: if they acceded to Lee's demands, they would suffer the vengeance of their own people; if they did not, they would suffer the vengeance of the Americans. For the time being, the matter went into abeyance.

The next effort to secure the murderers took place on 17 May. There were rumors that the Nez Perce were sheltering the murderers, and accordingly, Lee with his new recruits set out for their country. This was in violation of the peace commissioners' promise to the Nez Perce that no whites, excepting Craig, their agent, and emigrants passing through, would enter their domain without their express permission. That the Nez Perce had in fact sheltered the murderers, thus justifying the American incursion, was never established. On the other hand, they may not have been particularly zealous in impeding their escape, for by the time the Americans reached the Nez Perce country, the murderers were well beyond the mountains.

By now, the Americans had had enough and had grown weary of trying to determine in the process of the pursuit which Indians were genuinely friendly to their cause and which were not—a determination that had plagued them from the beginning and now enraged them. As Maj. Joseph Magone wrote of the troops in the Nez Perce country, "I would have given more general satisfaction to the men by ordering them to wipe from the face of existence those professed friendly Indians, without distinction or mercy." Now, too, the shortages, as well as the chicanery associated with them, had become intolerable. In early June, Palmer received two reports from The Dalles with renewed charges of adulterated flour. This was particularly galling since the flour, so inferior to the Hudson's Bay Company product, was from a mill owned and operated by none other than the governor himself. "The army," wrote Cris Taylor at The Dalles, "belch forth bitter curses upon the people of the valley."[111]

The first officer to call it quits and return with his troops to the valley was Capt. William Martin, the commander of the Yamhill County volunteers. "We are unwilling to be a football for any set of tyranical demogogues," Martin wrote to the *Spectator* on 1 June, in what was an obvious reference to the political infighting between Palmer and the loan commissioners. Palmer was about to call it quits, as well. He wrote to Jennings on 5 June: "My hands are . . . tied . . . . I am anxious to get rid of a post [from] which I receive nothing but the curses of those whose business it is to aid in supporting our government." The previous day, he had written the governor that he had

> just been informed by the Loan Commissioners, that they have no funds on hands to meet the expenses of this department . . . . In absense of all other funds and the decision which the Loan Commissioners have made . . . places it entirely beyond the power of the Commissary to furnish the army with its pressing wants.[112]

But perhaps of greater moment was the change of season; soon the corn would silk and the grain would head. In the end, it may have been that, with the spring, these farmer soldiers simply wanted to go back to their fields and their women. In any event, the withdrawal began. Only small contingents were left at Fort Waters, as the Whitman mission was now called, and at Fort Lee. But in some respects, the disbandment of the troops increased Palmer's duties and vexations rather than reducing them. While he was still responsible for providing supplies for the two contingents in the field, he also faced the task of collecting from the returning volunteers all property belonging to the provisional government, namely, horses and gear. The volunteers were not always cooperative; they still had not received a penny of pay for their services, only their keep—adulterated flour and tattered breeches.

During this time, Palmer also may have been distracted by certain concerns extraneous to his duties. For one thing, elections were coming up on 5 June, a process that Oregonians found all-absorbing. The elections were for county and provisional government officers and for several measures as well, one of which called for the prohibition of liquor. In a community where many drank their spirits by the dipperful but where there were also a number of fanatical proponents of temperance, the measure elicited considerable controversy. The matter was further complicated by the contribution that liquor had made to Indian troubles in the valley. The controversy and the fiercely competing candidates could not have left Palmer uninvolved.

There was also a personal matter. On 27 June, Palmer received a confidential letter from Absalom Hembree, his commissary agent in Yamhill County. Hembree's letter did not concern commissary matters but rather Palmer's fifteen-year-old daughter, Sara. Sara, Hembree reported, had been converted to Methodism at a local camp meeting; she had also been "converted" to twenty-six-year-old Andrew Smith. How Palmer interpreted the meaning of the word "converted" in this context is unknown. What is known is that in Oregon City the following day, Palmer saw to it that Sara and Andrew were married.

Meanwhile, the volunteers were slowly drifting down from the upper country and, in some cases, with property whose ownership was not entirely clear. In late June, Berryman Jennings reported from The Dalles that the fort anvil had disappeared, a serious loss, and that horses belonging to the government had vanished. "The boys must be watched," he concluded. Palmer agreed. A few days before, he had written the governor that "the officers seem to have but little control over the men. They have apparently become perfectly reckless." The Reverend George H. Atkinson, the newly arrived Congregational missionary, was similarly distressed by the returned volunteers he encountered on the streets of Oregon City. He, too, found them "reckless" and also "vociferous and very profane." W.W. Walter, one of the profane, made no bones about it: "we were as wild as a band of Indians."[113]

The official time and place of discharge was 5 July at McSwain's farm on the Clackamas, but many of the volunteers had arrived early to be on time for what in those years was the most important holiday and celebration of the year: the Fourth of July. "I would like very much myself," C.W. Crook wrote from the Whitman mission in May, "to lean back under the cool shade in the valley on the 4th of July and talk about *American Independence.*"[114] It was a sentiment, genuine and strong, shared by his fellow volunteers, these sons of the soldiers of the Revolution.

Elaborate celebrations were held throughout the valley, but the most official event took place in Oregon City. The center of festivities was the town's famous hostelry, Sidney Moss' Main Street House. The Main Street House, it may be remembered, was the home of the Oregon Lyceum, or debating society, and the stage on which the Lyceum's most colorful member, Charles Pickett, had pranced his antic part. * It was at the Main Street House, then, that the celebrants gathered, the volunteers cantering up on horses flamboyantly "decked out in Indian trappings," according to Walter, and without doubt making a general show of themselves. Inside, Mr. and Mrs. Moffat sang a "National Air," followed by twenty-six toasts. To the acute distress of some, Prohibition had in fact been approved by the people on 5 June, and thus the toasts were drunk with what the *Spectator* called "Adam's Ale," which is to say, water. Nonetheless, these toasts "were responded to with as hearty a cheer as though accompanied by copious draughts of sparkling wine." The final toast and the one that no doubt raised the heartiest cheers was to the volunteers:

* Pickett by now had left the Sandwich Islands for California, but he still kept in contact with his friend, Lee. In March, Pickett had written him for some "squashed Indians heads"—skulls that had been subject to the head-flattening practice of the Chinook-speaking Indians—for a museum he intended to establish in San Francisco.

> At their country's call, they reared themselves like a mighty lion from his lair, drew their swords, and brandished their steel in the face of their foes, convincing their enemies and the world at large, that the same spirit which burned and animated the souls of the warriors of the revolution, has been transmitted unadulterated and untarnished to their posterity.[115]

WITH LIMITED SUCCESS, Palmer continued to collect the provisional government's property and to scavenge supplies for the two up-country contingents. In August, it was finally decided that the loan commissioners would pay the volunteers and meet other expenses by refunding the entire debt and issuing new scrip. All of this was done on the assumption that the cost of the war would eventually be assumed by the United States. But as historian J. Henry Brown concluded, "it seems that the U.S. Government was more interested in prosecuting an unjust war for political purposes against a weaker nation [Mexico], than rendering aid to her own distressed people."[116]

It must have been a bitter irony to Oregonians that on 9 August, two months after the war had ended, the brig *Henry* arrived in the Willamette loaded with arms and ammunition sent from United States army stores in San Francisco. But as Bancroft later pointed out, it may have been just as well that the *Henry* had not arrived while the war was on. The Cayuse War was by far the least bloody of the Oregon Indian conflicts, and the reason was simple: as often as not, the powder horns were empty.

Still, the war did much harm. It further embittered the already galled relations between Protestants and Catholics, the British and the Americans, the whites and the Indians—a bitterness that would take many years to pass.* But perhaps the most damaging consequence of the war lay in H.A.G. Lee's action in late June. Unable to find volunteers willing to stay on and garrison the fort at Whitman's mission, Lee, now superintendent of Indian affairs, offered Cayuse land to all who would remain. Governor Abernethy sanctioned the action, and the 13 July *Spectator* announced it:

* The bitterest and most lasting of all of these conflicts, between Catholics and Protestants, was finally laid to rest at Whitman College in July 1986. The occasion was a conference celebrating the 150th anniversary of the arrival of the first Protestant missionaries to the Columbia Plateau. The keynote speaker was a Jesuit.

> In consideration of the barbarous and insufferable conduct of the Cayuse Indians, as portrayed in the massacre of the American families at Waiilatpu, and the subsequent course of hostilities against the Americans generally; and with a view to inflict upon them a just punishment, as well as to secure and protect our fellow-citizens, immigrating from the United States to this Territory, against a course of reckless aggressions so long and uniformly practiced upon them by the said Cayuse Indians.
>
> I, H.A.G. Lee, Superintendent of Indian Affairs, hereby declare the territory of said Cayuse Indians forfeited by them, and justly subject to be occupied and held by American citizens, resident in Oregon.

The offer was a gross violation of all that the whites had promised the Cayuse again and again and by all parties, and which consisted of the simple declaration that only the guilty would be punished.

Now, by Lee and Abernethy's action, the whole tribe was to suffer the

American vengeance for the Whitman massacre. It is true that Palmer—at the Whitman mission, in council with the Cayuse, Nez Perce, and Yellow Serpent on 7 March—had stated that the Cayuse "had forfeited the land by making war upon the Americans," but he had immediately added that the Americans did not want their land and thus maintained the promise that the innocent would not be punished.[117] Still, his assertion of the right, if not the act, may very well have been the origin—the imprimatur, as it were—of Lee's action.

The confiscation of the Cayuse land made it clear to the Indians of the Northwest that the Americans spoke with a "forked tongue"—said one thing, did another. It also made it clear to the whites that if the Indians misbehaved, they would be justified in taking their land by way of punishment. This belief of the rights of whites to Indian land and the Indians' loss of trust in the word of whites were seeds that Palmer himself had sown, dragon's teeth whose deadly crop he himself would reap.

As for the Cayuse, driven from their homeland, their tragedy was almost Greek in its nature and dimensions. Frances Victor put it well: "The very thing was about to happen which the Cayuse had killed Whitman to prevent, namely, the settlement of their lands by white people." The terrible malediction of the *Spectator* had come to pass: "Let the places that once knew them, know them no more forever."[118]

FIVE

Settling In

A MYSTERIOUS CRAFT APPEARED on the Willamette River in August 1848. William Rector observed: "[it] was the occasion of much speculation as to what was its true character." The small ship

was not concined to any one nor haled from no place and displays no flag, the editor of the little paper untertook to interview the comander but found him very reticent even to insulting. the editor published the arival of the misterious craft and recomended tying him up unless he gave some account of himself, intimateing that he was a piret.[1]

The commander apparently was not tied up as a pirate, but instead went cruising up and down the river, buying flour and bacon at modest prices as well as all the picks and shovels he could find—the latter purchases, in particular, were found to be most puzzling. When his ship could hold no more, the commander, a Captain Newall of San Francisco, informed the gulled locals that gold had been found at Sutter's Mill in California.

It is estimated that two-thirds of the able-bodied men of Oregon threw down what was at hand—axes, awls, chisels, plows, pens, scales, forceps, tankards, and Bibles—and departed for California.

The following is a portion of a poem published in the *Spectator* at the time, which historian J. Henry Brown says "contains more truth than poetry."

> There wealth untold is bought and sold
> And each may be partaker!
> Where fifty tons of finest gold
> Are dug from every acre!

At sound of gold both young and old
　　Forsook their occupation,
And wild confusion seemed to rule
　　In every situation.

An old cordwainer heard the news,
　　And though not much elated,
He left his pile of boots and shoes
　　And just evaporated.

The cooper left his tubs and pails,
　　His buckets and his piggins;
The sailor left his yards and sails,
　　And started for the "diggins."

The farmer left his plough and steers,
　　The merchant left his measure,
The tailor dropped his goose and shears
　　And went to gather treasure.

A pedagogue, attired incog,
　　Gave ear to what was stated
Forsook his stool, bestrode a mule,
　　And then absquatulated.

A boatman, too, forsook his crew,
　　Let fall his oar and paddle,
And stole his neighbor's iron-gray
　　But went without a saddle.

The joiner dropped his square and jack,
　　The Chapenter his chisel,
The pedlar laid aside his pack
　　And all prepared to mizzle.

The woodman dropped his trusty axe,
　　The tanner left his leather
The miller left his pile of sacks
　　And all went off together.

The doctor cocked his eye askance,
   The promised wealth descrying,
Then wheeled his horse and off he pranced
   And left his patients dying.

The preacher dropped the Holy Book
   And grasped the mad illusion;
The herdsman left his flock and crook
   Amid the wild confusion.

The judge consigned to cold neglect
   The great judicial ermine,
But just which way his honor went
   I could not well determine.

And then I saw far in the rear
   A fat, purse-proud attorney
Collect his last retaining fee
   And start upon his journey.

And when each brain in that vast train
   Was perfectly inverted,
My slumbers broke and I awoke
   And found the place deserted.

—O.P.Q.

In J. Henry Brown, Brown's *Political History of Oregon* (Portland, Ore.: Lewis & Dryden, 1892), 453.

The most serious of these derelictions was the plow, for after all, the people left behind had to eat. The *Spectator* pleaded with Oregonians to stay on the farm—until their own printer hurried south, which for a time obliged the newspaper to cease publication.

Palmer was among the throng. Early in September, he and William Lysander Adams joined a group of 150 "stout, robust, energetic, sober men" and, with provisions for six months loaded into fifty wagons, started south.* Their route lay up the Willamette Valley and on to the Rogue River, the latter new country to Palmer but with which, in time, he would

An Ohio-born schoolteacher and Campbellite parson,

become well and tragically acquainted. They followed
the Rogue into the Cascades and by late October had arrived at Goose Lake on the Oregon-California line. To
their astonishment, they found the lake populated by
vast numbers of pelicans; they also found its water pu-
trid. The next day, however, they followed a deer and
came upon a clear stream where they feasted, drinking
good water and eating badger. Peter Burnett remarked
at the time that "the tail of the badger, the ear of the
hog, and the foot of the elephant are superior eating."[2]

Traveling along the Pit River, they came by late October to the red oaks that signified their proximity to the
Sacramento Valley. They soon reached their destination, Long's Bar on the Yukon River. "Below, glowing
in the hot sunshine, and in the narrow valley of this lovely and rapid stream," Burnett wrote,

> we saw the canvas tents and the cloth shanties of the
> miners. There was but one log-cabin in the camp.
> There were about eighty men, three women, and five
> children at this place. The scene was most beautiful to
> us. It was the first mining locality we had ever seen,
> and here we promptly decided to pitch our tent. We
> drove our wagons and teams across the river into the camp, and turned out our
> oxen and horses to graze and rest.[3]

Adams came to Oregon in 1848. He was a superb political satirist, an editor of the Oregon Argus, *a probate judge, and a collector of customs under Lincoln. After several years of travel in Europe and several more on his Yamhill farm, Adams at the age of fifty-two decided to take an M.D. degree in Philadelphia. He returned to Oregon, where he practiced medicine for thirty-two years. He died at the age of eighty-five, having fathered ten children by two wives.*

Here, and in several other communities, Palmer and his group met fellow Oregonians. Some of these communities still remain as place names—Oregon
Gulch, for example, and Oregon House. Then there was Hangtown, founded
by Oregon miners and apparently deserving of its name; Bancroft writes that
the Oregonians there were "clannish and aggressive" and very quick to use
"the rifle or the rope."[4]

Palmer left no record of his mining days except to later tell Bancroft that he
had acquired two thousand dollars' worth of gold, after which he returned to
Oregon by ship, apparently in the early spring of 1849.

Palmer found that the gold rush had benefited Oregon in most respects.
For one thing, it had provided a nearby market for Oregon products. Also,
and at long last, it provided a currency to replace a method of exchange that
was awkward to say the least: one bushel of wheat equaling one dollar. And
indeed, later commentators believed that the Oregon settlement might not
have survived—or, if so, but lamely—without the California gold rush.

On the other hand, Oregon had not been contaminated by the California glitter. "After all it will be seen," wrote Bancroft,

> that the distance of Oregon from the Sierra Foothills proved at this time the greatest of blessings, being near enough for commercial communication, and yet so far away as to escape the more evil consequences attending the mad scramble for wealth, such as social dissolution, the rapine of intellect and principle, an overruling spirit of gambling—a delirium of development, attended by robbery, murder, and all uncleanness, and followed by reaction and death.[5]

From such wickedness Oregon, unlike its unfortunate neighbor to the south, had been preserved.

For Palmer, his profits from the goldfields meant that he was finally free to settle down, for as far as is known, he still had not established himself on his claim at Dayton. This, however, was not yet to happen.

ON THE MORNING of 13 March 1849, a flotilla of canoes arrived at Portland. The lead canoe carried the "Cincinnatus of Indiana," the "Marius of the Mexican War," and, his latest title, the governor of the Oregon Territory, Joseph Lane.* For good or for ill, Oregon was at last a territory. Governor Lane was not welcomed by all. The Whigs were enraged that the territory should be governed by a Democrat, and most Oregonians resented anyone who was imposed on them from the outside. Palmer, however, was not among these discontents. Not only were both he and Lane Democrats, but they were also fellow Hoosiers, and perhaps most important, both had served together in the Indiana legislature.

It was probably due to this friendship but also to Palmer's qualifications that Governor Lane asked Palmer to guide Lt. George W. Hawkins to Fort Hall. Hawkins had come out by ship with Lane as the latter's official escort. The purpose of his present mission was to carry supplies to Fort Hall for the expected arrival of the American Rifle Regiment.

The American Rifle Regiment—which was to earn for itself a rather dubious reputation in Oregon—was authorized in 1846 by Congress to garrison posts along the Oregon Trail. But before the regiment could carry out that duty, it was diverted to serve in the Mexican

*Born in North Carolina in 1801, Joseph Lane served in the Indiana legislature from 1822-46, when he left to fight in the Mexican war. Following the war, it was reported that Lane, on being asked by President Polk whether he wanted the Oregon territorial governorship, is supposed to have replied, "I'll be ready in ten minutes," and he in fact held that post from March 1849 to June 1850. Lane later served as territorial delegate to Congress and as the state's first senator. In 1860, he was demo-

war. This now concluded, the regiment was on its way to Oregon to garrison the trail posts as well as Oregon City. The regiment consisted of six hundred men and thirty-one officers. Its ranks included a fair number of scalawags as well as such distinguished figures as ethnologist George Gibbs and artist William Tappan, both of whom Palmer would come to know.

Palmer and Hawkins set out for Fort Hall on 25 June with fifteen hundred pounds of supplies and a herd of cattle. They followed the same route Palmer had taken to the goldfields. At Goose Lake, the party encountered a General Wilson and his wife en route to California, where, according to some accounts, he was to serve as customs collector and superintendent of Indian affairs.

cratic candidate for U.S. vice president with John Breckinridge. On the approach of the Civil War, he lost favor due to his pro-slavery and pro-Southern sympathies, thereafter living in retirement in southern Oregon until his death in 1881. See Joseph Lane, Auto-biography, microfilm, Bancroft Library.

The general asked Palmer to join his party as guide, and Palmer agreed to go along; the remainder of the trail to Fort Hall was well marked, and thus Lieutenant Hawkins no longer needed his assistance. Palmer's service with the general and his wife would prove to be more of an adventure than he may have expected.

The first incident occurred when the general's teamsters, refusing guard duty, mutinied. Accordingly, Captain Morris, who commanded the general's escort, expelled them from the camp. But one of the teamsters was the driver for the general's wife, and she insisted that he be returned to her. Captain Morris insisted that she must choose between the teamsters and the escort; she chose the teamsters and the escort departed. Palmer opted for the general's lady.

The next incident occurred when a man named Brown accidentally shot himself in the arm while crossing the Humboldt River. Two physicians traveling in another party were called in to amputate the shattered arm, but according to Palmer, they did a "bungling job of it." The amputation had to be done again, and Palmer "sharpened a butcher knife" and did it. Brown was unable to travel, so he and Palmer and the general's son stayed in a cabin in the mountains for two weeks. Starting out again, Palmer had what he called the most difficult outdoor experience of his life.

> Where we crossed Feather River there is a bar with a gravelly and sticky bottom . . . . The river was running perfectly full of slush ice in large masses . . . . We stripped off naked, put our clothes on our shoulders and started across. It was the worst job I ever had in my life wading that stream.[6]

On reaching Sacramento, Palmer's duties were over, and accordingly, he went to San Francisco and took ship for Oregon. His fee had been fifteen hundred dollars, and this together with the two thousand dollars he had brought back from the gold rush probably gave him all the capital he needed to establish himself on the Yamhill claim, and in the spring of 1850, he did so.

ALEXANDER HENRY was among the first whites to see the Yamhill River country and its inhabitants. As quoted earlier, he found the latter "the most miserable, wild, and rascally looking tribe I had seen on this side of the Rocky Mountains."[7] As for the landscape, his only comment is on the Yamhill, which he calls the "Yellow River," an accurately descriptive name, since its waters are often muddied.* However, another fur trader, John Work—traversing the valley in 1834—provides a full description of the region:

> * *"Yamhill" is said to be a corruption of* a-ya'mil, *the local Indian word for the Red Hills of Dundee, northeast of the river.*

> a fine valley not very wide, surrounded with a number of rising hills thickly covered with oak. The soil all the way is very rich and the pasture though not rank more luxuriant than in the large level plains. On the summit of the hills the soil inclines in some places to a reddish tile . . . . The river has generally steep clayey banks, & is difficult to approach on account of the underwood.[8]

The next visitor to report on the Yamhill was Charles Wilkes, commander of the United States Exploring Expedition of 1838-43. Wilkes, too, found the region pleasing and fertile. He also called on its first settler, Louis La Bonte, and his wife, a Clatsop Indian named Little Songbird, and who had started farming in 1836 on the "neck," a reach of land between the Yamhill and the Willamette. "The most perfect picture of content," Wilkes wrote of Louis and Little Songbird.[9]

By 1842, eight families had settled on the Yamhill, and from the emigrations of 1843 and 1844 came many more. By the time Palmer arrived, it was a populated place, and many of the settlers were from Indiana. That was typical: people from the same place in the States settling together in the same place in Oregon. This probably was a factor in Palmer's choice of the Yamhill, but it had other advantages as well. As Palmer later wrote: "the valley is fine prairie land, soil light and rich, occasionally interspersed with fine groves, and well adapted to agricultural purposes."[10]

Palmer's land claim in this little Eden lay six miles southwest of present-day Dayton. However, for reasons unknown, he sold this claim and bought land on the south bank of the south fork of the Yamhill from his son-in-law,

Andrew Smith, the camp-meeting Lothario. It was a good spot. Here was the head of navigation on the Yamhill, the farthest point to which boats from the Willamette could come whatever the season. Commercial service on the Yamhill had begun in 1850, with a sixty-five-foot flatboat powered by four Klickitats and capable of transporting 350 bushels of wheat. Then, in 1851, a little paddle wheeler called the *Hoosier* began a scheduled run. The location was to become and would remain for many years the principal wheat-shipping port for the Yamhill Valley.

It was here, then, on a bluff above the river and beside an Indian trail, that Palmer built a house in the spring of 1850. It was in the popular Classic Revival style—white clapboard, paned windows, brick chimneys at either end—and served both as a residence for his family and as a hotel. Palmer's friend, Cris Taylor, built a store nearby, and that fall, the two men laid out a town and named it Dayton for Taylor's home in Ohio. Palmer and his family were finally established in Oregon. There was to be only one more move. Sometime in 1851 or 1852, Palmer sold his house-hotel to J.B. Jacobs and built himself a new house a little west of the town center. The Palmers would remain there for the rest of their lives.

THERE HAD BEEN MANY CHANGES in the decade since Palmer had first seen Oregon. Most important, the white population had grown from two thousand to thirty thousand. Settlement had spread from the valley into the foothills, some to the lower reaches of the tributary streams pouring down from the mountain ranges, some higher up where the falling water could be used to power mills. The greatest change lay in the increase of cultivated land—wheat and oats, hay, potatoes, onions, the young orchards finally beginning to bear, all protected from the growing herds of cattle by a zigzag of split-rail fences. With the mills, the crude cabins of chinked logs were giving way to the simple elegance of Greek Revival farmhouses, lilacs at the door, and, inside, objects unknown in the forties—cookstoves, sewing machines, perhaps a settee and a spinet from around the Horn. Indeed, it may have been now, having permanently established themselves, that the Palmers' own mahogany came out, as well as their library—some of these appointments perhaps from Sarah's patrician Quaker home in Philadelphia.

Growth and change were reflected in another significant development. By now, there were thirty registered towns in the valley, and by the mid-1850s, they were linked by fourteen steamboats on scheduled runs. The towns themselves—Dayton, for example, and its neighbor, Lafayette—were not all that impressive, the buildings of a flimsy, slapdash kind, much clutter and muck about, but a columned courthouse went up in Lafayette, and some towns boasted an academy where a youth could learn a little Latin and how to play the flute. As for the capital, Bancroft tells us that "a sort of gay and fashionable air was imparted to society in Oregon City by the families of the territorial officers . . . which was a new thing in the Willamette Valley, and provoked not a little jealousy among the more sedate and surly."*[11]

There was also development at either end of the valley. In 1850, gold was discovered in the Rogue River Valley, and the towns of Jacksonville and Ashland were founded while Roseburg had its beginnings in 1852 as a way station on the Oregon-California trail. But it was at the other end of the valley that Palmer saw the most impressive development—the town of Portland.

At the head of navigation on the Willamette and with the best low-grade pass through the hills to the rich wheatlands of the Tualatin Valley, Portland had become the place where "the wagons could meet the ships" and thus drew ahead of the other river towns. In addition to docks, Portland had a brick building with arches, Classic Revival cottages on sixteen elm-planted blocks, land set aside for parks, a library, and a music shop. Despite the unkind remark of a woman bound for California, who referred to Portland as "rather gamey," Oregon now had its metropolis.

*An example of this surly attitude toward the "gay and fashionable air" at Oregon City is reflected in a comment on the then territorial governor, Gen. John P. Gaines: "The People in this country think less and less every day of governor gaines. they say it is to much like being governed by a petticoat to be governed by him." Thomas C. Shaw to Joseph Lane, 22 December 1851, MSS 1146, Oregon Historical Society.

In general, by the early 1850s there had been growth in all areas: the economy, transportation, education, government, the amenities of everyday life. What, one wonders, did Palmer think about all this progress?

American historian Richard Hofstadter has written of

the enduring American obsession with an escape from society—in the first instance from the society of Europe and then from that society as it was repeated, re-created, and imitated in the American east—into the original innocence and promise of nature, as represented in the vast interior of woods and prairies. On the other hand, "here lay the nub of the intimate American quarrel with history, the difficulty of combining the pastoral, or still worse, the primitivist, sense of the ideal human condition with another equally deep intellectual craving, the belief in progress."[12]

And so, one wonders. A woman on her mare—the children up behind—riding down to camp meeting, reins in at some point on the trail to shade her eyes and gaze at the long, green valley with its meander of river, at the houses and barns, schools and churches, shops, taverns, and all the rest that year by year increase. The wilderness domesticated. And she surely was grateful. Should a man ride by—Palmer or another like him—he, too, reins in for a moment to look down on what he and his fellow settlers have wrought and feels such pride. But if Hofstadter is right, then mingling with that pride there was also regret.

THERE IS LITTLE INFORMATION on Palmer's first years in Dayton. He planted an orchard of 160 apple trees, his sons helping him, and he built a sawmill on the creek behind his house. It can be assumed that he worked to sell, or give away, town lots to encourage the growth of Dayton. He was active to some degree in community affairs, for in 1851, he was made a trustee of the Oregon Academy in nearby Lafayette. And he was involved in politics.

When the people became dissatisfied with Samuel Thurston, Oregon's territorial delegate to Congress, Palmer was one of the men the party suggested might oppose him. But none of the proposed candidates was more popular than Joseph Lane, who as a Democrat had to resign his governorship when Taylor, a Whig, became president. It was Palmer, as chairman of the Yamhill Democratic Committee, who first put forward Lane's name in 1851. Lane was elected and continued as delegate until statehood in 1859.

One favor deserves another. On 31 December 1852, Palmer wrote a letter to Lane in Washington that contains the following curious passage:

> Now General, did I not believe you would be bored horribly by applicants for office asking your influence, and none others more entitled or better qualified to discharge the duties than myself, I would ask for something but as I have never been an office seeker it is better perhaps to not attempt it at this late day. I have never solicited anyones influence in my behalf and as favors of that kind are seldom bestowed unsolicited, of course I need expect none. But do try and have good honest men appointed.[13]

Four and one-half months later—about the time needed for a letter to reach Washington and a reply to come back—Palmer learned that he had been appointed superintendent of Indian affairs for the Oregon Territory.

The Troubles
of 1853

T HE FIRST OFFICIAL AMERICANS to parley with the Indians of the Oregon Country were Meriwether Lewis and William Clark. Thomas Jefferson provided the explorers with medals that showed a peace pipe superimposed upon a tomahawk and bearing the legend "Peace and Friendship." And indeed, one of the principal purposes of the expedition was to effect a peace and friendship that would be conducive to future commerce in both the commercial and social sense. Jefferson instructed the explorers to trade with the natives in a "friendly and concilatory manner" and, most important, to gather information about them that would "better enable those who may endeavor to civilize and instruct them *to adapt their measures to the existing notions and practices of those on whom they are to operate.*"[1] Tragically, the italicized portion of Jefferson's advice [author's italics] was seldom heeded.

Excepting the trappers, the missionaries were the first Americans to engage in prolonged commerce with the Indians, and they were not about to "adapt their measures" to the Indians' "existing notions and practices," but instead were intent upon the expiration of Indian ways.[*2] The same could be said of the first official Indian agent, Dr. Elijah White, and the code of laws with which he hoped to replace the Indians' "notions and practices."

White is among the more colorful and disreputable figures in Oregon history. His contemporary, historian William H. Gray—albeit a historian given to exaggera-

* *Until recently, the tape recording accompanying the diorama of the Whitman massacre at the Whitman National Historic Site ended*

tion and sometimes more—described White as a "puff-ball of folly and ignorance" while, and as noted earlier, Charles Pickett referred to him as "the Gilded Chamberpot." Two such different personages as Dr. McLoughlin and Narcissa Whitman found him, in the latter's words, "quite ignorant of the Indian character." Nor was Bancroft impressed. He described White, who was in his thirties at the time, as a man of "slight, elastic frame" with manners "of that obliging and flattering kind which made him popular, especially among women," and as "affectedly rather than truely pious." Also, "the longer he dwelt upon this coast, the more he became smooth and slippery like glass, and flat withal, yet he could be round and cutting on occasions, particularly when broken on the wheel of adversity."*³ Modern historians have been no kinder.

thus: "The tragedy of Dr. Whitman was that he was not understood by the Indians." Typically, the reverse was not considered.

Yet White had his redeeming features. He defended Dr. John McLoughlin, often when it was not expedient to do so. Also, he seemed to have true sympathy for the Indians' plight. Finally, and however disreputable in certain respects, he was colorful. Some of his contemporaries, equally disreputable, did not possess even that saving grace.

As noted earlier, White had first come to Oregon in 1837 as physician to the Jason Lee mission. After allegedly misusing mission funds and Indian women, he was relieved of his duties in 1840. Back in the States, he was approached by certain persons who, determined on the acquisition of Oregon for the United States, proposed to him that he return to Oregon as official Indian agent, a foot in the door, as it were. White was happy to oblige, for this would make him the first official American to reside in the Oregon Country. Thus, he would not only score—indeed, infuriate—Lee and the mission community, but he would be well positioned for some future office, the governorship, for example. The fact that the Indian appointment, not to mention any "governorship," was wholly irregular—since the Oregon Country was still not yet American territory—in no way dampened White's ambitions.

* *Bancroft was never to change his view of White. Many years later, he found that White was practicing medicine "a stone's throw" from Bancroft's own premises in San Francisco. Although White was now in his seventies, he was "active on his feet and well preserved though how much of him was padding, and what was the true color of his well-dyed hair and whiskers I cannot say." See Bancroft, History of Oregon, vol. 11, 391.*

When White was appointed as Indian agent for the Oregon Country in

1842, the commissioner was Thomas Hartley Crawford. Mr. Crawford, whom one associate described as a "sharp-featured old gentleman with a bald head somewhat shaped like that of a chicken," undoubtedly communicated to White the Department's policy. "Indians," Crawford had written, "must be civilized as well as, if not in order to their being Christianized."[4] That is, the Indians were to jettison their traditions and acquire the ways of the whites. This was Elijah White's charge, and he attempted to carry it out. In the spring of 1842, he departed for Oregon, the leader of a wagon train noteworthy for its squabbles.

On his arrival in Oregon, the state of Indian-white relations was a vexing one for all concerned. Heretofore, it had been the policy of the government to extinguish Indian land titles and set up military posts *before* permitting settlers to occupy frontier regions. That had not happened in Oregon for the simple reason that the region was not yet United States territory. The resulting injustice to the Indians, apprehension on the part of the whites, and confusion for all is well put by White himself:

> This legislative body [the provisional government] have again and again peti-
> tioned the congress of the United States to extend jurisdiction over Oregon,
> making sensible, and even moving appeals, urging the moral wrong of strip-
> ping the Indian race of their lands, game and fisheries, without rendering com-
> pensation for what is to them so valuable; also of leaving American citizens,
> who were encouraged to emigrate to that country, surrounded by hordes of In-
> dians without any protection from the home government. The irritation on the
> part of the natives arising from the whites pouring in, in such numbers, and de-
> spoiling them of their rights, often jeopardizes the dearest interests of the set-
> tlers, and reflects great discredit on the government, for not *righting* the wrong
> of the Indians, and *protecting* her own citizens.[5]

The first call on White's offices came in November 1842 from Whitman and Spalding, for they were having problems with the Cayuse and Nez Perce, respectively. In the case of the Whitmans, the Cayuse had burned down a mission mill, and during one of Dr. Whitman's absences, a brave had appeared at Narcissa Whitman's bedroom door.

Accordingly, White set off in high fettle for the Walla Walla and the Clearwater. He was not particularly well received at Whitman's mission, for few Cayuse bothered to present themselves. So, he went on to the Clearwater, where his reception was of a very different order, greeted, as he was, by no fewer than twenty-two chiefs. After ministering to the sick and praising the Indian children for their accomplishments, White got down to business. He began with statements of his good intentions and assurances of the respect and affection in which the Nez Perce were held by their Great White Father in Washington. Eight of the chiefs replied. "First arose Five Crows," White wrote,

> a wealthy chief of forty-five, neatly attired in English costume. He stepped gravely but modestly forward to the table, remarking: "It does not become me to speak first; I am but a youth, as yet, when compared to many of these my fathers: but my feelings urge me to arise and say what I am about to utter in a very few words. I am glad the chief has come; I have listened to what has been said; have great hopes that brighter days are before us, because I see all the whites are united in this matter; we have much wanted some thing; hardly knew what; been groping and feeling for it in confusion and darkness. Here it is. Do we see it, and shall we accept?"*
>
> Soon the Bloody Chief arose—not less than ninety years old—and said: "I speak to-day, perhaps to-morrow I die. I am the oldest chief of the tribe; was the high chief when your great brothers, Lewis and Clark, visited this country; they visited me, and honored me with their friendship and counsel. I showed them my numerous wounds received in bloody battle with the Snakes; they told me it was not good, it was better to be at peace; gave me a flag of truce: I held it up high; we met and talked, but never fought again. Clark pointed to this day, to you, and this occasion; we have long waited in expectation; sent three of our sons to Red River school to prepare for it; two of them sleep with their fathers; the other is here, and can be ears, mouth, and pen for us. I can say no more; I am quickly tired; my voice and limbs tremble. I am glad I live to see you and this day, but I shall soon be still and quiet in death."[6]

* Five Crows, whom Palmer later was to meet on the Umatilla, was a Cayuse chief, but his mother was Nez Perce, which may explain his presence on this occasion.

After seven other chiefs had delivered a similar welcome, White launched into his program for the Nez Perce. First, they were to choose a paramount chief for the whole tribe. This violated tribal tradition, which provided for a number of chiefs. Nevertheless, the Nez Perce followed White's suggestion and elected as their head chief Ellis, son of Bloody Chief. White no doubt had it in mind that one chief would be easier to deal with than a plethora of lesser chiefs. But in this case he was wrong, for Ellis turned out to be very difficult indeed.

Next, White presented a code of laws created by himself and according to which, he informed the Nez Perce, they were expected to live. "The first attempt made by whites west of the Rocky Mountains to teach the Indians to govern themselves according to alien standards," Charles Carey wrote in his *General History of Oregon*.[7] And indeed, the laws had been designed primarily for the benefit of the whites. For example, it was customary for the Indians to freely enter each other's dwellings and to borrow and use each other's effects without permission. Both actions were now prohibited, the latter punishable with twenty to fifty lashes. These laws, of course, reflected the Whitmans' and Spaldings' concern for privacy and the inviolate nature of personal possessions and had no relation at all to Indian practice. White's laws were also inequitable in that they specified punishment for offenses by Indians—a certain number of lashes, a form of punishment that the Indians found particularly degrading— but none for offenses committed by whites. There was only the general pre- scription that whites were to be "punished." Finally, there was the question of who was authorized to punish whites. The answer was simple: no one.

Having delivered his laws like Moses from the mount, White lectured the Nez Perce on the evils of begging, distributed fifty hoes to the "industrious" poor, and departed, well satisfied with himself.

En route, he stopped at Whitman's and again was disappointed when most of the Cayuse chiefs declined to appear. One who did expressed reservations about the laws of the whites: "three-fourths of them [the whites]," he charged, "though they taught the purest doctrines, practiced the greatest abomina- tions." White could do little more than urge the Cayuse to gather more of their people for another meeting with him in the spring. He then departed for the valley, stopping at Wascopam, now The Dalles, to promulgate his laws to the Indians there. He was later informed by one of the missionaries stationed at Wascopam that "the clean faces of some, and the tidy dresses of others, show the good effects of your visit."[8] So ended the first foray of the first American official among the Indians of the Northwest.

The following spring, White again received reports of unrest in the upper country, reportedly due to the Indians' alarm at the increasing number of whites on their land. One of these same whites, arriving at this time, possessed a remarkable understanding of the Indians' anxiety and expressed it as well as it has ever been put. Peter Burnett, the Tennessee attorney who was later to fig- ure so largely in Oregon and California history, began by contrasting the atti- tude of the Indians toward the Hudson's Bay Company with their attitude toward the Americans:

> The Indians soon saw that the [Hudson's Bay] Company was a mere trading es-
> tablishment, confined to a small space of land at each post, and was, in point of
> fact, advantageous to themselves. The few Canadian-French who were located

in the Willamette Valley were mostly, if not entirely, connected by marriage with the Indians, the Frenchmen having Indian wives, and were considered to some extent as a part of their own people. But, when we, the American immigrants, came into what the Indians claimed as their own country, we were considerable in numbers; and we came, not to establish trade with the Indians, but to take and settle the country *exclusively* for ourselves. Consequently, we went anywhere we pleased, settled down without any treaty or consultation with the Indians, and occupied our claims without their consent and without compensation. This difference they very soon understood. Every succeeding fall they found the white population about doubled, and our settlements continually extending, and rapidly encroaching more and more upon their pasture and camas grounds. They saw that we fenced in the best lands, excluding their horses from the grass and our hogs ate up their camas. They instinctively saw annihilation before them.[9]

It was, then, apprehensions such as these that were behind the unrest reported to Dr. White in the spring of 1843. In late April, he set out again for the upper country. At Wascopam, he was confounded with the first unexpected result of his laws. Those who had been whipped for offenses were irate that they had not been rewarded for the pain inflicted. If the lashing could not be compensated for with gifts, then White's laws were not acceptable.

At Whitman's mission there was great dissatisfaction with the laws as well. Some were using the laws to intimidate or terrorize others, and also they had created a division between those who honored them and those who did not, the former charged by the latter with being servants of the American "women." Even Narcissa Whitman pointed out that forcing the Indians to accept the laws was an insult to their pride. Finally, Yellow Serpent, the powerful chief of the Walla Walla, questioned the very legitimacy of the laws in the statement quoted earlier: "Where are these laws from? Are they from God, or from the earth? . . . I think that they are from the earth, because, from what I know of white men, they did not honor these laws." Complaints about the whippings continued, and question was raised as to why the Americans had not paid the paramount chiefs. After much discussion, tempered by much feasting, an accommodation of sorts was finally reached, culminating in the election of Five Crows as the Cayuse high chief. For the time being at least, the Cayuse and Nez Perce had been partially reassured of White's good intentions, and White returned to the valley: "thus ended, more fortunately than might have been anticipated, [his] second official essay for the protection of the citizens of the United States in Oregon," Bancroft wrote.[10]

White remained on as Indian agent in the Oregon Country for two more years. Despite his posturing and his shallow understanding of Indian character, he sincerely desired that their condition be improved and that justice be done to them. In his report to the Secretary of War in November 1843 he wrote:

> It appears to me morally impossible that general quiet can long be secure, unless government take almost immediate measures to relieve the anxieties and better the condition of these poor savages and other Indians of this country . . . . Sir, I know how deeply anxious you are to benefit and save what can be of the withering Indian tribes, in which God knows how fully and heartily I am with you, and earnestly pray you, and through you our general government, to take immediate measures to satisfy the minds, and, so far as possible, render to these Indians an equivalent for their once numerous herds of deer, elk, buffalo, beaver, and otter, nearly as tame as our domestic animals, previously to the whites and their fire arms coming among them, and of which they are now stripped, and for which they suffer. But, if nothing can be done for them on this score, pray save them from being forcibly ejected from the lands and graves of their fathers, of which they begin to entertain serious fears.[11]

Despite these sentiments and what were probably good intentions, White failed the Indians in the end. When Yellow Serpent's son was killed by a white in California, White promised to conduct an inquiry into the matter. He also promised gifts and money to Nez Perce chief Ellis and made promises to other Indians as well. But by the spring of 1845, frustrated by the many problems of his office, he was only too ready to accede to the provisional government's request that he carry a memorial to Congress. And all the promises went by the board. So, Oregon's first Indian agent. In general, it had not been an auspicious beginning.

FOUR YEARS ELAPSED before another United States Indian agent appeared in Oregon. One reason for this hiatus was that Congress and the executive, not to mention the Department of Indian affairs, had been overwhelmed by a sudden increase in the number of Indians they had to deal with during the years in question. Between 1845 and 1848, a million square miles of territory were added to the United States by way of Texas, the Oregon Country, and the Southwest, annexations that brought two hundred thousand more Indians under the government's jurisdiction. Naturally, an adequate staff and policy were not in place to handle the problem. Still, an attempt was made.

Following the solution of the Oregon border dispute with Great Britain in 1846, Washington, as noted earlier, appointed Charles Pickett as agent. However, by the time his commission arrived in Oregon, Pickett had already moved on to the enticements of Honolulu. The office continued vacant until filled locally by the exigencies of the Cayuse War. Palmer and Lee, of course, were the two officials to hold the post, but their service was distinctly ad hoc, and it cannot be said that they had any real Indian policy. The exception to this was the assertion by Palmer and the action by Lee that resulted in the confiscation of Cayuse lands for white settlement. Also, Lee issued an order that no missionaries were to reside in the upper country until United States forces should arrive to keep the peace. Shortly after issuing this order, late in 1848, Lee resigned since, as Bancroft put it, "the compensation bore no proportion to the services required."[12] Between them, Palmer and Lee had served for less than a year. Governor Abernethy did not appoint a successor for the simple reason that no one would take the job.

In short, Indian policy in Oregon—as in the country as a whole—had until now consisted of unworkable laws, broken promises, war, the confiscation of Indian lands, and drift.

The drift ceased with the arrival in March 1849 of the territory's new governor, Joseph Lane. Lane also held the office of Indian superintendent *ex officio*. Lane's two principal concerns were the establishment of schools and a proper administration of Indian affairs. To accomplish the latter, he met with the Indians of the valley, the Columbia, Puget Sound, and the southern Oregon coast. The valley Indians were the first to gather with him, and they did so with high expectations, for they had been repeatedly promised that once Oregon was a territory the Great White Father would compensate them for the loss of their land and game. Yet Lane brought them neither blankets nor shirts—not even a bead—only words. Still, Lane had a way with Indians, with most people for that matter, and it seems that to a large extent he beguiled away their disappointment, at least for the time being. He also learned his lesson and took presents when he visited the other tribes.

Coincidental with these visits, Lane gathered material for a report requested by Washington on the region's roughly twenty-four thousand natives so that Washington might formulate policy. In the meantime, he had formed a policy of his own: "the moment I am informed that any injury has been committed by them upon our people, they will be visited by sudden and severe chastisement." On the other hand, as he had informed the legislators in July:

> Surrounded as many of the tribes and bands now are by the whites, whose arts of civilization, by destroying the resources of the Indians, doom them to poverty, want and crime, the extinguishment of their title by purchase, and the locating them in a district removed from the settlements is a measure of the most

vital importance to them. Indeed, the cause of humanity calls loudly for their
removal from causes, and influences so fatal to their existence.

Bancroft's gloss on this is "the usual official robbery under form of the extinguishment of the Indian title, and their removal from the neighborhood of the
white settlements, was unblushingly urged." Indeed, Bancroft was not sympathetic to the governor's treatment of Indians in general and referred to him
as a "good butcher of Indians, who . . . cursed them as a mistake or damnable
infliction of the Almighty."[13]

The record, however, does not quite support Bancroft's charge. On more
than one occasion, Lane strongly condemned whites for their mistreatment of
Indians. On hearing that miners were traveling to the Spokane country, he instructed his agent there to caution miners against abuse of the Indians. A band
whose village was burned by a white seeking their land received Lane's protection and the white was driven off. Most persuasive of all, however, is Frances
Victor's assertion that Lane's gallantry, audacity, and courage earned him the
esteem and affection of many Indians.

Lane's call to the legislature to alleviate the Indians' condition resulted in a
memorial to Congress asking the government to purchase the Indian lands of
the Willamette Valley and remove the Indians to a place remote from settlement. For the time being, this was the announced policy toward the Indians in
the valley, though it awaited execution. Next, there was the question of what
to do with the Indians of the upper country, particularly the Cayuse murderers
of Marcus and Narcissa Whitman.

After Lane consulted with Oregon's old Indian hands—John McLoughlin,
James Douglas, Peter Skene Ogden, William McBean, Bishop Blanchet, and
perhaps Palmer and other Americans—all agreed that he should demand the
surrender of the murderers. He set forth the reasons in his October 1849 report
to the Secretary of War:

> The eyes of the surrounding nations are upon us, watching our movements in
> relation to this cold blooded massacre and if the guilty be not punished they will
> construe it as a license for the most attrocious outrage and scenes of a similar
> character will be enacted by other tribes who by our example toward the guilty
> Cayuse will be incited to gratify any malicious spirit with the blood of Ameri-
> cans, and our suffering the guilty in this instance to escape a just punishment,
> will be to them an assurance of their own safety. Indeed the chiefs of some of
> the neighboring tribes have informed me that they already have had difficulty in
> restraining their tribes joining the Cayuse and they are anxious the murderers

should be brought to punishment, as it would deter their own bands from crime.[14]

In line with this policy, Lane addressed a series of letters to the Cayuse and Nez Perce chiefs. The letters are remarkable for their blend of bluster and blandishment. If the murderers are not given up, Lane threatened, "the Cayuse nation will be destroyed." But he also assured them that "for your goodness I love you." In general, his message to the chiefs was essentially the same as his 7 May 1850 message to the legislature: "the whole tribe will be held responsible, until those, whoever they may be, concerned in that melancholy and horrible affair, are given up for punishment." In fact, Lane was in no position to act until United States forces, in the form of the Mounted Riflemen, appeared.[15]

By the time the Mounted Riflemen arrived in Oregon in October 1849, they had lost forty-five wagons, three hundred horses and mules, and seventy men either dead or deserted.

Lane seems to have been impressed by the Mounted Riflemen. But Bancroft, perhaps, took the view of the Duke of Wellington, who charged that his soldiers were "the scum of the earth . . . enlisted for drink." "The Oregon officers," Bancroft wrote, "were seldom sober and indeed one, Maj. J.S. Hathaway, attempted suicide when 'Mania a potu.'" In addition, the men proved to be exceptionally unruly. "Their presence in the metropolis of Oregon," wrote Frances Victor, "was anything but delightsome to its inhabitants, who were soon made as unhappy by the advent of the troops as they had been previously by the want of them."[16]

Unruly or not, they were troops, and Lane planned to use them against the Cayuse if need be. However, before he could do so, 120 riflemen deserted for the goldfields of California. With a stunning insouciance, they provisioned themselves by informing settlers along the way that they had been sent to buy cattle on government credit.

In an exercise that he no doubt undertook with zest, Lane went off in hot pursuit and succeeded in rounding up and bringing back to Oregon City seventy of the deserters.* He was now free to turn his attention to the Cayuse.

And the Cayuse were in a trap. Hostile or neutral—and thus untrustworthy—tribes lay on three sides of them; the whites were on the fourth. In general, the Indians of the upper country were weary of the disloca-

* *After a winter of racket, drunkenness, and random shots, the Mounted Riflemen were finally removed to Fort Vancouver. To cele-*

tions created by the Cayuse War and its aftermath, and *brate, the citizens of* they feared a resumption of the war now that United *Oregon City burned* States troops were in Oregon. Hoping to draw the poi- *down their barracks.* son and with the incentive of a substantial reward of-fered by the whites, the Nez Perce endeavored to capture those thought to be culprits and did catch and kill Tamsucky. Finally, Young Chief of the Cayuse, without allies and convinced of Lane's determination, secured the capture of several of the alleged murderers and made it known that he was ready to sur-render them. There was no other way out.

Lane received the prisoners at The Dalles. He assured them that they would have a proper trial but that they would be obliged to pay for their own defense. The fee was fifty horses. It seems inordinate. It may be that the Cayuse misun-derstood, that they thought of the fifty horses—or, at any rate, a portion of them—as restitution, compensation for their crimes, for this would have been in line with their own practices. In other words, they may have believed that the fifty horses were more a fine than a fee and that, once paid, they would be free.

On the party's return to the valley, a curious exchange took place between the guards and one of the prisoners, Tiloukaikt. The latter's words are among the most quoted in the literature of Northwest Indian-white relations. The guards invited Tiloukaikt to share their mess. Tiloukaikt replied, "what hearts have you to offer to eat with me, whose hands are red with your brother's blood?"[17] His statement is like a flare in the night, and in its brief light we see with a rare clarity the mind of the Indian, the mind of the white, and the minds of those who have never let Tiloukaikt's words be forgotten.

On another occasion, Tiloukaikt was asked why he had suffered himself to be taken captive or thereafter had not attempted escape. "Did not your mis-sionaries teach us that Christ died to save his people," he replied. "So die we to save our people."[18] What did he mean? Tiloukaikt was not a sweet-tempered man. He detested the missionaries, physically attacking Whitman in one in-stance. That at this point in his extremity the proud Cayuse had finally come to the faith seems doubtful. More likely, these were angry words, spoken in irony by a bitter man.

The trial began in Oregon City on the morning of 22 May, and the town thronged for the occasion. The five Cayuse, jailed on an island in the river, were led across the little bridge connecting the island to the town and taken to the courthouse, where they were joined by their counsel, Territorial Secretary Kintzing Pritchett, as assisted by Maj. R.B. Reynolds and Capt. Thomas

Claiborne of the Mounted Riflemen. The attorneys for the defense first claimed that United States law had not extended to Oregon at the time of the massacre, and thus the court had no authority to try the Cayuse. The court rejected the claim, although even the prosecution apparently had some doubts in the matter. Next, the attorneys asked for a change of venue to Fort Vancouver, insisting that Oregon City was so predisposed against the Cayuse as to preclude a fair trial, but that plea was rejected as well. A jury was impaneled with "those liable to be embittered against the Indians . . . carefully excluded."[19]

The Cayuse pleaded not guilty. The question remains today whether they were or not. Suggesting innocence is the fact that these Cayuse were not among those first accused by the survivors of the massacre. Also, much of the testimony of the survivors following their rescue and return to Oregon City—as well as at the trial itself—was confused and contradictory. Furthermore, Captain Claiborne told Bishop Blanchet that two, and perhaps more, of the Cayuse were innocent. On the other hand, Ruby and Brown in their book on the Cayuse wrote that the Cayuse themselves continued to maintain that these five were among the murderers. In any event, the jury found them guilty. According to Joe Meek, the United States marshal, on the reading of the verdict, three of the condemned "were filled with horror and consternation that they could not conceal."[20] Their attorneys' request for a new trial was refused.

Interestingly, there was on the part of some a reluctance to accept the jury's verdict. Captain Claiborne claimed—though rather implausibly—that Lane, departing Oregon City before the conclusion of the trial to settle Indian difficulties in the south, had signed "a promise to suspend the execution if there were a sentence of death against the accused."[21] But if such a statement were signed, it was never seen.

On the other hand, there is no question that Pritchett believed the Cayuse should be granted a reprieve so that the case might be appealed to the United States Supreme Court. "Secretary Pritchett . . . said that he would not agree to allow these men to be executed although he knew that his life was in danger."[22] Pritchett, believing that he was governor *pro tem* in Lane's absence, was prepared to act on the reprieve when reminded by the judge that there was no certainty that Lane had in fact left the territory. Thus, Pritchett was not empowered to act. He did not.

Meanwhile, the Cayuse had signed statements prepared by Bishop A.M.A. Blanchet protesting their innocence. But the issue was clear: the Cayuse would be either legally executed or lynched by the mob. "Much doubt was felt as to the policy of hanging them, but the *popularity* of doing so was undeniable," wrote the 21 August 1850 *New York Tribune* later commenting on the trial.

The hanging took place on 3 June at two in the afternoon. Joe Meek was the hangman. Kamiasumpkin begged to be stabbed to death rather than submit to the indignity of hanging by a rope, and Tiloukaikt fought frantically against the tying of his hands. A crucifix was held before them while Meek cut the drop ropes with a tomahawk. Their bones lie today in Oregon City in an unknown place.

IT WAS AT ABOUT THIS TIME that hundreds of goldseekers were using the trail from Oregon to the California goldfields. With the increased use of the trail came problems with the Rogue River Indians. The Rogues were a diverse group of tribes who were not about to be trifled with. These were not the languishing Indians of the Willamette Valley but a hardy and fierce people who lived in a bracing environment. Until the gold rush, they had been spared the debilitating effects of white contact, and they meant to resist that contact with all the force they had.

It was with these Indians that Lane was to end his career as Indian agent. In the late spring of 1850, a group of miners returning to Oregon with a quantity of gold were robbed of it by the Rogues. The miners applied to Lane to recover it, and he was happy to oblige. Among other things, and as noted earlier, it removed him from Oregon City during the trial and execution of the Cayuse, a proceeding that he himself had inaugurated but about which he may have had certain misgivings. Indeed, there probably was some truth in the earlier quoted *New York Tribune* statement that "much doubt was felt as to the policy of hanging them [the Cayuse]." In any event, and according to Bancroft, Lane took his time in reaching the Rogue, which suggests that he may have left Oregon City a little sooner than required.

He set out with thirty men, half of whom were Klickitat, Rogue River enemies. Arriving at the river, Lane called for a parley with the Rogues but stipulated that all at the parley should be unarmed. During the meeting, another tribe of Rogues arrived armed and raised the war cry. With the aid of the Klickitat, Lane took the Rogue River chief captive and disarmed the other Indians. There was no violence.

The Rogue River chief remained in Lane's camp for several days. On the morning of the first day, the chief's wife was given permission to join her husband. What else occurred during those days must have been of an unusual nature, for the Rogue River chief took Lane's name and thereafter was always known as Chief Joe. He also asked Lane to give new names to his wife and son and daughter; Lane named the wife Sally and the children Ben and Mary. (Lane and Mary were to meet again under circumstances most curious.) Finally, Chief Joe gave Lane a young slave boy as a gift.

When the chief was released, another parley was held, and the Rogues promised not to harm travelers on the trail and not to oppose settlement in exchange for government reparations and an agent to guard their interests. Both sides made promises they could not keep. Lane could not guarantee the good behavior of the whites and an expeditious Washington any more than Chief Joe could guarantee the good behavior of his young braves or the acquiescence of the chiefs of the other Rogue River tribes. As for the miners' gold, the Rogues had thrown it into the river, thinking it worthless.

Lane's career as Indian superintendent ended with a peace achieved mainly by discussion and goodwill, not by aggression. The exception to this was the Cayuse affair. Lane genuinely believed that if the Whitmans' murderers, or the surrogates for them, were not punished, the Cayuse and other tribes would feel free to act with impunity. Lane also believed that there could be no peace unless the Willamette Valley Indians were removed to a place distant from white settlement. He well knew that, whatever happened, the valley Indians would lose—for the most part, had already lost—their land. The object was to place them on other land, distant from friction with the whites and where they might live inviolate. There could have been, and were to be, worse Indian agents than Joseph Lane.

TWO DAYS AFTER THE FIVE CAYUSE WERE HANGED, Congress passed the Oregon Indian Act. The act established a commission to purchase Indian land in the Willamette Valley and to remove those Indians to a region east of the Cascade Mountains. It also created an official Oregon Superintendency of Indian Affairs. The commissioners appointed to purchase the land were John P. Gaines, Oregon's new Whig governor, and lawyers Alonzo A. Skinner and Beverly S. Allen; the new superintendent was Anson Dart of Wisconsin.

In February 1851, the three commissioners summoned the tribes to the banks of the Willamette at Champoeg. Bancroft disapproved of the circumstances in which these negotiations took place: "With a pomp and circumstance in no wise in keeping with the simple habits of the Oregon settlers; with interpreters, clerks, commissaries, and a retinue of servants they established themselves." This grandness was in considerable contrast to the bedraggled tribes skulking in from their ramshackle camps in the valley. It was also in contrast to the prices the commissioners were offering for the Indians' land. On occasion, the government had paid as much as ten cents an acre for Indian land, but in this instance, the commissioners were told that "a very small portion of that price will be required."[23]

By April, the commissioners had bought a parcel eighty miles long by twenty miles wide from the Santiam, and they had secured another thirty by forty miles from the Tualatin. In May, more purchases were made from the Yamhill, the Molalla, and the Luckiamute. By the time the commissioners wound up their work—"five weeks of absurd magnificence," as Bancroft called it—they had negotiated six treaties and had extinguished Indian title in about half the Willamette Valley.[24]

But all was not well. Most of the sums paid the Indians were for the most part to be in goods and services, that is, agricultural implements and teachers. But the Indians were not interested in farming, and they saw no point in having teachers; as they told the commissioners, they would soon be dead and so what was the benefit? The Indians also refused to go east of the mountains. And they had good reason. For one reason, they were gatherers, not hunters, and there was little to gather beyond the mountains with which they were familiar and could trust. The relocation would also mean leaving the graves of their ancestors, and though leaving ancestral graves meant little to the perennially restless Americans, it meant much to them. Finally, and again with good reason, they feared the Indians east of the Cascades.

The commissioners capitulated, partly out of sympathy for the Indians and partly because some whites wanted to keep the Indians' cheap labor—indeed, slave labor, in some cases. A compromise was reached that gave the Indians small reservations on the margins of the valley. These tended to be the poorest agricultural lands, yet the Indians were encouraged to take up farming. Also, some of these reservation lands had already been claimed by whites. In short, what appeared to be solutions only turned out to be problems.

The work of the commissioners received its final defeat when Congress refused to ratify the treaties. A number of reasons were given for the rejection, but it was probably due to Lane's opposition, as territorial delegate, to the Indians remaining in the valley. With the dissolution of the commission in April, all Indian affairs fell on the shoulders of Anson Dart, the new superintendent of Indian affairs. Dart's shoulders were relatively broad, but the weight placed on them was perhaps more than they could be expected to bear.

In the spring of 1851, gold was discovered in the Klamath River. Miners in Indian country almost always meant trouble. Settlers had a stake in peace. For one thing, they had their womenfolk and children to protect. They had barns and crops that could be burned and oxen that could be killed. Also, Indians were often employed by settlers. There were many accounts of good relations between settlers and Indians. Miners, on the other hand, often were young, single, and rambunctious. This led, among other things, to the giving of their attentions to Indian women, an attention not always appreciated. The men were transient, and their personal possessions were few. In short, they had little stake in peace and, in fact, often relished a fight.

Trouble began when threatening behavior on the part of the Indians, provoked possibly by the whites—"unprincipled and ungovernable," as Dart described some of the miners—prompted the miners and some settlers to petition Oregon City for troops. However, the Mounted Riflemen, who had turned out to be more a curse than a blessing, had had orders to depart Oregon, except for a small contingent left at Fort Vancouver. It so happened that one departing division on its way to California passed through the south at the time of these troubles and paused at the Rogue to carry out an operation against the Indians. They killed fifty. Retaliation occurred in September when five whites exploring the Rogue from the coast were killed by the Rogues. Such were Dart's problems in the south.

Dart had problems at home as well. Of the twenty-thousand-dollar budget allocated for the Oregon superintendency, only three hundred dollars remained after the commissioners' five weeks of "absurd magnificence." Also, the three subagents authorized to assist Dart in his work wandered off and more or less disappeared—mainly because there was not enough money to pay them a decent wage. Finally, Dart was hampered by the lack of clear directives from Washington.

Luke Lea, the U.S. commissioner of Indian affairs, had informed Dart that it was his duty to "civilize" the Indians by encouraging them in agricultural pursuits, preventing tribal wars, and suppressing the liquor trade. In fact, Lea had no policy for civilizing the Indians, and as he candidly confessed in a report to the secretary of the Interior,

> The great question, How shall the Indians be civilized? yet remains without a satisfactory answer. The magnitude of the subject, and the manifold difficulties inseparably connected with it, seem to have bewildered the minds of those who have attempted to give it the most thorough investigation. The remark is not more striking than true, that "there is nothing in the whole compass of our laws so anomalous, so hard to bring within any precise definition, or any logical and scientific arrangement of principals, as the relation in which the Indians stand

towards this government and those of the States." . . . I therefore leave the subject for the present, remarking, only, that any plan for the civilization of our Indians will in my judgement, be totally defective, if it do not provide, in the most efficient manner, first, for the ultimate incorporation into the great body of our citizen population.[25]

Dart shared Lea's one certainty in this matter, that Indians must be assimilated into white society, but it stood in direct opposition to Lane and others who believed in strict segregation. This division of opinion was to bedevil Indian policy for many years and, in a sense, has yet to be resolved.

In June 1851, having done what he could to settle matters in the south, Dart traveled to the upper Columbia, where he held a friendly council with the Nez Perce and the Cayuse. Among other things, Dart told the Indians that they were free to practice their native religions, a gesture that must have gained the Indians' sympathy, however much it infuriated the missionaries. He next went to the coast, where in treaties with those tribes he purchased land on both sides of the Columbia extending 60 miles up from the mouth as well as 130 miles of land up the northern coast and 80 miles down the southern coast. Returning to the valley, he purchased the land comprising Oregon City and Milwaukie from the Clackamas Indians. All in all, Dart negotiated thirteen treaties in the spring and summer of 1851 and acquired six million acres at an average of three cents per acre.

These delicate and arduous negotiations concluded, Dart departed for Washington to urge their ratification by Congress. Not one of the treaties was approved. There appear to be three reasons for this grave reverse. First, there were certain technical objections to the manner in which the treaties had been negotiated. Second, some settlers complained that part of the land designated as reservations on the coast and in the Willamette Valley had already been claimed by whites under the Donation Land Law of 1850. Finally, Lane continued to adamantly oppose the Indians remaining in the valley.

It is difficult to suppose that Dart received a hearty welcome when he returned to the valley. The settlers were unhappy because he had not secured the extinguishment of Indian title, and the Indians were once again disappointed in not gaining the benefits promised by the treaties. And there were more troubles in the south. Chief Sam of the Rogues had demanded that a settler trade his two-year-old daughter for a horse and two Indian children. Also, another miner had been killed. To avenge these acts, some eighty volunteers, mainly miners, gathered at Jacksonville to proceed against the Indians. Alonzo A. Skinner, a subagent in southern Oregon, arranged a truce between the volunteers and the Indians, but it was of brief duration, and again, more Indians were killed. Late in July, a dinner was held at Table Rock to honor the volunteers. A number of toasts were made, most to the valor of the volunteers. One, however, was ominous, for it ended, "may you live to see the time when the Indians of Rogue River are extinct."[26]

Dart suffered on for a year and a half under the most difficult circumstances. Finally, he resigned his position in June 1853, discouraged by his inability to effect a solution of the Indians' status and by a salary no longer adequate to his expenses. He may also have disagreed with Commissioner Lea's drastic change of attitude toward the Indians. In 1851, Lea had written that the Indian is "intellectual, proud, brave, generous . . . . That his inferiority is a necessity of his nature, is neither taught by philosophy nor attested by experience." In the following year's report, however, he made a most curious about-face.

> Much of the injury of which the red man and his friends complain has been the inevitable consequence of his own perverse and vicious nature. In the long and varied conflict between the white man and the red—civilization and barbarism—the former has often been compelled to recede, and be destroyed, or to advance and destroy . . . . The consequence of the onward pressure of the whites, are gradually teaching them the important lesson that they must ere long change their mode of life, or cease to live at all. It is by industry or extinction that the problem of their destiny must be solved.

In the same report he also wrote:

> When civilization and barbarism are brought in such a relation that they cannot coexist together, it is right that the superiority of the former should be asserted and the latter compelled to give way. It is therefore, no matter of regret or reproach that so large a portion of our territory has been wrested from its aboriginal inhabitants and made the happy abode of an enlightened and Christian people.

And Secretary of the Interior Steward agreed: "The only alternatives left are, to civilize or exterminate them."[27] In short, conform or die.

Dart agreed that the Indians must *"live among us as part and parcel of our own people,"* but he certainly did not agree that the Indians by their "perverse and vicious" nature had brought their misfortunes upon themselves. Instead, he believed that, more often than not, these misfortunes had been visited upon them by the whites, and furthermore, he was "well persuaded that with few exceptions the Indians of Oregon are the most peaceful, friendly and easiest managed, with proper care, of any uncivilized tribes within the bounds of the United States."[28]

Despite Dart's general goodwill toward the Indians, he accomplished little during his term, except to bring opprobrium down upon his office from both Indians and whites. Still, the goodwill was something. Even Lane, no admirer of Dart, admitted in a backhanded way that Dart was "on the side of the Indians generally," and Bancroft summed him up as "a fair and reasonable man, who discharged his duty under unfavorable circumstances with promptness and good sense."[29]

SUCH, THEN, WERE PALMER'S PREDECESSORS—White, Lee, Lane, and Dart. All were well disposed toward the Oregon Indians. All believed that the Indians should be compensated for the land and game they had lost and would lose through further settlement. This was true even in the case of Lee who, excepting his seizure of Cayuse lands for their refusal to give up the alleged murderers and his desperation for men to man Fort Waters, pleaded for fair treatment of the Indians. All of them also believed that it was the duty of whites to "civilize" the Indians so that their condition might be bettered—a belief by no means peculiar to the benighted past but one that in one form or another has affected Indian policy down to the present. Finally, none of the commissioners seems to have been guilty of peculation at the Indians' expense—though one reason may have been that there was little to peculate. In short, Palmer was not handicapped in these respects by the men who had come before him. Men worse, much worse, were to follow him.

At the same time, however, all of Palmer's predecessors as commissioners of Indian Affairs had failed to extinguish Indian land titles and to gain compensation for the Indians. This meant that when Palmer took office, both whites and Indians were dissatisfied with the anomalous position in which they found themselves. This was his gravest problem.

There were certainly other problems as well. One of these confronted him immediately. Sitting down for the first time at his desk in the superintendency office in Milwaukie, Palmer discovered that no one had the key to open the drawer containing all of the agency records. When the key was found some days later, Palmer was appalled to see from the records that, notwithstanding numerous claims against the superintendency, there was "not a dollar of funds in my hands."[30] He was further appalled that the dollars spent had accomplished so little. Before long, Palmer had to borrow from his own salary of twenty-five hundred dollars a year to keep the superintendency solvent.

Further crippling Palmer's efforts was Washington's failure to formulate a general policy toward the Indians, which in effect meant a prohibition against all treaty making. This especially concerned Palmer because by 1853 settlement was extending beyond the Willamette Valley into the upper country, and he was well aware that "settlement of the whites there without the consent of the Indians would inevitably provoke their hostility."[31] Finally, Palmer was apprehensive about conditions on the Rogue River where animosities still flared.

How qualified was Palmer to face up to the responsibilities of his new job? Timothy W. Davenport, an early Oregon physician and scholar, knew Palmer when the latter took on his duties, and Davenport had no doubts. "Palmer was not at all a doctrinaire or idealist," Davenport wrote,

> full of fanciful notions as to the perfectibility of any race, or that all the Indian needed to make him an equal with the white man was justice . . . . he was a plain, unpretentious, practical and honest man, strong in the conviction that all people show their best traits when well treated . . . . He was strong in body, delighted in adventure, and the rough and ready work of an Indian superintendent in early times was well suited to his nature.[32]

Such, then, was the man who now took on the incubus of Oregon Indian affairs.

IN HIS FIRST DAYS in the superintendency office in Milwaukie, Palmer dealt with routine matters. Reports from the upper country claimed that the Indians there had grown "saucy"—a favored adjective for Indians who the whites felt did not know their place—and that some were stealing the emigrants' cattle, assisted in their thievery by "white Indians" from the Umatilla, apparently traders who had allied themselves with the Indians for nefarious purposes. At about the same time, Maj. Benjamin Alvord,* stationed at The Dalles, wrote to the *Oregonian* that "many of these Indian tribes have behaved so well towards all the whites as to merit the most just and considerate treatment of them by the people and the government."[33] The reports were confusing.

Palmer's principal task at the outset, however, was to organize his office and to appoint agents and subagents to assist him in his work. He chose Joseph M. Garrison, Samuel H. Culver, and Robert R. Thompson as agents and Josiah L. Parrish, Philip F. Thompson, and W.W. Raymond as subagents. These men were to serve at Port Orford, Astoria, Rogue River, Salem, and The Dalles. The *Oregonian*, founded as a Whig organ in 1850, naturally complained about the Democratic appointments, stigmatizing those selected as "obscure individuals."[34] Although the

* With the departure of the Mounted Riflemen in 1851, a skeleton company of artillerymen was assigned to The Dalles. Major Alvord took command of an augmented force the following year.

newspaper did not damn Palmer by name—perhaps because he was so widely respected, even by many Whigs—it was in a perfect fury over the general success of the Democrats. So much so, in fact, that editor Thomas J. Dryer scattered his shot over every aspect of their behavior.* Palmer also hired Cris Taylor, a Whig and his closest friend, to stop the illicit liquor trade with the Indians. It was an impossible task, partly because Indian testimony against whites was not admissible in court, and the Indians were not eager to inform on the purveyors of their firewater. Also, whites were determined, come what might, to bootleg drink to the natives. After the miners, no single element contributed more to Indian unrest than "blue ruin," as it was often accurately called.

In the first months of his service, Palmer gave agent Joseph Garrison a special mission. He was to meet an emigrant train pioneering a new southern route from Fort Boise to the Willamette Valley and collect information on the Indians of southeast Oregon. Palmer was convinced of the supreme importance of gathering all information possible on an area and its inhabitants before taking action in the area, a seemingly rudimentary precaution often overlooked. In this instance, however, he was to be disappointed, for heavy snows in the Cascades forced Garrison and his party to turn back. Palmer was not sympathetic. Garrison's difficulties, in Palmer's judgment, were "over estimated"; perhaps a view to be expected from a man who, barefoot, had climbed high up the slopes of Mount Hood. In any event, Garrison did not long remain in Palmer's services.

Closer to home, Palmer was plagued by the anomalous position of the Willamette Valley Indians. Because no treaties had been ratified, the question of what land was owned by the Indians and what was owned by the whites had not been settled. As a result, daily conflicts erupted between the two groups. In a letter of early June, Palmer suggested to agent Parrish that he

> visit the Indians, and some of the settlers in that neighborhood and try to bring about a better feeling among them. The refusal to ratify the treaties entered into with them last year leaves the whole matter as it was before the council was

* For example, on the Sunday following Palmer's assumption of office, Lane and his followers, including Palmer, no doubt, took a celebration cruise on the SS Multnomah. "This desecration of the Sabbath on the part of Gov. Lane and his pliant followers" was, according to the 21 May 1853 Oregonian, characterized by "a band of music and much noise and confusion." And it was in this month of particularly vituperative exchanges between the politically opposing newspapers that the Oregon Statesman, the Democrats' organ, took to referring to the Oregonian as "the Sewer."

held, and until the possession of right to the lands be acquired by treaty, they must be allowed to remain amongst us, to fish, hunt and dig roots or follow such other occupations as best suit them, keeping in mind, however, that they are not to intrude on the cultivated fields of the whites or otherwise interfere with the property of the settlers.

Do try and prevail on the people to use forbearance and treat them kindly, as an opposite course can but tend to augment their already heavy grievances and prolong their stay among us as it will increase the obstacles attending the acquisition of their territory.

Palmer's counsels of moderation and patience may have had their effect, for Parrish in his reply stated that he had had no recent cause to use "the lash" in gaining the Indians' cooperation.* Even clearer evidence of the importance Palmer gave to white "forbearance" is in a letter written a few days later to a Yamhill settler who complained of Indian behavior. Palmer responded: "Many of the Indian difficulties are caused by an unwarranted assumption of power to redress our own and sometimes immaginary wrongs."[35] Palmer could be as blunt to whites as he was to Indians.

Palmer also insisted that the Indians settle differences among themselves according to their own codes. This made sense from the Indian point of view, he believed, and also from the point of view of his agents and himself; otherwise, they might find themselves attempting to negotiate in a morass of conflicting custom.

By early summer, Palmer had come to certain conclusions about what the policy toward the Indians should be. On 23 June, he wrote the new U.S. commissioner of Indian Affairs, George Manypenny. Manypenny was a man genuinely concerned for what was then considered the Indians' good, but as Palmer was to find, he was severely hampered by shortages of both money and staff. The heart of Palmer's policy was contained in the following portion of his letter:

> That these Indians cannot long remain on the reserves in the heart of the settlements, granted them by treaty, even though Congress should confirm those treaties, it is too clear to admit of argument—vice and disease,

* It is uncertain to what degree Palmer had Lane's support in his Indian policy. In May, Palmer's first month as superintendent, the following appeared in the 28 May 1853 States-man*: "Lane opposes the payment of large sums of money to Indians for imaginary titles to lands, but holds that the government should occupy the lands, and furnish Indians in need with blankets, clothing and food, such as is necessary to their comfort. There is nothing more farcical and grossly wrong than to treat with such miserable specimens of humanity as the Indians of this valley, (no more*

the baleful gifts of civilization are hurrying them *competent to contract* away, and ere long the bones of the last of many a *than the wolves of the* band may whiten on the graves of his ancestors. If the *prairies)."* benevolent designs of the Government to preserve and elevate these remnants of the aborigines are to be carried forward to a successful issue, there appears to be but one path open,—a home, remote from the settlements must be selected for them, then they must be guarded from the pestiferous influence of degraded whitemen . . . . let comfortable houses be erected for them, seeds and proper implements furnished and instruction and encouragement given them in the cultivation of the soil; let school houses be erected and teachers employed to instruct their children, and let the missionaries of the gospel of peace be encouraged to dwell among them. Let completeness of plan, energy, patience and perseverance characterize the effort, and if still it fail, the Government will have at least the satisfaction of knowing that an honest and determined endeavour was made to save and elevate a fallen race.[36]

Palmer also addressed the question of where the reservations should be. The upper country, he argued, was not suitable for the Willamette Valley Indians, whereas the coast was clearly ideal. Most important, it was remote and in Palmer's judgment would remain so, isolated as it was by mountains on one side and a forbidding coast with few harbors on the other. The coastal lands abounded with fish and game, and there were a number of small valleys where the Indians might farm. Palmer also believed that the valley and coastal Indians, sharing certain ways and traditions, would be compatible. He added this caution: "They [the Indians] have become distrustful of all promises made them by the U.S. and believe the design of the Government is to defer doing anything for them until they have wasted away."[37]

The urgency in Palmer's letter may have been due to events on the Rogue River a few weeks before. Certain citizens of Jacksonville believed that a sub-chief named Taylor had murdered seven whites on Galice Creek the previous December. Taylor at first maintained that the men had drowned, but "under pressure" he finally confessed to the killing, pleading for mercy on the grounds that he had used a small knife to torture the whites rather than a large one. Reportedly, his trial and hanging took less than thirty minutes.[38]

Their appetites whetted, the Jacksonville group then went off to find two white women who were allegedly being held and tortured by the Rogues. They found no women, but they did capture six braves. These they released, after tying their hands, and shot as they fled. It was now, apparently, that the Rogues began to stockpile weapons, stealing them when possible but also trading for them with the whites, one woman for one gun. "Thus," A.G. Walling wrote, "the Indian warriors placed themselves on a war footing, while the whites were figuratively sunk in luxurious ease"—the ease before the storm.[39]

Back in the valley, there was a certain ease as well, caused in part by the hottest July the whites could remember. True, disquieting news had arrived that there was smallpox among the Indians on the Clearwater River—Palmer asked for permission to vaccinate them—but on the other hand, he had received good news from Port Orford. Agent Culver reported that, for his five thousand charges, there was an abundance of food and a scarcity of liquor and that, in general, contentment reigned.

It was good news, too, that in the valley a bumper wheat crop was about to be harvested, while for the most important of holidays, the Fourth of July, a truce between the warring political parties was to be observed. "It is hoped that partisan and sectarian feeling will be unknown," the *Statesman*'s editor wrote on 28 June, "and that we may come out as a *people* to pour the heart's full treasure on our country's altar."

The grandest of these celebrations took place in the capital where, highlighting the occasion, the foundations of the statehouse were now in place. "Not less than two thousand met to renew their confidence in free institutions," the *Statesman* reported on 12 July, with music, church services, speeches, the reading of the Declaration of Independence, a masquerade parade, dinner, and eighteen toasts. The most gallant of these toasts declared: "Providence has greatly favored Oregon, having given us a fertile soil, a salubrious climate—precious metals and 'Heaven's last best blessing,' woman."

Finally, and always good news, word arrived that the first of the year's emigrants were crossing the Cascades. It meant so much—relatives and friends to see again, girls to marry, fruit scions for an orchard, the root of a rambling rose, breeding cattle, perhaps a dentist's drill, old copies of *Harper's Weekly*, someone ready to sell a banjo—for the settlers were still very much alone, here on the far western shore where there was still little but the land, the sky, the water.

THE EUPHORIA OF THAT JULY of 1853 passed with the month. On 4 August, a southern Oregon miner named Richard Edwards—who was said to have made off with a Shasta woman—was ax-hacked to pieces by some Shasta braves. At twilight on the following day, a mule cantered into Jacksonville, its saddle and withers soaked with blood; the butchered owner was found on the outskirts of town. The next day at sunrise, a miner on his way to his site was waylaid and murdered. Two isolated farmhouses were fired. The "luxurious ease" of the whites had ended.

On 7 August, a mass meeting was held at Jacksonville calling for the extermination of the southern Oregon Indians. To show that they meant business, a group of citizens hanged two Shastas along with a nine-year-old Indian boy who had tagged along with some settlers seeking refuge in the town. "Nits breed lice," the miners said as they hanged the boy.[40] The citizens sent a plea to Captain Alden at Fort Jones just over the California border, and he arrived several days later, with a force of regulars and volunteers. Now, too, a man named Ettinger was sent to Salem to request aid.

Ettinger arrived on 18 August, delayed, he complained, because people along the way had refused to lend him a fresh horse, despite the urgency of his mission. His mission had two purposes: to inform the government of the state of things in southern Oregon and to get troops. Ettinger put the matter plainly. "The people there now demand extermination of the hostile Indians, and are resolved not to stop short of it. Indians are shot down whereever they are found."[41] As for the troops, Governor George Curry met the request by securing Lt. A.V. Kautz, six artillerymen, and a howitzer from Fort Vancouver and by organizing a volunteer force of forty under the command of James W. Nesmith.

Palmer, meanwhile, not yet aware of the troubles at the Rogue, was about to depart for a month-long exploratory expedition to the coast. His purpose was to select an area for the reservation he had proposed to Commissioner Manypenny in June. Agent Parrish planned to accompany him as interpreter and his clerk, Edward Geary, as map maker. He had also invited some of the principal Indian chiefs in the valley to join the party so that they might pass on the site. Their route to the coast was probably to have been the Indian trail along the Nestucca River—the present-day road from Carlton over the mountains to Beaver. On the coast itself, the party's intention was to explore the principal rivers from source to mouth between Tillamook and Coos Bay or, in other words, about half the coast. The day before the group planned to leave, however, Palmer was informed of the Rogue River Indian troubles. It probably did not come as a surprise to him, for earlier in the month, he had written to Gen. E.A. Hitchcock, commander of the Pacific Division in California, asking that troops be sent to defend the whites *and* the Indians. Palmer set out immediately for Jacksonville.

Palmer's purpose, as in the Cayuse War, was peace and the negotiating of a treaty to codify that peace. However, his treaty-making efforts were not to be well received at the Rogue. Indeed, they were to put him in danger. At about the time of Palmer's departure, the *Oregon Statesman* warned:

NO TREATIES AND NO QUARTER.

The people of the South are so much exasperated against the Indians on account of their recent murders and destruction of property that it is said to be unsafe for a man to *talk* about treaties in their hearing. The "humane" individual who ventures to do it, finds himself roughly *treated* as a reward. Something of the temper of the people of that section may be gathered from the subjoined extracts from articles in the *Yreka Herald*; we copy italics and capitals.

The present outbreak has justly led all to the conclusion that *extermination is the only way to secure peace.* We have "drawn the sword, and thrown the scabbard away," and the tomahawk will no longer be buried but in the sculls of the red foe.

Let it be our last difficulty with Indians in this section of the country. They have commenced the work with their own accord, and without just cause. Let our motto be EXTERMINATION! *and death to all opposition, white men or indians!*[42]

Meanwhile Lane, who had been informed of the war at his farm in Roseburg, arrived at Jacksonville on 21 August and took over command from Captain Alden. Here, he heard of the inconclusive skirmishes that had so far occurred and in which six whites had been killed and several wounded. He immediately mounted an attack. It proceeded under the most disagreeable of circumstances: the summer heat, the dense undergrowth, the broken terrain, the clouds of choking smoke from the areas fired by the Indians to obscure their trail, plus "the yells of the Indians, the howling of dogs and the sharp, continuous crack of the rifles," as Lane's aide, William T'Vault, wrote. Both Lane and Alden were wounded and three whites were killed. "The best men generally are the first to fall," T'Vault judged, "and the most clamorous for extermination are not the most interested."[43]

At some point during the battle, the Indians learned that Lane, whom they much admired, was on the field. Although the Rogues were well fortified and had plenty of weapons and ammunition, Lane's presence apparently prompted them to sue for peace. Lane went to the Indians' camp, where they were burning the bodies of the dead so the whites could not desecrate them, and went into council with chiefs Joe, Sam, and Jim. The chiefs assured Lane that they were ready to remove to a reservation, and they agreed to hold a treaty council in early September. Lane wrote Palmer at Yoncalla on 31 August to inform him that his presence was expected at the council. An unusual truce prevailed. The combatants pastured their horses together, Indian women brought water to the wounded whites, while their men helped carry the litters of the wounded twenty-five miles through the mountains to Jacksonville. "I find no mention," Bancroft wrote, ". . . of humane or christian conduct on the part of the superior race."[44]

In fact, not far away, members of the "superior race" were behaving in a manner far from humane. A miner named Bates lured some Grave Creek Indians into his cabin with a promise of food and then shot them all, an act severely condemned in the pages of the *Spectator*. Also, a band of volunteers from Crescent City arrived in Jacksonville bearing a banner lettered with one word: EX-TERMINATION. Now, too, Lieutenant Kautz arrived with the howitzer and James W. Nesmith and his valley volunteers cantered into camp, described by an observer as General Sam Houston had described the Texas Rangers: "Anything but gentlemen and cowards." Brave ruffians, in other words.

Yet they may not all have been as tough as they appeared. One volunteer wrote of the march:

> It has rained for two days past and we have had horrid times in camp, being on a forced march, we pack nothing except what is necessary to keep body and soul together—a little flour and bread, no tents, no axes and but few blankets. Sleeping on the wet ground beneath the lowering storm cloud, one often dreams . . . how sweet it is to die for one's country.

Whether the last phrase reflected a conventional sentiment of the time or expressed a certain sarcasm, it is hard to say, but the latter seems more likely. If this volunteer was overly sensitive to outdoor life in August, then another would appear to have been even more so in another vein—indeed, a pale romantic who could write of the Rogue and its environs as being "scenery as sublime and grand as the fervid description of the Rhone by Byron" and goes on to his own description of the river as "clear, limpid and beautiful—here meandering through grass-turfed and flower-decked banks and there flashing and sparkling in the sunlight in foaming rapids and beautiful cascades." As for the Indians whom this volunteer had come to fight, he found them full of "firmness, determination and chivalry . . . even their daughters acted with a heroism which would have done honor to a more enlightned race." He was particularly struck by "Mary"—probably the girl named by Lane in 1850 at the request of her father, Chief Joe—"tall and delicately formed with hair as dark as the raven's wing . . . dark lustrous eyes . . . the features Grecian in their cast." He then stated the Indian side of the conflict about as well as the Indians might have done themselves:

A few years since the whole valley was theirs alone. No white man's foot had ever trod it. They believed it theirs forever. But the gold digger come, with his pan and his pick and shovel, and hundreds followed. And they saw in astonishment their streams muddied, towns built, their valley fenced and taken. And where their squaws dug camus, their winter food, and their children were wont to gambol, they saw dug and plowed, and their own food sown by the hand of nature, rooted out forever, and the ground it occupied appropriated to the rearing of vegetables for the white man. Perhaps no malice yet entered the Indian breast. But when he was weary of hunting in the mountains without success, and was hungry, and approached the white man's tent for bread; where instead of bread he received curses and kicks, ye treaty kicking men—ye Indian exterminators think of these things.[45]

AND INDEED, OPPOSITION to a treaty and agitation for extermination continued, voiced by many and in print by the *Oregonian* and, to some extent, by the *Spectator*, both Whig publications. On 3 September 1853, the *Oregonian* published a 30 August letter from a Rogue River correspondent who claimed that "the whites of Rogue River valley will pay but little attention to any treaty stipulations entered into by those in authority with the Indians"—that is, Palmer and Lane. On the same day, the *Oregonian* editorialized:

> It is easy to foretell the end of this war. The whole Indian race in southern Oregon will be exterminated. Indeed, this seems to be the only alternative left. Self-styled philanthropists at a distance may prate about the cruelty and wickedness of such a course; but were they in the position of our citizens—subjected to the ruthless hand of savages—they too, would be in favor of exterminating the race. Treaty stipulations amount to nothing with these Indians; their most solemn pledges are disregarded whenever the opportunity to plunder presents itself. Therefore, one course only is left for the whites, and that course will inevitably be adopted.

The day before, the *Spectator* had reported that "the extinction of the entire race in that region is the almost unanimous sentiment," and this notwithstanding the newspaper's later statement of 26 September that the war was a "long, meditated revenge of the Indians for the many wanton murders committed by the miners." In any event, the newspaper's 2 September edition concluded that "no treaty with the southern Indians can be entered into that the whites will feel safe under after it is made."

And indeed, this was the nub of the matter: a treaty, the opponents argued, would not guarantee their safety, for neither the Indians nor the whites would observe it. Bellicose miners and partisan editors were not the only persons to hold this view. T'Vault, Lane's aide and certainly no exterminationist, wrote that "many good men go for a war of extermination."[46] After all, a majority of Oregonians were descendants of families that had been fighting Indians for two hundred years and had not yet thrown off a long accumulation of hostility. Also, many held the common nineteenth-century Darwinian view of the survival of the fittest. What is remarkable in the passions of that time and place is not the number of hotheads bent on extermination but the number of cool heads bent on tolerance and justice.

PALMER ARRIVED IN JACKSONVILLE on 5 September to find, according to his diary, "great excitement among the troops and miners and much opposition to the proposed treaty of peace. There are more rowdies assembled here than I have ever saw at one place." This belligerence of the whites made it difficult for Palmer and Lane to find and approach the Indians.

> Today [7 September] General Lane and myself and several others went out to visit the Indians but a few could be found. They affeared treachery on our part and are very shy. it is with the utmost difficulty that they can be approached. a few whites are carrying them news and trying to break up the treaty agreement.[47]

Finally, however, and after much distrust on the part of the Indians, whites and Indians met in full council on 8 September at Table Rock.

The setting, according to Judge Deady, was "worthy of the pen of Sir Walter Scott."[48] Table Rock, a massive, square abutment of gray granite, looms out some one thousand feet above the valley of the Rogue. The camp of the Rogues lay against its ramparts, a slope of meadow shaded here and there by giant oaks. According to Nesmith, it was a beautiful morning, the meadow golden in the sun. Lane, Palmer, Nesmith, Deady, and several others wore red hunting shirts. Chief Joe, in contrast, wore a long, black robe, priestlike. His troops, feathered and painted in the investiture of war, lolled above, higher on the slope, while far below on the plain, a company of white-belted dragoons set their horses in formation, their scabbards and carbines flashing in the sun. It had been agreed that the whites would come to the Rogues' camp unarmed—thus the reason for the dragoons remaining below.

The whites, according to Frances Victor, "were received with a sullen etiquette not easily translated into cordiality." Also, the exchange of remarks—or, more precisely, long orations—on the part of both whites and Indians was most onerous, for the Rogue River had to be translated into Chinook Jargon, the Jargon into English, and vice versa. It went on all day, with one significant interruption. "About the middle of the afternoon," Nesmith reported, a young Indian came running into camp stark naked, with the perspiration streaming from every pore. He made a brief harangue, and threw himself upon the ground apparently exhausted. His speech had created a great tumult among his tribe. General Lane told me to inquire of the Indian interpreter the cause of the commotion; the Indian responded that a company of white men on Applegate Creek, and under the command of Captain Owen, had that morning captured an Indian known as Jim Taylor, and had tied him to a tree and shot him to death. The hubbub and confusion among the Indians at once became intense, and murder glared from each savage visage. The Indian interpreter told me that the Indians were threatening to tie us up to trees and serve us as Owen's men had served Jim Taylor. I saw some Indians gathering up lass-ropes, while others drew the skin covers from their guns, and wiping sticks from their muzzle.[49]

Lane succeeded in quieting the Rogues, partly because Chief Joe apparently had given one of his sons to Lane as a hostage. But Lane's conciliatory response must have mollified the Indians as well. He stood up and spoke with much gravity:

Owen who has violated the armistice and killed Jim Taylor, is a bad man. He is not one of my soldiers. When I catch him he shall be punished. I promised in good faith to come into your camp, with ten other unarmed men to secure peace. Myself and men are placed in your power; I do not believe that you are such cowardly dogs as to take advantage of our unarmed condition.[50]

And they did not.

Three days later, though not authorized by Washington to do so, Palmer and Agent Culver concluded a treaty of cession and peace with the Rogues. It was, Palmer believed, the only way that peace could be assured. Something had to be done, and Palmer was always ready to risk censure for what he considered right action.

The Rogues agreed to cede to the government thirty-five hundred square miles, rich in timber, good agricultural land, and gold. The Indians were also required to surrender all of their weapons except those required for hunting and to pay indemnities for the property they had destroyed. In return, the Indians were permitted to retain one hundred square miles for a temporary reservation out of the thirty-five hundred ceded. The government also agreed to pay them sixty thousand dollars, less fifteen thousand dollars for the indemnities; the remainder would be provided in sixteen annual installments of clothing, blankets, farm implements, stock, and structures for the chiefs. Finally, the government agreed to assign an agent to the reservation. Bancroft concluded that although conditions made the treaty imperative, it placed "the conquered wholly in the power of the conquerors, and in return for which they were to receive quasi benefits which they did not want, could not understand, and were better off without."[51]

All agreed that, at less than three cents an acre, the purchase was a steal. Whether Palmer wished to more amply recompense the Rogues is not known. What is known is that he was constrained by two obstacles. The first lay in the Indian Department's policy of paying on the basis of population rather than land area. There were about a thousand Rogues, which meant that each Rogue River Indian would supposedly receive six hundred dollars. Second, Palmer was inhibited by the fact that Congress would not ratify a treaty that it considered extravagant in its provisions. Ratification was difficult enough for then as now, requiring a three-fourths majority of Congress. These considerations complicate any judgment, especially one made now, of the justice of the Palmer treaty. Whatever the case, this treaty became the model for those he subsequently negotiated.

Before returning to the Willamette Valley, Palmer made the first of these subsequent treaties with the Cow Creek Indians, neighbors of the Rogues and sometimes blamed for the depredations of the latter. Vicious attacks by whites had obliged them to flee to the mountains. This, in part, motivated Palmer to provide them with the security of a reservation. In return, the Cow Creek ceded eight hundred square miles for twelve thousand dollars, an exchange so advantageous to the whites that it was said Palmer accomplished more with two bushels of potatoes—the feast he provided—than had all the days of elaborate feasting at Champoeg.

As Palmer had expected, there was great opposition to the Rogue River Indian treaty, particularly from the exterminators, the Whigs, and the *Oregonian*. The 24 September *Oregonian* wrote:

> It appears from the latest advices from Rogue River, that another treaty of peace has been made with the thieving, murderous bands of Indians, who have continued under former treaties to steal and destroy the property of the whites; and whenever opportunity offered, to murder the defenseless and unprotected.
>
> Some men's "bowels of compassion" and feelings for the *poor Indians*, are wonderfully exercised whenever it is for their political interests that they be so.

The following week the newspaper was quite overcome with rage. If Lane had been the "Mary Ann" of the Mexican war, he was indubitably the "Gassy Ann" of the Rogue War for having made peace with the Indians. And the treaty, the *Oregonian* thundered, was nothing but "bumbuggary."

Similar allusions were made in Jacksonville, where a drunken miner went about the town seeking money to buy General Lane a petticoat. However, and in a sense surprisingly, in view of the character of the population, Jacksonville soon came to its senses. An indignation meeting called to protest the treaty was canceled. On 24 September, Jacksonville citizens gathered to announce that the rights of the Indians must be remembered and that "we look upon any person who would attempt to violate any of the provisions of this treaty, as unworthy of the esteem of his fellow man, and undeserving of the rights and privileges of citizenship."[52] Prudentially, the group added that anyone found selling arms to an Indian would be given 150 lashes and immediately expelled from the valley—a tacit admission that one of the principal causes of the war had been the Indians' success in amassing firepower from the very whites they planned to shoot.

It turned out to be an expensive war in more ways than one. Although the Rogue War lasted less than a month and only three or four hundred men were in the field, more than a hundred whites were killed, including noncombatants. The mass killings of modern war make the figure seem insignificant, but for the time and population of Oregon, it was high. The deaths were keenly felt, for many among the combatants were relatives or neighbors. It was not, as in modern wars, an army of strangers. On the Indian side, there were as many deaths, if not more, and a similar familial grief over the fatalities.

The war cost $7,000 a day, or a total of $258,000, for which, of course, the federal government was billed. The figure covered a number of items, including 29,100 candles, 19,000 bars of soap, and 10,184 pieces of lead. According to one commentator, the citizens of southern Oregon had never seen such bright nights, been so clean, or fired so many shots. No wonder the Whigs were enraged to see this cornucopia of benefits showering down in such profusion on their detested enemies, the Democrats.

On the whole, and at least for a time, the treaty was fairly well observed by both Indians and whites, though incidents did occur. The most curious in its sequel followed the murder of James Kyle by two Rogues on 6 October near Jacksonville. Under the conditions of the treaty, the Rogues were obliged to hand over the culprits, in this case a relative of Chief Joe's and another young brave. The Rogues, wishing to honor the treaty, surrendered the braves even though it must have left them heartsore, for the accused were much favored by the tribe. The citizens of Jacksonville were inclined to lynch the two men, but the treaty called for a proper trial, and Agent Culver promised both whites and Indians that a trial would take place in November. But Judge Obadiah McFadden of Pennsylvania, recently appointed to the bench by President Pierce, did not appear, and Jacksonville complained to the *Statesman* on 6 December:

"Why has he not come. Is he an old fogy with silk gloves, and too delicate to travel in the mist? . . . We have no disposition to keep prisoners at an expense of sixteen dollars per day each for the accomodation of delicate judges." The Rogues were also distressed by the failure of the judge to appear. Finally, losing patience, they were convinced that the promise had been broken, and they arranged for the escape of the accused.

PALMER, COMPLETING HIS NEGOTIATIONS with the Cow Creek Indians, started home—going down the valley, passing the plowmen, now, in late September, preparing the land for the sowing of winter wheat. He no doubt stopped in Salem to report to the governor, to see how the foundations of the statehouse were coming along, and to jaw with friends. A few weeks earlier, on 26 August, the *Spectator* had reported that the capital was "as quiet as a goose pond after a shower." In the literal sense, however, this could no longer have been the case, for shortly before Palmer's arrival, a set of brass band instruments had been delivered. And so, in the stillness of a place where, excepting mills, machinery did not exist, the cacophony of the practicing musicians must have been audible, indeed.

Traveling on to Oregon City, now called by some "the New York of the Willamette valley," Palmer found a number of excitements. In his absence, two paddle wheelers, the *Fenix* and the *Oregon*, had collided while racing on the river. Only a month or so before, the *Canemah* had exploded, its boilers overfueled while racing. And there had been yet another jailbreak. Exploding riverboats and jailbreaks seemed to be about as endemic to early Oregon as malaria.

In addition, the emigrants were arriving in large numbers, "lean, lank and hungry," crowding the streets. Sixty-five hundred had made the crossing with the largest herds yet seen in Oregon. Also, and to the relief of many, there were 105 more girls than boys.

By now, Palmer had moved the superintendency's office to Dayton, a more convenient location for him and also closer to the coast, where he hoped to establish a reservation. On arriving in Dayton, he may have been pleased to hear that in his absence Lafayette had formed an agricultural society and had made plans for a library.

But all the news was not good. Palmer's clerk, Edward R. Geary, was prostrate with fever, and affairs in the office had been neglected.* He also had letters waiting for him from two of his agents. R.R. Thompson on the Umatilla

* *Geary, a Presbyterian minister, later be-*

complained that the Indians were "very haughty" and　*came superintendent of*
"coppying their white brothers in many particulars."　*Indian affairs.*
Also, "they are very indignant when I send them out of
the kitchen . . . they seemed to think I came here expressly to feed them."
Thompson's health was "on the decline and if it get much worse I shall be
compelled to return to the valley." Agent W. W. Raymond wrote from Tansy
Point at the mouth of the Columbia. Raymond—who was "lacking in system
and energy," Palmer judged—was an ineffectual but well-intentioned agent
whom Palmer was to suffer for all of his time in office. Raymond reported that
sailors from the ships anchored in the estuary carried on an extensive liquor
trade with the Indians, turning them into "perfect maniacs." He also pleaded
for flour, sugar, and molasses to compensate the Indians "for the roots our
hogs and cattle have destroyed." Finally, he lamented that disease was so rampant among his charges that "they will soon become extinct."[53]

The most discouraging news of all was from George Manypenny. Palmer
had expected a draft from the commissioner, for the superintendency was
quite without funds. Raymond's flour, sugar, and molasses was the least of it.
Palmer had also promised supplies to the Rogue and Cow Creek Indians, who
desperately needed them now that winter was coming on and they no longer
occupied their traditional hunting and gathering grounds. Thus Palmer's profound disappointment when he found that Manypenny had sent him not
money but a sermon.

The commissioner had heard that trading, among other unnamed activities, was occurring between whites and Indians on the Sabbath. "The Sabbath," Manypenny reminded Palmer, "as an institution of the Great Father of
the nations, its observance is required alike of whites and Indians." Superintendents must not only promote the physical well-being of the Indians, but
they are also obliged

> to advance their political prosperity; to diffuse knowledge among them; to su-
> perinduce an habitual observance of morality; to make them participate in all
> the advantages and the blessings of a Christian society.[54]

Palmer's words on finishing this letter from far Washington are not known—
or whether he noted that the day, 5 August, on which it had been written was
the same day the riderless mule had trotted into Jacksonville, its withers
soaked in blood.

PALMER'S FIRST MAJOR ACTION on returning to Dayton was to write his annual report to the Indian Department. Sent on 8 October, it was a document of

forceful frankness: "A general feeling of anxiety and distrust pervades the tribes and bands from the sea-board to the Rocky Mountains." Palmer ascribed this condition to "the conduct of evil minded whites" and to the fact that no treaties had been ratified. "If existing treaties are not ratified and new treaties not negotiated with dispatch, a general Indian war will follow."[55]

Palmer recommended the manner in which the treaties should be negotiated. Referring obliquely to Governor Gaines' "five weeks of absurd magnificence" at Champoeg, Palmer insisted that the Indians should not be "paraded, petted, and feasted at public expense . . . as it inclines them to indolence and extravagance . . . and impresses them with the belief that our Government has a reckless disregard of expenditure." He also recommended that negotiations take place in seasons when "their wants are so numerous and pressing, that they yield a ready ear to terms, and comply with such as may be dictated." These appear to be the words of the canny, New England sharp dealer—and in part, no doubt, they are—but Palmer was probably sincere in adding, "I would only avail myself of their necessities the more effectually to promote their general welfare."[56]

After stating that reservations east of the Cascades would be required—a change in his view—as well as at the coast, Palmer concluded with his two most immediate concerns. At Port Orford, newly arrived miners promised trouble, for "many . . . are of the most reckless and desperate character." Finally, and most important of all, the superintendency desperately needed funds. Palmer had been obliged to borrow money at 5 percent. He did not mention, however, as he had to others, that he was considering resignation. Possibly, he was saving this as a final threat to pry funds loose.[57]

Palmer included in his annual report a rather sunny description of conditions at the Rogue River. His treaty with the Rogues was unauthorized, and it may be that he hoped Agent Culver's report would convince Manypenny of the wisdom of his action. But within a few weeks, Palmer was far from certain that peace prevailed in the south. "The reports from Rogue River are very confusing," he wrote to Culver on 4 November. "Sometimes it is reported that you are in a state of war." Palmer suggested that there were "certain" whites—Whigs—in the Rogue River Valley who would deliberately incite trouble for political purposes, "to fasten odium upon those who have favored the entering into treaty stipulations"—himself and the Democrats.[58]

Finally, news from Port Orford continued to be bad, for Agent S.M. Smith had written him that the miners there had "no regard for laws, order, or life."[59]

Of all Palmer's correspondence that November, none is more revealing of the general problem he faced than a letter from an Indian complaining of depredations by whites and a letter from a white complaining of depredations by Indians. The first letter was from William Chinook, who had joined the party of John Frémont when the explorer visited The Dalles in 1843. Methodist missionary H. K. W. Perkins persuaded Frémont to include nineteen-year-old Billy Chinook in his party and also asked that Frémont enroll Chinook in a school upon the party's return to the east. Chinook did in fact study in Philadelphia and Washington where, according to the *Oregonian*, he was "feasted and caressed." In 1845, he accompanied Frémont to California. Chinook returned to The Dalles in 1851 to claim land and settle on Mill Creek with his wife and a large herd of cattle.* On 3 November 1853, Chinook wrote Palmer:

> We are tormented almost every day by the white people who desire to settle on our land and although we have built houses and opened gardens they wish in spite of us to take possession of the very spots we occupy. We remonstrate and tell them that this is our land, they reply that Government gives them to settle in any part of Oregon Territory and they desire to take land in this very spot.
>
> Now we wish to know whether this is the land of the white man or the Indians. If it is our land the whites must not trouble us. If it is the land of the white man when did he buy it?
>
> Now if we as Indians have no power to defend our right against the whites; will you inform us how we are to do . . . soon all the good land will be taken. Where will we go, where will we make our homes. If we lose our country what shall we do. I know that the whites are strong, that they have ammunition and guns and power; we cannot resist them, but we ask them to leave us our homes for we are poor and have no power. Be so kind as to answer us and tell us what you think.

* *In 1859, Chinook removed to the Warm Springs Reservation, where he served as an interpreter and a scout. Chinook died in 1890. His tombstone reads: "A faithful and true friend of the white man." Lake Billy Chinook, a Deschutes River reservoir, is named for him. Chinook's letter is one of the few written statements by an Indian for the period. See Oregonian, 14 May 1853.*

Two weeks later, Palmer received a letter from Robert Hull:

> I emigrated to Oregon in the fall of 1848 under the Territorial Government which gave to each settler one section of land. I made me a claim on the Molala some time before the land bill was passed in Congress. When I heard of the land bill I was perfectly satisfied with the same; it stipulates that the Indians should

be removed beyond the Cascade Mountains. I was on my claim sometime before I knew that I was on the Indians' camping ground, but the land bill requiring them to be removed I remained satisfied thinking that Government would soon take them away. I have continually had to suffer from them ever since, every fall they have stolen some of my cabbage and potatoes. They would tell me that I have stollen their lands. A number of times they have thrown down my fence. Year after year has passed and they are still among us. When we got a change of government, I thought then surely they will be taken away but they are still among us. I am not the only individual that has suffered from them. A few days ago an Indian that is well known among the settlers by the name of old man Yelkir came to my house. I had just been getting supper. He had the ribs of a side of venison. He said he wanted to swap for some flour. I did not like the look of his meat. I told him I did not want to buy it; he said I must either buy it or give him some flour. I told him I would do neither. He came towards me; he took my hat from my head and struck me. I got my gun as quick as possible, thinking to shoot him down; but I did not know whether I would be justified or not. I want to know of you whether I should be justified or not. I want to know of you whether I shall take the law into my own hands, and shoot them down or not, or shall I wait a little longer expecting to have them moved? I want you to write and let me know.[60]

On 20 December, Palmer addressed the questions raised by Chinook and Hull in two letters, one to Hull, the other to Manypenny. He strongly urged Hull not to take the law into his own hands. The Indians, he wrote, "have the greatest cause of complaint," while "on the part of the whites, a little forbearance should be exercised." He agreed that the 1850 Donation Land Law authorized Americans to claim and occupy land, but only after Indian title has been extinguished—and that, in Oregon, had not yet occurred. Furthermore, Palmer was still not authorized to deal with the Indians for that extinguishment except where it was necessary to keep the peace. He advised patience and recommended that, in the case of threat or injury from the Indians, Hull apply to the civil law, "ample to protect the rights of our citizens."[61]

On the same day, Palmer wrote to Manypenny, enclosing a copy of Chinook's letter, "a picture of Indian wrongs no less true than sad and painful." He stated that though whites had encroached upon the ancient camping and root grounds set aside as reserves by Dart under the earlier, unratified treaties, this was not a matter of immediate concern since the valley tribes were so few in number and so debilitated. However, Palmer warned,

South Western, middle and upper Oregon, where the Indians are numerous and warlike, these wrongs are keenly felt and arouse the vindictive spirit of revenge, and in all probability without some prompt and efficient intervention of the Government war will result, to quell which, besides the sacrifice of human life, will require an expenditure many times greater than is at present necessary to obtain their lands by treaty and secure their lasting gratitude and friendship . . . . The occupation of the plains of middle Oregon by our citizens at an early date is as certain as any future event depending on human volition, and the question is now fairly before us. *Shall it be with outrage and blood, or with peace and goodwill.* Early treaties with the tribes of that region will prevent the former and secure the latter, to be secured, I believe, in no other way.[62]

The case could not have been stated with more cogency and eloquence.

Notwithstanding Palmer's apprehensions, December was not entirely cast in gloom. Manypenny wrote to say that money was on the way, and Palmer sent much-needed supplies to the Rogue and Cow Creek Indians. Blankets were in particular demand, for now that the Indians were confined to the reserve, they were no longer able to work for whites in exchange for clothing, as had been their custom. Food was in very short supply as well, because the war had interrupted their gathering and storing activities. Also, for those who had not lived before in the region of the reserve, the location of foodstuffs was unknown.

Cheered by his success in getting supplies to the Indians and by the promise of money from Washington, Palmer may also have been diverted by the arrival of the legislators in Salem early in December. This was always an occasion for hope—for favors, money, position—or despair, depending on one's party affiliations. But there was also much opportunity for gossip, intrigue, high jinks, and humor. And Palmer had a well-developed sense of humor and liked to exercise it. Despite his dire predictions to government of war and blood, it is likely that his humor and his perennial optimism kept him fresh and vigorous, whatever the tribulations of his office.

Also provoking much interest at this particular time was the 2 December arrival of the new territorial governor, John Wesley Davis, an Indiana physician who had gone into politics and succeeded to the point of becoming Speaker of the House in 1845. Davis was very much a Democrat. "I endorse everything the Democratic party ever has done, and everything it ever will do," he crowed.[63] This advocacy made him most welcome to the Oregon Democrats—though anathema, of course, to the Oregon Whigs.

Davis was also welcomed by many because he brought with him forty thousand dollars. This was to be spent on completing the statehouse and on building a sorely needed penitentiary. The money would also serve certain "unspecified" purposes. In general, historian Bancroft pointed out, the only thing wrong with Davis was that he was from the East.

What the new governor thought of his territory is hard to say. In a certain sense, he must have found it rather insubstantial, for a day or so after his arrival, both the Methodist church and the Masonic hall collapsed in a gust of wind. He may have also found the rowdiness objectionable. Palmer could have told him of the dozens of letters he had received complaining of drunken Indians on the streets; no doubt Palmer would have received as many, if not more, complaining of drunken whites if the latter had been in his charge. Coincidental with the governor's arrival, an "Ethiopian" and a white got into a fight over an Indian woman, the Ethiopian losing his ear. And despite the frequent jailbreaks, the jails were overflowing. Finally, the governor could not have been happy with the contractor for the u.s. mail service; letters from Hillsboro to Oregon City took three weeks.

Despite these various discomfitures, good spirits usually won the day. Certainly, many were looking forward to the grand balls promised for New Year's Eve. And the weather had been mild, the warmest winter anyone could remember. A few days before Christmas, editor D.J. Schnebly of the *Spectator* gathered pinks and bachelor buttons in his garden. In the foothills of the Cascades, however, the weather was less mild, and on 29 December, Agent Parrish wrote Palmer to say that the Santiam were starving.

SEVEN

Massacre and Politics

I F DECEMBER 1853 had been the mildest the settlers had ever known, January 1854 was the coldest. The Columbia froze from the Cascades to the Cowlitz, teams able to cross on the ice at Portland and Vancouver, while in the valley, the meadows slept beneath a snow blanket eight inches thick. There was snow in the south as well, but it was streaked with blood. At Cottonwood Creek near present-day Lakeview, four miners were murdered. The miners, some said, were hunting not only gold but also squaws. On the south coast, Agent S.M. Smith at Port Orford wrote Palmer on 1 January that miners were molesting the Indian women there as well. He added, however, that most of the miners were "well-disposed, law abiding and order loving men, who will not permit the rights of the Indians to be invaded."[1]

It was true that there were among the miners men who, partly out of principle and partly out of concern for their own safety, deplored the barbarity of some of their fellows. A miner on the Illinois River wrote Samuel Culver in January to complain of a "company of desperados" from Sailor Diggings who had attacked the local Indians with the aim of exterminating them, even though they "have been peaceable and friendly." But now, by reason of the Sailor Diggings whites, the safety of the Illinois miners was endangered. "We now appeal to you for relief that we may safely pursue our labor and not again be subjected to quit our homes in the dead of winter by the outrageous proceedings of men whom we look upon as regardless of our peace and welfare."[2]

Agent Smith could assure Palmer that there were other men like the Illinois miners, but that did not alter the Indians' general sense of grievance. Smith quoted one chief in his letter to Palmer:

> I cannot understand white men. You make promises but do not fulfill them. I sold my country long ago to the great American Tyee [chief]. The great American Tyee promised to pay my people—he has not made good his words. Now his people come here, take my land without permission and do not pay me. What do your people mean?[3]

Miners on the Coquille wrote to Palmer as well, but in their case complaining of harassment by the local Indians and asking him what course they should follow. Palmer replied that he was not as yet empowered to make treaties and urged the miners to exercise "prudence and forbearance" and, most important, to keep liquor away from their more belligerent companions. But Palmer's advice came too late.

There was at this time a ferry on the Coquille River about a mile above present-day Bandon. On 26 January, a group of miners were lounging at the landing when a bullet whizzed through their midst—fired by the local chief, they charged, though the chief later said he was shooting at a duck. That incident exhausted their patience.

The miners met the following day to determine a course of action. First, they heard complaints against the Indians: they had ridden miners' horses without permission; called miners "God damned Americans" and told them to clear out; and ransacked their cabins when the miners were absent. George Abbot reported that after the incident at the ferry landing, he had requested a talk with the chief, who had refused, saying that he intended "to rid his country of all white men; that it was no use talking to him, that if they [the whites] would take out his heart and wash it, he would still be the same."[4] The chief was invited to the meeting, but he failed to appear, later claiming he feared to do so.

At the end of the meeting, two resolutions were passed:

> That the Indians in this vicinity are in a state of hostility toward the whites from their own acknowledgements and declarations . . . . That tomorrow morning, the twenty-eighth instant, as early as possible, we will move upon and attack the Indian village.[5]

The miners informed Agent Smith at Port Orford of their intentions, but so late as to preclude his arrival on the Coquille River to mediate—probably their intention.

The miners attacked at dawn on the following morning. They killed fifteen men and one or possibly two women and then burned the Indians' village. At a meeting held that evening, the chief appeared, and according to Frances Victor, "a treaty of peace and friendship" was concluded. The miners returned what property they had not burned as well as the twenty or so captives taken. Finally, they resolved to write a report on the whole affair, one copy for the governor and another for Agent Smith.[6]

Arriving that evening or the following morning, Agent Smith was not in the least impressed by the miners' "punctilio of meetings, formal resolutions and reports . . . a most horrid massacre, or rather an out and out barbarous murder." How, he wrote Palmer, "could anyone believe that 75 men, women and children with three serviceable guns could expell 300 miners."[7] Smith recognized that the Indians had been troublesome, but he refused to believe that they were of any real danger to the whites. Smith's rage over the affair was such that he sent his report to the California newspapers. When the news story appeared, the miners threatened Smith with fifty lashes; in the end, he resigned and left the area.

Palmer gave full credence to Smith's account of the incident. He wrote to Lane, now territorial delegate, that it was "an unprovoked attack by reckless villains wholly unwarranted and unsupported by the least shadow of grounds or necessity." He then leveled a general indictment: "This system of plunder and murder so frequently repeated against this unfortunate race of beings without I may say almost an effort on the part of the government to restrain them is a blot upon our reputations that can scarcely be wiped off." The civil authorities, he maintained, "are wholly powerless [to restrain the lawless whites] and many of the settlers, either from interest or fear from these lawless bandits . . . give aid and encouragement." Under such circumstances, Palmer concluded, "can it be expected that the Indians will remain guiltless of an occasional act of retaliation."[8]

THE KILLINGS ON THE COQUILLE were not the last to occur on the south coast in early 1854. At about the same time as Palmer's letter to Lane, and in some respects an illustration of it, a massacre took place on the Chetco River at present-day Brookings. For some time, the local Indians had run a ferry across the river's mouth. With the arrival of the miners, the ferry became more profitable. This excited the greed of a man named Miller, who attempted to appropriate the craft. The Indians resisted. Palmer told the story in his annual report:

Nine well-armed men, att[a]cked the village, and as the Indians came from their lodges twelve of them were shot dead by these monsters. The women and children were permitted to escape. Three men remained in the lodges, and returned fire with bows and arrows. Being unable to get a sight of these Indians, they ordered two squaws, pets in the family of Miller, to set fire to the lodges. Two were consumed in the conflagration; the third, while raising his head through the flames and smoke for breath, was shot dead. What adds to the atrocity of the deed is, that shortly before the massacre, the Indians were induced to sell the whites their guns, under the pretext that friendly relations were firmly established. The Indians kept up a random fire from the opposite village during the day, but without effect, and at night fled to the mountains. The next day all the lodges on the north bank were burned; and the day following, those on the southern, two only excepted, belonging to the friends of an Indian who acted with Miller and his party. This horrid tragedy was enacted about the fifteenth of February, and on my arrival, on the eighth of May, the place was in the peaceable possession of Miller . . . . Twenty-three Indians and several squaws were killed prior to my arrival . . . . Miller was subsequently arrested and placed in the custody of the military at Port Orford; but on his examination before a justice of the peace, was set at large on the ground of justification, and want of sufficient evidence to commit . . . . Arrests are evidently useless, as no act of a white man against an Indian, however, atrocious, can be followed by a conviction.[9]

Finally, on 21 February 1854, the *Statesman* reported an incident near present-day Agness on the Rogue: "Some whites attacked . . . squaws and children . . . a few days since; they killed 8 squaws, one child and wounded a young Indian. Comment is unnecessary."

These outrages on the south coast convinced Palmer that he had to negotiate treaties immediately, with or without authorization. He first tried to gain authorization by presenting the matter to O.C. Pratt, the territorial judge, and Benjamin Harding, the territorial attorney general. Palmer argued on the basis of emergency:

When the lives and property of our citizens engaged in their lawful callings are in danger and an expensive and bloody war seems impending, only to all appearances to be avoided by the purchase of the lands of the Indians, the occupancy of which by the whites is the cause of the difficulty, then I apprehend such an emergency exists.[10]

Both men denied his plea. Palmer then wrote to George Manypenny on 27 February to state that the exigencies of the situation demanded that treaties be negotiated, even if not authorized, and that he intended to do so.

PALMER BEGAN WITH THE TUALATIN INDIANS. They were an influential tribe, and he believed their readiness to negotiate would encourage the other tribes to do so as well. But the Tualatins were not cooperative. First, the Indians did not want to sell their land and live on a reservation; and second, if they were forced to leave their land, they wanted money in payment, not goods. Palmer was absolutely opposed to this arrangement, for he was convinced that the money would drain down the bunghole of a whiskey barrel. He was stalemated.

In his dealings with whites who were less than understanding of the Indians' plight, Palmer could be very blunt. In his dealings with Indians who were not acting in what he judged to be their own interests, he could be very blunt as well. His letter of 21 March to the recalcitrant Tualatins is an example of that bluntness and of Palmer's generally stern manner in treating with his charges. Although he was genuinely and profoundly sympathetic to the Indians, Palmer never allowed his feelings to turn mawkish but accorded the Indians a seriousness appropriate to that dignity which he considered innate in them. On 21 March 1854, Palmer wrote to "the Chiefs and Head Men of the Tualatin Band of Calapooia Indians":

> I have been informed that some of you are still opposed to the sale of your country and to remove to another to be designated by your Great Father the President.
>
> Our rule of action is that when a majority are in favor of a measure it is decided that way and binding on all. It would be well for you to do so too. I have once made you a proposal. You would not listen to it. It was not made to deceive you but for your good. Your refusing to sell your land and remove to some other place need not injure me. Why should I care about it? Nor will it injure the government. The reason why I wish you to sell is because I know it will be for your good. The whites are determined to settle on your land. We cannot prevent them and in a few years there will be no place left for you. Then what will you do? Will you live in the mountains like wolves? The deer and other game being killed off you will have nothing to eat, your women and children crying for food, and freezing from cold; there will be no one to care for you. I tell you this will be so. Then be wise. Take good counsel. Sell your lands. Agree to remove to such places as the Government may hereafter select for you, where they will protect you and provide for your wants . . . . If you agree to sign the treaty, I will pay you as soon as that is done, two yoke of oxen, two logs chains, one plow, ten hoes, six axes, thirty blankets, twenty-two ready made dresses, thirty pairs shoes, thirty hickory shirts, twenty four cotton flags, twenty four spear knives, five cases powder, two pounds lead, or ball and shot, four nests camp kettles, twelve hundred pounds flour, fifty pounds of coffee,

two hundred pounds sugar, twenty five pounds tea, three dozen tin cups, twenty four tin pans, one beef, ten bushels of wheat for seed and twenty bushels potatoes, two bushels of peas, one bushel corn, ten bushels of oats and half a bushel of beans for the same purpose.

If you desire to do as I have proposed, come down to Dayton and sign the treaty and I will deliver them to you; and as soon as the treaty is approved of by our great chief, we will make you another payment; and you will be permitted to reside at your present home until a selection is made for you, and no one shall molest you or your property.

He signed the letter "Your friend, Joel Palmer."[11]

The Tualatins did come down to Dayton, and on 25 March, the treaty was signed. In exchange for an area of 1,476 square miles, each family was promised forty acres on the reserve—at such time as it might be established—as well as annuity goods for twenty years. Writing Joseph Lane in Washington, urging early ratification, Palmer argued against one sure objection:

The provisions of this treaty may be thought by some too liberal toward these poor degraded beings and that they are not entitled to the consideration given them. Their very weekness and ignorence is one of the reasons why we should liberally provide for them. No one will for a moment pretend that the amounts proposed to be paid them is any consideration, comparatively speaking, for their country.[12]

Thus was Palmer caught, caught between his conscience and his critics, realizing on the one hand that the Indians were not receiving just compensation and on the other hand arguing that they were being overcompensated out of sympathy for their destitute condition.

ON 27 MARCH, PALMER RECEIVED $2,086 from Washington, which allowed him to embark on his long-delayed tour of the south. The Chetco and Coquille affairs required his attention, and he still had to explore the coast for a suitable reservation site. Incidents on the upper Rogue River in the vicinity of Jacksonville called for his presence as well.

It will be remembered that in the previous year, the Rogues, in accordance with the treaty, had handed over for trial the two Indians accused of killing James Kyle and that the trial had not occurred due to the failure of "that old fogy with silk gloves," that is, the judge, to appear. Since the promised trial did not take place, the Rogues felt free to arrange for the escape of the accused men. However, on the remonstrance of the whites, the Indians had again handed the men over, and they had been tried and hanged. The Rogues were much exercised by this denouement, in part because the two men had been favorites in the tribe, but mainly because the same justice was not meted out to whites who killed Indians. Samuel Culver quoted the Rogues in his report to Palmer: "If we see that you do the same to your people, then we are convinced of the justice of your laws."[13] But they saw no such justice, and this, then, was one reason for their growing discontent.

There were other problems on the Rogue as well. The Indians on the reserve had suffered much from the bloody flux, or dysentery, and shortages of food. Those who lived off the reserve and who were not included in the treaty had engaged in scattered violence. Also, intertribal hostilities had broken out. The 15 April 1854 *Oregonian* welcomed the development: "It will save the whites the trouble of exterminating them."

Palmer started south in early April, going as far as Salem on a paddle wheeler. At Salem, after visiting his daughter Mary, who was enrolled at the Willamette Institute, Palmer met the pack train he had sent ahead from Dayton under the care of his son, Lorenzo. The train carried supplies for the Rogue and Cow Creek Indians: two plows, axes, and hoes, as well as oats, beans, and seed potatoes. Flour would be purchased on the way. Earlier, Palmer had shipped three thousand dollars' worth of supplies by sea to Port Orford, which he hoped would be there by the time of his arrival, planned for late April. This necessity for providing such quantities of foodstuffs for the Indians gives some idea of the degree to which their traditional source of subsistence had been destroyed.

His work in Salem completed, Palmer, his friend Cris Taylor (serving as his clerk), and Lorenzo started up the valley in the spring rains, passing what many still called Skinner's Mudhole—present-day Eugene. From there, they began the climb into the Calapooya Mountains and the Umpqua country. Palmer found the local Indians to be "wretched, sickly and almost starving." He ascribed their condition partly to their improvidence and the severe winter, but there were also more basic causes:

> Through the operation of the law lately enacted, prohibiting the sale of firearms and ammunition to Indians, they can no longer procure game, rendered scarce and timid by the presence of the white man; and the cultivation of the soil, together with the grazing of large herds of domestic animals, has greatly diminished the subsistence derived from native roots and seeds.

Without the "assistance offered by a few humane settlers," Palmer claimed, they would not have survived the winter.[14]

After giving the Umpquas supplies and presents, Palmer ordered the subagent, William Martin, to provide them with land to cultivate—much of their region had been occupied by settlers—and to bring to trial any white who might harm them. For the Indians on the Grave Creek hills near present-day Galice, however, Palmer had little sympathy due to their "constant aggressions." He made no bones about it: "I declined making them any presents and told them to expect nothing until they should merit it by their *good conduct*."[15]

At Rogue River, Palmer found the Indians "excited and unsettled." The severity of the winter, shortages of food, and disease had killed large numbers of the Rogues on the reserve. "Consternation and dismay prevailed," Palmer wrote Manypenny.[16] Many Indians had fled, and others were preparing to go to the mountains for security. Palmer distributed his supplies and turned his attention to finding Tipsey, chief of a Shasta band of Rogues. The previous year, goods had been sent to the band on the condition that they live on the reserve; they had not. Furthermore, they had killed a settler and his dog, placing the corpses of both at the doorway of the settler's own house. The band's chief, Tipsey, was a curious figure. At the end of the 1853 hostilities, Lane, out hunting with a companion, inadvertently stumbled into Tipsey's camp, where he feared he would be killed. Instead, the chief gave him food and shelter. It was known, however, that Tipsey—a tall, powerful man with a graying goatee—was exceptionally reserved in manner and did not care to associate with whites. He refused gifts from them, although he did allow his women to receive them. He lived much of his time in seclusion with his band in the mountains. Palmer and forty dragoons spent five days searching for Tipsey. Failing to find him, Palmer returned to deal with other Rogue River bands, whom he eventually persuaded to come in to the reserve.

It can be assumed that Palmer carefully observed the behavior of his agent on the Rogue, Samuel Culver. Palmer had written Joseph Lane: "Agents are apt to consider the office is created especially for their benefit rather than for the performance of their duties."[17] In the case of Culver, Palmer would soon have proof that the agent was more concerned for the "benefit" rather than the "duties" of his office.

PALMER ARRIVED AT THE COAST in mid-May. He first visited the scene of the Chetco massacre. Most of the surviving Indians fled from him, excepting two boys and an old woman. He left some tobacco and shirts for them with a settler who was in their trust and proceeded up the coast to the Coquille River, where the other massacre had taken place. There he was met by Agent Josiah Parrish, who had replaced the intimidated Smith.

Perhaps it was his visits to the Chetco and the Coquille together with the eyewitness accounts of the two massacres that led Palmer to make the most vehement statement of his career regarding white treatment of Indians. On 12

May, he wrote from Port Orford to Gen. John Wool in San Francisco, requesting more troops to restrain

> lawless persons . . . outrages at variance with every principle of justice and revolting to humanity have been committed against the Indians . . . . How mortifying that we have so reckless a population as to demand the presence of troops to protect the natives against the barbarities of our own citizens . . . . Scenes have been enancted here by whites . . . against Indians that would disgrace the most barbarous nations of the world.[18]

It took a brave man to write such statements in the Oregon of 1854.

Palmer had probably planned to continue up the coast, but lacking funds, he was obliged to return to the valley by way of ship to Portland. Before leaving, he carried out one of the principal duties of a superintendent: "to gather information as to the number of Indians, their location, condition, extent of country claimed by each band, their means of subsistence, the character of the country they inhabit." There were thirteen hundred Indians in the Port Orford district, "athletic and robust" in appearance and, with the understandable exception of the Chetco and Coquille, friendly to the whites. The Indian women had formerly been known for their chastity, but "sad changes . . . have taken place in this regard, and many serious difficulties have had their origin in the licentiousness of the miners."[19]

ON PALMER'S RETURN TO THE VALLEY at the end of May, he found all manner of excitements. There was, for example, the case of Nimrod O'Kelly, Oregon's first convicted killer—the victim, Jeremiah Mahoney had, Nimrod claimed, "intruded" on his land. At the time of Palmer's return, O'Kelly, to the consternation of many, had been released from jail after a very short confinement. The reason given was his advanced age. Then there was the case of Charity Lamb who, with her daughter, had axed her husband to death while he was eating his dinner. It was alleged that Charity and her daughter had been seduced by a neighboring farmer who had moved on to California, where Charity and her daughter planned to join him after disposing of Mr. Lamb. These upheavals in society were matched by upheavals in nature; Mount St. Helens erupted.

Violent happenings such as the above almost replaced politics as a subject of conversation. But not quite, for the June elections were approaching. Fiercely debated was a proposed measure to bring prohibition to Oregon again. Also controversial was a measure that would have Oregon apply for statehood. And then, of course, there was an issue of long standing, the question of where the capital should be located. Construction of a statehouse in Salem had already begun, but there were still those—particularly the "pensioned aristocracy," as the Democrats called the Whig officeholders—who wanted the capital returned to Oregon City. Indeed, the citizens of Oregon City still held under lock and key the state library, a decided inconvenience to the Salem bureaucracy. But the most serious political issue of all—indeed, for Palmer, ominous—was described in the *Spectator* on 26 April. The subject of the article was the American party—commonly called the Know Nothings—a secret order, with all the hocus-pocus of cryptic signs and special handshakes, that was devoted to the exclusion from public life of foreign-born Americans and Roman Catholics. In time, this group and the ambiguous nature of Palmer's association with it was to have a major impact on his career.

While preparing for another trip to the coast to continue his reservation survey, Palmer received bad news from the south. Tipsey, chief of the Shasta band of Rogues—whom Palmer had pursued in April on the upper Rogue—had been killed by a Klamath chief named Bill. "What better evidence Bill and his people could have given of their friendship to the whites . . . it would be hard to tell," Culver wrote Palmer.[20] And indeed, the desire to ingratiate himself with the whites appears to have been one of Chief Bill's purposes.

Following the killing, Chief Bill had started out for Fort Jones, presumably to seek protection there from Tipsey's people. Stopping to bathe in the Klamath River, he had been shot by the Cottonwood miners, scalped, and thrown live to the fury of the rapids. The motivation is tangled. These Cottonwood miners were the same men who, in January, had lost four of their fellows—said to have been "squaw hunters"—to Chief Bill and his band. The miners, however, claimed the four were killed by the Klamath while out seeking horses that the Klamath had stolen. Here, as in many of the Indian-white conflicts, the confusion of fact and falsehood, plain mistake and rumor, makes determination of the truth impossible, however clear the results. The results in this case, as Culver explained it to Palmer, were grave: "This chief Bill has stood between the Shastas and whites as Joe and Sam have between the Indians and whites here. In other words was our best friend . . . . We are worse off now than before."[21]

BEFORE PALMER LEFT FOR THE COAST, the elections determined that the majority of Oregonians still preferred whiskey to "Adam's Ale" and territorial status to statehood. Palmer was also grateful to hear that Congress had ratified his treaties with the Rogue and the Cow Creek Indians, perhaps the best news that he had so far received as superintendent.

Where Palmer began his coast survey is uncertain, but it may have been on the Coquille near present-day Bandon. At any rate, it was there on 28 June that he wrote Parrish at Port Orford to say he was conducting a census of the local Indians and that he was "much annoyed by the mosquitoes and gnats" in the process.[22]

Palmer went on to explore the region that lay between the Umpqua River at present-day Reedsport and the Nestucca River near Tillamook, a distance of 120 miles. His practice was to spend a day or two following each of the major streams to their headwaters in the Coast Range. It was along these streams— the Umpqua, Siuslaw, Alsea, Yaquina, Siletz, and Nestucca—that the Indians lived. Except for the Siuslaw, Palmer classed all these bands as Tillamook. He judged that nature provided well for the coastal Indians:

> Muscles deeply encase the rocks rising from the ocean near the coast; several species of clams abound on the beach, and crabs in the bays; while salmon, herrings, sardines and other fish, in perpetual succession, visit the streams. The mountains yield a profusion of berries, and the low-lands, in the proper season, swarm with wild fowl.

Palmer found the Indians "peaceable, healthy and well clad," and in the case of the Siuslaw chiefs, who often had eight or nine wives, lusty. He also recorded that whites had seldom visited them and that he was the first white some had ever seen.[23]

Although one purpose of Palmer's survey was to report on the number and condition of these bands, his principal concern was to determine whether the region was suitable for a reserve. The Yaquina, he decided, was the only stream accessible from the sea, meeting his requirement that the place be isolated and thus not invite white penetration. Also, the region was large enough to accommodate all the Indians west of the Cascades. But in other particulars he was disappointed: "They [the Indians] would be required to live in small, detached communities, in scarcely accessible valleys, and a great number of farmers, mechanics, teachers and agents would be required for their proper instruction and control."[24] Once again, Palmer began to consider relocating the valley and southern tribes to country east of the Cascades.

PALMER RETURNED TO THE VALLEY on the trail that followed the Nestucca and which brought him out within a few miles of Dayton. At his office he found a letter waiting from Perit Huntington, a settler at Yoncalla.* No document of the period illustrates more   *Huntington came to* clearly the plight of an Indian who, deprived of his tra-   *Oregon as a miner in*

ditional food sources, had attempted to provide for *the early 1850s, became*
himself in the manner of the whites. Huntington wrote *a farmer, and in 1863*
on behalf of an Indian named "Dick Johnson" who had *was appointed superin-*

> settled upon and commenced cultivating a small tract *tendent of Indian*
> of land . . . . he had perservered until he now has *affairs.*
> twelve acres enclosed and in the best state of cultiva-

tion of any tract of similar size I have ever seen in the Territory. He has also
made in addition between five and six thousand rails for fencing a pasture and
built a good hewed log house. He has provided himself with farming tools, a
cow and work horses and is altogether better prepared for farming than one half
the white settlers in the country. Dick has been personally known to me and to
the people of this settlement for four or five years and his characer for honesty
and industry has invariably been good.

Some twelve or eighteen months since a Mr. Bean took a claim which included a little more than half of Dick's enclosure. He has had more or less difficulty with Dick ever since and about eight months since gave him a severe
beating.

A Mr. Kennedy about two weeks ago took a claim adjoining Bean which
takes in Dick's house, spring, the remaining part of the field, and the ground
which Dick had laid out for a pasture. Dick applied to the settlers of the neighborhood for assistance, and a number of them went to see Kennedy and endeav-
oured to bring about some compromise or induce him to leave. Kennedy refused to leave, to pay Dick for his labor or make any other arrangement whatever, saying that the "law" would give him the place and that he intended to
have it anyhow.

Dick then applied to Martin, the Indian Agent, for redress. Martin came in
and saw Kennedy and Bean—*advised them to remain* and told Dick *not to do any
work outside of his fields* but to remain and occupy what he had already actually
inclosed . . . if he is cut down to this limit which Martin assigns him he cannot
stay on the place . . . .

Public opinion is very strongly in Dick's favor, and there are not five men
within ten miles of his place who would not sign a petition to have him protected in his possessions . . . .

This situation if he is forced to leave the place is really deplorable, for when
he commenced cultivating the soil, his people (the Klickatats) cast him off and
will not permit him to come back to them, and if he is not suffered to remain
among the whites his only chance is to go into the mountains and make his living thieving.[25]

After "a careful investigation from all the information in my possession," Palmer wrote to Huntington, Agent Martin, and Kennedy, making very clear his position in such cases. First, the Northwest Ordinance of 1787 stated that Indian lands "shall never be taken from them without their consent; and in their property, rights and liberty, they shall never be invaded or disturbed." On the basis of these provisions, Palmer maintained that the claiming of Johnson's land by Kennedy was "subversion of every principle of justice." *[26]

He next made the point that the Indians' loss of their traditional food sources "leaves them no alternative but either to follow the pursuits of the whites in cultivating the soil or starve." Palmer concluded by saying that his department respected Johnson's rights, that Kennedy would do well to abandon his claim, but if no settlement could be reached, Agent Martin was to "mark off," and thus confirm, the boundaries of Johnson's land.[77]

What Palmer did not mention in these letters, though he was fully aware of it, was that Kennedy also had rights as given him by the Donation Land Law. The problem lay in the conflict between the Territorial Act of 1848, which confirmed the Indians in the possession of their land, and the Donation Land Law of 1850, which opened the same land to white settlement. Treaties were to have settled the conflict by extinguishing Indian title to the land, but until now, only the treaties with the Rogue and Cow Creek Indians had been ratified. In short, at this time, both Kennedy and Johnson had equal right in law to the same land. The fact that this was no seasonal hunting ground but land built upon and cultivated by Johnson gave the latter a stronger claim in equity, but this still did not dissipate the legal impasse. Thus, the principals were left with nothing but exhortation on the one hand, obduracy on the other, turmoil in general, and finally, death.

For the Johnson case ended in tragedy. In late July, Palmer learned from Martin that forty men had joined to force Kennedy from Johnson's land. At the end of a six-hour meeting with Kennedy, however, the men decided that the Donation Land Law might make their action unlawful. They therefore took their case in the form of a petition to President Pierce. They also urged the President to remove Agent Martin, believing him to be prejudiced against Indians in general. Lindsay Applegate, for example, charged that when hoes

It might be asked how in good conscience Palmer could cite such provisions when he himself had informed the Cayuse six years earlier that they had forfeited their land. He probably would have answered in the words of the Northwest Ordinance that such forfeiture was permitted in the case of "just and lawful wars," that is, the Cayuse War.

promised to the Indians were not forthcoming, Martin told them they might till the land with their fingers. This matter of Martin may be one reason the petition was not sent to Palmer, for Palmer and Martin were old friends from the Cayuse War. It is just as likely, however, that the petitioners recognized that Palmer had done all he could, and that they must go to a higher authority. Martin himself stigmatized their action as politically motivated; he was a Democrat, and Huntington, Applegate, and others of the forty were Whigs.

In late August, Martin wrote Palmer that he had marked off the 360 acres claimed by Johnson and that Kennedy and Bean had promised not to molest the Indian, though they still maintained that under the law the land properly belonged to them. Their fear of further retribution may have secured this promise not to attack Johnson, for by now, Kennedy's house had been set afire—by Johnson, it was said, on the urging of the whites who supported his claim.

There is no further record of developments in the Johnson case until 7 December 1858, when the *Statesman* reported that Johnson and his father-in-law had been murdered by a party of whites and that one of the whites had immediately moved into Johnson's cabin, taking over all of his livestock, implements, and other effects. Several Indians witnessed the killings, but because Indians could not testify in court, charges were never brought against the killers. Thus, in the case of Johnson and Kennedy, was the conflict between the Territorial Act and the Donation Land Law finally settled.

DURING THE SEVERAL WEEKS in which Palmer remained in Dayton before departing for southeastern Oregon to search for possible reservation sites, he received five reports from the field. All but one were despairing.

"The feeling of hostility desplayed by each party," Culver wrote of the whites and Rogues, "it would be almost impossible to realize . . . men of standing and those in all respects worthy entertain sentiments of the most bitter and deadly hostility entirely at variance with their general disposition."[28] In other words, it was not only the hot-tempered, transient miners who were calling for the severest measures against the Indians but also the more responsible members of the community. Culver ended by pleading for supplies for the Indians who, prohibited from hunting, and their roots and seeds destroyed, were starving.

At Port Orford, Josiah Parrish was also despondent. In his report to Palmer, he first gave an overview of his district, which stretched from Coos Bay to the California border, an area of some three thousand square miles, one hundred fifty miles long and about thirty wide. It was a beautiful place. The many streams were bordered by fertile prairies, especially in the south, and rhododendrons, lilies, acacia, honeysuckle, and tulips abounded. Here, twelve bands comprising about fifteen hundred Indians resided, living from the sea and streams, in the spring gathering the stalks of the wild celery and sunflowers and in the summer a plenitude of berries. They were, Parrish said, a friendly people, both among themselves and to the whites.

But this stretch of coast was no longer Eden. It had become "dotted with towns and villages of miners." And it was the miners who, during the past six months, had burned down four Indian villages. "I believe in no single instance have the Indians been the first agressors," wrote Parrish. "Many of the whites on this coast seem to have lost nearly all sense of humanity and they are ready to butcher an Indian for the smallest offense."[29] This was a deterioration, indeed, from six months previous, when Smith had written that most of the miners were "well-disposed." One cause, no doubt, was the enormous increase in the number of miners who, hearing tales of the south coast's golden sands, had swarmed to garner them.

Parrish saw only one solution. "I would beseech the government in their [the Indians'] behalf, that the most efficient measures should be taken for their speedy removal to a place of quiet, and, if possible, to one of safety." This tough ex-blacksmith and missionary concluded with a plaintiveness uncharacteristic of him. "Here I am in trouble, called in almost every direction, and no means to help myself, and far from home. I will not say that I am discouraged for this word is not in my book—but things are very dark."[30]

The final verses in this dirge came from Agent W. W. Raymond and a settler at the Cascades. Raymond reported that a sailor named Jack provided a continuous supply of drink to the Clatsop, and the settler complained of a similar supply to the Indians of his neighborhood, "keeping them constantly whooping and hollering, day and night, and fighting each other."[31]

PALMER MUST HAVE BEEN HAPPY to leave these melancholy tidings and escape to the bright, sage-scented high country east of the mountains. Although he never said as much in his official correspondence or his diaries, Palmer seems to have preferred the trail to the office. His purpose in this journey was to determine if the Klamath Lake region would be suitable for a reservation for the Willamette Valley Indians. He also wished to make contact with the Klamath because there was no agent in the region. Also, the Klamath had plagued the emigrants of the southern route with various molestations, which Palmer was determined to stop.

Palmer and eight men, including Cris Taylor, left the valley on 4 August, eager to reach the higher elevations, for the valley shimmered with far more than the usual heat. Indeed, Palmer had the very highest elevation in mind. Earlier, he had agreed to join Thomas Dryer, editor of the *Oregonian*, and several others in an ascent of Mount Hood. On reaching the place of rendezvous a day late, however, Palmer found that Dryer had gone on without him—a case of poetic injustice since Palmer, after all, was the first white man to have scaled high enough on the mountain (Crater Rock) to determine the feasibility of its ascent.

The party's route took them up the Barlow trail where, having crossed the mountains, they turned south. Employing a Tygh guide with the unpropitious name "Kup-up," they followed the Deschutes River, passing through Warm Springs and a landscape that Palmer described as "stony and broken in the extreme."[32] Here and there, however, they skirted forests of pine and juniper and, on occasion, camped in meadows of tall grass. On 19 August, they reached the lake.

The Klamath lived in semisubterranean, earth-domed lodges near the marshes and lakes, and they consumed plants and waterfowl. They had had little contact with whites and still used bows and arrows instead of guns. At the time of Palmer's visit, about four hundred Klamath lived in six villages on the lakeshore. On 21 August, Palmer called the Indians into council.

> After explaining to them the objects of my mission and our determination to punish those who committed acts of violence and theft against our people, and listening to their replies and promises of good conduct, I made them a few presents and the council broke up with an apparent good feeling.[33]

Thus was Palmer somewhat assured that the emigrants of that year traveling the southern route would not be molested.

Palmer was also pleased to find the Klamath region suitable for a reservation. About 150 square miles in area, it was of sufficient size to accommodate both the Willamette and Umpqua valley Indians. The soil was good, and near the lake there was "an abundance of nutritious grasses." The valley Indians' principal objection to the area was the severity of the winters, but Palmer judged from the slight construction of the Klamath lodges that those fears were groundless. In general, he was satisfied. "Isolated and remote from other tracts adapted to settlement," he reported, "this region seems peculiarly marked out as the asylum of these remnants of the aborigines."[34]

BY 30 AUGUST, PALMER WAS BACK in Dayton refreshed by his time on the trail, reassured of the safety of the coming emigrants, and certain that he had found a place where the Indians of the interior valleys might live unharmed and at peace. Whatever good spirits he may have enjoyed, however, must have been dashed by news from the south and east that awaited his return.

A letter from Culver informed him that whites had killed two Indians. One of the murderers had fled to California and the other had escaped from jail. The Indians were now more convinced than ever that no white would ever be punished for crimes against them.

The news from the east was the worst since the December morning six years before when word of the Whitmans' massacre had reached Oregon City. Another massacre had now occurred. On 20 August, the Ward party of twenty-one emigrants from Kentucky had been attacked by Snake Indians near Fort Boise; only one young boy had survived. There had also been brutality against the women. No crime inflamed the passions of the settlers more. In this case, a Miss Ward had been tortured to death: "The marks of teeth were plainly visible upon her left cheek. A hot iron had been thrust into her private parts."[35]

Just at this time, Governor Davis resigned, probably for reasons of health. For as noted earlier, "there was no fault to be found with him, except that he was imported from the east."[36] Davis was replaced by the highly popular local, George Law Curry, or "Young Curry," as he was known—due, according to Malcolm Clark, to his eagerness and impetuosity. The new governor sent out a call for two companies of volunteers to proceed to Fort Boise to punish the Snakes. But at Fort Vancouver, Captain Bonneville refused to provide arms and ammunition, saying that it was too late in the season to embark on a campaign. James Nesmith, the appointed commander of the volunteers, agreed, and the call for volunteers was rescinded. Some of the citizenry objected, but in the end the weather prevailed. Nonetheless, the Snake attack combined with the bad news from both the south and the coast made many people, including Palmer, wonder if they were not in for a general Indian war.

Palmer's first chore on returning to Dayton was to write up his annual report for Commissioner Manypenny. This consisted of accounts of his journeys to the south, the coast, and the Klamath region. In each, he described the character of the country and the condition of the Indians. He included R.R. Thompson's annual report for the upper Columbia, which he had not visited, and a summary of his own surveys and dealings in the Willamette Valley. He made only two recommendations. First, a military post should be established on the Boise River to ensure the safety of the emigrants. Second, a reserve should be established in the Klamath region. Palmer concluded his report with a statement of what he believed Oregon Indian policy should be:

> Treaties for the purchase of the country of the more numerous and warlike tribes of this Territory, and the removal and concentration of all at suitable and convenient points, where the agents of the government can watch over, instruct, and protect them, and thus convince them of our humane intentions, can alone secure peace while they exist, or elevate them in the social scale above their present savage state. When thus collected and colonized, Congress should enact a wise and equitable, yet stringent code of laws for their government, at first to be wholly administered by citizens of the United States. But as the Indians should advance in civilization and intelligence, let the administration of the laws pass into their own hands; and so also the other powers of government, until they should at length be vested with power to enact and administer, under the constitution of the United States, all their local and municipal regulations.[37]

On 12 August 1854, Palmer was gratified to receive from Manypenny the authority to begin the very measures that he had proposed. He was finally authorized to negotiate treaties of peace and cession and was given funds to initiate the process. The authority brought with it, however, certain stipulations: annuities had to be paid in goods and services, and the payments must be terminated after twenty years. Also, reservations were only to encompass those tribes that were compatible in their customs and interests.

Palmer was greatly encouraged. "The next two years," he judged, "will be an important period in the history of our Indian relations in as much as . . . within that period we will be able to extinguish indian title to all the lands in Oregon and make permanent provisions for their colonization, civilization and enlightenment."[38] As always, Palmer was optimistic. Nonetheless, it remained to be seen whether his new powers had come in time to avert a general Indian war.

At this time, the Oregon superintendency went through another important change. Three agents resigned, and four new men were appointed. Parrish gave as his reason lack of funds with which to carry out his duties—although Palmer believed that "his private affairs appear to interfere materially with the duties of an agent," perhaps a reference to Parrish's wife, who suffered from "brain fever." Martin resigned because he declined to move from the Umpqua to the Rogue River, the place to which Palmer had removed the Umpqua agency, but he also resigned for what Palmer called "other causes"—probably the Dick Johnson affair.[39] Poor health appears to have been the cause of Philip Thompson's resignation, for he died soon after. All, however, were embittered because of their very difficult position in having to mediate between whites and Indians and the woefully inadequate compensation they received for their efforts.

To replace these men, Palmer appointed Ben Wright, Nathan Olney, Edwin P. Drew, and an additional agent, Absalom J. Hembree. Only Ben Wright's appointment was controversial: it was charged that in the autumn of 1852 he and a group of volunteers under his command had invited two Modocs to their camp and then murdered them. That Palmer should have appointed such a man as an Indian agent seems most curious, indeed. C.S. Drew, a sometime volunteer officer and hardly a partisan of Palmer's, denied the truth of the charge against Wright in his 1860 report to Congress:

> The appointment of Wright, at the instance, and during the administration of Indian Superintendent Palmer, whose sympathy for, and confidence in, the Indians was unlimited, is the most positive proof that the charge so often reiterated against him is entirely destitute of any foundation whatever. Instances are known where Superintendent Palmer took the word of a lying, thieving Indian in preference to that of one of his agents, whose statement could have been corroborated by the oaths of numerous respectable witnesses. Is it a supposable case, then, that he would have been instrumental in getting the appointment to an agency of a man who treacherously murdered Indians by the wholesale? Certainly not. *[40]

What Palmer himself believed is suggested in a letter to Lane on 30 December 1854: "It is evident when he is at war with Indians he is a perfect *Anthony Wayne* of a fellow and feels warranted in playing their [the Indians'] own game." In any event, Palmer was convinced that Wright would make a good agent, and evidence suggests that Wright as agent exhibited no hostility toward Indians but, indeed, the reverse. "After he became Indian Agent," wrote Rodney Glisan, a United States Army doctor in the region at the time, "his sympathies seemed to lean, if either way, in favor of the Indian, and against the white man. He stood like a wall of adamant between the two races in their numerous quarrels."[41]

*Drew was not alone in his view of Palmer as too sympathetic to the Indians, for even Palmer's friend, Lane, accused him of too often taking the Indians' side.

Upon appointment of the new agents, Palmer sent letters of instruction to each. The letter to Olney is a good example of the evenhandedness he expected of his agents, here referring to the Ward massacre by the Snakes in August:

> The impunity with which these savages have for years robbed and murdered defenseless immigrants has doubtless impressed the opinion that we are weak or indifferent to the wrongs inflicted on our citizens and has rendered them *more* insolent and audacious. They will therefor need signal and terrible proof of their mistakes in this regard, and this should by no means fail to be accomplished. But at the same time all un-necessary sacrifice of human life should be avoided, and to this end you will use all possible effort to ascertain and discriminate between hostile and friendly bands. The punishment inflicted should plainly appear to be the dictate of stern justice rather than revenge . . . . Women and children should if possible be saved that they may at the same time be impressed with the sense of our power and humanity. Where the innocent and the guilty are punished alike, there is no stimulus to good conduct but the reverse.[42]

Remembering the time, place, and circumstances, Palmer's statement, however sententious, is one of remarkable restraint. After all, this was the second major massacre of whites by Indians with which he had been closely associated. The killing of the Whitmans, the ravishment of some of the surviving women, and the war that followed had not been forgotten. Here now was fresh outrage. And it was personally brought home to Palmer by the fact that the young boy who was the sole survivor of the Snake massacre was put in his charge until such time as he could leave the boy with foster parents on the Umpqua.

PALMER BEGAN THIS SOUTHERN JOURNEY on 22 October. His general mission was to prevent an Indian war, but he had other, more specific, purposes as well. Congress had agreed to ratify Palmer's treaty with the Rogue and Cow Creek Indians, provided those tribes were prepared to confederate and share their reserve with other tribes. The reason for Washington's insistence on confederation of many tribes on one reserve was the resulting economy of administration and the fact that the settlers were opposed to a multitude of small reservations scattered about the countryside. Palmer's purpose was to convince the Rogue and Cow Creek Indians of the wisdom of Washington's policy.

Palmer's second charge was to negotiate treaties of cession with the other tribes of the south—the Shasta, Grave Creek, and Umpqua. Finally, he was bent on determining the truth of the continuing rumors concerning Samuel Culver, his agent in Jacksonville.

Palmer met with the Rogues on 15 November, and they reluctantly agreed to share the Table Rock reserve with other tribes. Two days later, he negotiated a treaty with the Shasta and the Grave Creek, who ceded their lands in return for various annuities and agreed to confederate with the Rogues at Table Rock. Then, on 29 November, he persuaded the tribes of the Umpqua River Valley to cede about seven thousand square miles in return for annuities of $140,000 and to confederate with the Cow Creek on a temporary reserve. Palmer hoped that, in time, this confederation could be moved to the Klamath region.

Palmer's achievement was considerable. He reported to Manypenny: "As with all tribes, they urge serious objections against leaving their accustomed haunts and evince great skill and cunning in meeting arguments designed to induce them to do so." But

> the reckless habits of a portion of the mining population from whom the natives
> have received so many severe chastisements and wrongs together [with the]
> prospects of being provided with a home, an asylum for their aged and infirm,
> protection for their women and children, as well as the prospects afforded by
> cultivating the soil, of an abundance to guard against hunger, induced the more
> conservative to listen favorably to our proposals.

Finally, "the proposal to establish schools and hospitals among them contributed very much to overcome their objections."[43]

These treaties, which were ratified in 1855, along with those concluded in 1853, effectively extinguished Indian land title in southern Oregon, except for a narrow area along the coast and a small, remote enclave of southern Molallas on the western slopes of the Cascades. The principal dispute between whites and Indians was to be resolved, at last. However, a large number of Indians still inhabited the countryside and had to be brought to the reserve; for as long as they were off reservation land, the possibility of hostility between them and the whites loomed large. Settlers on the Coquille had complained to Palmer: "They were roaming over our settlement hunting and being insolent . . . like a wandering bunch of Arabs subsisting upon the inheritance of others."[44] In addition, Palmer believed from information picked up in Jacksonville that whites were encouraging dissension among the Indians and, he suspected, providing them with weapons. These whites apparently hoped that the Indians would carry out the process of extermination against each other, thereby saving them the trouble. In any event, it was essential in Palmer's view to get all the southern Oregon Indians on the reserves as soon as possible. But here he was faced with a dilemma.

As early as September, Palmer had been informed by sources he considered trustworthy that Samuel Culver, his agent in Jacksonville, was not carrying out his duties. It was charged that Culver was spending more time on his mining claim than on the reserve. Far more serious, he was accused of growing hay on the reserve and pocketing the proceeds from its sale. "Too often," Palmer wrote to George Manypenny, "have persons appointed to office on this coast appeared to regard their place as a sinecure, and official duties of secondary importance." In this case, he was particularly angry because of the fact that if the Indians had benefited from the hay themselves, it would have helped reconcile them to the reservation, and furthermore, this benefit would have served as an example to nontreaty Indians. As he informed Culver, "at this critical time too . . . when the utmost caution and vigilance on the part of the agent is required to prevent the breaking out of a war that must result in their extermination renders your course the more to be regretted."[45] Accordingly, Palmer had suspended Culver until he could go to Jacksonville and investigate the matter.

On arriving in Jacksonville, Palmer heard from a committee of citizens that Culver was innocent. Although Palmer was convinced of Culver's guilt, he had to admit that the evidence against him was not conclusive. There was another consideration as well: Palmer needed Culver to bring the Indians in to the reservations. The matter was further complicated when some important Democrats threatened to call a meeting to denounce the suspension of Culver, which, after all, had brought dishonor on a fellow Democrat. Palmer does not appear to have given a fig for the threat. However, because of the slim evidence against Culver and in particular because of his need of Culver to bring the Indians in, Palmer reinstated him as agent.

Culver's return to grace was brief. Apparently, Palmer found new evidence of Culver's wrongdoing, for several weeks later he fired the agent for good. Among other things, Culver's "throwing himself on his dignity with his lofty mien toward all whom he regards as his inferiors unfits him for an agent." And finally, "he has really been the agent of a set of intriguing politicians rather than an agent to the Indians."[46] Palmer was probably referring to Culver's family connection with Judge Pratt, who was seeking to replace Lane as territorial delegate. In any event, the hay, the pride, the politics—it was all too much. It was politics rather than hay, however, that was at the heart of the matter, and for that reason, Palmer had not heard the last of Samuel Culver and the "intriguing politicians."

Before departing for the valley, Palmer saw Lane's old friend Chief Joe. He was dying. Barely able to speak and weeping, the chief told Palmer that his wife, two of his daughters, and an adopted son had died, that his tribe had deserted him, and that he longed for death. His lament was a kind of metaphor for the tribe itself. In 1852, the census had counted 1,154 Rogues; now, two years later, there were only about 500 left.

PALMER REACHED SALEM in the first week of December and found the town in turmoil. The legislature was again in session, and two issues in particular divided its bellicose members: the location of the capital and voting procedures. Now that at long last the statehouse was almost completed, a combination— or perhaps a collusion—of Jackson and Benton county members had mustered enough votes to have the capital moved to Corvallis. This would be the third site occupied by Oregon's restless seat of government.*

As for the second issue concerning voting procedures, the "Salem Clique," that is, the wing of the Democratic party controlled by Asahel Bush, editor of the *Oregon Statesman*, desired a *viva voce* vote instead of the customary secret ballot. The *viva voce* vote required every man to publicly announce his choices so that the whole world would know where he stood on both candidates and issues. The secret ballot, argued its opponents, was the vote of a coward, not of a man. However, the true reason for the movement for the *viva voce* lay elsewhere.

The secret Know Nothing party appeared to be gaining in membership. As mentioned earlier, the Know Nothings were pledged to oppose for public office any man who was not a native-born American, particularly if he happened to be a Roman Catholic. For this reason, the Know Nothings had much support in Oregon from the remnant of the Mission party, who still held the Whitman massacre to have been instigated by the priests. In addition, however, the Know Nothings also hoped to wrest power from the grasping hands of editor Bush and his Salem Clique, but they wished to do so without revealing themselves, that is, by way of the customary secret ballot. The *viva voce* meant, as Bancroft put it, "a severe ordeal for some who were not ready openly to part company with the democracy." The Whig *Oregonian* was, of course, enraged:

* *The quid in this quid pro quo was that Jackson County would get the proposed university. "It was not even pretended that the money to be spent at Jacksonville would benefit those it was intended to educate, but only that it would benefit Jackson county," wrote Bancroft, adding that it was planned to use the first installment of money to build a place of repose for the Jackson County politicians, that is, a courthouse. See Bancroft, History of Oregon, vol. 2, 351.*

> They [the Salem Clique] have said, in plain terms, that "*we* are your owners," and *we* will drive you with the *viva voce* system, as we drive cattle into the corral with the *lash*. Bare your backs, therefore, and receive the blows patiently, ye followers of Oregon democracy. Let there be no writhing, squirming, or twisting; come up to the yoke and receive it; it was made for you—to "*crush out*" the spirit of liberty of voting for whom you please.[47]

The Know Nothings were not alone in running afoul of the Salem Clique and the Democratic party leadership. On returning to Dayton, Palmer found that he, too, was deeply in trouble with the party due to his firing of Culver; for indeed, the Culver affair was far from over. In fact, it was rumored that, because of the firing, there was a movement to remove Palmer from the office of superintendent of Indian affairs.

In his 30 December letter to Lane, Palmer reported that many "apparently" sincere friends believed he had acted hastily in discharging Culver. "Your course," he quoted them as saying, "is distracting the Democratic Party," to which Palmer replied:

> Very well, if the party is to be sustained by fraud and corruption, the sooner we are broken down and beaten the better for the country; the Democratic party needs no such props. As a party we cannot maintain our position by attempting to screen one of its members in the perversion of his official functions either for pecuniary interests or the advancement of favorites.[48]

On this ominous note—ominous for Palmer as well as for the Indians of Oregon—did the year end.

EIGHT

Know Nothings

EIGHTEEN FIFTY-FIVE BEGAN with a renewed attack on the Know Nothings. On 2 January, Asahel Bush published a long and scolding "exposé" of what the *Statesman* liked to call "the midnight order" and "the disciples of the mask and dark lantern."* One of those accused of membership in the organization was none other than the superintendent of Indian affairs. From what is known of the public life of Joel Palmer—and a great deal is known—this alleged membership in the Know Nothings is considered one of the few blemishes on an otherwise blameless career. Thus, it warrants some consideration. On 1 January, James Nesmith wrote to Joseph Lane:

* *The Know Nothings did go to absurd lengths in their concern for secrecy. Persons could signal their membership to each other not only by a special handshake but also by "placing the little finger of the right hand in the ear, and scratching the same."* See *Statesman*, 26 April 1854.

> General Joel Palmer, the man who was *once* our mutual friend, and who I would have defended under all circumstances, has turned a traitor to his party, his friends, his God, and his country; by takeing the damnable oath to support, vote for, and defend, the midnight conclave. Besides he has used his position to build up the accursed order. He has kept a Whig Know Nothing [Cris Taylor] in his office ever since he has held it at 5 dollars per day, besides he recently entered into an arrangement to expel Mr Geary his chief clerk who is a good democrat, and a warm friend of yours from his office and appoint [A.E.] Bonnell a Whig and the leader of the Know Nothings in his place. These facts have been

recently developed. Every democrat who has heard of it, curses the traitor long loud and deep, and pray that he may speadily be hurled from the place which he has so effectively disgraced.[1]

Palmer answered the charge on 14 January in a letter to Lane. Although candor was one of Palmer's signal characteristics, he could, on occasion, be oblique, if not disingenuous. His letter to Lane was both. "Sometime since," he wrote, "I learned that an effort would be made by Pratt through his and Culver's friends to cause my removal."[2] Palmer was referring in part to Pratt's desire to replace Lane as territorial delegate; thus, it was to Pratt's and Culver's advantage to discredit Palmer because he was Lane's principal supporter. Palmer told Lane that several legislators had signed a petition asking President Pierce to remove him from office because of his association with the Know Nothings. The real reason, Palmer claimed, was his sacking of Culver and his loyalty to Lane.

There is no doubt that Judge Pratt was unhappy that Palmer had fired his brother-in-law. There is also no doubt that Pratt and other Democrats found it unpardonable that Palmer should have attacked a member of his own party; some even charged that he was "destroying the Democratic Party."[3] But the Salem Clique sincerely believed Palmer was a Know Nothing, and it would appear from Palmer's own words and other evidence that they were right.

After again asserting that Culver and Pratt were the vipers of the plot, Palmer went on to give this curious and equivocal account of his relations with the Know Nothings:

> I know but little about this order, and that little has given me no very exalted opinion of it. I have felt there was a necessity for some counteracting influence against foreign combinations and powers in our little Oregon as I have and still believe they wield an undue influence over the acts of many of our leading men, and I feel willing at all times and under all circumstances to join in any legal and proper means to lessen that influence and break up such dependencies. But I at the same time am satisfied that the danger to be apprehended from that influence is not such as to warrant the resort to midnight conclaves and secret organisations. There has undoubtedly been very many persons entered this order with good and pure motives, others from mere curiosity to ascertain its objects . . . . I am not ready to pronounce a man a criminal who for the purpose of knowing something of an order that appears shaking the foundations of former political organizations, and who upon stepping upon the first round of the lader cries hold.[4]

Could it have been Palmer himself who placed his foot on the first round of the ladder and then cried hold?

In early April, James Nesmith, who was now a u.s. marshal, wrote Judge Deady regarding Palmer and the Know Nothings. Although Nesmith was a "monumental he-gossip," in Malcolm Clark's words, Deady had no reason to doubt his veracity in this case. "He [Palmer] reluctantly admits having joined the damned Nothings," Nesmith wrote, "but says that was only prompted by *curiosity* and that he *now* has no sympathy with them and won't be drummed out of the Democratic Party. I guess that he is sorry that he was found out." Nesmith also frankly admitted that when the Salem Clique found Palmer enrolled in that "hostile organization they concluded to let him *drop*."[5]

That Palmer should have been associated, if temporarily, with the Know Nothings is plausible. His background together with the nativistic program of the Know Nothings made him a likely recruit. Palmer's family had been in the United States for two centuries, and he had grown up in northern New York where, in the 1820s, "foreigners" were practically unknown. Similarly, the Whitewater Valley, when he went there to live in the 1830s, knew almost nothing of aliens and their ways. Then, in the 1840s, there came a change. Immigration to the United States increased enormously, and the quiet, homogeneous, little Quaker valley was suddenly deluged with Irish and German Catholic immigrants come to build the canals. They were different: in religion, in manner, in customs and beliefs, in speech and costume—in almost everything. And there were thousands of them. The established, indigenous, Anglo-Saxon, Protestant population felt threatened, particularly by Catholicism, which these sons of the Revolution associated with Old World absolutism. The first Catholic church opened in the Whitewater Valley in 1845, the year Palmer left—a coincidence? Perhaps, perhaps not.

Finally, there is a tradition in the Palmer family that Joel Palmer remained hostile to the Roman Catholic church all his days. Catholics and the lingering influence of the Hudson's Bay Company were no doubt in his mind when he wrote Lane of "foreign combinations and powers in our little Oregon," and which he vowed to "join in any legal and proper means to lessen that influence and break up such dependencies." But he added, "I at the same time am satisfied that the danger to be apprehended from that influence is not such as to warrant the resort to midnight conclaves and secret organisations."[6] In short, it is certainly possible that Palmer did place his foot on the first round of the Know Nothing ladder, but he may also have turned back. That first step, however, was not forgotten by the Democratic party. This, added to the fact that he supported Lane, made him a marked man.

Palmer was not cowed by the outcry from his party. In a letter to William Martin, his former agent on the Umpqua, he urged Lane's reelection as delegate to Congress and then digressed to his own situation:

> I expect to be removed, the great men of the nation representing Salem Democracy have willed it and have sent on a strong petition asking my removal and of course it will be done. I have no regrets about it, the office has been offered without my asking and it is likely to be taken without consulting me and it will go unregreted. I have no desire for office and do not care a fig so far as my political standing is concerned but no man prizes more highly than myself the confidence and good will of my neighbors and citizens generally and I am willing to make any sacrifice on my part to obtain it, not for political distinction or for sake of office, but it is a consolation to reflect that a community regards a man for his goodness of heart and as an honest man. The spleen and spite of a few demagogical cracked brained politicians has no influence in causing me to lose slumber but if I believed a really good man suspected my correctness or doubted my motives it would give me pain. but enough of this. Let us buckle on our armor and do battle for old Jo.[7]

IN THE MEANTIME, both Whigs and Democrats were thrashing about in the results of the recently completed legislative session and the campaign for territorial delegate. The *viva voce* law had passed, to the discomfort of many who did not care to speak their minds, a situation that was to discomfit Oregonians for the next seventeen years. The capital was in fact moved to Corvallis, and editor Bush and his press with it. The editor, however, was not pleased with Corvallis society, "the most tickyasse, pickayune, grabbing people it was ever my lot to fall amongst." Money had gone to Jacksonville for the "university"—that is, the courthouse. The penitentiary remained in Portland, although the *Oregonian* urged that it be removed to the new capital to save the cost of transporting criminals—the Democrats in the legislature—to its dungeons. And once again, the legislature decided to ask the people if they cared to join the Union. This, of course, brought up the subject of slavery. In late spring, a group of free-soilers, concerned about the issue, met in Albany—"a collection of *old grannies*" and "nigger-struck *dames*" the *Statesman* called these founding members of the Republican party in Oregon.[8] In any event, the people once again declined to join the Union.

As for the campaign for territorial delegate, the contestants were Lane and former governor Gaines. Pratt, despite his machinations, had dropped by the wayside. Editor Dryer of the *Oregonian* was, of course, a supporter of Gaines, and in the manner of a militia boy standing on a stump to cock-a-doodle like a rooster and announce his readiness to "take on" anyone, Dryer offered to go anywhere and do battle, verbal or otherwise, for his candidate. In the end, it did come down to "otherwise" with respect to the candidates themselves. In The Dalles, debating on the platform, Lane called Gaines a damned liar, and Gaines, sometimes referred to by Democrats as a "petticoat," socked Lane in the jaw. Political life in early Oregon may have lacked decorum, but it did not lack vitality.

IN THE MIDST OF THE TURMOIL, Palmer, uncertain how long he would remain in office, attempted to carry out his duties. News from both the Umpqua and the Rogue was bad. Dr. G.H. Ambrose, Culver's replacement on the Rogue, reported that not enough seed had been sown the previous season at Table Rock, which meant the Indians would starve if they were not permitted to leave the reserve to search for food. The local whites strongly opposed their release and refused to sell seed to Ambrose for the coming year because the government had not yet paid them for the seed sold the year before. Palmer wrote that he was completely without funds and could do nothing. The reason, he believed, was "the movement of leading men in this Territory to cause my removal."[9]

Other matters at Table Rock also distressed Palmer. Earlier in the year, he had—in accordance with the Table Rock treaty with the Rogues—appointed a commission to determine the compensation due the settlers for their losses in the Rogue River disturbances of 1853. The commission now recommended a compensation of forty-six thousand dollars, about a third of which was to be deducted from the sum to be paid the Rogues for their land. Palmer considered some of the settlers' claims "an outrage and a species of public plunder,"[10] and he must have felt deeply the bitter irony that at this time when the Rogues were starving, they were obliged to pay a portion of these unjust claims.

There was bad news as well from Ben Wright at Port Orford. The Crescent City Militia, commissioned by the state of California, was moving up the coast, killing Indians as they came—sixty so far, it was said—and intended to continue on into Oregon. Wright had warned the "exterminators" that if they entered Oregon, the consequences would be most "fearful."[11]

However, Wright also relayed some good news. He had jailed and put on bread and water two whites who had molested Indian women. Upon the molesters' release, Wright wrote, "they came out docile."[12] This may have been one of the first instances of whites punished for mistreating Indians.

A short time later, news of a similar nature arrived from Agent Ambrose at Jacksonville. A white who had killed an Indian in a fight had been sentenced to two years in jail for manslaughter. Also, a farmer at Winchester, whose calves had been killed by an Indian, wrote Palmer that his neighbors had sought to take revenge on the Indian but he had persuaded them to leave the matter to the courts. At last it seemed that at least some whites wanted to give Indians the protection of the law.

Palmer's most satisfying accomplishment during the winter and spring of 1855 was to confederate the Willamette Valley tribes, concluding treaties that extinguished all Indian land titles in the valley and designating a 125-mile stretch of coast for their reserve. For now, he had determined that it was impractical to move the Indians in the Willamette Valley east of the Cascades. Palmer was also encouraged by the arrival in late March of a draft from Washington for three thousand dollars. Due to a shortage of coin, however, Palmer had to sail to San Francisco and the mint to get the money. On his return in early May, he began preparing for one of the most important episodes of his career.

NINE

Walla Walla

S HALL IT BE WITH OUTRAGE and blood, or with peace and good will?" Thus had Palmer written Manypenny in December 1853, referring to the settlement of the Columbia plateau.[1] Again and again, both before and after that date, he had pleaded the urgent necessity for treaties with the tribes of the region. Now, at last, it appeared that the time had come and that it might not be too late for "peace and good will."

So far, few whites had settled on the plateau, and the Indians' root and berry grounds and fishing stations were still intact. Also, the few settlers who were there carried on a satisfactory trade with the Indians in horses and cattle. Still, and with good reason, the Indians feared increased settlement. After all, they knew what had happened in the eastern United States, in the Willamette Valley, and at their own Wascopam, which Lewis and Clark had noted as the Indians' great trading center. Now, with a garrison and a steeple and called The Dalles, no Indian was welcome in it. These were the fears that in the spring of 1853 had led a delegation of Yakima, Cayuse, and Walla Walla to call on Maj. Benjamin Alvord at The Dalles garrison and tell him that they "did not object to persons merely hunting, or those wearing swords, but they dreaded the approach of the whites with ploughs, axes and shovels in their hands."[2]

And axes and shovels were precisely what they were threatened with. Isaac I. Stevens, governor of Washington Territory and also its superintendent of Indian affairs, had appeared the previous year in their lands with magic glasses and tripodal sticks to trace a fateful course for what, with a startling abruptness, would soon round the bend of history—what Nathaniel Hawthorne a few years earlier had called "the long shriek, harsh, above all other harshness," that is, the railroad.[3] Stevens, in addition to his other duties, had been commissioned to survey a northern route for a transcontinental line to end at Puget Sound. Anxious that his route be chosen—three others were under consideration as well—it was imperative that the question of Indian lands be settled. Accordingly, in January 1855, Stevens wrote Palmer about the matter and also discussed their shared responsibility for tribes that lived in both Oregon and Washington.

Through their agents, both men set out to determine the willingness of the tribes to attend the great council proposed for May at Walla Walla and which would settle by treaty the disposition of their lands. Palmer instructed Thompson at The Dalles to urge the John Day, Deschutes, Wasco, and what was left of the Cayuse to attend the council, for "it is very questionable whether our people can be much longer restrained from making settlements in that country." But the John Day, Deschutes, and Wasco had gone to the mountains to gather roots, and the Cayuse, understandably, were not particularly receptive. One Cayuse chief, Thompson, reported

> was aware we knew more than they did, but that their knowledge was suffi-
> cient for them. They knew the names of the earth, sky and things as they were
> and did not desire to change them if they could. They did not ask the whites for
> their laws or superior knowledge. All they wanted was to be left alone.[4]

Meanwhile, James Doty, Stevens' secretary, and Andrew Bolon, his Indian agent, approached the Indians on the Washington side of the river. The Cayuse were uncooperative there as well, and Kamiakin of the Yakima was equivocal, to say the least. But Yellow Serpent of the Walla Walla and Lawyer* of the Nez Perce agreed to attend the council; both appeared ready to sell their lands.

* Lawyer's name apparently derived from the belief that this Nez Perce favored diplomacy over war.

In general, however, the prospects for the council were uncertain. The previous year, various chiefs of the Columbia tribes had gathered in alarm at the Grande Ronde River to discuss how to keep the whites out. Major Rains at The Dalles, like his predecessor, Alvord, feared resistance. Father Ricard of the Yakima Mission reported that there were plans to kill the council whites before they could assemble. Stevens admitted that "there were unquestionably a great many malcontents in each tribe," and even Palmer—so anxious for so long to at last conclude these treaties—apparently had second thoughts. Stevens reported: "At this time [mid-May] the Oregon officers expected little from the council, and evidently believed that the whole thing was premature and ill-advised." And indeed, Palmer subsequently advised George Manypenny that "the signing of the treaty was adverse to the will of the Nation, as expressed prior to the delegations coming to the council." Still, matters went ahead. *Isaac I. Stevens: Young Man in a Hurry* was the title Kent Richards gave his 1979 biography of Stevens; the Walla Walla Council is an instance of the title's aptness. For Stevens was determined. The malcontents "might embolden all not well disposed, and defeat the negotiations. Should this spirit be shown, they must be seized; the well affected would then govern in the deliberations."[5]

PALMER LEFT FOR WALLA WALLA in mid-May, meeting Stevens at The Dalles. It took them three days to reach the council site, camping at night on the Deschutes, the John Day, and the Umatilla. The rivers were so high that supplies sometimes had to be transferred from the pack mules to canoes; in contrast, the land burned with heat, the sky an "intolerable glare," wrote Lawrence Kip, a young West Pointer who had gone along for the lark.[6] Arriving at their destination on the third day, the sky turned black and cracked with thunder, letting loose a tempest—which to some may have seemed an omen.

The council grounds were at Mill Creek, only six miles from the place of the Whitman massacre, now the site of Whitman College. The land lay empty then, a fan-shaped plain, bounded on either side by high, brown, barren hills, at its end the mass of the Blue Mountains slouched against the sky. The plain itself was palely green with spring, a darker green the long serpentines of cottonwood and willow which edged the meander of streams flowing across it. Kip could not get over how cold the nights, how hot the days, how magnificent the sunsets.

The first order upon arriving on 21 May was to set up quarters. The men built a log storehouse for the enormous quantity of foodstuffs brought along to feed the tribes: beef, potatoes, bacon, flour, coffee, and sugar. Then they constructed a long arbor roofed with boughs, beneath which forty to fifty chiefs would banquet, "so that, as in civilized lands, gastronomy might aid diplomacy," Hazard Stevens, Governor Stevens' son, later wrote.[7] In addition, a number of tents were erected, and a second arbor built for the deliberations. At the end of this first day, a message arrived from Yellow Serpent—whom the whites may have expected to receive them since this was his domain—to say that, because of the rain, he was remaining in his lodge.

Two days later, Lt. Archibald Gracie arrived with troopers from The

Dalles garrison. The whites were now fully assembled: Palmer and his staff of twelve, Stevens' staff of thirty-five, forty troopers, and several missionaries and settlers. Although five-sixths of the Indians invited to the council lived in Washington Territory, Palmer and Stevens held equal rank as the chief officers of the party. They were very different men.

Palmer, at forty-five, was a tall, strong man with an open, regular-featured face framed by a chinstrap of black whiskers and a full head of coarse, black hair. The eyes were small, unusually deep-socketed and flashing—usually with humor, sometimes anger—and though the mouth was firm and set, there was no hint of meanness or pique about it. Above all, it was the strong, big, straightforward face of a man who meant what he said. Stevens was seven years younger and slightly grotesque, a tiny man with a big head and a dragging limp. But it was a compelling face, darkly handsome and full of force, fine eyes, and in the play of face and eyes, a curious tension between anxiety and arrogance.

The two men were as different in background as they were in appearance. Stevens had grown up in Amherst, Massachusetts, in a family that had lived there since 1641. He had attended Philips Academy and then West Point, where he was graduated first in his class. From his appointment as a lieutenant in the engineers until he became governor and superintendent of Indian affairs, all of his experience had been as an engineer; Stevens tended perhaps to look on life as a machine and men its parts. Palmer's years as a canal builder gave him something in common with Stevens, but by and large, they had lived in very different worlds. This was particularly the case with respect to Indian affairs. Palmer had spent much of his life dealing with Indians; Stevens' first experience had occurred only a few months before when negotiating a treaty with the tribes of Puget Sound. An instance of his ignorance of Indian ways is reflected in one of his orders to Bolon, his agent. Bolon, when recognizing—though "appointing" might be the more accurate term—the chiefs and sub-chiefs of the various tribes, was to record the information on a special form and send a copy to Olympia, as though the ephemerality of Indian leadership could be arrested if put on paper, alphabetized, and filed.

WHILE WAITING FOR THE INDIANS to arrive, there was much in the way of commissary preparations—after all, literally thousands of Indians were expected—and also, much discussion of a particularly vexing question: which tribes should be combined and where and how large the reservation should be. In the midst of these unresolved matters, word came that the Nez Perce were arriving. To greet them, the Americans removed to a little knoll above the plain. Among the Americans was Stevens' son, Hazard, then thirteen. Some years later Hazard, writing his father's biography, remembered the arrival of the Nez Perce:

Soon their cavalcade came in sight, a thousand warriors mounted on fine horses and riding at a gallop, two abreast, naked to the breech-clout, their faces covered with white, red, and yellow paint in fanciful designs, and decked with plumes and feathers and trinkets fluttering in the sunshine. The ponies were even more gaudily arrayed, many of them selected for their singular color and markings, and many painted in vivid colors contrasting with their natural skins,—crimson slashed in broad stripes across white, yellow or white against black or bay; and with their free and wild action, the thin buffalo line tied around the lower jaw,—the only bridle, almost invisible,—the naked riders, seated as though grown to their backs, presented the very picture of the fabled centaurs. Halting and forming a long line across the prairie, they again advanced at a gallop still nearer, then halted, while the head chief, Lawyer, and two other chiefs rode slowly forward to the knoll, dismounted and shook hands with the commissioners, and then took post in rear of them. The other chiefs, twenty-five in number, then rode forward, and went through the same ceremony. Then came charging on at full gallop in single file the cavalcade of braves, breaking successively from one flank of the line, firing their guns, brandishing their shields, beating their drums, and yelling their war-whoops, and dashed in a wide circle around the little party on the knoll, now charging up as though to overwhelm it, now wheeling back, redoubling their wild action and fierce yells in frenzied excitement. At length they also dismounted, and took their stations in rear of the chiefs. Then a number of young braves, forming a ring, while others beat their drums, entertained the commissioners with their dances, after which the Indians remounted and filed off to the place designated for their camp.[8]

Later in the day Lawrence Kip, the young West Pointer, went off to pay a call on the Nez Perce. He was received by Lawyer, who showed him the wound in his side suffered a few years earlier in an encounter with the Blackfeet; he also showed Kip locks of Blackfoot hair, which Kip reported "he wore about him." That evening, the energetic Kip and Lieutenant Gracie entertained at dinner in their tent, a buffalo robe for their table, the food simple but enjoyed "with appetite which required no French sauces to provoke."[9]

The following day and despite the heavy rains, some thirty Nez Perce chiefs gathered beneath the arbor to dine, Palmer and Stevens in frock coats and stocks sitting tailor-fashion on blankets at either end. Each chief was served four pounds of beef, two pounds of potatoes, and half a pound of corn, all of which, according to Hazard Stevens, they "gorged like famished wolves."[10]

But Yellow Serpent was still absent and, furthermore, had sent a message that cast a shadow over the Americans' hospitality: he would prefer on coming to bring his own provisions. When the Americans presented a gift of tobacco to the messenger to take to him, the messenger refused it and, according to Stevens, was heard to say as he rode away, "you will find out by and by why we won't take provisions."[11]

Relations with the Nez Perce, however, remained cordial, and that evening young Kip again visited Lawyer. He found the chief reading the New Testament, wearing a stovepipe hat circled with ostrich plumes, and posing for Gustavus Sohon, a German artist on Stevens' staff.

The following day, Doty heard rumors that the Walla Walla, Cayuse, and Yakima had combined and were determined to oppose the treaty. However, that evening several hundred Cayuse and Yakima arrived, and though "whooping and screaming like deamons," some of the Cayuse chiefs condescended to shake hands with the whites. But that was all. They refused to smoke, and in a manner the whites no doubt would have described as "haughty," they rode off almost immediately to their camp, a mile across the plain, behind a serpentine of cottonwood.[12]

That the Cayuse were deeply distrustful of the whites' intentions is certain. Only a month before, Agent Thompson had written Palmer that the Cayuse feared for their country, feared that the whites "would put it on their backs and carry it off."[13]

The next morning, the whites rode over in the rain to the Nez Perce camp, where Christian members of the tribe were holding Sabbath services, and a chief was delivering a sermon on the Ten Commandments. Young Kip, inquisitive as always, elected to visit the Cayuse instead. Their activities were of a very different nature, "the young warriors lounging about their lodges, preparing their arms or taking care of their horses." Indeed, that evening, there was much discussion among the whites as to the disposition of the Cayuse and Yellow Serpent's troubling absence. Disturbing, too, was the word from some priests who had arrived the day before from the Yakima Mission. According to the priests, the Yakima chief, Kamiakin, was not well disposed toward the council, and they quoted him as saying, "if the governor speaks hard, I will speak hard, too."[14]

From the beginning, Kamiakin had held himself aloof from the Americans. "A tall, large man, very dark, with a massive, square face, and a grave, reflective look," he lived near present-day Yakima, where he had extensive, well-tended farms and large horse and cattle herds. He impressed everyone who met him. Stevens found him to be a combination "of the panther and the grizzly bear. His countenance has an extraordinary play, one moment in frowns, the next in smiles, flashing with light and black as Erebus the same instant . . . . He talks mostly in his face, and with his hands and arms."[15]

The previous month, when Doty and Bolon had called upon Kamiakin to discuss the council, he had at first refused to see them. When he finally did so, he refused the presents they offered him, saying that he had never accepted as much as a grain of wheat from the Americans, and for the very good reason that "presents" were later interpreted by the Americans as payment for the purchase of Indian lands.

Despite this hostility to the whites, Kamiakin finally did appear. According to Dr. Lansdale, one of Stevens' staff, Kamiakin was "moderately friendly but still reserved." Now, too, Yellow Serpent arrived. Though stating his friendly feelings for Americans, the whites, in fact, found him querulous. He requested that an additional translator be assigned to the council, "that they might know they translated truly." When he saw Nez Perce boys in the Americans' camp, he said, "I do not wish my boys running around the camp of the whites like these young men." Stevens' impressions of Yellow Serpent were mixed: "He was well advanced in years, and somewhat childish and capricious in small things, but his form was as erect, his mind as firm, and his authority as unimpaired as ever."[16]

BY 29 MAY, MOST OF THE EXPECTED INDIANS had arrived, and accordingly, at two that afternoon, the council was formally opened. Joel Palmer and Isaac Stevens sat beneath the arbor with their secretaries, agents, and interpreters, while the Indians gathered in a vast semicircle before them. The number of Indians is in dispute, with one source claiming two thousand, another saying one thousand, and Kip estimating five thousand. Whatever the actual number, there was a significant representation of the region's population of about fourteen thousand Indians. This may not have pleased Stevens, who preferred dealing with tribal notables. It is possible that he either was ignorant of or disregarded the Indian belief in communal ownership of the land and that, in theory at least, no chief or group of chiefs had the power to sign away what belonged to all.

After the smoking of pipes, Stevens introduced the interpreters and asked the Indians if they were satisfied with those chosen. They were, though Stickus for the Cayuse admitted that "there may be some words hard for them to make us understand."[17] Next, Stevens announced that the chiefs were the guests of General Palmer and himself and that there were provisions sufficient for all. But Young Chief of the Cayuse refused, saying that they had adequate provisions for themselves and for the Yakima as well.

By now, it had begun to rain, and so the council adjourned until the following day or whenever the weather might clear. The delay may have discomfited the anxious Americans but not the Indians. "We will talk slow," said Young Chief, "not all in one day. No snow falls at this season of the year."[18] And slow it would be, for the council would last for two more difficult weeks.

The following day, the weather did clear, and all assembled again. The two commissioners sat on a bench at the entrance to the arbor, while the Indians in a great circle sat on the ground before them, "reposing on the bosom of their Great Mother," Kip reported. A Nez Perce chief, Eagle-From-The-Light, reposed upon the pelt of an enormous grizzly bear, the teeth and claws arranged to face the frock-coated commissioners. "It [the grizzly] tells me everything," the chief informed Stevens.[19]

Palmer began the session, addressing the Indians as "my friends." This form of address, which he used alternately with "my brothers," reflects the difference in attitude Palmer and Stevens brought to the council, for the previous day—and through most of the council—Stevens had addressed the Indians as "my children." Palmer, as if to correct and downplay the condescension, stated at the outset, "we both come here to talk to you as men and not as boys." He then introduced Governor Stevens, who again greeted the Indians as "my children."[20]

For the next several days, Stevens and Palmer held forth on a variety of matters. Stevens, after thanking the Indians for their earlier hospitality to him and his survey party, stated that history had shown that white men and red men could not live together in peace. For this reason, the Great Father, Andrew Jackson, had moved the Indians to a reservation in a "fair land" west of the Mississippi where, Stevens implied, the Indians had lived happily ever after. Thus did Stevens come to the issue: "Now we want you to agree with us to such a state of things; you to have your tract . . . the rest to be the Great Father's for his white children."[21]

Palmer also resorted to history, although somewhat more accurately: "Three hundred and sixty years shows us that the white man and the red man cannot live happily together." He also reminded them that "their customs and mode of life were different they did not understand each other." What could be done in the present circumstances?

> If there were no other whites coming into the country we might get along in peace; You may ask, why do they come? Can you stop the waters of the Columbia river from flowing on its course? Can you prevent the wind from blowing? Can you prevent the rain from falling? Can you prevent the whites from coming? You are answered No! Like the grasshoppers on the plains; some years there will be more come than others, you cannot stop them. Our cheif cannot stop them, we cannot stop them.

And furthermore, Palmer went on to argue,

> this land was not made for you alone, the air that we breathe, the waters that we drink, was made for all. The fish that come up the rivers, and the beasts that roam through the forests and the plains, and the fowls of the air, were alike made for the white man and the red man . . . . Who can say that this is mine and that is yours.

In short, the whites were coming and had a right to come, but so far they were few, so "now while there is room to select for you a home where there are no white men living let us do so."[22]

Palmer concluded by listing for the Indians the goods and services the government would provide them: blankets and clothing, hatchets and hoes, shops and mills, doctors and teachers, millers and mechanics, and a variety of other benefits. "You can rely on all its [the treaty's] provisions being carried out strictly."[23] Alvin Josephy, in *The Nez Perce Indians and the Opening of the Northwest*, stated that Palmer's promise to the Indians has never been forgotten because of its falsity. But it is impossible to determine to what extent this was guile on Palmer's part, to what extent optimism—probably a measure of both. In general, Palmer kept his promises. It was noted earlier that at the beginning of his life in Oregon he had been asked by the Cayuse chief Tamsucky to bring him red velvet from the States and that, in fact, he had done so. Throughout his career as superintendent and later as Indian agent at Siletz, he battled to provide the Indians with those goods and services stipulated in the treaties. Palmer was not entirely without guile, but in the giving of his word he was rarely duplicitous.

THE INDIANS SAID VERY LITTLE during the first days of the council. When they finally spoke, they listed four objections to the whites' proposals. First, they did not believe Stevens and Palmer, again and again expressing their distrust. "You have spoken in a round about way; speak straight . . . . You have spoken in a manner partly tending to Evil. Speak plain to us," Yellow Serpent demanded. Yellow Serpent also found it suspicious that the whites refused to hold council on Sunday, supposing that perhaps they were reluctant to lie on the Sabbath. "Why should you fear to speak on Sunday?" he asked. "Perhaps you have spoken straight, that your children will do what is right," said Kamiakin doubtfully. "I ask my friends to speak straight and plain to us," said Stickus. "Your words since you came here have been crooked," said Howlish Wompoon. "I wonder if we shall both tell the truth to each other," said Red Bear, stating perhaps more accurately than any the full "truth" of the matter.[24]

There was good reason for the Indians to doubt the commissioners. The past was filled with broken promises, and Stevens had most fatally begun the council with "crooked" words. Underestimating the Indians, he apparently believed he could gloss Andrew Jackson's transportation of the Cherokee, Creek, Seminole, Choctaw, and Chickasaw, but the Columbia Indians knew very well that this allegedly beneficent act had in fact been "a trail of tears" and the tribes' destination no "fair land." The Indians were not quite the "children" that Stevens fancied them to be.

The Indians' second concern was that the commissioners had not consulted them on the location of the reservations, had drawn up boundaries "without our having any voice in the matter," as Young Chief said.[25] The commissioners' intention, of course, was to remove the Indians from their ancestral lands—or portions of those lands—so as to reserve certain areas for the railroad and for the benefit of emigrating farmers. This is not to say that the needs of the Indians were overlooked, but certainly, they were secondary.

The Indians had good reason, of course, to fear that they would be forced to leave land that held great material and spiritual significance for them. Young Chief said, "that is what I love, the place to get our roots to live upon . . . . The salmon comes up the stream." Camatspelo put it even more graphically: "How do you show your pity by sending me and my children to a land where there is nothing to eat but wood?" But the other significance, the spiritual, appears to have been equally, if not more, important to them. This lay in their relationship to the land and in a manner almost entirely alien to the Americans. For one thing, the land contained the graves of their ancestors, their tie to the past and without which they would be alone in the present, a traumatic deprivation for any people. In a sense, it seemed to the Indians that the loss of their land left them without a future, too, for it was, as one Nez Perce said, "for those that come that we are speaking."[26]

Secondly, the Indians, as animists, believed every rock and tree of their homeland, every stream and lake, animal and bird—all things—were imbued with spirit, and thus, their land was literally alive to them, not dead matter. Accordingly, to leave these places, sanctified by both death and life, was a very different matter for them than for the whites leaving the pestilential river valleys of the border states where most of them, in any event, had not lived for long. To expect the whites to have understood this Indian symbiosis with the land would be to expect them to understand something they had not experienced.

But it is the Indians themselves who best expressed, and with the transcendence of great poetry, this identification between themselves and their land. Said Stickus:

> If your mothers were here in this country who gave you birth, and suckled you and while you were sucking some person came and took away your mother and left you alone and sold your mother, how would you feel then? This is our mother this country as if we drew our living from her. My friends all of this you have taken.

Said Young Chief:

> I wonder if this ground has anything to say: I wonder if the ground is listening to what is said. I wonder if the ground would come to life and what is on it; though I hear what this earth says, the earth says, God has placed me here. The Earth says, that God tells me to take care of the Indians on this earth: the Earth says to the Indians that stop on the Earth feed them right. God named the roots that he should feed the Indians on: the water speaks the same way: God says feed the Indians upon the earth; the grass says the same thing: feed the horses and cattle. The Earth and water and grass says God has given our names and we are told those names; neither the Indians or the Whites have a right to change those names: the Earth says, God has placed me here to produce all that grows upon me, the trees, fruit, etc. The same way the Earth says, it was from her man was made. God on placing them on the Earth desired them to take good care of the earth and do each other no harm.

Then, abruptly, and with an incongruity reminiscent of Lawyer's stovepipe hat encircled with ostrich plumes, Young Chief went on to say, "God said: You Indians who take care of a certain portion of the country should not trade it off unless you get a fair price."[27] This, perhaps, is what the anthropologists mean when they speak of "a culture in transition."

Perhaps the most moving declaration came from the Yakima chief Owhi:

> God gave us the day and night, the night to rest in, and the day to see, and that as long as the earth shall last, he gave us the morning with our breath; and so he takes care of us on this earth and here we have met under his care. In the earth

before the day or the day before the earth. God was before the earth, the heavens were clear and good and all things in the heavens were good. God looked one way then the other and named our lands for us to take care of. God made the other. We did not make the other, we did not make it, he made it to last forever. It is the earth that is our parent or it is God is our elder brother. This leads the Indian to ask where does this talk come from that you have been giving us. God made this earth and it listens to him to know what he would decide. The Almighty made us and gave us breath; we are talking together and God hears all that we say today. God looks down upon his children today as if we were all in one body. He is going to make one body of us; we Indians present have listened to your talk as if it came from God.

God named this land to us that is the reason I am afraid to say anything about this land . . . . I am afraid of the Almighty that is the reason of my hearts being sad: this is the reason I cannot give you an answer. I am afraid of the Almighty. Shall I steal this land and sell it? or what shall I do? . . . Shall I give the lands that are part of my body and leave myself poor and destitute? . . . I cannot say, I am afraid of the Almighty.

I love my life is the reason why I do not give my lands away. I am afraid I would be sent to hell. I love my friends. I love my life, this is the reason why I do not give my lands away. [28]

The Indians' final concern was that they would be obliged to live with tribes other than their own, for the plan finally announced by Stevens on 4 June called for only two reservations, one for the Nez Perce and one for the Yakima. The Spokane, Cayuse, Walla Walla, and Umatilla were to live with the Nez Perce on the former, while the Palouse, Colville, Okanagan, Wenatchi, and Klickitat were to live with the Yakima on the latter. Official policy called for large reservations, and agents were urged to combine compatible tribes on one reservation. But the Cayuse, Walla Walla, and Umatilla did not want to share land with the Nez Perce.

Distrust of the whites, a profound reluctance to leave their land, and a disinclination to join with other tribes on a reservation seriously impeded the progress of the council. There was also simple confusion, an inability on the part of the Indians to fully grasp the commissioners' proposals. "I walk as it were in the dark," said Young Chief, "and cannot therefore take hold of what I do not see . . . . When I come to understand your proposition then I shall take hold." The following year, the Walla Walla and the Cayuse wrote Stevens: "All the promises and advises were as presents of curious objects sent us from a great distance of which we did not understand the real importance." [29]

AND SO, THE COUNCIL DRAGGED ON. The whites refused to parley on the Sabbath, while the Indians now and then called for a day of rest or feasting, wearied as they were by so much they did not understand. The weather, meanwhile, veered from one extreme to another. One morning the valley was an "oven," Kip wrote, while in the afternoon came a thunderstorm "worthy of the tropics."[30] And then there was the night when Mill Creek overflowed, threatening to flood the whole camp.

Despite the vagaries of both weather and proceedings, certain events occurred that helped determine the outcome of the council. On 3 June, the sixth day of the council, Lawyer, the Nez Perce chief, moved his entourage to the camp of the whites. His motives for doing so are not clear. Hazard Stevens later claimed that Lawyer wanted to protect the whites from a threatened massacre by the Cayuse and perhaps the Walla Walla and Yakima. Alvin Josephy believes the reverse—that Lawyer sought protection with the whites because of a plot by the Cayuse and others to kill him. Whatever the reason, the move made it clear that Lawyer and at least his faction of the Nez Perce were ready to accept the commissioners' proposals—or so it seemed at the time. Also, it signaled a rift between the Nez Perce and the other tribes, and indeed, from then on there was growing dissatisfaction on the part of the Cayuse, Walla Walla, and Yakima.

On preparing for the Walla Walla council, Stevens had instructed Agent Bolon to secure selection of a head chief for each tribe and in particular to choose those persons "who are best affected toward the American Government and people." But it had not worked out that way in every case, and the Americans grew more and more apprehensive. On the evening of the day after Lawyer's move, Kip observed that "until a late hour we heard from the Indian camps the sound of their singing and the beating of their drums, and could see the figures flit before the fire." The next night, Kip was even more uneasy: "There is evidently a more hostile feeling toward the whites getting up among some of the tribes." He reported that when he and Gracie went that night to the Cayuse camp to watch the races, the Cayuse braves tried to turn them back. "If . . . this hostile feeling at the Council increases, how long will it be before we have an actual outbreak?" Kip asked. And indeed, the whites were in a precarious position, for their force of one hundred would not endure for long if the several thousand Indians should turn on them.[31]

In the midst of these uncertainties, bad news arrived. Gold had been discovered north of the Walla Walla country in the Colville region. This meant that miners would soon be passing through the Indians' lands. Palmer made no bones about it: "among those who come there will be some bad people, those bad people will steal your horses and cattle."[32] It was more urgent than ever to settle the land question.

This urgency together with the growing hostility of the non-Nez Perce tribes finally forced the commissioners to make certain concessions. On 8 June, they announced that in deference to the wishes of the Cayuse, Walla Walla, and Umatilla, they would create a third and separate reservation. Furthermore, the annuities for each head chief of five hundred dollars per year for ten years would be extended to twenty years. Yellow Serpent was granted certain other privileges as well, and he agreed to the proposed terms. Young Chief also appeared ready, if reluctant, to accept the commissioners' proposals. Kamiakin and the Yakima, however, remained dissatisfied.

Into this impasse, and greatly complicating it, rode Looking Glass, a Nez Perce who for some time had disputed the paramount chieftainship with Lawyer. Looking Glass had first heard of the council when passing through the Bitterroot Valley. In his seventies at the time, he had immediately struck out with twenty of his braves, riding three hundred miles, sometimes through shoulder-high snow, arriving at the council grounds seven days later—furious and flourishing a Blackfoot scalp. "My people, what have you done?" he cried, still in his saddle. "While I was gone, you have sold my country."[33]

Thus had Looking Glass "kicked the fat into the fire," as Dr. Lansdale put it. The commissioners adjourned the council until the following day, and that evening, there was much discussion in the white camp as to whether Looking Glass would oppose the treaty. There was also much excitement in the Nez Perce camp, where Kip saw Looking Glass' braves "dressed in buffalo skins, painted and decorated in the most fantastic style . . . exhibiting themselves as much as possible and singing songs in honor of their exploits."[34]

The next day, the excitement carried over into what James Doty called "a stormy session." The storm began with Looking Glass. "Why do you want to separate my children and scatter them all over the country? I do not go into your country and scatter your children in every direction." But Looking Glass' principal concern was that the proposed Nez Perce reservation be extended farther west. Palmer, beginning to lose patience, replied: "If we change the line to where he says he would have to stay here two or three days more to arrange the paper. We are all tired . . . . Shall we say one thing today and another thing tomorrow?" But Looking Glass was obdurate: "I want you to talk plain just like the light." Palmer reminded the Indians that the government was giving back to the Nez Perce in the form of a reservation most of the land it was buying from them. Looking Glass still refused to accede, and Palmer finally lost all patience. "We did not come here to talk like boys . . . . Pee-o-Pee-mox-a-mox [Yellow Serpent], Young Cheif and the Nez Perses say yes! None of their people say no! Why do we talk so much about it? I have done."[35] With no agreement reached, the council was adjourned until the following Monday.

That night, however, the commissioners achieved much of what they sought, but it would appear that they did so by adding threat to their other arguments. According to two settlers present at the evening meeting, Stevens told the interpreters to tell the chiefs that "if they don't sign this treaty they will walk in blood knee deep." Threats, the promise of increased annuities to the chiefs, and probably a great weariness finally combined to force the chiefs' submission. Yellow Serpent for the Walla Walla and Kamiakin, Owhi, and Skloom for the Yakima signed the treaties. It is said, however, that Kamiakin refused the treaty goods and that in signing the treaty he bit his lip so fiercely that it ran with blood. *[36]

The following Monday, with the treaties in his quiver, Stevens told Lawyer: "We want no speeches. This will be the last day of the council." Lawyer signed first, followed by Looking Glass and the other principal Nez Perce chiefs. And Kip wondered, wondered what Stevens "has been doing with Looking Glass since last Saturday, we cannot imagine, but we suppose . . . 'every man has his price.'" In total, fifty-six chiefs signed the treaties that ceded sixty thousand square miles to the United States.[37]

And so, the council was over, one of the largest, longest, and most significant of any Indian–white council in United States history. Stevens, overconfident, was certain of his triumph. On the following day, he wrote George Manypenny that the council's "effect on the peace of the country hardly admits of exaggeration. Had no Treaty been effected, there would probably have been blood shed and open war the present year."[38] The reverse turned out to be the case, and Stevens proved wrong, when several months later a war broke out that would rage for three years and involve elements of all

Fifteen years later, William Winans, director of the Colville Indian Agency, visited the aged and impoverished Kamiakin, bringing with him the six hundred blankets provided for in the Walla Walla treaty and which at the time Kamiakin had refused. As a token of peace and friendship, Winans asked Kamiakin to now accept the blankets. Kamiakin stood up and, pointing to the ragged sleeve of his shirt, said: "See, I am a poor man, but too rich to receive anything from the United

the tribes present at the Walla Walla council.

From the beginning, Palmer had believed that the council was premature and that if it had been delayed, as he had wished, the war might have been postponed, even perhaps avoided. Once the council had been convened, however, Palmer did his best for its success. Still, in one of his last statements to the gathered Indians, there was a note of doubt: "We commenced a long way apart but now we are together. We are one. I hope we shall always remain as one and have one heart." As quoted earlier, Palmer had stated his misgivings to Manypenny with particular reference to the Yakima: "It is pretty evident that the signing of the treaty was adverse to the will of the Nation, as expressed prior to the delegations coming to the council, and that on the return of the chiefs they were beset by their people and denounced as traitors to their tribe." In the same letter, Palmer, by implication, admitted that at the end of the council he had been seriously at fault in joining Stevens in a proclamation that opened the ceded lands to settlement. "The immigration of persons into their [the Indians'] country seeking locations for settlement immediately after the treaty, and before any resulting visable advantages, alarmed them, and placed an additional argument in the mouths of the opposers of the treaty."[39]

States." See Stevens, *A True Copy of the Record,* 6.

However, even without the premature white settlement, the war might have occurred, for there is some evidence that the tribes had already determined on it. It was stated earlier that threats, increased annuities to the chiefs, and weariness combined to persuade the chiefs to sign the treaty. But it may have been, as Robert Ignatius Burns concluded, that "the Indians were using the treaties in the same way they believed the Whites used them—as an instrument of deception." For example, the Yakima chief Owhi told the Swiss Jesuit Joset that "the war commenced from that moment," that is, the moment of the signing of the treaty, and Joset wrote that "the chiefs agreed to a mock treaty in order to gain time and prepare for war."[40]

In Hazard Stevens' view, the Yakima were not alone in planning for war:

> All the circumstances and evidence go to show that, with the exception of Steachus, the friendly Cuyuse, they all—Young Chief, Five Crows, Pu-pu-mox-mox [Yellow Serpent], Kam-i-ah-kan, and their sub-chiefs—all signed the treaties as a deliberate act of treachery, in order to lull the whites into fancied security.

Kamiakin, in a certain sense, disputed this. During the Yakima War, he told a captured white, whom he later released, that it was Looking Glass who had first proposed the war and who intended to initiate it by killing Stevens.

Kamiakin, as well as Skloom, Yellow Serpent, and others, believed that the whites should be given a three-year grace period in which to meet their promises. But when the false news of Stevens' murder came back, Kamiakin reportedly said, "we were all of one mind, which was to drive the white people out of the country."[41]

Whatever the truth of these matters—the prematureness of the treaties, the manner in which they were negotiated by the whites, the motives of the Indians in signing them—the fact is the war occurred, and it is difficult to see how in the circumstances of the time it could have been otherwise. As Palmer warned, there was no way to stop the whites from coming. "Can you prevent the wind from blowing? Can you prevent the rain from falling?"[42]

That the settling of the Columbia plateau was inevitable cannot be disputed. That this settlement together with the reservation system destroyed the integrity of plateau Indian life cannot be disputed either. Prior to Walla Walla, that life had a wholeness multifarious in its tightly interwoven parts: land and water, sky, bird and beast, stone and star, root and seed, the bones of the dead, the hearts of the living, all bound into one by myth and belief—a structure as sound and sheltering as the eagle's nest. With the arrival of the missionaries, the texture raveled a little, but it was Walla Walla that finally tore the structure apart and scattered it. Men like Palmer, with their good intentions, sought with teachers, doctors, and preachers, with carpenters, farmers, and blacksmiths, to build the Indians a new structure—a citadel of enlightenment and progress. But in fact, what replaced the eagle's nest was a flimsy hovel in which the spirit, deprived of its ancient sustenance, finally died.

TEN

War

WHILE STEVENS WENT TO FORT BENTON in Montana to hold council with the Blackfeet, Palmer held council at The Dalles with what he called the tribes of "middle Oregon." He met with fourteen of their chiefs on 25 June and concluded treaties that, together with the treaties with the Cayuse at Walla Walla, ceded almost all of the northeast quadrant of Oregon to the United States. The negotiations, however, were not without difficulties. For example, some of the tribes did not want to confederate with the Wasco, as the treaties demanded. Also, many considered the proposed reservation at Warm Springs to be too distant from the Columbia. In fact, one band of Wasco, refusing to leave the banks of the river, declined to sign the treaty. "I have said I would not sell my country and I have but one talk," said their chief. *[1]

Overcoming most of these difficulties, Palmer returned to the Willamette Valley to find the citizenry preparing for the principal event of the year—the Fourth of July. Never had the Oregon Territory seen such a celebration. In Portland, the Volunteer Fire Brigade marched in bearskin hats and buckskin aprons, each man carrying an ax, the fire engine wreathed in flowers. Equally colorful was the Portland Light Horse Cavalry, prancing through the streets under the command of a Captain Pillow. After the parade, the Constitution was read and there were a number of orations. Then, "to satisfy the cravings of na-

* *The chief may have been influenced by John Edwards, a white who warned the Indians that they were being bilked and not to sell their lands. Edwards was subsequently arrested for disorderly conduct.*

ture," the 7 July *Oregonian* reported, the celebrants repaired to the Metropole Hotel for refreshments and the endless toasts. "May their 'fuse' never be choked in case of conflagration, or their members doomed to the gloom of perpetual celibacy," was one of the toasts drunk to the Volunteer Fire Brigade. Finally, fireworks were set off in the evening to be admired by "thousands." There is no record of celebrations in Dayton, but in neighboring Butteville, thirty-eight toasts were drunk, and at 4:00 p.m., as the 4 August *Statesman* reported, all were invited to "tip the light fantastic toe" at a ball that continued until midnight.

In addition to these cheering festivities, Palmer found waiting for him cheering letters from his agents, in particular Dr. Ambrose in the south, who assured him there would be no war "this season" and that "peace and harmony are once more restored."[2] Free of that concern, Palmer set out at the end of July for Gold Beach to negotiate treaties extinguishing the last of the Indian titles to the coast.

He arrived on the lower Rogue on 26 August. There, in a grove of myrtles three miles upstream from the river's mouth, he convened a council of twelve hundred Indians assisted by subagents Drew and Wright. In the midst of the council, an incident occurred that initially, at least, came near to disrupting the council and, for that matter, provoking war.

During the proceedings, according to the earlier mentioned army doctor, Rodney Glisan,

> an Indian and a white man had a quarrel, which resulted in the latter being
> wounded in the shoulder by the former. The Indian fled. Captain Ben Wright, a
> sub-Indian Agent, being on the treaty ground for the purpose of assembling the
> Indians preparatory for the treaty, happening to hear of the difficulty, and wish-
> ing to prevent further bloodshed, went personally and arrested the Indian with
> a view of having him properly tried, and punishing him for his misdemeanor if
> found guilty. At night, whilst he, some others, and the prisoner, were lying as-
> leep in a small shanty, a shot was fired by an unknown person, which shattered
> the prisoners's arm. Wright having dressed his wounds, placed him between
> himself and the wall; thus, with his own person, affording protection to the In-
> dian. The night passed off quietly, but it was evident that the populace intended
> getting forcible possession of [the Indian] in the morning with the view of
> hanging him, and the Agent rose early and took his prisoner to the treaty
> ground, and there placed him in a small hut. He had scarcely done so, when the
> mob assembled to the number of sixty persons, armed with Colt's revolvers,
> and demanded the prisoner. Wright stood in the door, and by his determined

manner and strong arguments, managed to keep them at bay until the arrival of a detachment of fifteen United States troops, who had opportunely reached the opposite side of the river; and for whom he secretly dispatched a messenger. The prisoner was then turned over to their protection. The crowd hung around for some time blackguarding the soldiers, but finally dispersed.

On the following day, the twenty-seventh of August, a constable took the prisoner in charge with the intention of taking him before a magistrate some three miles down the river. At the solicitation of the constable, and request of General Palmer, General Superintendent of Indians in Oregon, who had arrived in the meantime, a corporal's guard of troops was furnished the prisoner. After the latter had been properly committed by the magistrate to stand his trial at the next term of court, he was remanded to the corporal for conveyance to prison. As the guard was ascending Rogue River late at night (moonlight) three men came alongside. The corporal ordered them to keep off, but instead of doing so they commenced firing into his boat, killing the prisoner, who was at the time between the corporal's knees, and another Indian rowing the boat.

The corporal then commanded his men to return the fire. The three men were instantly killed, each receiving a ball through the chest. The five corpses were taken to camp. The Indians fled from the council ground in consternation. An attack was expected on the general's camp by the exasperated citizens. A gentleman was dispatched to the mouth of the Rogue River to explain the matter to the Vigilance Committee. On arriving there he ascertained that the three men, who had met such an untimely fate by their rashness, were to have been supported by a strong party in another boat. But this party is said to have gone home to bed, after hearing the fateful shots, without even ascertaining the fate of their companions.[3]

Although the incident disrupted the council, its implications must have eventually predisposed the Indians to accept Palmer's proposals. This may have been the first case in Oregon of whites killing whites in defense of Indians, or at least in defense of the principle that even Indians had a right to a trial. The Indians must have been astonished and impressed. The whites were enraged.

A similar incident of whites protecting Indians from other whites had occurred a month earlier at Fort Lane near Jacksonville and with similar results—the rage of much of the white community. In early summer, Lieutenant Switzer had captured fourteen Illinois River Indians accused of thievery and murder and had brought them to Fort Lane where the commander, Capt. Andrew Jackson Smith, and Agent Ambrose determined to keep them until their trial, "as much to prevent whites from killing them as to discourage them from running away." They were soon joined by two Rogue River Indians, charged with participating in a massacre of eleven whites on the Klamath River in late July. On 5 August, two hundred California volunteers arrived at Fort Lane demanding the two Rogues and warning that if they were not released "we will . . . go and take them where they may be found, at all and every hazard."[4]

Capt. Andrew Jackson Smith of Bucks County and West Point, son of a captain at the siege of Yorktown, was not accustomed to being addressed in such a manner by civilians. "He stormed furiously, declined to submit to dictation, and invited the bold Californians to put their threats in execution."[5] The volunteers retreated but vowed to take the fort by storm in three days if the Indians were not released to them. Captain Smith prepared, aiming his loaded cannon at the approaches to the fort. Meanwhile, the volunteers hatched a plan whereby they would get the soldiers drunk and then enter the fort, but this was frustrated when Captain Smith forbade his men to leave the fort. After a time of staring into the mouths of Captain Smith's cannon, the volunteers returned to California.* The soldiers' actions in defending Indians against whites in these two instances was strongly condemned. The 22 September *Statesman*, commenting on the incident at the coast, wrote: "Three men were deliberately and cruelly shot by U.S. soldiers as a *penalty* for shooting an Indian. They took it upon themselves to *punish* citizens, when the law had devolved that duty upon courts." It was an interesting point: in defending the Indians' right to trial, the soldiers denied the whites their right to trial by killing them.

* The two Rogues in question were later taken to Yreka under official escort. A grand jury failed to return an indictment, and the Rogues were released, whereupon they were shot by the mob.

As might have been expected, the *Oregonian* was far more exercised by these matters than the *Statesman*. On 11 August, the newspaper charged that "troops are stationed among us solely for the protection of our savage enemies" and that Fort Lane was nothing but "a place of safety for every Indian who is so fortunate as to take the life of a white man." But it was the *Oregonian*'s long editorial of 25 August on the killing of the whites at the lower Rogue that best exemplified the newspaper's position, and not only the newspaper's position. There is no question but that the Whig *Oregonian* used the Indian question as a cat's-paw in its attacks on the Democrats, but there is no question either that the attitudes voiced in the editorial were also the attitudes of many Oregonians.

It is a fact well known throughout the country that the citizens generally accuse the government officers with sympathizing with the Indians in all their difficulties with whites; that the government officers endeavour to prevent the whites, who are constantly suffering from all manner of depredations, murder, rapine, robbery, and crimes of every hue, at the hands of the Indians, from revenge and retaliation. The Indians also understand this is to be so. Therefore, whenever they become repressed by the citizens who endeavour to restrain their depredation, they rush to the government officials and seek protection.

The people in Oregon, particularly in Rogue river valley, and through the southern portion of our territory, have suffered untold evils by these red devils. Their stock is constantly being stolen, crops destroyed, houses burned, men shot down in the paths and gulches of the mountains, or murdered at midnight in their cabins and houses. Men are driven from their homes to seek safety and shelter for their wives and children, and the whole country kept in constant alarm and commotion by a few hundred filthy animals in the shape of men. It seems to us that the government by its officers should either protect its citizens or allow the citizens, unmolested and unopposed, to protect themselves, which they are abundantly able to do if the official dignitaries will not interfere, and which *they will do, regardless of either the civil or military power,* unless these Indian depredations are checked, and the guilty punished in a speedy and proper manner. The decapitation of every Indian in Oregon would not atone a thousandth part for the valuable lives they have destroyed during the last five years within our borders. Had we a treaty made by the citizens of Oregon and presents given in the shape of *powder* and *ball* through a *rifle barrel,* in place of by government officials, we might then hope its stipulations would be faithfully kept, and peace, safety and harmony prevail in our midst, and not till then.

By "government officials," the *Oregonian* clearly included Indian agents such as Palmer, but it was the army that the newspaper particularly criticized. And it was true that most United States officers in Oregon tended to be more sympathetic to the Indians than to the whites. This was partly because the army had experienced few difficulties with the Indians compared to those suffered by settlers and miners. When they did not come by sea, the army crossed the plains in large, armed companies, not in the relatively defenseless trains comprised of many women and children. Also, when the soldiers reached Oregon, they did not live on isolated farms or mining claims but in fortified encampments. They were not fighting for their homes.

Secondly, the officers tended to be upper-class easterners and southerners who, by background, were inclined to the nineteenth-century romantic view of the Indian as "noble savage." In any event, and for whatever complex of reasons, the army was often at odds with civilians over the treatment of Indians. And this from the top down, that is, the commander of all Pacific forces at the time, Gen. John E. Wool who, according to Frances Victor, entertained a "strong bias against the people as distinguished from the army" and who had an "especial dislike of volunteer forces."*[6] This three-way rancor of the military, civilians, and Indians was to bedevil the relations of all three for years to come.

> ** His dislike is perhaps understandable, for it had been the onerous duty of this "Xenophon of the Mexican War" to command twelve thousand volunteers in that war, volunteers who were of no more a docile disposition than the volunteers of Oregon.*

As for Palmer and his agents, in the two incidents under consideration, Palmer fully approved of the army's stance, while Ambrose wrote that he was

> tired of the senseless railing against Captain Smith and the Indian agent [himself] for doing their duty, obeying the laws and preserving our valley from the horrors of war with a tribe of Indians who do not desire it, but wish for peace, and by their conduct have shown it.[7]

That Dr. Ambrose's position was not exactly a popular one is suggested by the fact that his words appeared in the press under the pseudonym of "miner."

PALMER CONCLUDED TREATIES with the so-called Confederated Coast tribes on 8 September 1855. He then set out on his return. Rather than taking a ship, he traveled inland to the valley, now busy with reapers gathering in the especially abundant harvest of 1855. At home in Dayton, he found that in his absence a fair number of new emigrants had arrived—always a matter of excitement—and further, that a grand new paddle wheeler, the *Sara Hoyt*, had been launched in Portland on a flood of champagne. The news waiting for him in his office, however, was less diverting, for Dr. Ambrose's letters from Jacksonville had turned pessimistic.

Widespread thievery had exhausted the whites' patience. "Our frontier settlers are many of them bachelors," Ambrose wrote,

> and when they are absent from their houses at work, no one left to guard what they own; and not infrequently, when they return from their work at night, do they find their little stack of provisions minus; it had been abstracted during their absence by Mr. Indian crawling down the chimney, or knocking a board off and crawling through a crack . . . . After a repetition of the thefts a few times, and the individual, after a hard day's work, has had to walk two or three miles to get his supper and lay in another small lots of provisions, which in a few days may probably go the same way, he gets peevish and angry, and embit-

tered against the Indian race, and would about as soon shoot one as eat his supper.

In addition to the thievery, there were acts of plain wantonness: cattle shot, for example, rail fences burned. But most frustrating, "not an Indian can be found who is guilty of any of the above acts. One band lays the charge to some other band; they in return, charge it upon another band; and so it goes from one to another, and all go unpunished."[8] Most serious of all, four whites had been murdered. In one case, it was as if the Indians wished to convey a message to the whites: the man's heart had been ripped out, and in its place they had put a stone.

In the midst of these alarms of imminent conflagration in the south, word came of conflagration in the east. Agent Bolon of Washington Territory, investigating the murder of some miners in the Yakima country, had had his throat slit by Kamiakin's nephew and both he and his horse set afire. The Yakima War had begun.

Palmer left immediately for The Dalles, arriving on 2 October. His purpose was to dissuade the Oregon bands from allying with the Yakima, as in the Cayuse War he had sought to prevent those bands from combining with the Cayuse. Agent Thompson told Palmer that, except for the Tygh, who believed that their treaty goods had been deliberately infected, the tribes of his agency had no hostile intentions. But it was clear that the Yakima were bent on war. Kamiakin had warned Nathan Olney, whom he said he loved like a son, to keep clear of the field of battle, and furthermore, he made it clear that he would punish any tribe that did not join the Yakima in their campaign.

Following his discussions with the Columbia tribes, Palmer sent messages to the more distant bands and also ordered Nathan Olney to go among the Walla Walla, Cayuse, and Umatilla to discourage them from allying with the Yakima. As usual, Palmer placed more confidence in friendly but firm persuasion than in military force. In this case, he strongly doubted the efficacy of the military, for he considered Maj. G.O. Haller's one hundred men, who had gone in pursuit of the murderers, insufficiently trained to confront the "bravery and sagacity of these Indians."[9]

Palmer, now certain of war in Washington and fearful of its spread to Oregon, returned to the valley on 7 October, reaching Dayton at nightfall. On that same evening, J.A. Lupton and forty men from Jacksonville—"miners and men-about-town," Walling called them—camped on the Rogue opposite the mouth of Little Butte Creek, the present-day site of Eagle Point.[10] The eastern boundary of the Table Rock reservation lay a mile or so away, and Fort

Lane a few miles farther on across the river. In the immediate vicinity of the whites, there were two camps of Indians. At daybreak the next morning, the whites charged the camps and killed twenty-four Indians, sixteen of them women and children and four old men. Lupton, mopping up, came upon an Indian prone in the brush. The Indian, too badly wounded to rise and run or grapple, raised his leg, drew his bow with the sole of his foot, and released an arrow into Lupton's lung, mortally wounding him. The Rogue River War had begun.

ELEVEN

The Fires
of Autumn

NEITHER THE YAKIMA nor the Rogue River War could have come as a surprise to Palmer. On 8 October 1855, he wrote to George Manypenny that

the crisis of the destiny of the Indian race in Oregon and Washington teritories is now upon us; and the result of the causes now operating, unless speedily arrested, will be disastrous to the whites, destructive to the Indians, and a heavy reproach upon our national character.[1]

Palmer's solution was to immediately remove all Indians to reservations and to equip them with enough provisions and tools for both comfort and work. He estimated the cost, in addition to the regular appropriations, at one hundred thousand dollars—a fraction of the cost of an Indian war, as he pointed out. But it was too late; the wars had begun.

The circumstances of the Rogue River massacre are a tangled skein of assertions by various interested parties. Agent George Ambrose maintained that a few days previous, he and Capt. A.J. Smith had warned the Indians of the area that there might be trouble and that it would be well for them to seek refuge on the reserve or at Fort Lane. In fact, Smith reported, the Indians had been on their way to the reserve when they were attacked. But Frances Victor claimed that the reserve was a safe hiding place for wayward bands and that Lupton and his men had believed that the Indians they attacked were thieves. Others asserted that Lupton had been convinced that these were the Indians who had killed two whites in the Siskiyous and, furthermore, that they had not been on their way to the refuge but were intent on further mischief. Walling attributed the attack to a personal motive. "It is the prevailing opinion that he [Lupton] was led into the affair through a wish to court popularity." In any event, and as Walling concluded, "by some it has been termed a heroic attack, worthy of Leonidas or Alexander; others have called it an indiscriminate butchery of defenseless and peaceful natives."[2]

Whether "heroic attack" or "butchery," the attack provoked an immediate response from the Indians, so immediate that Frances Victor wondered whether the Indians had been hoping for just such an incident. Ambrose supported that opinion, writing Palmer that John, a chief of the Applegate Rogues, "had been in waiting for some time for a pretext to commence hostilities, only desiring the assistance of some other Indians, which this unfortunate occurance secured to him."[3]

The Indian reprisals began with a fury the following day. Chief John killed a young carpenter at Table Rock, allegedly yelling at the boy, "I want no house," and indeed, until the end of his life, John opposed reservation life. John was soon joined by two other Applegate Rogues, Limpy and George, and together they went down the river, killing two packers on their way. Finally, they reached the homestead of J.K. Jones. Their activities there were subsequently reported by Captain Hewitt of Fort Lane:

> His house was burned to ashes, and Mr. Jones, who was sick at the time, was burned in it. Mrs. Jones was found about thirty yards from the house, shot through the lungs, face and jaws horribly broken and mutilated. The bones of Mr. Jones were found, the flesh having been mostly eaten off by the hogs. We found Cooper, who had been living with Jones, about one hundred and fifty yards from the house, shot through the lungs, the ball having entered his left breast.

The Rogues then went on to the Brown homestead.

> Mrs. Brown and child were found in the well, head downward; she had been stabbed to the heart; also stabbed in the back and the back part of the head. The child was below her, and had no marks of violence upon it. Mr. Brown was found in the house, literally cut to pieces. His arms and legs were badly cut, and I should think there were as many as ten or fifteen stabs in his back. After burying the remains of the bodies as well as circumstances would permit, we proceeded to the house of Mr. King, which we found burned to ashes and the most horrible spectacle of all awaited us—Mr. Jones, who had lived with him, and two little children were burned in the house; the body of Mr. King, after being

roasted, was eaten almost entirely up by the hogs. Mrs. King was lying about thirty yards from the house almost in a state of nudity, shot apparently through the heart, and her left breast cut off; she was cut open from the pit of the stomach to about the center of the abdomen; intestines pulled out on either side. We performed the last sad rites over the slain, and returned to our camp.[4]

At the Waggoners' homestead, Mr. Waggoner was absent, having gone to point out the trail to Sailor Diggings for Dr. Sara Pellet, a temperance lecturer from Oberlin College, on tour in southern Oregon. Thus, Waggoner's wife and child were alone. The Rogues abducted them; their scalps were found the following year at Cow Creek. At the Harris', the Rogues killed Mr. Harris, as well as the hired man, and abducted nine-year-old David Harris. Mrs. Harris and her daughter barricaded themselves in the house and fired at the Rogues until the Indians withdrew, rampaging on to Grave Creek where they killed three more whites.

One of the Rogues' last stops on this bloody day was the house of a man named Haines. When the volunteers got to the Haines' farm

they beheld a sight never to be forgotten even by the bravest of men. Mr. Haines had been murdered and scalped, and then his body thrown across a bench in the house. Three of the little boys lay near the door on the outside of the house, their heads split open with a tomahawk. The fourth boy, the baby of the family, lay at the east corner of the house. The Indians had taken him up by the feet and had beaten his head against one of the logs of the house. The top of the little fellows head lay at a short distance from the body . . . . The Indians made Mrs. Haines and little Mary Haines prisoners, and took them down Rogue River to Hellgate, where they scalped the little girl and threw her body over the bluff into Rogue river.[5]

It is impossible to judge the accuracy of these accounts. "I have lived in an Indian country too long to put confidence in more than one-twentieth part of the Indian atrocities that are reported," wrote Rodney Glisan, the army doctor who had served for eleven years on the frontier and who at the time, and as noted earlier, was stationed on the south coast.[6] Glisan was skeptical for good reason, but even though the events of 9 October may have been exaggerated, great havoc was in fact wreaked.

PALMER RECEIVED THE TERRIBLE NEWS from Rogue River and bad news from The Dalles at about the same time. Agent Thompson reported from The Dalles that Major Haller and his one hundred men had been surrounded by three hundred Yakima and their allies. Under heavy fire, the Americans had barely escaped and in the process had lost their howitzer. The Indians' success could only win them recruits from the bands that had remained neutral. *

As for the news from Rogue River, Palmer's reaction to Lupton's attack on the Indian camp was among the most bitter of his career. "If it becomes a fixed policy," he wrote Manypenny,

> to permit wholesale butchery of defenseless women
> and children of those of our friendly bands of Indians,
> who, in accordance with treaty stipulations, locate
> upon temporary or permanent reservations, and com-
> ply with all the requirements of such treaties, and the
> regulations and directions of the agents of the government placed among them,
> the officers of the Indian department may as well be disbanded. Pledges of aid
> and protection by the government to such as enter into treaty stipulations are
> but empty bubbles, made only to be violated by our people. We, as agents of
> the government, are made the instruments by which to prepare them for the
> slaughter; our pledges are broken, confidence destroyed; and, unless supported
> in our efforts to maintain the faith of the government, we might as well close
> the office in this superintendency.

* In a letter a few days later concerning this rout, R.R. Thompson wrote that "the military do not wish to have it called a repulse." See Thompson to Palmer, reel 5, 14 October 1855, 353.

At the same time, Palmer had no sympathy for the rampaging Rogues.

> Great wrongs have undoubtedly been done to the Indians but when war comes
> between the races who can hesitate to act . . . . War is upon us and what ever its
> origin, when defenseless women and children are murdered and the property of
> our citizens destroyed by the ruthless savage, no one can hesitate as to the
> course to be pursued toward those in the attitude of enemies.[7]

While supporting punitive action against these enemies, Palmer foresaw that whites in their aroused state might not always make the distinction between hostile and neutral Indians. Therefore, he acted to isolate the neutral Indians from the whites as well as from the inflammatory influence of the hostiles. Palmer ordered Agent Ambrose to place on the Table Rock reservation or at Fort Lane all nonhostile Indians in his district. In the valley, temporary encampments were established to which all valley Indians were ordered to repair. Then, in late October, Palmer went to The Dalles to set up three temporary reserves. At the same time, he issued a general order that any Indians refusing to live in the sanctuaries would be treated as hostiles. Thus did Palmer hope to shelter his charges from the coming storm.

The rising of that storm on the Rogue began when news of the Indians' mayhem reached Jacksonville. Twenty volunteers joined fifty-five troopers from Fort Lane and set off in pursuit of the rampaging Indians. At Waggoner's place, the volunteers surprised a group of Indians who were plundering the property and who "greeted them with derisive yells, dancing, and insulting gestures."[8] When the troopers appeared, however, the Indians fled.

Meanwhile, news of the mayhem spreading, settlers and miners "forted up" or else took refuge in Jacksonville. By 11 October, 150 men had enlisted in the volunteer force. But it was a force quite insufficient, for it was estimated that the enemy numbered about four hundred. However, a larger volunteer force was precluded by a shortage of weapons—the Indians, according to Frances Victor, having earlier "and slyly" bought up all the weapons they could find. The shortage of weapons and thus, of men, necessitated a call for aid to the army at Fort Vancouver and the government at Salem. A scenario for opera bouffe soon developed. It happened that at the same time a messenger set out from Fort Lane to Fort Vancouver to request men to help in the Rogue River War, a messenger set out from Fort Vancouver for Fort Lane to request men for help in the Yakima War—the two messengers no doubt passing on the road. The messenger from Fort Vancouver arriving first, Major Fitzgerald and ninety troopers departed from Fort Lane, leaving the force in the Rogue War sorely depleted.

As for the request to government, it, too, was touched with farce. When Governor Curry received the request for help from Fort Lane, he issued a call for six hundred volunteers to serve in two battalions of five companies each. The northern battalion from Linn, Douglas, and Umpqua counties planned to rendezvous at Roseburg—the southern battalion from Jackson County at Jacksonville. Each battalion was to elect its own officers. With the elections, a fourth adversary was added to the conflict: politicians. From now on, there would not only be war between Indians, army, and civilians but also between Whigs, Know Nothings, and Democrats.

Five days after calling for the two battalions, Governor Curry ordered the southern battalion to disband, alleging that it was "waging a war of extermination against the Indians."[9] Although there was some truth to the charge and though many in the south favored such a war, the principal reason for Curry's action was that some Whigs and Know Nothings had been elected as officers of the battalion. This could not be countenanced by the Democratic administration. Accordingly, a new battalion was formed with officers more acceptable to Salem.

It was also alleged at this time that the Whigs and Know Nothings had deliberately provoked the war. Agent Ambrose wrote Judge Deady that the Whigs and Know Nothings had told the Indians "that just as soon as winter should set in they would all be killed." When this failed to rouse the Indians, the Whigs and Know Nothings "were compelled to begin it themselves and accordingly they raised a company of men (Lupton's force) and made several simultaneous attacks upon the Indians." Ambrose concluded, "I have no doubt but it is the deepest laid political plot ever concocted in this territory."*[10] That is, the Whigs and Know Nothings provoked the war and then, by election of officers from their own ranks, took over its prosecution and all the benefits—political and monetary—thereof. And there were certainly those who believed that "monetary" benefits were a factor as well as politics. Palmer was one of these, having seen firsthand the profits made from the Cayuse War of 1848 and the Rogue River War of 1853.

> * Ambrose's charges directly contradict those he made to Palmer on 9 October, when he claimed that Chief John and others had been waiting for a pretext. Either he had changed his mind or he had some political purpose in his new analysis.

The *Statesman* had its suspicions as well, which, self-servingly, it did its best to spread in its 20 October issue:

> We have private intimations that it has been the organized and deliberate purpose of some individuals in the south to incite Indian depredations and disturbances, so as to create opportunities to plunder the public treasury. It is difficult to believe that men can be so mercenary and fiendish.

Walling, writing on the causes of the war, put it more pointedly: "Speculative gentlemen mused upon the profits of an Indian war . . . . 'A good crop pays well, but a good lively campaign is vastly more lucrative.'"[11]

Although the new officers of the southern battalion were mainly true-blue Democrats, the concern over Whigs and Know Nothings, particularly the latter, did not subside but rather was raised to a frantic pitch. The *Statesman* railed and railed, seemingly more exercised by the presence of Know Nothings in the south than by the marauding Indians. On 3 November, the newspaper reported that Governor Curry was distressed to know that the superintendent of Indian affairs employed Know Nothing Whigs—a reference to Palmer's close friend and associate, Cris Taylor. On 17 November, the newspaper demanded that all Know Nothings resign. It was Palmer whom they had in mind.

Indeed, Palmer was now assailed from all sides. His own party had as much as asked him to resign, and the *Oregonian* and the Whigs had made it clear what they thought of him and his policies. After calling for the extermination of the Indians on 20 October, the *Oregonian* cried: "This idea of *humanity* to Indians in this country is preposterous, if not criminal." Attacked by bitter political foes on one side and by the Indian wars on the other, Palmer's survival as superintendent seemed doubtful.

MEANWHILE, THE WARS WENT ON. In the south, three battles occurred before the snow drove both Indians and whites to their winter fires. The disadvantages under which the whites suffered in these battles is best described by Samuel Culver in a letter to Palmer the year before. Remarking on the experience the Indians had gained over the years in their skirmishes with whites, Culver concluded:

> this experience, together with the remarkable country they have to operate in renders them formidable, and none are better aware of the advantage they posses in this respect than themselves. The country is composed of narrow valleys and mountains covered with timber, and an undergrowth so dense that they can conceal themselves within a few yards of persons passing or pursuing, shoot them with impunity, and make their escape unseen and almost certain. The valleys are narrow—so much so that the Indians can quit their hiding-places in the shade of evening, have time to reach any of the settlements, do their work of destruction, plunder, and perhaps murder, and return to their secure retreat before morning.[12]

It is an account that might have been sent by another kind of agent, a century later, from Vietnam.

The first of these fall battles occurred on 17 October at Skull Bar at the mouth of Galice Creek, about twenty miles down the Rogue from present-day Grants Pass. Here was located a small mining camp, a ménage of miners, Chinese, and captured Indian women. Captain Lewis and a company of volunteers were sent to guard the camp, taking up their position on the bar. The position could hardly have been more ill-suited for defense, let alone retreat. On one side, the bar faced a high, steep slope of fir and hazel; the hazel was the "undergrowth" that Culver had said provided such excellent concealment. On the other side of the bar—precluding retreat—ran the Rogue, swift, cold, and deep. Here, then, were the soldiers garrisoned in two board shacks, an old corral serving as breastworks.

On the morning of 17 October, six volunteers attacked the hazel-embowered slope and received "galling" fire from the Indians, forcing the volunteers to retire to their corral-breastworks. A second attack by the volunteers was no more successful. Throughout the exchanges, according to Walling, "considerable conversation of an unfriendly nature passed between the different sides." Now, too, the Indians began shooting lighted arrows at the wooden shacks and corral and into the mining camp, as well, the latter finally burning to the ground. During the night, however, the volunteers improved their defenses to such a degree that, on the following morning, the Indians retired.

Five volunteers were killed and six severely wounded. The Indians had plenty of ammunition and arms. The 20 October 1855 *Statesman* was later to write that "as in the war of 1853, the Indians have all the guns in the country." Though the Battle of Skull Bar had no particular effect on the overall war, Captain Lewis stated that he and his men "fought the hardest battle ever fought this side of the Rocky Mountains."[13]

The second of these fall battles of 1855, the Battle of Hungry Hill, took place on 31 October and 1 November in the Grave Creek Hills near the confluence of Grave Creek and the Rogue. Here, there assembled that most unstable of compounds, a mixed force of regular army and volunteers. Lt. George Crook was at this time camped nearby at Six Bit House, so colorfully named for the cost of meals and one night's stay. Crook's description of the volunteers he encountered there is probably a fairly accurate picture of these Oregon cavaliers, notwithstanding the element of satire. Furthermore, it may make more explicable the events of the Battle of Hungry Hill and other battles in the Rogue River War:

> There came a company of southern Oregon Mounted Volunteers raised for the ostensible purpose of operating against the hostile Indians, and camped near us. When they unsaddled they threw their saddles, bridles and spurs on one pile. The next morning when they went to saddle up the ones who came first found the best. A perfect pandemonium ensued. I thought I had heard obscenity and blasphemy before, but this beat anything I had ever heard.
>
> The name of the Capt. of the company at Six Bits House . . . was Bowie, a Methodist exhorter. He was a short, stout man. He was left-handed, and wore an old artillery sword about one foot and a half or two feet long. He didn't seem to have any control over his men. After exhorting them for a long time to get ready, probably about two-thirds had saddled their horses. He succeeded in getting some of them into line.
>
> He drew his little sword with his left hand, and brandished it over his head,

and bawled out, "Tenshun the company!" Some answered back, "Go to hell!" while others said, "Hold it, Cap, until I go to the rear," only in not such choice language.

"Now," says he, "at the command 'prepare to mount,' catch your horses by the bridle with your left hand, put your foot in the stirrup, and mount." Suiting the action to the word, in attempting to mount, his foot slipped out of the stirrup and his chin struck the pommel of the saddle and his corporosity shook like a bag of jelly. He looked out at some of the men who were on their horses, when he said, "That's right boys, get up thar."

We finally got under way, and a motlier crew has never been seen since old Falstaff's time. They were mounted on horses and mules of all sizes and degrees, some wore plug hats, and others caps; all were mostly armed with the old-fashioned squirrel rifles. The Captain rode at the head of his company, while I brought up the rear.

We had not proceeded far before we came to a thicket where the Indians could ambush us and inflict great damage on us without our injuring them in return. The Captain halted the company, and said, "Tenshun the company!" drew his sword as before, "Now, boys, look well to your caps. Guns on right shoulder! Keep your eyes well about you! Look behind every stump and tree! You may be attacked at any moment, and in case of attack be prepared to resist the attackment!" The men would answer back with some obscenity.

I made the remark that if we were attacked, I would rather be in front than in rear, as there I might have some show of getting away from the Indians, but in the rear I should certainly be trod to death. The joke was not particularly relished by the cavalier who heard it. No Indians showed themselves, and we passed unmolested. *[14]

There is no doubt that the volunteers were obstreperous, but in this case they may have had reason for being so. Volunteer Harvey Robbins complained that at Roseburg "the citizens . . . seem to treat the volunteers with but very little respect. One man has even forbade our cutting wood on his claim." That this should have irked the volunteers as the cold night came down is understandable. On the other hand, it is understandable that the farmer in question may have been irked with the volunteers, for Robbins adds that upon the farmer's refusal, "we just went to his wood that was already chopped and helped ourselves." The men were further

*Crook, an Ohio farmer's son, was graduated near the bottom of his class at West Point and went on to become one of the nation's foremost authorities on Indian affairs. Over six feet tall and broad-shouldered, Crook's "uniform" on campaign usually consisted of a flannel shirt, canvas

exercised that night when some locals attacked their camp, one faction seeking to kill the Indian prisoners the volunteers were guarding and another demanding their release and freedom. Conditions did not improve. Robbins recorded in his diary: "Rained all night. We have no tents yet. The citizens will not even let us sleep in their barns."[15]

These, then, were the obstreperous and disgruntled volunteers who joined the regular army to serve under the disputed command of West Pointer Capt. A.J. Smith in the Battle of Hungry Hill. The original plan of the campaign had been to set out at eleven o'clock on the night of 30 October to surprise an encampment of Rogues on a hill several miles distant. However, before this could be done, someone lit a campfire, which warned the Indians of the army's approach. The following morning, a new attack was mounted with great enthusiasm, if little order. Lt. Cyrenius Mulkey reported that the troops "were in about the greatest state of confusion that I have ever seen a company of men in my whole life. Everybody for himself, and everybody howling, 'Where are the Indians?'"[16] They soon found out: charging the hill where the Indians were encamped, they met with devastating fire and lost several of their men.

trousers, moccasins, and a slouch hat. To keep his whiskers out of the way, he braided them and tied them at the back of his neck. One commentator described him as "plain as an old stick." Quoted in the Crook biography by Jerome A. Greene in Soliders West: Biographies from the Military Routine, ed. Hutton, 115.

Meanwhile, the Indians retreated to a canyon on the far side of the hill, which was their main fortification. The whites unknowingly poured down into it. "I do not think that any one ever saw a battle fought at such a disadvantage as this was," wrote Mulkey.

> Here were four hundred of our men scattered all over the battlefield in this thick woods, and every man for himself in the brush where they could not see each other . . . . What made it worse, they were shooting at every bush that happened to be moved by either Indian or white man, so you can see that in many cases our men were shooting at each other.[17]

Again the force suffered serious casualties.

The men spent the night at what they named Bloody Springs for the number of dead and wounded. It was by now very cold in the mountains, and they had no food. The following noon, Captain Smith, according to Capt. T.J. Cram, "having found . . . that no confidence could be placed in the promised support of the volunteers, ordered a return to Fort Lane." Twelve whites had been killed and twenty-six wounded in the Battle of Hungry Hill. No one knew the number of Indian losses, but they were estimated to be far less. It is impossible to say who might have been responsible for this debacle, whether volunteers or army. Walling wrote, "as neither side in the controversy is supported by any but interested evidence, we cannot at this date satisfactorily discuss the question." In any case, Lieutenant Crook pithily described the result: "The troops withdrew to the settlements, and left the Indians monarchs of the woods."[18]

There is one curious aspect of the battle that deserves some attention. Mulkey claimed that the Indian troops were commanded by a woman:

> got a good view of the squaw, Sally Lane, who was commanding the battle . . . . The squaw was on horseback, and was giving directions to the Indians . . . . I have never seen but one person who had as powerful a voice as had Sally Lane, and that was her father, Chief Joseph Lane . . . . She was a large stout woman, and had a voice like a man, only more so.[19]

Mulkey's account of the battle appears to be straightforward, and there is no reason to doubt his word concerning "Sally Lane," though he had been misinformed as to her name, which was Mary.

The mysterious Mary appears in several sources. Joseph Lane, who named her, described her as "quite a young queen in her manner and bearing and for an Indian quite pretty."[20] He described how she came to his tent during the 1853 Rogue War to wake him with the warning of a plot against him.

Lane was not alone in finding Mary a pretty woman. As quoted earlier, a young volunteer in the 1853 campaign described her as "tall and delicately formed with hair as dark as the raven's wing . . . dark, lustrous eyes . . . her features Grecian in their cast."[21]

There is also the report of Lafayette Grover, Oregon governor and United States senator, and a man whom Bancroft considered an unusually reliable source. Grover was with Lane during his negotiation with Chief Joe in 1853, and what Grover says of Mary suggests that in addition to her striking appearance, she was a woman of authority:

> It [the negotiations] looked very black, and dangerous. After a while there was a daughter of the old Chief called Mary, Queen Mary . . . . She spoke to our interpreter and after she had talked to her father sometime she told the interpreter that the council could go on.

In 1857 at Grand Ronde, Philip Sheridan also encountered Mary, "an excellent woman . . . who by right of inheritance was a kind of queen of the Rogue Rivers."[22]

It is curious that no other participant in the Battle of Hungry Hill mentioned Mary. The answer may lie in a statement Mulkey made nearly sixty years after the battle. He had never read a detailed account of the Battle of Hungry Hill, he said, and added: "I think that all of the officers were like myself ashamed to give the battle in detail," and perhaps especially the detail that they were defeated by a force led by a woman.[23]

THE LAST OF THE FALL CAMPAIGNS occurred when a large band of Rogues retired for the winter to the river bars of the Rogue in a region called The Meadows. In late November, a force of about four hundred volunteers and fifty regulars decided to rout from the vicinity of Black Bar a group of these Rogues numbering some two hundred. Setting off for the campaign, the men were in good spirits, "nothing but talking, dancing and all kinds of mischief," wrote one of the volunteers to his intended.[24]

On arriving at The Meadows, the strategy decided on was to ferry the troops across the river to Black Bar and from there make their assault. Harvey Robbins, who was among the troops, described their position: "The river runs here in a deep canyon. The side on which the Indians were is covered with fir timber and brush so thick that we could not see them. The side on which we were was open with the exception of a few scattering trees."[25]

Their first task was to construct rafts, though some of the men elected to pan for gold instead. According to Robbins, an officer ordered the men "to get behind something and keep a close lookout for Indians, but the boys were disposed to laugh at him." Ensconced on a bluff above to cover the charge was Captain Judah with what Walling called his "toy . . . a heavy twelve-pound howitzer . . . the inseparable companion of all his expeditions to fight the Indians. On this occasion he had brought this piece with infinite difficulty and labor, to The Meadows." Judah's firing of his ordnance had "the effect only to set the wild echoes flying through the hitherto silent solitude."[26]

While this futile fire went on, the troops were attempting to launch their rafts. Now within range of Black Bar, the Indians opened fire, killing one man and wounding twenty-two. The men retreated. According to Walling, "at least one Indian bit the dust, for George Cherry killed a brave and carried the scalp tied to his war-horse's bridle."[27] Thus ended the Battle of Black Bar.

WHILE MINOR SKIRMISHES CONTINUED in the south and hostile Indians burned and sacked the Table Rock agency, there were now fears that the war would spread to the Willamette Valley. On 21 October, Edward Geary wrote to Palmer at The Dalles reporting on these concerns: "There is much fear and quaking among our citizens residing at the eastern base of the Coast Range in consequence of the signal fires seen looming up on the Cascade summits." He continued:

> it has been rumored that for some days there was a large number of armed Indians encamped on the headwaters of the Santiam, believed to be in great measure strangers to the valley and also that most of our Indians have mysteriously disappeared from their temporary reservations.[28]

Finally, armed Indians had been seen prowling in the vicinity of John Perkins' mill.

Geary had set out to investigate these matters. In Salem, he found there was not "the shadow of a shade of foundation" to the allegations that the Santiam were grouping for an invasion of the valley. As for those armed Indians near Perkins' mill, Geary judged them to be "the shades of the earlier aborigines [who] like Ossian's heroes, [were] on the hills of mist pursuing deer formed of clouds, and bending their airy bows."[29] The Indians who so mysteriously disappeared from the temporary reservations, he implied, had left out of the fear that apprehensive whites would attack them. Finally, Geary was silent on those signal fires flaring from the summits of the mountains; he may have concluded that they were stars.

Nonetheless, fears persisted and night patrols were formed in Portland. This provoked the Salem *Statesman* to question the manliness of the inhabitants of that bastion of Whiggery by publishing an editorial on 13 October headlined: "PORTLAND INVESTED / MARTIAL LAW DECLARED / COMMITTEE APPOINTED TO 'MANAGE' THE TOWN INDIANS / NERVES UNSTRUNG / DOGS RUNNING, ETC." Editor Dryer of the *Oregonian* replied on 20 October:

> That public calumniator, pensioned slanderer, cowardly libeller and miserable lickspittle, Asahel Bush, of the *Salem Statesman*, is attempting to create the impression that the people of this city are a set of nervous old women and cravenhearted cowards . . . . In this long labored article to abuse us, he asserts what every man in this community knows to be a *lie*—a cowardly, slanderous *lie* . . . designed and known to be a *lie* when published . . . . The course pursued by the citizens of Portland in relation to the Indian war now prevailing was absolutely necessary and called for, as the present state of affairs most fully show. In all the public meetings which have been held in this city, in relation to the Indian outbreak, Whigs and democrats alike participated. There has been but one feeling, one sentiment and one object, viz: to prepare for the worst emergency which is now fully realized—to unite as one man and to make common cause in defence of our country against these Indian marauders. Party strife and personal

bickering have been kept entirely out of sight. Yet, in the face of all this, and when the blood of men, women and children of our country is yet warmly gushing from the wounds of their mangled corpses, stretched upon the cold earth; . . . when the echoing screech of the victims of Indian barbarity has scarcely died away; when the wives and mothers are hurrying to and fro, seeking places of safety and protection; when men of all ages, professions and calling are arming and rushing to the battle-field—in short, in the midst of an Indian war raging all around us, this contemptible backbiter, practiced libeller and cowardly calumniator, Asahel Bush, seeks to plant a poisoned dagger into the public mind for party purposes, because we have been called upon by our neighbors and fellow citizens to address public meetings to devise ways and means for the protection and defence of our common country. If there is any animal meaner than the slimy creeping reptile, it is the cowardly slanderer, paid libeller and miserable lick-spittle of the Oregon *Statesman* who is known by the cognomen of Asahel [Ass-a-hell] Bush.

From the safe distance of the present, these fulminations appear comic. At the time, however, there was good reason for the valley to be apprehensive. After all, neither on the Rogue nor on the Columbia were the whites exactly victorious. On 24 November, the *Oregonian* reminded its readers: "In looking over the events of the last two months, we can only say things look rather squally . . . the Indians have had the best of every fight so far."

This was certainly the case on the Rogue. It was also the case on the Columbia. Following what Major Haller did not want called a "repulse" by the Yakima in early October, several other operations were mounted and augmented by five companies of Oregon volunteers. However, as Frances Victor put it, "now that the Indians were confronted with equal numbers, they were more coy. Their horses being fresh could carry them faster in flight than the horses of the calvary could follow in pursuit." In time, the whites did gain on the Yakima and surround them, "but owing to a misunderstanding the charge was made at the wrong point and failed, the Indians escaping among the rocks and trees."[30]

Then, surprisingly, an offer of peace came from Kamiakin, written out by the oblate priest, Father Pandosy. That Major Rains and his men did not entertain the friendliest feelings toward the amanuensis and his brother divines, not to mention the author of the proposal, is suggested by the fact that when the army reached the now deserted Yakima Mission, the men donned the priests' vestments to caper about in what no doubt was salacious pantomime.

As for Kamiakin's offer to negotiate peace, it drew from Major Rains what must be one of the most antagonistic and implacable statements in white and Indian relations:

> We will not be quiet, but war forever, until not a Yakima breathes in the land he calls his own. The river only will we let retain this name to show to all people that here the Yakimas once lived . . . . Your people shall not catch salmon hereafter for you, for I will send soldiers to occupy your fisheries, and fire upon you. Your cattle and your horses, which you got from the white man, we will hunt up, and kill and take them from you. The earth which drank the blood of the white man, shed by your hands, shall grow no more wheat nor roots for you, for we will destroy it. When the cloth that makes your clothing, your guns, and your powder are gone, the white man will make you no more . . . . the whites are as the stars in the heavens, or the leaves of the trees in summer time. Our warriors in the field are many, as you must see; but if not enough, a thousand for every one more will be sent to hunt you, and to kill you; and my kind advice to you, as you will see, is to scatter yourselves among the Indian tribes more peaceable, and there forget you ever were Yakimas.

And so the war went on, a "martial uproar," as Father Burns called it, with the whites achieving nothing.[31] But winter finally came, bringing a respite for everyone.

PALMER'S CONCERN IN THESE MATTERS was not the Yakima War itself, which was being waged in Washington and thus not in his jurisdiction, but rather the disposition of the Oregon bands south of the Columbia. However, Agent Thompson's reports from The Dalles, as well as his own observations, persuaded Palmer that these tribes would not ally themselves with the belligerents—if left to themselves. It was the possibility of interference that worried him. On 21 November, he wrote General Wool:

> The strong desire of a portion of our citizens to involve the tribes . . . with those now unfortunately engaged in hostilities against us, leads them to circulate exaggerated reports of their intentions and actions, well calculated to exasperate our people to acts of violence with a view of provoking retaliation which may afford an excuse for making war upon them.[32]

As he so often had before, Palmer found the source of Indian troubles in white designs. Needless to say, some believed that the source lay elsewhere. As one correspondent wrote the Oregonian on 3 November 1855: "I hope the people of Oregon are now satisfied with the reckless, insane and criminal manner in which the Indian affairs of this territory have heretofore been conducted."

Whatever the virtues or failings of Palmer's policies, the reality in late 1855 was, as stated before, that the whites had been far from victorious on the Rogue and the Columbia. "This result might have been expected under the circumstances in which they went into the contest," the *Oregonian* editorialized on 24 November:

> People in this country, we fear, are in the habit of vastly underrating the courage and the ability of the Indians to fight. The Indians have altogether the advantage of the whites, in a war of this character. They are far more numerous than most people imagine, they are better armed than the whites; they are better acquainted with the country; they choose their own time, place and mode of fighting; besides, they have no bickerings or jealousies among them; no *political* or *party* axes to grind; no political ambition to gratify; no white-livered renegades to throw obstructions in the way of their warriors, for party purposes. This is not, we regret to say, the case with the whites. We have among us, classes of men who sympathize with the Indian race; some few, unquestionably honestly, others, like the Pharisee who went upon the house-top to pray, while the Indians have no sympathy, but wage an indiscriminate war with the whites, of all ages, sex and condition. They have so far, killed more whites than our forces have Indians.

WHEN PALMER RETURNED from The Dalles in late October, he found, as noted earlier, a rising gale of opposition to the Know Nothings. Furthermore, there was now the explicit demand that he expel all Know Nothings and Whigs from his staff. These matters no doubt worried him, but of far more concern was the letter from Agent Ambrose waiting for him on his return.

Writing on 20 October, Ambrose informed Palmer that he was in a quandary and needed advice. Provisions for the reservation Indians were running out, Ambrose reported, but it was impossible to let the Indians leave the reservation to search for food because the whites would kill them; "hence you will see no other alternatives but to feed or to fight them." Palmer replied that he was "at a loss to know what to do." Finally, he returned to a course contemplated earlier: remove the reservation Indians and all other friendly bands to the Willamette Valley for the winter and transfer them in the spring to a permanent reservation on the coast. All remaining bands in the south could then be classified as enemies, leaving the army free to "pitch in," as Palmer put it.[33]

Palmer explained the situation to Commissioner Manypenny: "I am satisfied of the futility of attempting a permanent Indian settlement on the Table

Rock reserve, and that its abandonment at once is a wiser course." For one thing, the reserve was too small; for another, it was too close to white settlements; and for a third, it would be much cheaper to provide provisions for the Indians in the valley. The 334 Indians camped at Fort Lane "are in imminent danger of meeting the fate so boldly and recklessly threatened—that of annihilation; and unless they are immediately removed, the scheme will be undoubtedly carried into effect." And finally:

> The Umpqua Indians are but little more secure; one village having been already attacked by a body of lawless vandetti and put to death—men, women and children. These bands may also be located and comfortably provided for on the coast reservation, if the purchase of the tract referred to be consumated. This would concentrate all the tribes in the territory west of the Cascade mountains upon one reservation, which I regard as highly desirable; and *now*, if ever, this subject must be achieved, as I believe it the only measure by which they can be saved from extermination.[34]

The place that Palmer had in mind for these several bands was the Grand Ronde Valley on the south bank of the Yamhill about thirty miles west of the Dayton agency. Palmer considered it a suitable temporary reserve for the southern bands and thought that it would serve as an ideal permanent reserve for the bands of the Willamette Valley. Although not yet authorized to do so, he set about acquiring the Grand Ronde land. "I can conceive of no other means by which to avert an impending calamity, involving the destruction of those bands and a blot upon our national reputation."[35]

He first had to purchase land claims held by whites who were already settled in the valley. This accomplished, Palmer contracted with Joseph Jeffers to plant a crop of winter wheat and make other improvements on the reserve. He impressed upon Jeffers that "no person will be employed to service among the Indians who uses profane language, drinks as a beverage spirituous liquors or holds illicit intercourse with their women."[36] Palmer appointed Courtney Walker, a former trapper and missionary, to assist in transferring the Indians to the reserve.

But Palmer's plan met serious opposition. Ambrose, who had earlier represented the Indian situation as so desperate, now took a far more optimistic view. Palmer's plan, he wrote on 22 November, was "a matter which should require some consideration" and only to be entered into with the Indians' "hearty approval." A week later, Ambrose informed Palmer that the Indians "have an aversion to being removed . . . . They have erected comfortable temporary winter quarters, and are to all appearances, quite contented." A few days later, on 2 December, Ambrose was insistent:

> I regard it as almost impossible to remove the Indians at this time, for several reasons: first, the unusual severity of the winter at this early season; secondly, they are destitute of winter clothing . . . few of them have either shoes or stockings; many of them are sick . . . I do assure you, a trip to the Willamette at this inclement season of the year could not be accomplished without a vast deal of suffering among them.[37]

On the same day, Agent R.B. Metcalf, who had replaced William Martin on the Umpqua, wrote that it would be difficult to persuade his Indians to leave in view of the weather and their scanty clothing. Most important, however, both agents agreed that it would be folly to endeavour to remove them without an escort, and a military escort was not then available.

Behind the demand for a military escort lay perhaps the real reason for the agents' reluctance to bring the Indians to the valley. Certainly, they were concerned for the welfare of the Indians, but they were also certainly concerned for their own safety. For now there were threats that if the Indians were brought to the valley, they would be killed—along with those who brought them.

The residents of southern Oregon were happy to be rid of the Rogues, but the residents of the valley were far from happy to receive them.* Palmer himself was told that certain settlers had threatened "to shoot them [the Indians] and those that attempted to cause such a movement." There was also personal animosity toward him in this matter. G.M. Miller wrote from Eugene that persons opposed to the move were more guided by motives of revenge, against Palmer personally. Meanwhile, mass meetings were being held up and down the valley protesting the move. Even Palmer's admirer, Col. Nathaniel Ford, wrote, "I have always been your friend and I am as much so now as I ever was but it is my duty to protect my family."[38]

* *Recalling this period, Judge William M. Colvig, a prominent southern Oregon citizen, wrote: "The only honest acquisition of the Rogue River Indians was their name."* William M. Colvig, "Indian Wars of Southern Oregon," *Oregon Historical Quarterly* 4 (March 1903):228.

But Palmer was determined. On 1 December, he wrote General Wool for help:

> I have received intelligence that meetings of the citizens of the Willamette valley residing along the route to be travelled by the Indians in reaching the designated

encampment, as well as those in the vicinity of the latter, have resolved upon resisting such removal, and avow a determination to *kill* all who may be brought among them as well as those who sought to effect that object. This feeling appears so general among our citizens, I am apprehensive that they may attempt carrying it into effect. To avoid which, I have to request, if it be deemed practicable, that a command of twenty men be directed to accompany those Indians on their removal.[39]

Palmer then stated his reasons for his action:

Believing, as I do, that the cause of the present difficulty in southern Oregon is wholly to be attributed to the acts of our own people, I cannot but feel that it is our duty to adopt such measures as will tend to secure the lives of those Indians and maintain the guaranties secured to them by treaty stipulation.[40]

On 13 December, Palmer left for the south to organize the removal. It was a difficult trip, the streams swollen with heavy rains, the mountain passes deep in snow, and little forage for his animals along the way. Even the mails had been suspended due to the inclement weather. "The trip," Palmer later wrote Manypenny, "was performed through one of the severest storms that I have ever experienced in Oregon."[41] But Palmer made it, arriving in Jacksonville near the end of the month. He was greeted with the news that certain persons were telling the Indians that Palmer's intent was to remove them to an isolated place where he would have them all killed. Weather, whites, and Indians—all seemed determined to thwart him in his purpose. In the Willamette Valley, that determination was expressed in the most significant protest meeting of all: the legislative session of 1855-56.

AS USUAL, THE LEGISLATORS MET in a huff. Bancroft acidly summarized the reasons:

Oregon was somewhat soured over the Indian question, and toward the United States generally. The savages should have been more quickly and cheaply killed; the regulars could not fight Indians; the postal service was a swindle and disgrace; land matters they could manage more to their satisfaction themselves; better become a state and be independent. There was even some feeling between northern and southern Oregon; the former had labored and the latter had suffered, and both were a little sore over it.

Despite the problems crying for solution, the legislature accomplished little more than to pass yet another law on the location of the capital and to attempt to have Palmer dismissed and his policies abrogated. On 17 December, Andrew Shuck, from Palmer's own Yamhill County, offered a joint resolution for a memorial stigmatizing Palmer as "foolish and visionary" and "praying Congress to restrain the Superintendent of Indian Affairs from settling the southern Indians in the Willamette valley."[42]

As noted earlier, opposition to Palmer had begun in December of 1854, with his firing of fellow Democrat Agent Culver. This was considered gross disloyalty to the party. At the same time, there was the conviction that Palmer was or had been a Know Nothing, and as he himself knew, a group of legislators had earlier petitioned President Pierce for his removal. The obstacle to this dismissal was Palmer's old friend, Joseph Lane, still territorial delegate to Congress. In September 1855, in the midst of the *Statesman's* campaign against the Know Nothings, Editor Bush wrote Judge Deady that he had once again urged Lane to jettison Palmer. "He [Lane] promised to have . . . Palmer removed. We shall see. I told him it was said he was bumbugging us . . . . He denied it. I have not much hopes of Palmer's removal."[43]

Bush's doubts were justified, for Lane took no steps to remove Palmer. Now, however, circumstances had changed, for in addition to the Know Nothing charge, Palmer's enemies could claim that he was endangering their lives by bringing the Rogues to the valley and despoiling their Territory by giving a third of the coastal lands to the Indians for a reservation. All this was further exacerbated by Palmer's public statement that the Rogue and Yakima wars had been started by the whites. The combined effect of these various charges hardly made Palmer a popular man.

This became apparent in the debate that followed on Shuck's resolution condemning Palmer's policies—though an admixture of respect for Palmer was also present. The debate was prefaced by an admonition from the Speaker, Mr. Waymire:

> Before putting the question to the House, the chair would suggest that it is disinclined to interrupt members when addressing it; or to call members to order when they are out of order. The chair is aware of the fact that many members here are inexperienced in Parliamentary Proceedings. It is therefore, with some degree of reluctance that it sees itself under the necessity of using its prerogative, believing that the good sense of the gentlemen should suggest to themselves what is decorous. To address a member as "the old man" is not Parliamentary; to question a member's motive is not Parliamentary; to address a member by name is not Parliamentary. The chair hopes for the future that members will confine themselves within the limits of the rules. *

These strictures having been delivered, the Speaker then

* *A possible reason for the lack of the "Parlia-*

invited debate. H. U. V. Johnson of Washington County stated that though he was prepared to vote for that part of the memorial condemning the location of the Rogue Indians in the Willamette Valley, he "could not vote for that part which censured Gen. Palmer."[44] This would be a point of contention throughout the debates; all agreed that they did not want the Rogues in the valley but disagreed on whether Palmer himself should be censured.

mentary" is that it was customary to keep a keg of whiskey with a dipper in the House cloakroom, a felicity that prevailed into the twentieth century.

William Tichenor of Coos County was also reluctant to attack Palmer personally. "I have not reflected [reproached] upon Gen Palmer. I have as high a respect for him as any man in the territory but we are not willing to submit our right to the *ipse dixit* of any man." R. P. Boise of Polk and Tillamook counties was more critical. Until the establishment of Indian agencies, settlers had had few difficulties with the Indians. As for Palmer, he "would not say that Gen. Palmer wished to do wrong, but . . . he was a visionary man; and the fact that he is going to bring the fierce and savage Rogue river Indians and settle them in the Willamette valley, was a plain proof of it."[45]

But it was Delazon "Delusion" Smith of Linn County who took Palmer most to task. First of all, though "he would not advocate the doctrine that might was right . . . the whole history of settlement upon the continent proved that the destiny of the Indian race, was to fade out of existence before the advances of the Caucasian, or Anglo Saxon race,—that sooner or later religion and civilization shall possess the earth, as the waters do the deep." This matter established, Smith then went on to Palmer:

> Water does not seek its level or the stone gravitate with more certainty than that this conduct of our Indian department was the original source of the disaffection, which has led to the war that is now upon the country . . . . Sir, the arable land of this valley belongs to the "pale-face man" and he will possess it, and *we will possess it* in peace. If the superintendent does not know history, we will teach him his duty, Sir.[46]

With this final thrust, the House adjourned for the day.

Four days later, on 21 December, the memorial again came under discussion. There now appeared in Palmer's defense George Brown of Multnomah County. Brown refused to vote for the memorial so long as it characterized Palmer as "foolish and visionary." On the other hand, he agreed with Delazon Smith on the fate of the Indians: "The fact is the Indians cannot be civilized and christianized. It is the 'manifest destiny' of the Anglo-Saxon race to conquer . . . this was the case from the time when they rolled forth from the craggy rocks of Germany and conquered Britain." A. R. Burbank of Yamhill County agreed that "foolish" should be struck out of the memorial, and Thomas Smith of Jackson County held that Indian agencies were the cause of some of the Indian troubles, not General Palmer himself. Hyer Jackson of Multnomah County asserted that though he was no apologist for Palmer, he did not wish "to decry him in his absence"—an interesting point since the debates did not begin until Palmer had departed for the south. Jackson said he would not vote for the memorial if it suggested that Palmer was responsible for the war.[47]

These defenses raised the dander of Fred Waymire of Polk County. The effectiveness of the defenses of Palmer he compared to "a bob-tailed horse in fly time." Drawing himself up, he advised the assembled gentlemen "that when a man is pregnant with a speech and can't get rid of it, he ought to be delivered." According to the *Statesman* this provoked considerable laughter in the House. Waymire then proceeded to deliver. As was well known, he reminded his colleagues, Palmer had once kissed an Indian. It had been hoped that when appointed superintendent of Indian affairs he would not do so again, but in fact, he had "promoted the interests of the Indians to the detriment of the whites . . . . Dollars and cents and the convenience of his royal highness, Gen. Joel Palmer, is the only consideration that induced him to bring the Indians into the valley." For this reason,

> the women of Polk County, they won't speak to him. They would not give
> him a meal's victuals, they say, because he is a greater enemy to them than the
> Indians . . . . The object of both Wool and him [Palmer], I believe, is to get a
> war nearer home, when our wives may be compelled to cook their meals when
> it is rainy.

Once again, Brown came to Palmer's defense, joined now by Augustus Burbank of Linn County, and an amendment was proposed that would strike from the memorial the designation of Palmer as "foolish and visionary." This provoked Waymire to call for a reading of the memorial to see how it would "jingle as amended." The jingle did not please him.[48]

Now, Captain Tichenor of Tillamook County rose and returned to the theme of the Indians' perfidy. "It is not until the white man goes to make much of them and tries to elevate them," he charged, "that they become insolent and troublesome." Tichenor was particularly distressed by the Indians' propensity for thievery. They came aboard his ship, he reported, to "steal pipes and hide them in a place where you would not imagine though they had no clothes on!" He took his superiority over the Indians as his "right of might. If God did not intend it to be so, why did big fishes eat up little ones!" Brown took exception:

> He justified the right of might, the law of brute force. Now if the gentleman

wishes to return back to the savage state of our ancestors, why that will do. But we have advanced a step beyond the savage state. We do not cultivate our scalp for our neighbors, as the Indians do—and perhaps the gentleman's constituents do.[49]

Waymire entered the fray again, wishing to return the discussion to Palmer. "It is a notorious fact that he is the cause of all our difficulties north and south . . . . Turn him out . . . the biggest fool in the valley." Brown objected strenuously: "The gentleman from Polk, it seems, has been running around in his country among the lowest class of people, to have them pronounce Gen. Palmer a fool. It is the policy of government that I think is in the wrong, and not the conduct of the individual carrying out that policy." Mr. Boise of Linn County rallied to his friend Mr. Waymire: "There are no 'lowest class' in Polk County."[50]

Waymire finally came to the nub of the matter. "It is talked of out of doors, and only need we be mealy-mouthed on this floor. The superintendent is accused of being a Know Nothing and having made Know Nothing appointments." Waymire then went on to say that he had promised his wife that he would get the matter of Palmer settled. "I want a vote to be taken tonight that I may let the old woman know when I go home that I was right."[51]

The pack was off. "He has entered the unhallowed portals of a Know Nothing wigwam," Johnson charged. "He probably belongs to the Know-Nothing lodge," said Hutson. "I say the same here," said Risley. "His head should roll from the block," said Smith. The vote was taken. The memorial passed, without amendment, with only four opposed.[52]

ON 28 DECEMBER, through deep snows and subzero temperatures, Palmer set out on his return to the valley. He had done what he could: bought clothing in Roseburg for the nearly naked Umpqua; gained the agreement of the Molalla* to confederate with the Umpqua; and ordered Agent Metcalf to remove the Umpqua and their confederates to the reserve as soon as the weather permitted. As for the Rogues, their removal, too, was to wait on more clement weather.

*These Molalla were not the Willamette Valley tribe but a tribe from the headwaters of the Umpqua River.

Palmer probably reached Salem in the late afternoon or early evening of 30 December. He may, then, have been in time to see the whipping flames and great black bags of smoke at the center of the town and to have heard that most terrible of sounds, the roar of fire devouring air. Perhaps it seemed to him a fitting climax to the year, for after all, it had been a year of fires—the fires of political acrimony, the fires of Indian-white hostilities, the fires of civilian-military animosity—fires that, unlike the actual fire in Salem, would not slowly smolder out, but rage on to eventually engulf Palmer himself.

As for the actual fire that Palmer saw that night at the end of the year, it was the just-completed statehouse* that lit the sky. Whoever set it afire set it well, for it burned right to the ground and would not be replaced for many years.

* *Early in the session, a law was passed locating the capital once again in Salem. After the burning of the statehouse, a second law was passed referring the question of location to the people. However, the people refused to vote on the matter, for as Bancroft quoted the* Statesman *as writing, they were "tired of the subject," their patience exhausted. So, at long last, after four moves and many stratagems, the capital came to rest in Salem—though even then the fact would not be legally confirmed for another decade.* Bancroft, *History of Oregon,* vol. 2, 353.

TWELVE

The General and the Politicians

ON PALMER'S ARRIVAL IN SALEM he was, of course, immediately informed of the House's charges against him, and he immediately set out to refute them. His tactics were two: letters to the newspapers and a request for a personal appearance before the Territorial House.

Debate on Palmer's request was granted on 7 January 1856. However, the following day, the members had second thoughts. Waymire wanted the matter reconsidered for the most ingenious of reasons: the more the general sought to vindicate himself, he explained, the more foolish he would appear. "I want to save him from any such exposure," Waymire claimed. He then went on to the old heart of the matter: all Palmer's employees were Know Nothings and Palmer had asked General Wool "to shoot down our citizens." Finally, Waymire was "*bored* almost to death by the explanations of the General." Boise agreed that Palmer wished to use General Wool and his troops to shoot down what Palmer had called "the lawless rabble," a reference to Boise's own constituents! Burbank shilly-shallied. He did not think Palmer had been referring to the people of the Willamette Valley, let alone to Boise's constituents! On the other hand, he was not prepared to listen to "bunkum" from the general and, in the end, opposed his appearance.[1]

Smith had other reasons for denying Palmer a hearing. There was no precedent for such an accommodation in the histories of the Greek and Roman empires, nor indeed at the national capital. It could only turn the legislature into a "bear garden."[2]

Perhaps what angered the House members most in all these matters was that Palmer was alleged—no doubt correctly—to have insulted them. Boise reported that the general had stated that at the Grand Ronde reservation he would endeavor to make the Indians "at least as civilized and intelligent as the members of the present assembly." For his part, Smith had been informed that Palmer, in referring to the House, had said: "Whom the gods wish to destroy, they first make mad." The members voted eight to three to deny Palmer's request to appear in the chamber of the House.[3]

But they could not deny him the adjacent halls, where Palmer had been "taking every member of this body by the button-hole."[4] One of the matters the general was no doubt at great pains to explain was his letter to Gen. John Ellis Wool that had so often been referred to in the debate.

Gen. John Ellis Wool had a distinguished military career before, during, and after his service in Oregon—though many Oregonians would have disputed the "during." In the Mexican war, as mentioned earlier, he accomplished the daunting task of mustering and training twelve thousand volunteers in six weeks and thereafter leading them on a march to Saltillo that "for sheer audacity and control . . . ranks with Xenophon." Largely responsible for the victory of Buena Vista, Wool was voted a sword and thanks by Congress. From 1854-57, he served as commander of the Department of the Pacific, and it was this service that brought him to Oregon. Late in the Civil War, the general saved Fortress Monroe, among other accomplishments. Commenting on his Civil War service and other services, William A. Ganoe wrote that though a "rigid disciplinarian . . . he had great personal benignity." As for the physical man, one of his officers described him as "a small, neat man with violet-colored eyes . . . . very sharp, like a bald eagle's."[5]

General Wool and General Palmer entertained great respect for each other. Wool had first visited Oregon in November 1855 and was initially well received. Who could help but be impressed by the valor and energy of a man who, on being asked where his headquarters were to be, replied, "in the saddle"? But that energy soon took the form of an acute appraisal of the Oregon scene, while at the same time the valor was translated into an exceptional frankness of speech.

> The less you have to do with them [the Oregon volunteers] the better it will be for the service. Many of them, as well as most of the Oregonians, are for exterminating the Indians, and accordingly do not discriminate between friends and foes. The course thus far pursued by Gov. Curry and the volunteers has only tended to increase our Indian enemies, whilst it has subjected the regular service

to great inconvenience and expense. This, too, by exhausting the resources of
Oregon and Washington, and without accomplishing the least good.[6]

These words were written by Wool to one of his associates, but there is little
doubt that he publicly stated these sentiments as well.

Wool's opposition to the use of volunteer forces when they were supposedly straining at the bit, ready for combat "at the first tap of the drum," and
his refusal to provide supplies to those in the field enraged most Oregonians.
General Wool did not give a damn. The 19 January 1856 *Oregonian* reported
that he had informed the New York newspapers that "this was not the first
time he had had *dogs barking* at his heels." Oregonians did not care to be called
dogs. Furthermore, the *Oregonian* wrote,

> General Wool's efforts to bring the volunteer service into dispute, and to influ-
> ence the congress of the United States to repudiate the payment of the expenses
> of this war, will be just as successful as an effort would be to make the people of
> Oregon bow down and lick the dust from his "heels" in place of "barking" at
> them.

For this was at the bottom of the matter. It was bad enough to defend the Indians and disparage the volunteers and citizens of Oregon, but it was intolerable
to threaten that cornucopia of United States funds with which Oregonians expected to cover the cost of the war, and perhaps the cost of some other things
as well—this was intolerable! And indeed, Wool did threaten the cornucopia:
"As long as individual war is permitted and paid for by the United States, and
which is expected by all citizens of Oregon, we shall have no peace, and the
war prolonged indefinitely, especially as it is generally asserted that the present
war is a God-send to the people." Later, referring to the governors of Oregon
and Washington, he was even more outspoken: "These two governors appear
to be running a race to see who can dip the deepest into the treasury of the
United States."[7]

This was the firebrand with whose name Palmer was now associated and
specifically in Palmer's letter to Wool of 1 December 1855 requesting a guard
to accompany the southern Indians in their removal to the valley. It was in this
letter that Palmer wrote, "believing, as I do, that the cause of the present difficulty in Southern Oregon is wholly to be attributed to the acts of our own
people . . . a numerous population who regard the treasury of the United
States a legitimate object of plunder."[8] Although Palmer himself was outspoken, he probably did not intend these remarks to be made public. But Wool,
perhaps to prove that he was not alone in his remonstrances, did just that,
thereby adding considerable fuel to the already raging fire.

ON HEARING OF THE HOUSE'S DENIAL of his request to appear before them, Palmer sent a letter to George Manypenny announcing that he was "not unwilling" to relinquish his office should the administration desire it. He warned, however, that any superintendent chosen by the legislature

> will feel under obligation to carry out the will of the body, which is wholly adverse to that expressed in your instructions . . . . On the other hand, should one be appointed from abroad, he must have the military force of the government to maintain the laws and enable him to carry out his instructions.

Neither alternative could have appealed to Manypenny, who had great confidence in Palmer. In early December, the commissioner had authorized Palmer to use one million dollars as he saw fit in the circumstances created by the two Indian wars. And in January, Manypenny had written Palmer that the Secretary of the Interior believed that "in the existing emergencies the direction and management of Indian affairs in Oregon will be confided to your discretion, believing as he does, that promptness, humanity, firmness and wisdom will mark your course."[9] In Palmer's present plight, however, these expressions of confidence meant nothing for the simple reason that they had not yet reached him and would not for a matter of weeks.

Palmer's letter to Manypenny after the denial of his request to appear before the House was followed the next day by another. Though declining to refer to the memorial, he did set out in detail his recent accomplishments together with an assurance that the people of the valley no longer opposed his temporary settlement of the southern Indians at Grand Ronde—an assurance that some would have found questionable. But Palmer was determined to keep his superintendency. He took other measures as well. Although the memorial condemning him had passed the House with little opposition, it had not yet been sanctioned by the Council or upper house. It is certain, therefore, that Palmer was busy "button-holing" the members of that body. Also, on 15 January, he wrote to the *Statesman* asking that it publish President Pierce's order establishing the coast reservation—so opposed by the memorialists—adding that so far as he was concerned, "the effort of those seeking to manufacture public opinion can have no influence in deterring me from the performance of a public duty."[10] Palmer wrote to the other newspapers as well, requesting that they publish those official documents, such as Pierce's and Manypenny's, that justified his actions. Only one newspaper complied, the *Oregonian*, no doubt to embarrass Asahel Bush and his clique.

The final gun fired by Palmer in his offensive was to dismiss his secretary,

Edward Geary. Relations between Geary and Palmer had been uneasy for some time, since Palmer believed that Geary wished to take his place. At this particular time, it came to Palmer's attention that the Democratic members of the House had met in caucus and—going beyond the memorial, which had only censured Palmer—agreed to demand Palmer's removal and to make Geary his replacement, if Geary would agree to abandon the Coast and Grand Ronde reservations. Geary did agree, for he seems to have genuinely believed the establishment of a reservation on the coast unwise, that in time the coast would prove an important resource and thus should be left open to settlement.

Geary's position directly contradicted Palmer's and Manypenny's policy, and in mid-January, Palmer wrote a short, tough letter of dismissal. There were three charges: Geary's "bungling manner" with the accounts; his susceptibility to "faction" (that is, the Salem Clique); and most important, what Palmer called his lack of sympathy for the laws of Congress and instructions of department heads. Geary wrote back a conciliatory reply that, together with Geary's letter to the caucus expressing his high regard for Palmer, suggests that Palmer may have dealt with his secretary a little severely.* In the meantime, the matter of the memorial still had not been settled. On 24 January, the Council finally returned it to the House, but with objections to some of the phrasing, particularly the characterization of Palmer as "foolish and visionary." The three members voting against retaining the characterization provoked Representative Boise to call "the first a know nothing, the second a whig, and the third might as well be both."[11] The memorial was returned to the Council with the controversial phrase intact. The question now was how the Council would vote.

* On the other hand, Agent R.B. Metcalf, who strongly disapproved of Palmer's Know Nothing connections, wrote Lane on 26 February 1856 that Geary "is a man that ought never to hold other than a subordinate position, he is treacherous, tyrannical, and ambitious. And would be the first man to turn against you when it became his interest to do so. His treatment of Palmer was the most unwarranted and unqualified treachery, so much in justification of his removal by Gen. Palmer." R.B. Metcalf to Joseph Lane, 26 February 1856, Lane Collection, Lilly Library, Indiana University, Bloomington.

THIRTEEN

Winter on
the Rogue
and Columbia

EANWHILE, THE WARS WENT ON, though muffled
somewhat by the winter snows. In early January 1856, a volunteer in the south wrote the *Oregonian* that his company was
blessed with "ten gallons of whisky so we manage to kill time
besides 'bout seven or eight Ingins per day."[1] This success in killing Indians
was only half true. Following the ignominious defeat of the whites at the
Battle of Black Bar at the end of 1855, the troops had encountered Charley's
band of the Rogues who, because they were without weapons—or because
they were genuinely so inclined—sued for peace. The volunteers killed all the
men, with the women and children fleeing to Fort Lane for refuge. The volunteers took a similar action against some of Jake's band of the Rogues. Both actions were much condemned by both Palmer and Wool. Thus, in these cases,
the volunteers' boast was true—but, in other instances, it was not.

Early in January, a combined force of volunteers and regulars engaged a
group of Chief John's band, who had fortified themselves in three deserted
cabins on Applegate Creek. The first casualty occurred when a white decided
to test the Indians' marksmanship. Placing himself behind a tree, he put his hat
on a stick and protruded it beyond the tree, while at the same time peering
around the other side of the tree to watch the fun. An Indian rifleman at a distance of fifty yards fired, his bullet penetrating not the hat but the volunteer's
head.

After repeated attempts to dislodge the Indians, the whites sent for a howitzer. In due course, the howitzer arrived but sans powder, for the mule carry-

ing the powder had fallen into a creek. Finally, the second load of powder arrived, a shell dispatched, and one of the cabins demolished. By now, however, it was dark, so the attack was suspended until morning. A guard, meanwhile, was posted around the remaining cabins to prevent the Indians' escape. Yet during the night, the Indians somehow made their way through the guards, and as Walling put it, "when they [the volunteers] arose the next morning their birds had flown and the cages were empty." On inspection, it was found that the "cages" had been most cleverly equipped with loopholes, underground passages and other features that would have made the Indians impregnable but for the howitzer. On viewing the cabins, Ambrose remarked that the "Indians ingenuity or cunning could hardly be excelled by the whites." Frances Victor, usually more generous, could not allow the Indians their ingenuity. It was, she wrote, "surprising in savage military science, but was probably learned from communication with white men."[2]

On 29 January 1856, a *Statesman* correspondent from Grave Creek reported on another humiliating defeat.

> The Indians in the two or three last attacks have been successful in killing some of our best men, and that without any loss on their part. It seems that the attack on Capt. Baily and his command of 70 or 80 men was made about 8 or 9 o'clock while a large fire was burning, making a light for the boys to wrestle by.

The correspondent concluded: "Thus it was that the Indians surprised 75 men, killing two, and caused them to retreat."

Far more serious for the war in the south was the loss of troops. Many men whose period of enlistment—usually three months—was over had declined to reenlist; others had simply gone home. By mid-February, only one-third of the original force was left. As Frances Victor explained, "there was neither pay nor glory . . . nothing but self-sacrifice." A *Statesman* correspondent from Deer Creek suggested yet another reason:

> The first companies that went out were composed to some extent of men who imagined that there would be but little or no fighting to do and that they would make four or five dollars a day . . . at the expense of a great deal less physical exertion than was required to maul rails or milk Spanish cattle. They have got over that.[3]

And then there was that farcical, but at the time, serious, rebellion by the women of Jacksonville. Meeting at the Methodist church, they demanded that at least some of the men return and protect them; otherwise, they would in the future "withhold all comforts of home." The men who were left in town responded by running a petticoat halfway up the town flagpole. The next day, the women chopped the flagpole down. It is impossible to determine the truth of the details of the story, but it appears to have occurred. What is certain is that many of the Jacksonville volunteers did return to "the comforts of home."[4]

For a variety of reasons, then, the forces in the south were gravely depleted. The result was that the roads and many settlements were left without protection and the field was given over to the Indians. Everyone blamed everyone else. Asahel Bush and the *Statesman* pointed the finger at the Whigs and Know Nothings, provoking the *Oregonian* to its loudest screech of the war. "Philemon," writing from Jacksonville on 12 January—probably a pseudonym for Editor Dryer—described Bush as a

> miserable poltroon; cooped as he is within the polluted walls of the *Statesman* office, steeped in liquor and dyed in iniquity—inflated with ignorance, arrogance and self-conceit—this aspiring genius dictates to the freemen of Oregon how they should proceed in matters of war.

But that was precisely the question: how should the freemen of Oregon proceed in matters of war? The one person qualified and authorized to make decisions, General Wool, had been denounced as both a traitor and a tyrant. As for Governor Curry, he was Bush's creature and proceeded in terms almost entirely political. Finally, there were the volunteers, to whom all policies, procedures, strategies, and orders constituted an offense not to be tolerated by the "freemen of Oregon."

MATTERS WERE NO BETTER in the northern war. In a major battle on the Walla Walla, the whites were far from successful. There was also, as usual, much trouble with the volunteers. In late January, Palmer received a copy of a letter from Father E.C. Chirouse at the Umatilla Mission to a priest at The Dalles. Chirouse, after comparing the volunteers to "the madmen of the Revolution," complained that they were running off the friendly Indians' cattle and stealing their provisions. Also, Agent Thompson reported from The Dalles: "Many things have occurred since the commencement of hostilities which for the honor of our manhood and boasted civilization I dare not pen." Because of the volunteers' activities, he wrote, it was difficult to keep the local Indians from becoming disaffected. In January, he complained again, and it was not only the volunteers' behavior toward the Indians but also toward the settlers. "If the settlers protest to the useless destruction of their property, their lives are threatened. One of them writing to a friend says that if their lives were in danger when surrounded by hostile Indians, they are doubly so now."[5]

But one of the most disturbing indictments of the volunteers came from the Indians themselves. It reached Palmer in the form of a copy of a letter to Governor Isaac Stevens from the Walla Walla and Cayuse:

> They [the volunteers] appear as ignorant and wicked as we are. They look upon us and treat us as belonging to a different race from man. They have nothing but contempt and hatred for our miserable condition. They say they want to destroy us all, thinking we are useless beings upon the face of the earth. That they are men and we are brutes without reason. Let them use the reason of men, since they are men.[6]

Finally, to Palmer's great sorrow and anger, Yellow Serpent was killed in December. The circumstances of the killing and whether or not it was justified are unclear. The volunteers claimed that the chief, a prisoner, was attempting escape. There is no doubt, however, that Palmer considered Yellow Serpent a friend of the Americans and to have "often exerted his influence in restraining the surrounding tribes from acts of aggression." He also considered Yellow Serpent a "victim of unscrupulous and designing men, in revenge for his boldness in avowing his preferences for Americans and denouncing those who were the oppressors of his people."[7] By "unscrupulous and designing men," it is not clear who Palmer meant; perhaps Hudson's Bay Company men, perhaps the priests. But by "oppressors of his people," he surely meant the volunteers.

There was also controversy over the manner of Yellow Serpent's death. One witness reportedly said: "They skinned him from head to foot, and made razor-straps of his skin," and some said as well that his ears and fingers were cut off for souvenirs. Frances Victor reminded her readers that the killing and mutilation took place not far from the site of the Whitman massacre and, furthermore, that the volunteers "were still smarting, too, under the recollection . . . of the Ward massacre of the year before, at which demoniacal scene babes were roasted alive before their mothers' eyes, and the mothers themselves tortured to death with hot irons thrust into their persons." Yellow Serpent "having chosen to place himself in combination with such offenders as these did not appear to the volunteers entitled to respect."[8] But Palmer and others argued that this did not excuse whites for engaging in those very practices for which the whites labeled the Indians barbarians.

IN THEIR LETTER TO STEVENS, the Walla Walla and Cayuse made a reference to Palmer that must have saddened him to read: "He [Palmer] told us that he was our great agent and he has disappointed and forgotten us." It was true that for the most part Palmer had disappeared from the eastern Oregon scene. For one thing, the Yakima War was in Stevens' territory. So far as Indian affairs on the Oregon side of the Columbia were concerned, Palmer, distracted by crisis in the south and political attacks in the valley, had to a large degree left matters in the hands of Agent Thompson. Nonetheless, he had not forgotten his obligations to the Indians of the region. In late January, for example, he wrote to Wool requesting that troops be dispatched to the Umatilla because he was

> firmly of the opinion that nothing short of the immediate occupancy of that country by regular United States troops can save these tribes from a participation in this war . . . and enable this department to maintain guarantees secured these Indians by treaty stipulations.

In the same letter, Palmer referred to another request for troops that he had earlier directed to Major Rains at Fort Vancouver. He desired these troops as an escort for the southern tribes in the process of their removal to the Willamette Valley. The presence of the troops was essential, Palmer wrote, in order to "awe lawless persons and give confidence to the Indians."[9]

For now the highly controversial removals had begun, and indeed, "lawless persons" and frightened Indians were two of the many problems impeding the removal. There had been many threats to disrupt the removal, and as for the Indians, many feared they were being removed in order to be killed.

DESPITE THEIR PLEA to be left to die on their own land, the Umpqua and associated bands began their journey to the Grand Ronde on 10 January under the direction of Agent Metcalf. The cold, sickness, inadequate supplies, scarce forage, conditions of the roads, and in particular, the Indians' propensity to desert plagued Metcalf all the way.

On the evening of the fifteenth, camped on Elk Creek near Yoncalla, seven Umpquas ran off into the night. The following day, whites circulated among the Indians telling them that Palmer was to be removed and that they would be shot if they went on to Grand Ronde. At the same time, Lindsay Applegate arrived to lecture Metcalf, denouncing him as inhuman for forcing the Indians to leave their native land. Metcalf wrote Palmer that if he did not receive a military escort, there would be a stampede in the camp. Palmer immediately sent a message to Fort Vancouver but was advised that troops could not be dispatched without the approval of General Wool, who at that particular time was in San Francisco rather than "in the saddle."

Metcalf got the caravan started again on 16 January. One woman had already died, and the agent realized that eight wagons were not enough to accommodate the increasing numbers of infirm. Indeed, so many complained of exhaustion that 18 January was spent in camp. That night, a boy died. Over the next several days, there were heavy rains, drenching everyone and everything and making the roads almost impassable with mud. Thus, there was a need for more fires than usual, and the whites along the way complained at the amount of wood the Indians were using. On 24 January, two more people died, so Metcalf hired another team and wagon for the old and sick who could not keep up. Earlier, Palmer had written Dr. Thomas Right at Corvallis asking him to go to the Umpqua when they arrived and attend the sick.

But Corvallis presented a problem—an old problem. Whites sold liquor to the Indians, and the caravan was delayed until Metcalf could find the drunken Indians. There was yet another delay the next day while Metcalf searched for another missing man; he found him, murdered and thrown into a creek. The heavy rains commenced again, and several oxen and horses gave out from struggling through the mud and were left behind. Metcalf and the Umpqua finally reached Grand Ronde on 2 February. It is doubtful that the reserve proved a blessed refuge after their long travail. Joseph Jeffers at the reserve wrote to Palmer a few days after their arrival: "The Umpaqua Indians . . . are suffering with the flux to the extent that it makes humanity shudder . . . and those that are sick suffer with the cold at night a nuff to kill them . . . the suffering of these people haunts me day and night."[10]

Still, the removal had been accomplished, a victory for Palmer. Now, too, he was partially victorious in the matter of the memorial. As noted earlier, the Council—objecting to the characterization of Palmer as "foolish and visionary"—had returned the memorial to the House, where a joint committee of Council and House was formed to effect a compromise. Changes were made, but the denigrating description of Palmer remained. This being the case, the Council on 30 January declined to sanction the memorial. The result was that the memorial went to President Pierce expressing the sentiments of the House only and not of the legislature as a whole. This fact, together with Lane and Manypenny's continued support, meant Palmer had prevailed. But it did not mean his enemies had abandoned their determination to remove him. As his agent for the Willamette Valley, Berryman Jennings, wrote him: "They will seek out every shady place to give you a stab."[11]

The matter of the memorial now concluded and the Umpqua established at Grand Ronde, Palmer's next concern was the removal of the nearly four hundred Indians from Table Rock and Fort Lane. This removal began on 22 February under the direction of Agent Ambrose.

The agent's first task was to shoe and clothe his charges, for all were barefoot and many almost naked. Palmer had contracted with a firm to provide these articles, but it had failed to do so, and Ambrose had to buy them in Jacksonville at highly inflated prices. He also found it necessary to hire two more teams and wagons; more than thirty of the band were sick.

The trek began well, with sunny and mild weather and passable roads. But on the evening of 28 February, camped on Jumpoff Joe Creek, an Indian leading his horse into camp was shot dead, probably by a group of volunteers camped nearby. Ambrose sent a message to Captain Smith at Fort Lane requesting more men for an escort. "That our country is infested with such a set of men," he wrote to Palmer, "none will question who are acquainted with the country."[12]

Believing the volunteers had gone ahead to harass the train when it started up again, Ambrose stayed in camp until the following day, when Captain Smith arrived with a reinforcement of sixty men. Meanwhile, a man named Love was identified as the killer, and Ambrose finally succeeded in getting him arrested. Love's defense, when questioned, was that the Indian he had killed was "a bad Indian."[13] Love escaped at some point but was caught and put on trial when the train reached Roseburg.

The remainder of the journey was plagued by a shortage of forage, straying cattle, and several deaths. Finally, on 25 March, after 33 days and 263 miles, the train reached Grand Ronde. Eight Indians had died on the way, but there had also been eight births. Thus, Ambrose was able to report that he had arrived with the same number of Indians with which he had started out.

THE REMOVAL OF THESE TWO INDIAN GROUPS relieved tensions in the south, but not entirely, for the Rogue Chief John remained a problem. This resolute foe of the whites appears to have been an exceptional man who never abandoned his proud resistance. Bancroft described him as having an intelligent face, earnest and determined, but "marked with that expression of grief which is often seen on the countenances of savage men in the latter part of their lives."[14]

In mid-February, Ambrose reported to Palmer that John wanted peace, but not the "peace" that had prevailed earlier. That peace had

> only served to lull his people into a belief of security in which they were killed for amusement by the whites. If the whites wish to fight it is alright, he prefers war to a dishonorable peace, that he would rather die fighting for his rights than to . . . have his people killed for nothing when ever it suited the caprice of some men to do so.[15]

In the circumstances, John's attitude, however understandable, was not encouraging.

Two days earlier, R. W. Dunbar, Collector of Customs at Port Orford, had
written Joseph Lane, confirming John's complaint:

> I cannot refrain from speaking of things brought to my notice *daily* . . . . Law-
> less whites who are more disposed to abuse the defenseless Indian among us,
> than to meet those whose arms are raised against the whites, are constantly mal-
> treating civil, peaceable Indians. All or nearly all of the present difficulties in
> Oregon, North and South, may be traced to this cause, we have a low miser-
> able set of *white men* among us who prey upon the Indian, coax, buy or steal
> their women, and if they refuse, they are beaten and abused. Many Indians beg
> for redress, and reason thus: "What would white men say, if we took in this
> way, their wives or daughters," and strange to say, many white men sanction,
> or wink at this conduct, tho thare are some who do not. Two days ago 3 or 4
> *men* who belong to the volunteer Company, Officers commissioned by the Gov
> —came in from their camp on business, got into a drunken spree with others,
> went to a peaceable Indian's *ranch* and tried to take the *squaws*, and upon refusal
> the head of the ranch was beaten, he applied to the *Fort* for protection. Maj
> Reynolds, U.S.A. promptly sent a file of men and warned the rowdies that he
> would put them in irons if they were found again in a like predicament. On the
> day previous some of the same, with others in a like condition, fell on an un-
> offending boy (an Indian) beat him, and ran him out of town with clubs, and a
> drawn pistol in the hand of one I am told holding the office of Commissary in
> said Volunteer Company . . . . What an example this is to the Indians who are
> told that the white man is his *friend*. And what inducements for him to join the
> party now so successfully at war with the whites. The class above referred to act
> out the worst principles of their natures and seem to regard the Indian as having
> no rights.
>
>   These lawless men are running riot over the country, and many of them
> throwing obstacles in the way of the removal of the Indians to the reservation
> selected for them because they will be forbidden to go upon the reservation.
> Why Sir, it is matter of serious concern that nearly every single man, in this part
> of Oregon is living openly with Squaws, it is lamentable, when a man of cool
> reflection knows, that one of the principal causes of our present Indian difficul-
> ties, grow out of this lawless conduct. A few of us the other day, declared
> against the mal-treatment of the Indians, but it was by others hushed up I
> hope that these coast tribes, may be allowed to go on the reservation at an early
> day.[16]

But Palmer had done what he could in the south, and now his concern was the Willamette Valley and the upper Columbia. As early as January, he had announced that the Indians in the valley must remove to Grand Ronde, but he met resistance not only from the Indians but also from those whites who desired the Indians' presence, "some for their trade, some for their labor," as Jennings, the agent for the valley, put it. Nonetheless, the tribes gradually came in, some bands arriving by boat from the upper valley. Conditions at Grand Ronde, however, remained deplorable, despite Palmer's efforts. Jeffers wrote of the twenty Luckiamute who had come in late January that he had given them straw to sleep on, but that he did not have enough blankets, and "they suffer with the cold and I cannot sleep myself thinking about them in open tents."[17]

IMPROVING CONDITIONS AT GRAND RONDE as best he could, Palmer turned his attention to The Dalles. He had two concerns. One was to investigate the alleged irregularities of his Dalles subagent, Nathan Olney. The other was to persuade the friendly Cayuse, Walla Walla, and Umatilla, as well as the Wasco and Deschutes, to flee from the dangers of the Yakima War and to take refuge at Warm Springs. Arriving in mid-March, he found the evidence against Olney insufficient to warrant his dismissal. As for the Indians, though disinclined to confederate, they did agree by and large to remove to Warm Springs.

It was at this same time that a certain softening of Palmer's attitude vis-à-vis the treatment of Indians by whites occurred. Heretofore, he had always blamed whites for the outbreaks of trouble, and as for the volunteers, he routinely gave them the back of his hand. Now, however, he wrote Manypenny that in the case of the Yakima War he was not altogether certain who the culprits were: this time it might have been the Indians who broke the peace. Also, he paid some of the volunteers a compliment: "We have in the volunteer forces many well disposed officers and men."[18]

This shift in attitude may have been the better part of valor. Palmer was still very much under attack, partly because he was considered to be "on the Indian side of all questions or troubles." His comments may have been an attempt to mollify his critics. But perhaps not. He may have refrained from blaming the whites for the war only because "the usual sources of correct or reliable information in regard to the action and disposition of these Indians seems to be entirely barren of everything like authenticity." And he also hastened to add that among the volunteers, "the reckless predominate."[19]

FOURTEEN

Victory
and Defeat

B Y THE SPRING of 1856, Palmer could be proud of two accomplishments: he had completed or begun the removal of the Indians from the upper country, the Willamette Valley, and the south to reservations—those sanctuaries where he believed they would be safe from the white exterminators and where, in addition, their "improvement" might commence; and in little more than two years, he had also extinguished Indian title to roughly two-thirds of the territory. Thus, it must have come to him as a cruel irony that the spring of 1856 turned out to be the bloodiest of his superintendency.

From the time of Ben Wright's arrival at the mouth of the Rogue in the previous year, peace had prevailed on the south coast. "He stood like a wall of adamant between the two races in their numerous quarrels," Dr. Glisan had written.[1] To further ensure peace, thirty volunteers established a camp at the "big bend" of the Rogue near present-day Agness. Their purpose was also to form a wall of adamant, but in this case, between the warring Indians of the upper Rogue and the mainly peaceful tribes of the coast.

In February 1856, this encampment was moved to within a few miles of Gold Beach. The reasons are unclear; perhaps there was alarm that "Indian locks" had begun to appear on the doors of a few Gold Beach houses. These locks consisted of a spray of greenery placed against the door of a house to signify that the inhabitants were to be spared in any rampage that might occur, that is, persons whom the Indians did not wish to molest. Thus, it may have been that the appearance of these locks caused apprehension and dictated the removal of the encampment from the big bend to the outskirts of the town.

This proximity proved to be particularly convenient on the night of 22 February, Washington's Birthday. In celebration, an all-night ball was held in Gold Beach, and the volunteers were invited. All but ten accepted. Early on the morning of 23 February, while the revelers danced, the ten volunteers remaining in camp were attacked by local Indians—only two of the volunteers escaping, the others killed. Later that morning, Ben Wright was butchered, his heart taken out, roasted and eaten. Before the day was over, the Indians had fired sixty houses between the big bend and Gold Beach and had killed thirty-one persons.

Meanwhile, in Gold Beach, the citizens and dancing volunteers, numbering about 130, fled to a half-finished fort on the north side of the river and sent a messenger to the army at Port Orford thirty miles up the coast. But the force at Port Orford was so small that sending even a portion of it to Gold Beach would have left the post defenseless. Major Reynolds did dispatch a whaleboat of supplies to the survivors, but on its approach to Gold Beach, it foundered in the surf. All six of the crew drowned, and upon washing up on the beach, their bodies were dismembered by the Indians.

At the fort, the survivors worked to stave off starvation and thirst, sneaking out at night to forage for supplies. They were also working to free a Mrs. Geisell and her daughter, who had been captured by the Indians. Finally, an exchange was effected—four Indian women and one hundred dollars for the two white women. The two white women were told by the Indians on their departure that in two days they would be back again, for by then, the Indians said, they would have captured the fort.

But they did not. On the thirty-first day of the siege, "to the straining eyes of the imprisoned inmates of the fort was revealed the ravishing sight of two companies of the United States troops marching up from Fort Humboldt." It so happened that one of the men in the United States force was a correspondent for *Harper's Magazine*. His description of the survivors suggests that the trooper found the survivors less ravishing than the survivors found the troopers. "There were rough buck-skin clad miners and mule-drivers, thick-lipped, flabby squaws and delicate looking American women, and dirty, noisy children, and a general mixture of all the mongrel and nondescript races of the mines, crowded together in the little fort."[2]

Such, then, was the debacle at Gold Beach. Over and above the killings, the destruction, and the hardships of the siege, it was clear that the war in the south had now spread to the coast. Palmer, who first heard of the killings on 2 March, laid out what he believed to be the causes in a letter to George Manypenny:

> the extraordinary success of the hostile bands in whipping the forces fought against, and the ease with which they had invariably gained a victory over them, inspired a belief that they were abundantly able to maintain their position, and rid themselves of the white population. In every instance where a conflict has ensued between volunteers and hostile Indians in southern Oregon the latter have gained what they regard a victory. It is true that a number of Indian camps have been attacked by armed parties, and mostly put to death or flight, but in such cases it has been those unprepared to make resistance, and not expecting such attack. This, though lessening the *number* of Indians in the country, has tended greatly to exasperate and drive into a hostile attitude many that would otherwise have abstained from the commission of acts of violence against the whites.
>
> The avowed determination of the people to exterminate the Indian race, regardless as to whether they were innocent or guilty, and the general disregard for the rights of those acting as friends and aiding in the subjugation of our real and avowed enemies, has had a powerful influence in inducing these tribes to join the warlike bands.
>
> It is astonishing to know the rapidity with which intelligence is carried from one extreme of the country to another, and the commission of outrages (of which there have been many) by our people against an Indian is heralded forth by the hostile parties, augmented, and used as evidence of the necessity for *all* to unite in war against us.
>
> These coast bands, it is believed, might have been kept out of the war if a removal could have been effected during the winter.[3]

Palmer concluded that measures would soon be taken to remove the tribes to Grand Ronde and eventually to the new reservation at the coast.

LITTLE MORE THAN A MONTH LATER, a second slaughter bloodied the spring, this time at the Cascades of the Columbia. With the Yakima War, as during the Cayuse War, the Cascades grew in importance, for it was here that materiel for the war was transshipped. This necessitated the building of warehouses and a blockhouse halfway up the portage on the northern side.

On the evening of 25 March, the soldiers stationed at the blockhouse passed their time drinking whiskey toddies. The next morning, from lack of sleep and crapulence, they dispatched one of their numbers to the store at the upper Cascades for a hair of the dog, that is to say, a canteen of whiskey. Before the soldier could return, the Yakima, together with what Lt. Philip Sheridan described as "free lances" from other tribes, attacked both the blockhouse and the store. At the latter, about forty persons had taken refuge. The Yakima attempted to drive out the garrison and the refugees by setting fire to the blockhouse and the store, throwing lighted brands on the roof of each. In the case of the blockhouse, these efforts were repulsed by the soldiers' howitzer. In the store, the refugees doused the flames with brine from the store's pork barrels. After several days of siege, regulars and volunteers arrived from Fort Vancouver, Fort Dalles, and Portland, and the Yakima fled. They left seventeen dead whites and twelve others badly wounded.

In little more than a month, at Gold Beach and the Cascades, forty-eight whites had been killed by Indians. In a population of about thirty-five thousand, this was a high proportion of fatalities, twice the number per capita than the worst year of the Vietnam War—and the year had only begun. More death was sure to come. Panic ensued as well as recrimination, much of the latter focused on Palmer. Look what "pampering" of Indians had led to, charged his critics: forty-eight dead whites.

PALMER, IT MAY BE REMEMBERED, had gone to The Dalles in early March to make arrangements for the removal of the upper-country tribes to Warm Springs. He started back for the valley on the eighteenth, passing the Cascades where, in a week, the Yakima attack would come, arriving home on the twenty-second. The mail that awaited him was not of a happy nature.

Berryman Jennings wrote Palmer on 19 March that there were those who held the superintendent responsible for Ben Wright's death. Then there were requests from settlers on the Alsea and at Canyonville that Palmer immediately arrange for the removal of their local tribes. The request by John Boyd of Canyonville was especially pathetic. The local Indians at Canyonville had given up their arms to the settlers in return for a promise not to be harmed. No sooner had they done so than "a set of scamps" killed one of the men and four women; the rest of the band fled to the mountains. "One of the band," Boyd wrote, "came in last night very near starvation and very anxious to go on the reservation. I told them to come in and I would furnish them with provisions until I heard from you."[4]

However, within a day or so of Palmer's return and these letters seeking the removal of the Alsea and Canyonville Indians, the citizens of neighboring

Lafayette held a meeting to protest the establishment of the refuge at Grand Ronde and even went so far as to send petitions to Governor Curry in Salem and Delegate Lane in Washington. Palmer was in a box, besieged on the one hand by those who desired the Indians' removal, besieged on the other by those opposed to the place of removal. On the same day as the Lafayette meeting, the news of the Cascades arrived, adding an avalanche of fuel to the already raging fire.

On 29 March, a telegram arrived from Oregon City demanding the immediate removal of all Indians from the town and its vicinity. But it was in Portland that the greatest consternation prevailed and to which Palmer hastened on 30 March. "Intense excitement caused by the massacre at Cascades. Resolutions had been posted by citizens to kill all Indians found about the place," Palmer wrote in his diary.[5] The following day, more threats were made to kill any Indians seen. Palmer lodged a complaint and obtained a warrant for the arrest of would-be exterminators, but he found that it could not be enforced. He then called a public meeting, attempted to mollify those present, and then, there being little more he could do, hurried on to Oregon City to collect the Indians there and remove them to Grand Ronde.

Palmer presented his estimate of the situation and its causes in a letter to George Manypenny on 11 April. Because of the attack on the Cascades, an

> outbreak of popular frenzy came well nigh upsetting and defeating the whole project [removal of the Indians to reservations]. Not a little of this un-necessary excitement, I am forced to believe, grew out of efforts of disappointed politicians . . . by circulating the most outrageous, exaggerated and groundless reports in regard to the acts of the Indians and agents of the Department tending to influence the minds of the people who were ignorant of the facts, and drive them to acts of desperation.[6]

This downplayed the legitimate fears of the people. As the newspapers had stated and Palmer himself had confessed, the Indians had won every battle in which they had so far engaged. And now these two massacres had occurred, neither insignificant in its numbers. Then, too, the army sent to protect the settlers from the Indians seemed more interested in protecting the Indians from the settlers. Furthermore, General Wool had made it clear that he believed the war had been instigated for the benefit of profiteers. Finally, the superintendent of Indian Affairs wanted to move the warring Indians to the Grand Ronde, right into the settlers' midst.

But Palmer was not to be daunted, even though he must have known that his persistence in the establishment of the Grand Ronde might well lead to his downfall.

REQUESTS FOR REMOVAL continued to come in as well as large numbers of the Indians themselves in the process of removal. By early April, more than four hundred Indians were at Dayton awaiting transfer to Grand Ronde, some camped at Palmer's farm, others in the Dayton bowling alley. There were more than a thousand Indians at Grand Ronde. This meant much overcrowding, with the result that many strayed beyond the borders of the reserve. This, in turn, led to fear and anger on the part of the neighboring settlers. Palmer ordered strong fences to be built since, as he tartly observed, "the Indians are in the habit of throwing down the fences when in their way of travel." Secondly, he hired a guard to police the fenced boundaries and thus "effectually cut off all communications from the Reservation to the settlement of whites." He also began construction of a road to the coast, hoping to encourage at least some of the Indians to depart for the coast reservation and thus relieve the crowding at Grand Ronde.[7]

At the reserve itself, there was still much sickness and shelter remained inadequate, although Palmer had sent down a quantity of cloth for tents. However, and in spite of these conditions, there seems to have been some diversion, though it took a form that distressed Palmer's Quaker notions of industry. On two occasions, he wrote to his supervisors at Grand Ronde to complain of the Indians' fondness for "ball playing": "This ball playing should if possible be discouraged or at least confined to one day in the week and the balance of the time employed in something that will be useful to them."[8] A far more serious problem was the Rogues' refusal to give up their arms. This both angered the tribes who had relinquished theirs and made the settlers living near Grand Ronde uneasy. The settlers fired off a petition to Palmer demanding that the Indians not be permitted under any circumstances to leave the reserve.

There were also individual complaints. A.D. Babcock of Union Farm charged that Indian cattle had come onto his farm and threatened Palmer should it happen again. Then, on 15 April, a letter from Dayton appeared in the *Statesman* addressed to Palmer and signed "W"—probably Fred Waymire—that must have raised Palmer's dander appreciably: "I will . . . briefly state that which I, and others, whom you are pleased to call 'a set of intermeddling sons of b-t-c-h-s,' complain." W then goes on to list these complaints. The first was that at Grand Ronde Palmer had settled Indians in the midst of a white community without that community's permission. Secondly, Palmer had compelled citizens against their own wishes "to relinquish to you in the dead of winter, their lands and their homes, for the accommodation of the natural enemy of the white man." Next, Palmer had in effect "dismembered" Polk and Yamhill counties, since the reserve occupied portions of each county, and in addition, had isolated Tillamook County from the rest of the territory.

The writer's last two charges were the most serious.

> You have aided and encouraged Indians to commit outrages upon the whites, by bringing armed bands of these [the Rogues and Umpqua] through the settlements and setting yourself up as the special advocate of the savage and denouncing our brave and self-sacrificing volunteers as murderers.

Finally, by refusing to answer the formal complaints of the citizens, "you have shown yourself as an unprecedented coward." Anticipating Palmer's rage at the insult, the writer recommended restraint: "For your sake I would advise you to be a little more cautious as to whom you exhibit yourself in these paroxysms of anger." The letter concluded with what could only be interpreted as a threat: "Adieu, for the present."

In the same week in which this letter appeared in the *Statesman*, two of Palmer's principal men at Grand Ronde, Metcalf and Jeffers, resigned, discouraged by the Grand Ronde problems and their own low wages. In the south, Dr. Ambrose, similarly discouraged, resigned as well.

Palmer's temper in response to these raining misfortunes is reflected in three letters he wrote within a week of their occurrence. The first was to General Wool, who was now back in Oregon and very much "in the saddle"—though the *Oregonian* believed he should be "on the retired list." Palmer wanted troops:

> In the dilemma in which I am placed—between disaffection among the Indians on the reservation and alarm and excitement among the citizens, and backing out of agents . . . I am likely to fail in the entire plan, unless I can obtain aid from the military department.[9]

Within a few days, Wool sent Lt. Philip Sheridan and nine dragoons to Grand Ronde to disarm the Rogues and to be a "presence" there.

Palmer's next letter, written on 22 April, was addressed to A.D. Babcock, the farmer who had threatened him should he not prevent the Indians and their stock from straying onto his land. This letter conveys as well as anything Palmer's fairness, his sternness, and his inability to suffer fools and rogues gladly.

> Your menacing letter of yesterday is just received. my first impression of throwing it aside, as too contemptible to make answer to has given way, and I will endeavour to answer it—as impudent, threatening, and bombastical, as it is. You well know I did not seek to coerce you in selling your land claim to the Government. I was desirous to purchase of you, and offered you a large sum

$750 for it—much, indeed, above its intrinsic value, but you saw proper to refuse it, thinking you might compel me to pay the exorbitant demand you made for it—you had a right to do so and I have no more to say.

Every effort has been made, and shall continue to do so, to render the proximity of the Indians, as little annoying to you as possible; yet the position of your land is such that Indians and their stock may sometimes get upon it without a possibility of being prevented. I gave no orders to have any Indians located upon your ground, and I much doubt if there be any upon it—should there be, however, they shall at once be removed. As soon as the line fence is completed we shall be able to keep all the stock of the Indians within the limits of the Reservation.

Perhaps you have it in your powers to make it a warm time in that region as you threatened, and you may (possibly) commit some lawless act against them or their property, which might cause retaliation by them—should you do either let the consequences that may follow be upon you. Remember this, that I hold your letter as an evidence of such design, and it shall stand forth in judgement against you. We live in a country of laws, where every man has his rights, and if aggrieved can be righted and justice done him.

You ought not to loose sight of the truth that these Indians are removed to the Reservation by order of the United States Govt. and that they are under its protection, and that any wanton act—such as you threaten in your letter—will be visited upon you its heaviest punishment. The letter of yours which I now dismiss was doubtless written in anger; had you given yourself time for sober reflection you would not I think have sent it. Let me advise you to be governed by the usages and courtesies of gentlemen should you ever write a second.

The point you speak of as having been reached by forbearance is not in my opinion attained nor will it be until you shall attempt to carry into execution some of the threats of vengeance your letter is filled with.[10]

But it is Palmer's 21 April letter to Agent Thompson at The Dalles that most clearly reflects his anger and bitterness:

The opposition of political hucksters to the coast reservation seems not to abate, and the desperate extremes to which they resort may ultimately defeat the policy of Government. The citizens, as well as the Indians, are kept in constant excitement and alarm; Nothing I fear but the sending out of three or four regiments of regular troops can save this country from a war with all the tribes . . . . The few troops scattered over so great an extent of country is powerless to do good. They are barely sufficient to defend themselves; let alone the defense of the settlers; and to think of punishing our enemies with such a force is

preposterous. I regard the volunteer organization so far as its influence in sub-
duing the foe an entire failure. We are now one hundred per cent worse off than
when this war commenced so far as prospects of peace are concerned; besides an
influence and impression among Indians adverse to the successful carrying out
any system of policy designed for bettering their condition, and impressions
which years of untiring energy and devotion of agents cannot surmount. I have
not been advised as to what action will be taken by the President, or Department at Washington, upon the memorial and petitions of our one horse legislative assembly last winter, asking my removal. You will notice by the article in
the *Statesman* of the fifteen inst that the hue and cry is likely to be kept up, and as
may be naturally supposed, causes serious obstacles in the way of maintaining
order among the Indians. Fire brands are thrown among them, in the way of
messengers, counselling a course of conduct adverse to any orders or directions
we may give; and when those professing friendly persons advise them, they often put more reliance in their statements than in those of agents; as it appears
more in accordance with their superstitious notions, and whims. I am as yet unable to trace these yarns to the proper source but hope some day to fasten them
upon the right leg.[11]

Thompson himself was not without troubles. At the beginning of the
Yakima War, Thompson had told the Indians that all those desiring peace
should come to The Dalles, where they would receive protection. Three hundred did so. However, removed as they were from their usual hunting and
gathering grounds, they were soon in want of food. Accordingly, when the
salmon runs began, Thompson gave them permission to fish the Oregon side
of the Columbia. No sooner did they do so than Oregon volunteers camped
nearby fired on them. "Indians, Indian agents and the policy of General Government are all alike condemned," Thompson wrote Palmer.[12] Yet the agent
was in a quandary—a choice between the devil and the deep—for he feared
that if the volunteers left, enemy Indians would burn down the town.

But the volunteers, too, were distressed by problems. For one thing, unfriendly Indians, in addition to some who were feigning friendliness, had made
off with five hundred of the volunteers' horses—the *Statesman* later estimated
the Indians stole a thousand horses all told from the volunteers—a serious matter, indeed. Then there was the old problem of supplies. On 21 April, the same
day as Palmer's bitter letter to Thompson, an equally bitter letter from a volunteer was published in the *Oregonian* and signed "A Horse-Fed Volunteer":

> They [the volunteers] expected to meet with ordinary hardships and privations,
> but they did not expect to starve . . . on account of the carelessness or incompe-

tency of the heads of departments . . . having been selected from second rate
groggeries . . . . Now, there are boys here who have the blood of '76 coursing
through their veins with railroad velocity, who say the country must and shall
be protected, but they cannot and will not endure such treatment.

No one was very happy.

ON 27 APRIL, GENERAL WOOL WROTE PALMER that he had "most favorable
news" from the south and urged Palmer to travel with him to Port Orford.
"We will put an end to the war in Southern Oregon," he promised. Palmer replied to this astonishing news on the same day. Conditions at Grand Ronde, he
wrote, were too unsettled to permit his departure, but he promised to join the
general in due course. He closed with some comments on his own personal
position and duties:

> The mails bring me no intelligence as to any movements in Washington city
> relative to removals [his own]; the reports may or may not be true. My course
> is clear—that is, to push ahead, regardless of cliques, factions, or political dema-
> gogues. This I shall do, and if sustained by the government, have hopes of ulti-
> mately seeing acts approved by all good men.
>
> I have no political aspirations to gratify, but have higher aims than those
> likely to be attained by selling myself to those political hucksters. Justice and
> humanity toward these weak, ignorant, and downtrodden aborigines, holds a
> higher claim, and he who disregards them gives aid to factions disreputable to
> our reputation as a nation, and violates his duties as a good citizen; but whilst I
> would strive to protect and maintain the rights of the Indians, I would by no
> means trample upon those of the whites: both claim the interposition of agents
> of the government; and as some good people are pretty generally convinced
> that it is easier and safer to effect a peace with those Indian tribes by negotiations
> than with the rifle, we may be permitted to effect such an object in southern
> Oregon.[13]

Palmer's statement that he would "push ahead regardless of cliques, factions, or political demagogues" no doubt refers to the kinds of charges that appeared in a letter written the week before by former agent Metcalf to Joseph
Lane:

> In my previous letters I have refrained from mentioning anything that would
> have a tendency to impair the confidence you have had in Gen. Palmer, but
> facts are so palpable now that he is your worst enemy; I feel that I am doing an
> injustice to you not to give you the information which will enable you to judge
> for yourself. There is no longer a shadow of a doubt but he is a most virulent

Know Nothing, and endorses soul and body all of their views; And he is now using the influence his Office gives him to betray the democratic party— Finding fault with all because some few have the audacity to oppose his Know Nothing plans. There is no doubt but he is now against us with all his untiring energies, aided by immense sums of money placed in his hands for disbursement.

Metcalf went on to accuse Palmer of having appointed six Know Nothings to his service and concluded that "there is not a prominent Democrat in Oregon who is not particularly hostile to Palmer . . . he should be removed because he is injuring you and the Democratic Party."[14]

It is doubtful that Palmer would have appointed an agent just because he was a Know Nothing, but he would probably have employed a Know Nothing if he was otherwise qualified. As for Metcalf's charge that Palmer was a Know Nothing at this time, it seems unlikely that Palmer would have continued that association. In any event, Metcalf's accusations were probably typical of those emanating from Palmer's enemies.

AS PALMER HAD WRITTEN TO WOOL, problems at Grand Ronde precluded his immediately joining Wool in the south. Indians continued to pour in, Santiam and Willamette Klickitat, as well as Indians from St. Helens and the Sandy River. By early May, some fifteen hundred Indians were on the reserve. Palmer attempted to relieve the overcrowding by sending some groups to the coast to fish and hunt, particularly those groups addicted to "ball playing," and with the hope that they would "familiarize" themselves with the coast environment and decide to stay.

At the reservation itself, there now existed a house for the subagent, a hospital, school, store, warehouse, smithy, mills for flour and lumber, and a dormitory for the staff. In addition to the subagent, there was a doctor, two teachers, five farmers, five carpenters, two blacksmiths, one wagonmaker, one tinner, and assorted Indian employees. The subagent's job was to encourage the Willamette Valley Indians to choose a tract of land to cultivate and on which to build a dwelling. The farmers were to advise the Indians in their choice of land, instruct them in the use of implements, and assist them in planting. Houses were to be built and furniture made under the supervision of the carpenters, while the tinner and smith were to make whatever metal articles the Indians required. As for the teachers, one was allotted to the children of the Willamette tribes and one to the Rogues and Umpqua. The teachers were to provide books and clothes, and they were also urged to "distribute presents to encourage the children to attend school."[15] Finally, food rations were laid down. Persons engaged in labor were to receive daily rations of one-quarter pound of fresh meat; one pound, two ounces of flour; one ounce each of rice and coffee; two ounces of sugar; and one-half ounce of salt.

In short, Palmer had by now succeeded in establishing the physical plant of the reservation, putting in place a staff with defined duties and laying out a program that he believed would provide for the Indians' livelihood, health, and education. In other words, a structure, however shaky—and in the case of diet, woefully inadequate—had been created.

Now, too, the Indians were apparently less restive, for Palmer dismissed half of the sixty civilian guards he had hired earlier. Also, objections to the presence of the Indians declined in the white communities near the reserve. And on 26 April, the *Statesman* printed a letter signed by twenty-three citizens of Dayton defending Palmer and his policies.

WITH THIS LULL in the general welter of events, Palmer at last felt free to depart for peace initiatives in the south. Indeed, he believed it imperative to do so. "If peace is not made before the drought comes on, the entire country is ruined," he wrote in mid-May to Metcalf who, despite his resignation, had not yet departed the service.[16] In Palmer's view, that peace could only come with the removal from the south of the remaining Indian population. To this end, he had earlier instructed his agents to persuade the Indians to hand in their arms and go to Port Orford to await removal.

Palmer himself set out for Port Orford on 13 May. His send-off, at least in one respect, was soured, for on the eve of his departure, there appeared in the *Statesman* another letter from the offensive "W" of Dayton. "You have, Sir," the writer stormed,

> cunningly undertaken to entrench yourself behind a score of your paid adula-
> tors who, seeing you only through the medium of broad golden coin, are very
> willing to endorse your every statement . . . it has purchased you the signatures
> of twenty-three men to a tissue of cunning prevarications.

He charged Palmer with carrying "the dark lantern"—that is, that he was a Know Nothing—and concluded with some "salutary advice":

> It is that you look well to the seams of your breeches; with the catastrophe of
> your great prototype, a certain amphibious reptile of olden times, mentioned
> by Aesop, before you as an admonition, you must be a daring man indeed to
> undertake the like fatal experiment.

This was an allusion to Aesop's frog who so puffed himself up that he exploded.

IT HAD BEEN NEARLY SIX MONTHS since Palmer had been to the south. By the spring of 1856, about two-thirds of the original volunteer force were gone, and the battles engaged in by those who remained were hardly redeeming. In late March, a force of about two hundred attacked an Indian encampment near the California trail. According to Walling, "a great many . . . ran away during the fight, or else could not be brought into it at all." A second battle at The Meadows occurred in late April. The Meadows was chosen as the point of attack, in part because it was believed to be the Indians' "rallying point and base of supplies." The volunteers also hoped the attack would drive the Indians downriver and away from the settlements. Added to these motives was a fierce desire for revenge for the death of two whites who had been killed by the Indians and badly mutilated. One of the men was found headless, the other with his genitals stuffed into his mouth, his heart hung on a nearby bush.[17]

Although it appears that some Indians were killed at The Meadows, commentators judged that not much was accomplished. The volunteers, Walling wrote,

> consumed twenty-five days' rations in two weeks, drove the Indians from their place on the bar to another place in some unknown region, and returned to civilization. It is useless to enter into any long explanations of why such slight results were attained. It must have been partly the insubordination of the troops, who while nominally under the command of their general, colonel, lieutenant-colonel, four majors and unlimited captains and lieutenants, domineered shamefully over these officers and acted their own pleasure in times of emergency.[18]

It was an old story.

Walling's complaint was echoed in a 15 May letter to Lane from his old friend R.W. Dunbar, collector of customs at Port Orford:

> I think Col Buchanan, has under his command now in Rogue River valley, some 400 men exclusive of officers, enough to whip out all the Indians but can he find them in the Mountain fastnesses! it will require many more than are actually engaged in the field. Positions ought to be taken and kept, which cannot be done with so small a force . . . . Much blame may be attributed to the people for bringing on this war; for speculation etc, but some part of the want of success in its prosecution may reasonably be attributed to the course Genl Wool has taken in regard to this perplexing question! The volunteer forces, by their own choice, refused to be placed under the rules of the regular army, claiming an independence, which in my opinion has worked ruin and defeat on almost every occasion . . . . It is but today, news reached this place, that Genl Lamerick,

having a large volunteer force under him south, was about to, or had resigned! On the grounds of utter indifference of his men to submit to any orders—what is said of these may be said to some extent of all, better men never went into the field, but blind to their own interests! Whole trains of horses, are taken by the Indians from our Volunteers, and done so too, under our best Officers, and this is of frequent occurrence.

Genl Wool . . . has manifested a degree of neglect towards Oregon, in not actively placing a sufficient force of Troops in the field, until the patience of the people were worn out, their property burned or destroyed, and their wives and children murdered before their eyes, or before relief could come! The stand he has taken, in the unfortunate controversy between the Territorial Officers and himself, has so far weakened the Military arm of the Territory, that nothing is left for it, but a dishonorable abandonment of the field! its reputation gone, its credit bankrupt! . . . I look upon it as the cause, of the inability of the Territorial Officers, to procure sufficient supplies and the exorbitant prices paid for those, which could be had.[19]

All of this awaited Palmer in the south—a war fueled, if not brought on, for reasons of monetary profit; a volunteer army hostile to authority and command; antagonism between professional and volunteer forces; shortages of supplies and scalpers' prices; and finally, the exasperation, the desperation, the wrath of a civilian population who, in the midst of all of this martial hubbub, found themselves virtually defenseless against Indian attacks. *

ON 16 MAY, PALMER ARRIVED at Port Orford on the ship *Columbia.* The town was not in a state of siege, but it was thought unsafe to venture beyond its limits until army troops showed up as an escort. Accordingly, Palmer spent his time conferring with the Indians who had come in, as well as sending messages of invitation to those who had not. He was outraged to learn from other Indians that whites claiming to be employees of the Indian service had come among them "to gratify their animal passions."[20] Indeed, the Indians believed they were being urged to come in so that their women might be violated.

On 20 May, Lt. E.O.C. Ord with fifty men arrived from Colonel Buchanan's new headquarters on the Illi-

* As is usually the case, ordinary life flowed on despite the multitude of disruptions. In the same week that Dunbar wrote Lane of the dire state of southern Oregon, S.F. Chadwick, a Douglas County judge (later to be governor), also wrote Lane, "Let me take you away from Washington for a moment—and place you on that favorite mule. Now start and ride this one in

nois River. Ord reported to Palmer that the prospects for peace were improving and that more and more Indians were surrendering. At last, there seemed to be a general weariness with the war. "Nearly all the agricultural pursuits are neglected, and the mining interests are at a perfect standstill," wrote one correspondent to the *Statesman* on 27 May. "Everybody out here [Roseburg] is heartily tired of the war, and would be glad to have it ended by treaty, or any other way," wrote another. Ambrose reported from Jacksonville that the Indians had had enough and were ready for the reservation: "in fact now they have no other means of living than by pillage, chased from their homes like wild animals, into the mountains." Finally, the war had been sharply criticized in the East, where the *New York Tribune* thundered that no appropriations should be voted in Congress to continue the war. "The Oregon Indian war is palpably a White contrivance to plunder the Federal Treasury," the newspaper charged.[21]

WITH LIEUTENANT ORD'S TROOPS as an escort, Palmer started out on 24 May for Buchanan's camp on the Illinois River, hoping to conduct peace negotiations with the remainder of the hostile bands. The escort did not prove altogether reliable, for two of the soldiers got drunk and tried to kill one of Palmer's Indian servants. On the twenty-seventh, Palmer and his party arrived at Buchanan's camp to find that Buchanan had removed to a place near the confluence of the Illinois and the Rogue, somewhat above present-day Agness, and to which Palmer now proceeded.

Here, he learned that on 21 and 22 May Buchanan had met with the principal hostile bands at what came to be called the Council of Oak Flat. At the council, Chief Limpy and Chief George had agreed to give up their arms and go to the reservation, but Chief John had refused. According to Frances Victor, John had addressed Buchanan as follows:

these oak groves this morning—the grass is high, the flowers rank, numerous and beautiful, and the larks are whistling here and there in sportive glee. The grouse is thumping out his muffled throbs in the little nooks and canyons, and the dove is cooing to the spring. Down we will go to the farm house—where we will take a bowl of bread and milk with cream an inch thick— strawberries if you prefer them. We will have a fine salad—some new potatoes, and a rich juicy piece of broiled ham, with a poached egg. Now the pipe, then at sun set you can return to your cares again. Is this not a shadow of the picture. Think of it— on the third day of May, to have new potatoes and a strawberry pie. I wish sometimes that Gentlemen of the House and Senate could step over here, and pluck a quail, and get a lunch, and snuff pure air occasionally,

You are a great chief. . . . So am I. This is my country; I was in it when those large trees were very small, not higher than my head. My heart is sick with fighting, but I want to live in my country. If the white people are willing, I will go back to Deer creek and live among them as I used to do. They can visit my camp, and I will visit theirs; but I will not lay down my arms and go with you on the reserve. I will fight.[22]

and look out upon really picturesque scenery." Chadwick to Lane, 13 May 1856, Joseph Lane papers, MSS 1146, reel 2, OHS.

Chief George and Chief Limpy had agreed that they and their bands would relinquish their arms at the big bend of the Rogue on 26 May, and Captain Smith with ninety men went to assist in the process and to escort the bands to Port Orford. On arriving at the big bend, Smith received a message from Chief George warning him that Chief John planned an attack. But before Smith and his men could prepare an adequate defense, John attacked with a force of three to four hundred men, outnumbering the whites by at least three to one. This superiority together with John's use of his forces—"the tactics and strategy of a consummate general," wrote Walling—plus Smith's poor defenses resulted in a number of successful charges from the Rogues.[23] By the next morning, Smith was surrounded and, most seriously, cut off from water.

"*Mika hias ticka chuck?* (You very much want water?) . . . *Halo chuck, Boston!* (No water, white man!)" taunted the Indians, according to Frances Victor.[24] Some of the Rogues even crawled to the soldiers' breastworks and there, with long, hooked poles, snatched away the whites' blankets and other effects. The greatest insult occurred when Chief John threw a rope to Captain Smith and suggested that he hang himself. By late afternoon, a third of Smith's men were dead or wounded.* Palmer, in the meantime, and as noted earlier, had arrived on the twenty-seventh at Buchanan's camp, where all were ignorant of Smith's fate. The following day, however, a messenger arrived with the news. Captain Auger and his troops were immediately dispatched to help. Palmer accompanied them. On their arrival, according to the 24 June *Statesman*, "a successful charge was made with Gen. Palmer . . . first and foremost in it." And furthermore, "Gen. Palmer used his pistol with good effect, till he obtained a musket as it fell from the hand of a dying soldier."[25] Palmer himself makes no reference whatsoever in his journal to these heroics, whether for reasons

* At the council, Captain Smith had told John: "We will catch and hang you, sir; but if you go on the reservation, you can live in peace. Do you see those wagons, blankets, clothes, horses? You will have everything good, plenty to eat, peace. If you do not come, do you see that

of modesty or because they never occurred. Opposition to Palmer and his policies was now mounting in pitch, and it may be that the Port Orford correspondent was a friend—possibly Dunbar—who, seeking to deflect criticism of Palmer, was at pains to tout his bravery, even though in this instance it had not in fact been exercised.

Whatever the truth of these matters, Captain Auger's charge was successful, and the Indians fled. The Battle of Big Bend and the Rogues' assault on Smith proved to be the most deadly of the army's Rogue River engagements: eleven killed and sixteen wounded. Without Chief George's warning, it is probable that the entire force would have been lost.

Palmer remained in the area for two weeks, urging the various bands to come in. It soon became apparent, however, that they were reluctant to do so for fear of becoming targets of the volunteers' fire.

rope, sir?" John, now with the captain at a disadvantage, retaliated: "Hello, Captain Smith! You go on the reservation? . . . a great many wagons, good traveling . . . many things . . . plenty to eat . . . plenty to wear . . . if you do not go to the reservation, take rope Captain Smith; do you see this rope, Captain Smith?" Quoted in Victor, *Early Indian Wars,* 409-10n.

At this point, the Indians may not have been the volunteers' only target. On 27 May, the *Statesman* devoted much of its front page to an article by the *New York Tribune*'s congressional correspondent in Washington, D.C. The subject of the article was the House of Representatives hearing of 31 March in which Lane requested nearly half a million dollars from Congress for "the President in making peace . . . with the tribes which have thus far been friendly" and "for the purchase of powder wherewith to prosecute the existing war." The Whigs rebutted the request by quoting extensively from General Wool's reports on the war and from Palmer's damaging letter to the general. These quotes could not have been more damaging to Palmer, containing such statements as "believing as I do, that the cause of the present difficulty in Southern Oregon is wholly attributable to the acts of our own people." Thus, in the view of many, had the manhood of Oregon been slanderously impugned before the world.

The reaction was fury. "We think," the *Statesman*'s Roseburg correspondent wrote on 10 June,

> it is the duty of Palmer to make a correction of this false report in regard to the origin of our Indian difficulties, make an apology to the people of Oregon, then all will be right; otherwise the Oregon mounted volunteers may make a requisition on Gen. Lynch for a supply of tar or hemp for his especial benefit.

Unaware of these threats, Palmer continued to urge the dilatory bands to surrender and to protect them when they did so. On 11 June, Chief John's three sons visited the camp, and Palmer tried to convince them that it was in their father's best interest to surrender. They promised to talk with him. Then on 13 June, with more than seven hundred Indians in his charge, Palmer set out for Port Orford. On arrival, he found the Port Orford Indians quiet—with his own bands, there were now more than a thousand Indians—but the whites were fearful of these large numbers, a fearfulness, Palmer believed, "induced by a set of grog shop dealers and squaw men."[26]

"Squaw men." It is not surprising that Palmer should have mentioned them in the same breath with "grog shop dealers," for like many others, he probably did not hold squaw men in high esteem. It was vexing, then, that with all Port Orford's problems upon his arrival, his time should have been taken up with the problems of squaw men.

There was, first of all, a letter from subagent Drew at Coos Bay complaining of the eight squaw men in his jurisdiction: "Were there nothing but Indians to deal with the task of the agents would be meager."[27]

Next, there was a letter from Mr. Stephen Dain of Port Orford, who had traded a horse and other goods for a squaw. Subsequently, the squaw left him "and came here to stay with her people chiefly through their influence and persuasion and partly I suppose," he was frank to confess, "from her own inclination." The crux of the matter was the horse. Somehow it had ended up under General Palmer when, in late May, he had departed Port Orford for Buchanan's camp on the Illinois. Dain now wanted it back:

> Will you . . . have the kindness to deliver the horse, saddle, bridle and spurs
> . . . . Besides the horse I paid the Indians twenty dollars in money and a lot of blankets, shirts, dresses and beads. As they have broke the contract . . . I think it no more than just that they should be compelled to return me the horse and money. The other things they are welcome to keep. I should much prefer myself to keep the squaw.[28]

Still another letter from a disgruntled squaw man awaited Palmer. Aseph Hinch—also of Port Orford, also love-sick, also bamboozled—wrote: "You may think [it] strange me thinking so much of an Indian woman. She is a half breed and she is shrewd and understands business . . . it is hard for me to see her go away." That she was shrewd and understood business appears evident from the fact that, before her departure, she extracted $238 in cash and goods from Hinch.[29]

How Palmer dealt with these gulled swains and the embarrassing matter of the horse is not known. Surely they distracted him from other concerns, for Indians continued to stream in, requiring much palaver on the part of Palmer, as well as his attention to their camp, which was inadequate to their large numbers, now about thirteen hundred. Then, on the evening of the nineteenth, there was a scare.

"A rumo[r] gained circulation," Palmer wrote in his diary, "that a plan was on foot to murder all my men, then the soldiers, and then attack the town." It is understandable that this should have caused great consternation. Though all the Indians had presumably surrendered their arms, there were no doubt some who had not, retaining them in secret. Then there was the plain bellicosity of the three hundred warriors that Walling estimated the camp contained, "warriors the like of whom for bravery, perseverance and fighting powers have rarely been seen."[30]

Although Palmer suspected that "lovers of excitement" had spread the rumors, he went to the Indians' camp and ordered the chiefs to spend the night—allegedly fixed for the attack—at the fort. The next morning, following their release and after discussing the allegations with them, Palmer became convinced that the rumors had been groundless and was "satisfied the whole thing was concocted by evil-disposed persons."[31]

Notwithstanding the fact that there were still more Indians to come—Chief John, in particular—fear of more plots disposed Palmer to plan for the evacuation of the Indians. Because many were old and sick and unable to travel by land, and because Palmer lacked transport for provisions that a long overland trek would require, he decided to send the Indians to the reserve on the *Columbia*. It turned out to be a terrible voyage. The seas were rough, and the six hundred Indians, accustomed to the calm of estuary waters, were terrified by the giant, breaking swells. And more than terrified, for all succumbed to seasickness, made worse by their being crowded into the limited quarters of the little ship. Also, blankets and apparel were in short supply, and so, exposed on the decks, they suffered the assaults of wind and spray and the driving rains. It was not, as Palmer himself confirmed in his diary, a happy scene: jostling one another for space on the crowded decks, flung this way and that by the heavy seas, cowering in the cold and in terror of the tempest, and finally, their retching sickness soiling everything—it must have seemed to them the coming of a foul death. Such were the conditions in which "the monarchs of the woods" departed their land.

The removals continued. On 8 July, the *Columbia* was back in Port Orford to transport another six hundred Indians. In the meantime, Lieutenant Ord had been sent down the coast to take Chief John into custody, for he had finally agreed to surrender. "A long file of fierce looking fellows," Ord wrote in his diary, in paint & feathers each with a fine rifle & at their head steps sternly & erect a hard faced guilty old man—in shirt sleeves & a small rimmed old Hat on top of his Head—its Old John I know at sight—advanced a short distance up hill . . . to my tent in center of my camp where one by one as they came up—they laid down their rifles—some rather with a look of defiance—took John into my tent after seeing the *arms* delivered up and gave him a drink.[32]

Three days later, Chief John arrived at Port Orford with thirty-five braves, ninety women, and ninety children. A week later, under escort of Major Reynolds, he and his people were taken overland to the coast reservation.

IT WAS SOUTHERN OREGON's happiest Fourth of July in some years. Now, at last, the Indians were gone, that threat to life—not to mention conscience. The elation was evident in a general rambunctiousness. In Jacksonville, the celebrations reached such a pitch that Sheriff White was called in to restore order. The 15 July *Statesman* reported that "resistance was made and a general row ensued, which terminated in the death of one man and the wounding of two others. It is thought the end is not yet."

At Scottsburg on the Umpqua, the Fourth of July celebrations were more sedate. The participants gathered in a grove to pray, sing, recite the Declaration of Independence, and drink toasts. They then retired to "the dinner table, playing the ancient and useful game of knife and fork in dead earnest." This was followed by "dancing, eating ice-cream and ball-room gossip." Dancing continued until dawn, of course, at which time fifty of the hardiest celebrants boarded the *Bully Washington* for a little excursion to the coast, "going down to see 'old ocean,' to hear 'his roar' and, in a poetic sense 'lay hands upon his mane.'"[33]

In Port Orford, the army outdid even old ocean's roar. At dawn there was a salute of thirteen guns, at noon thirty-one, at sunset another thirteen, and at nine o'clock five rockets were launched from the cliffs into the night sky. There were, of course, the usual street fights, and at the noon salute, one soldier was badly burned while improperly loading the cannon, apparently a victim of what Dr. Rodney Glisan said was the principal disease at Port Orford, "intemperance." Glisan also reported that the Fourth of July was the occasion for the official announcement at Port Orford: "All the officers assembled at the Colonel's quarters and partook of refreshments. We were then informed by Colonel B. that he had the pleasure of announcing the Indian war on Rogue River closed."[34]

BUT PALMER'S TROUBLES were far from over. Before leaving Port Orford on 21 June, he had probably heard of a protest meeting held in Roseburg condemning him. General Wool's errors were due to "the bad hands in which he fell on arriving in Oregon, and from which he received his information, *especially* the official report of Joel Palmer to Gen. Wool . . . which was well calculated to deceive the old General."[35]

Also on 21 June, the *Oregonian* reprinted General Wool's incendiary letter of 2 April to the *National Intelligencer* in Washington, D.C. It was the incensed reaction to this blast that greeted Palmer on his arrival in Portland on 23 June. Wool, as usual, was as fearless in print as on the field. Governor Curry's sending of Oregon volunteers to the Yakima War was "one of the most unwise, unnecessary and extravagant expeditions ever fitted out in the United States and for no other reason than to plunder the Treasury of the United States and to make political capital for somebody." Then he loosed a final volley: "The Oregonians say that the 'war is a godsend to the country.'" In the same edition, the *Oregonian* promptly returned fire. This was "brass button tyranny." Did not the general know that

> the citizens have scores of times, yes, hundreds, aided in exhuming the dead and mutilated bodies of their relatives and friends from the black and charred evidence of Indian inhumanity . . . . their cattle wantonly shot, or driven off; their flocks and herds despoiled, their cellars, granaries and down to their clothes-lines, robbed . . . by these *fiends* in human shape.

The *Oregonian*'s rage reached its apogee when it suggested on 30 August that Wool be "sent to the lunatic asylum or to the penitentiary."

In its rage with Wool, the *Oregonian* had not forgotten Palmer. As noted above, Palmer reached Portland with his six hundred charges on 23 June and, from there, dispatched the Indians by riverboat to Dayton. The *Oregonian*, of course, was on the scene and reported it as follows:

> They were mostly either old decrepit specimens of the race, or filthy squaws and naked children. We noticed but few . . . able to bear arms, carry a torch, or run away. Our opinion is that these were sent off to enable the *real* warriors the better to plunder and lay waste the country . . . . Why did not Gen. Palmer bring in the warriors whose blood-stained hands are clothed with human gore.[36]

This was patently unfair to Palmer who, as everyone knew, had deliberately chosen the old and sick for this removal by ship since he doubted they would survive the journey by land. As for the "real warriors," all knew as well that they were now Colonel Buchanan's prisoners.

It was not until three in the afternoon of the twenty-third that Palmer at last concluded the arrangements for the Indians' departure and saw them off at the Portland docks. He then went uptown in the pelting rain—it was the rainiest, coldest spring anyone had ever known—to attend to other matters. It was nearly midnight before he was able to sit down and report to George Manypenny. "I now regard the war in Southern Oregon as closed," he wrote—and it must have given him much pride to write the words. After all, it was he who had closed the war, one of the longest and bitterest in United States-Indian history. Even his enemies had to admit to the truth of this. Agent Metcalf, who shortly before had written Lane that Palmer was a virulent Know Nothing and urged his removal from the superintendency, now wrote to Bush that "if Palmer had not been there not an Indian would have ever surrendered to Col. B. or any of his command. This I say from a personal knowledge of the Indians, and their own assertions."[37]

But Palmer had done more than end the war. He had by treaty negotiations extinguished the majority of Indian claims to Oregon land, a matter that had bedeviled the territory since 1850. Next, he had organized and effected the removal of the Indians from their former lands to the reservations, thus saving the lives of many—if not the majority. Thirdly, he had set up the reservations not merely as refuges for the displaced tribes but as places where, with the aid of farmers and carpenters, teachers, and doctors, the Indians might improve their condition. Finally, he had brought to a close a decade of war and laid the foundation for more than a decade of relative peace.

All of this had been accomplished under the most difficult of circumstances: negotiating treaties with Indians who were reluctant to negotiate and seeking ratification from a Congress reluctant to ratify; the logistical complexities of removal, especially from the south, where both the Indians and the whites protecting them were threatened by harassment and worse; laying out reservations at Grand Ronde and Siletz in the face of resistance from both political parties and ordinary citizens; the obstacle of an insufficient budget with which to staff the reservations with competent and honest men; and finally, bringing the war to an end in opposition to those who, for racist or pecuniary reasons, desired its continuance.

His letter to Manypenny finished, Palmer was entitled to a deep sense of culminating accomplishment, and so it may have been that, blowing out his lamp, taking to his bed, he lay down to untroubled sleep.

It was on this same date, 23 June 1856, that Commissioner Manypenny wrote Palmer that he had been dismissed from his post as superintendent of Indian affairs for the Oregon Territory.

IT TOOK NEARLY TWO MONTHS for a letter to reach Oregon from the capital, and thus, Palmer, unknowing, continued in office. His first act on returning to Dayton was to fire subagent Nathan Olney, whose conduct both at The Dalles and at Port Orford he had long questioned. Palmer laid out the charge in a letter to Manypenny: "dissipation, gambling and debauchery among the native women."[38] Even worse, Olney had taken an Indian from the Port Orford jail and handed him over to the mob to be lynched.

As the summer progressed, Palmer's principal concern was the transfer of some of the Grand Ronde Indians to the coast reservation. In early July, he hired a Dr. Stell of Oregon City to accompany seven hundred Indians to the coast and to serve there as their physician. Palmer instructed Stell that "the old and infirm will claim your special attention since experience has shown that the young, healthy and able bodied would often crowd from the wagons and horses, the helpless, leaving them to perish." At the reservation, Stell was to report once a month on the number of births and deaths and the causes of death as well as "making such suggestions as to the habits, mode of life, diet, etc., as you may deem useful and instrumental in bettering their condition and subserving the cause of humanity."[39] Palmer spent a week at the coast in July, finally determining that the upper Siletz was the most suitable place for the reservation; it was there the headquarters were finally established.

In these and all other matters of the agency, Palmer suffered difficulties because of the rumors that he was to be discharged. "The probability of it has caused me great embarrassment in business operations and has tended not a little to create an excitment among the Indians," he wrote on 13 July. "In the meantime," he told Metcalf, "we must strive to give up the Superintendancy in as prosperous a condition as possible."[40]

The blow came on 11 August, when Commissioner Manypenny's letter finally reached Dayton. On 15 August, Palmer wrote his last letter as superintendent of Indian affairs. In it he summed up his hope for the future, words that also characterize all that he had worked for in the past: "I leave the office with a desire to see such measures adopted as may tend to maintain peace and advance these Indians in civilization."[41]

THE DISCHARGE OF JOEL PALMER, one of the most distinguished superintendents in the history of the Indian service, was inevitable. Although liked and respected when he took office in the spring of 1853, his policies as they evolved earned him the antagonism of almost the entire Oregon community. For one thing, he sympathized with the Indians in their adversity. Most Oregonians did not. The Whitman massacre, the Cayuse and Rogue River wars, the cattle killing, the arson and theft, and the very sight of the Indians—perhaps troubling to the conscience of these usurpers of Indian lands—all had led to an exasperation with the natives that Palmer's explicit sympathy could only have exacerbated. Inflaming the whites even more was Palmer's condemnation of the volunteers who, in the popular view, and despite evidence to the contrary, were the flower and gallantry of the territory's manhood. Finally, with regard to the wars, Palmer had dared state that they had in part been instigated by the whites for the plain purpose of profit. This put the fear of Washington into everyone, for if Palmer's charges were taken seriously, reimbursement for the cost of the war and, more important, the profits might not be forthcoming.

As if the above grievances were not enough, Palmer was condemned by almost all for establishing reservations at Grand Ronde in the valley and Siletz on the coast. With respect to Grand Ronde, the settlers of the area feared the Indians would break out and rampage, and indeed, such a possibility existed. With respect to the 125-mile-long Siletz Reservation, it was argued that it cut the valley off from access to the coast—and it did—from Eugene to Oregon City. It was further claimed that the Coast Range passes constituted avenues of both assault and escape, the Indians free to sweep down through the passes to depredate the valley and then retreat to safety behind the mountain ramparts.

Finally, Palmer was not a good party man, in the Oregon of his time a serious transgression. In hiring and firing, he apparently gave not a damn whether a man was Democrat or Whig. There was, too, his alleged membership in the anticlique Know Nothings. Disloyalty to party—in this case, to clique—could not be forgiven.

The killings at Gold Beach and at the Cascades and the publication of Palmer's correspondence with General Wool were the last straws. Manypenny and Lane had attempted to circumvent the protest and then to delay Palmer's dismissal, but the demands that Palmer be ousted could no longer be blocked, and the blow fell.

PALMER'S PLACE WAS TAKEN by Absalom Hedges, a faithful Democrat known for his affability and courtesy, and from the outset, "affability and courtesy" prevailed between Palmer and Superintendent Hedges. Only a month after Palmer's discharge, Hedges employed him to sow three hundred acres of wheat and set up blacksmith shops at Siletz. It also seems likely that Palmer was ready with advice for Hedges during the difficult first months of his superintendency. And difficult those first months were to be.

As noted earlier, Palmer, in his haste to provide refuge for the southern tribes, had not had time to adequately prepare Grand Ronde, let alone Siletz. Now, housing and provisioning remained dire, so much so that the Grand Ronde Indians were beginning to wander off in search of shelter and food.* As for Siletz, there were rumors of outright revolt. Also, there were serious problems with the small, scattered bands of Indians who refused to come in and who now prowled the countryside, frantic in their desperation and, occasionally, committing depredations.

The following year, the shortage of housing was not helped by the fact that the Rogues, on leaving for Siletz, burned eighty or so of their Grand Ronde houses. This was their custom when abandoning a camp—done, they said, for "luck."

The solution to most of these problems was money. There was none. Again and again, Hedges begged funds from Washington for food, structures, agents' salaries, and for the goods promised in the treaty stipulations. "They have left their homes and come to a strange land reposing faith in the agent of the Great Father and should not be deceived." To no avail. Finally, Hedges threatened to "turn the Indians loose," if funds were not provided.[42] Late in the year, there was a foot of snow at Grand Ronde, the horses starving, and only a week's supply of flour and beef left for the Indians. It was too much. On 19 December 1856, pleading ill health, Hedges resigned.

ALTHOUGH PALMER ACCEPTED THE BLOW of his discharge with grace, he by no means kissed the rod. With Hedges' resignation, a new appointment was in' the offing, and he was determined to have it. His plan was to present himself at Washington with an entourage of fifty Oregon Indian chiefs. Not only would this show Washington the esteem in which he was held by the Indians, but it would also be an opportunity for the chiefs to express their grievances and problems directly, in person, and not as heretofore, from far Oregon and through the filtered reports of agents. Palmer no doubt hoped the Indians would make it clear that his appointment would be the first step in the solution to their many difficulties.

But the chiefs refused Palmer's request. Some may have remembered the horrors of the ocean passage from Port Orford to Astoria and did not care to once again expose themselves to the furies of Father Neptune, which a sea voyage to the eastern seaboard would have certainly unleashed. Palmer, undeterred but alone, embarked at Portland on 20 January 1857, arriving in the United States six weeks later.

Palmer remained in the States for three months, visiting Washington, Philadelphia, and his old home in the Whitewater Valley of Indiana. In the two latter locales, he spent time with friends and members of his wife's family.

In the diary Palmer kept during the journey, the majority of the entries concern the minutia of travel. As in his diaries for other years, he writes almost nothing that is personal, self-revelatory, or that provides a clue to the inner man. In the 1857 diary, however, one exception gives a glimpse. At the end of March in the Whitewater, present at a local gathering, he wrote: "I made an ass of myself when called upon for a speech but could not connect two sentences. This is the fate of all fools and numskulls."[43] It is an engaging admission from a man who suffered no lack of confidence—so little, indeed, that he could afford a measure of self-ridicule.

Most of his time, however, was spent in Washington in an attempt to regain the superintendency. The most influential Oregonian in the capital was, of course, the territorial delegate, Joseph Lane. Though Lane and Palmer were friends, Lane, as noted earlier, had agreed to Palmer's dismissal. He now opposed his reappointment. Lane would soon face reelection, and he feared that his support of Palmer would lose him votes. Also, he believed that Palmer as superintendent might question certain of Oregon's war claims. Accordingly, Lane gave his support to his old friend and colleague James Nesmith.

But Palmer had support as well. Even in Oregon, a few stood by him: Col. Robert C. Buchanan, commander of the regular forces at the end of the Rogue River War; Morton M. McCarver, first Speaker of the House of the provisional government and later commissary general of the state militia; and Robert W. Dunbar, collector of customs at Port Orford. In Washington, Palmer's principal ally was Senator Jesse Bright of Indiana. Bright believed that the injustice done to Palmer could only be righted by his reappointment.

It appeared in April that Palmer in fact might regain his post. Joseph Drew, a leading Oregon Democrat, wrote Judge Deady from Salem that "we think Palmer will get the place."[44] In the end, however, Lane prevailed, and Nesmith was appointed superintendent on 1 May 1857.* For a time, Palmer lingered on in Washington. At one point, and even though he had lost the superintendency, he met with Commissioner Manypenny to urge upon him his plan for a delegation of Oregon Indian chiefs; he still believed in the importance of such a face-to-face council. Then in early June, he set out, sailing from New York, arriving back in Oregon the following month. Except for a brief period some years later, Palmer's offi-

* As James E. Hendrickson points out in his biography of Lane, Nesmith soon had second thoughts about the appointment, saying he felt "very much like the lucky cuss who won the

cial association with the Indians of Oregon ended, and he began a new life.

elephant at the raffle and did not know what to do with him." See Hendrickson, *Joe Lane of Oregon: Machine Politics and the Sectional Crisis, 1849-1861,* 144.

FIFTEEN

Last Years

PALMER SPENT THE REMAINING TWO DECADES of his life in business and politics. Even before he lost the superintendency, he had a few entrepreneurial irons in the fire. In 1854, he joined with others to promote a portage railroad at Willamette Falls. Nothing came of it. The following year, he became a director of a telegraph system that was to link Portland, Oregon City, Salem—and in due time, London, Paris, and Rome. But the line, strung from trees, blew down before the connection with Salem—let alone the capitals of Europe—could be consummated.

Palmer's next venture followed his return from Washington. In 1858, gold was discovered in the Fraser and Thompson river country of British Columbia, and Palmer set up as a trader, taking supplies to the miners by way of The Dalles and the Okanogan. Initially, the enterprise was successful, but with the depletion of the mines in 1860, Palmer was left with no market for his considerable supply of goods and was obliged to sell out at a substantial loss.

In 1862, gold strikes again drew Palmer, this time to eastern Oregon and Washington. With others, he organized a company to build a packhorse trail up the Oregon side of the Gorge as far as Hood River, but according to Stanley Sheldon Spaid, "the expenses always exceeded the receipts."[1]

Palmer next tried construction. His first project was the Oregon City Woolen Mills, and a major project it was. The building—190 feet long, 50 feet wide, 4 stories high, and built of brick—rested on a hewn stone foundation 10 feet thick at its base to withstand the Willamette floods. "The handsomest and most substantial structure in the state," the *Weekly Oregonian* reported on 27

283

January 1865. Palmer became president of the company, but he soon fell out with the board, suing the board for fifteen thousand dollars in wages; the court awarded him only a third of his claim. Another of Palmer's projects was a plan in 1864 to build a canal and locks at Willamette Falls. Investors could not be found.

Palmer's last business fiasco revolved around railroads—the Oregon Central and the Astoria and Columbia River. The former never laid a foot of track, the latter only some years after his death.

Almost all of Palmer's business ventures were failures. This may have been bad luck, but it would seem that Palmer had little business sense, more given to optimism than to prudence. In any event, the Palmers were often in straits and would have been so more often had it not been for Mrs. Palmer's income from a family trust.

If Palmer's financial ventures usually backfired, his political career prospered. His arena lay in the new factions and parties arising in the early 1860s out of the issues of slavery and secession. Palmer, opposed to both, became a Union Democrat, that faction of the Democrats opposed to secession. In 1862, the Union Democrats joined with the unionist Republicans, as the Whigs were now called, to form a new party. Running on the new party's ticket in June 1862, Palmer was elected by a large majority to the legislature, which then chose him as Speaker of the House. The old animosities had been forgotten, at least for a time.

Palmer's prominence in the party continued. In 1864, he was elected to the state senate by another large majority, while in 1866—before U.S. senators were elected by popular vote—the party caucus nominated Palmer to represent Oregon in the U.S. Senate. He refused. The state constitution, he claimed, did not permit a legislator to accept another office during his own term. Even though he was assured that the prohibition did not apply to U.S. senators, Palmer remained adamant, reportedly saying, "I took an oath to support this constitution; it applies to my conscience and I cannot accept the office if elected."[2]

In 1868, the Civil War over, the issues of slavery and secession settled, many of the Union Democrats went home. However some, like Palmer, remained with the Republicans, and in 1870, they nominated him for the governorship. Palmer's Democratic opponent was Lafayette Grover. Grover was a native of Maine, graduate of Bowdoin, first U.S. representative from Oregon, and later, governor and U.S. senator—in short, a worthy opponent. Palmer lost the election by 631 votes. The explanation handed down in his family is that, as a known anti-Catholic, he was defeated by the Catholic vote. However, an astute observer and Palmer's contemporary, Timothy Davenport, saw his defeat as "an opportunity for those of his fellow citizens who thought him too kind to the Indians, to register their disapproval."[3]

PALMER, NOW SIXTY, was not to run for public office again. This is not to say that he left politics. In 1871, he received a government appointment, and few things were more political than a government appointment. Why he sought this particular post is not clear. He probably needed the money, but in addition, it is likely that he was out to rescue a dream that had turned into a nightmare—the reservation system. On 30 April 1871, Palmer took over as Indian agent at Siletz.

IN THE FIFTEEN YEARS since Palmer's superintendency, the Oregon Indians had passed through hell. "It is not your wars, but your peace that kills my people," Chief John is reputed to have said.[4] There were many reasons.

By now, the government had established five reservations in Oregon: Grand Ronde (1856), Siletz (1856), Warm Springs (1856), Umatilla (1860), and Klamath (1864). In 1871, the year of Palmer's appointment to Siletz, Frances Victor surveyed the Oregon Indian scene for the *Overland Monthly*. She found the four thousand Indians on the three reservations east of the mountains in better condition than those in western Oregon. She ascribed this partly to a healthier climate, partly to the fact that the eastern Oregon Indians had less contact with whites. Still, their circumstances were far from ideal. Warm Springs land was "poor and worthless," and though the tribes gained a partial livelihood by fishing at The Dalles, Victor concluded that they would continue to be "life pensioners upon the bounty of the U.S. Government just so long as they or their descendants are compelled to occupy these volcanic wastes." At the Klamath reservation, the land was better but the altitude such that she believed it precluded successful farming. "Agriculture is being taught as best it may be," she pessimistically concluded. Finally, there was Umatilla. This reservation somewhat lifted her spirits, for Victor judged it the best in Oregon: nine hundred acres under cultivation, ten thousand horses, fifteen hundred cattle. However, "they are generally only savages yet." Victor's survey of the twenty-five hundred Indians on the western reservations was even more dispirited—"so much abject degradation."[5]

What had happened? For one thing, under Superintendent Nesmith, who held office from 1857 to 1859, the Oregon and Washington agencies were combined, making the superintendent responsible for nearly 35,000 Indians and 165,000 square miles. Next, even if the natives had had a background in agriculture, the soil and climate of most reservation lands made farming impractical.

Unable to sustain themselves, they were at the mercy of government handouts. These were often of an inferior quality—"flour" consisting of shorts and sweepings, that is, cattle feed—and haphazard in their delivery, winter clothes arriving in the spring. In their former life, before the white incursions, the Indians could usually count on the quality of their foods—the berries, game, roots, and nuts—and their timely provision could be depended on as well, for they were the products of the seasons. Winter might be a little late one year, but it did not begin in June.

Then there was disease. Though the Indians in their native life had a different concept of hygiene from that of the settlers, at least those who were nomadic did not linger in contaminated sites. The reservations, on the other hand, enforced settlement and thus were soon befouled. Also, denied their customary physical exertion—the hunt, war, and the migratory tramps—they succumbed to a debilitating lethargy. This, combined with a bad diet, close quarters, and lack of resistance to the diseases carried by the whites, made every reservation a giant pesthouse. And treatment was almost wholly inadequate. Medicines were in short supply or nonexistent, reservation physicians were not of the highest caliber, and hospitals were few and barely habitable. Finally, the Indians persisted in sweat baths that were usually deleterious and gambled away their clothing to become victims of exposure. The mortality rate, particularly in western Oregon, was horrendous.

"To advance these Indians in civilization." Those had been Palmer's last words as superintendent, his last wish for his charges' welfare. The doorway to this goal was to be the reservation, and education the keystone of the doorway. Hardly a stone was laid, let alone a keystone raised. Like the reservation physicians, the teachers were often second rate—if not third—and understandably. Teachers knew their salaries might be delayed for months due to shortages—or the "misappropriation"—of funds, that their schoolhouses would lack supplies and sometimes be without a roof, and finally, that the majority of their students would consider school a punishment. It all added up to the fact that, as often as not, the schoolhouse door was shut.

Finally, many of the agents on the reservations were not qualified for their positions. Most were political appointees, their appointments a return for some favor. If they had any sincere interest in the Indians' welfare, it was an accident. To the contrary, the principal concern of many was to line their own pockets—"villainy made easy," as Judge Matthew Deady wrote. This propensity to divert funds, together with the government's parsimony and delays, meant the reservations were woefully underfunded. Another problem that existed, even in the case of an honest and dedicated agent, was that the agent's authority dissipated the traditional authority of the chiefs, leaving them powerless as rulers of their people. In general, then, the tenure of most reservation agents was a sorry one. "If demoralization of these wards [the Indians] had been designed by the Government," T. W. Davenport wrote, "it is doubtful if the scheme to accomplish it would not have given better satisfaction to them than the past treatment by political Indian agents."[6]

SUCH WAS THE SAD TALE of the reservations in the sixteen years following Palmer's separation from Indian affairs. And nowhere was the tale sadder than at Siletz. As noted earlier, Palmer was responsible for choosing the site of the coast reservation, believing it would meet the Indians' needs. In area, it ran roughly from present-day Tillamook to present-day Coos Bay, 125 miles, and from the sea to the crest of the Coast Range, some 1,382,400 acres, of which 5,000 were arable. How suitable, in fact, this land was for farming has been a subject of controversy. Superintendent Nesmith considered it worthless. However, Superintendent Rector (1861-64), perhaps a more reliable source, claimed Nesmith disparaged the land for political reasons. Wallis Nash, an Englishman not embroiled in Oregon politics and a generally accurate observer of the Oregon scene, judged the land excellent. In general, however, the Oregon littoral had not proven adaptable to farming—as distinct from grazing—and certainly, at Siletz the profusion and tenacity of fern in the land made for many problems.

With the location of the reservation determined, three forts were built at the periphery to discourage the Indians from leaving and the whites from intruding: Fort Umpqua, to the south, at the mouth of the Umpqua; Fort Yamhill, to the north, at present-day Valley Junction; and Fort Hoskins, to the east, in Kings Valley.

This, then, was the reservation and its guardians. However, when the first Indians arrived at Siletz in the spring of 1856, there was simply the land, for few facilities of any kind had been prepared—unlike Grand Ronde, where farms and structures already existed. Also, the Siletz area was alien to southern tribes such as the Rogues. Most reservations had been located in an area adjacent to, or even within, the Indians' homeland, and thus, they were familiar with its climate and resources. Not so Siletz. The Rogues from the dry south suffered terribly from the damp. From November through March 1857, "dense floods of rain were pouring down day after day without cessation. The whole country was deluged with water," wrote J. Ross Browne, who was sent from Washington in 1857 to report on Indian affairs in the Northwest.[7] During much of this period, the Indians had no shelter, and they had to eat seafood, which the Rogues found repellent. Finally, the administration of the reservation by Agent Courtney Walker was so disorganized and impotent that most of the white employees fled in fear of the Indians.

Walker was succeeded in December 1856, at the end of the reservation's first year, by Robert Metcalf. Metcalf, though dishonest—four years later he was forty thousand dollars richer, according to Frances Victor—did bring order and certain material improvements to the reservation. By the spring of 1857, five hundred acres were under cultivation, and there were warehouses, a blacksmith shop, a slaughterhouse, plans for a hospital and school, and twenty-seven board houses. Yet the Indians were discontented. For one thing, Metcalf and his employees were rough, much given to using the lash. Philip Sheridan reported in the spring of 1857 on "the determined hostility of the agents placed over the Indians." Furthermore, Metcalf had "surrounded himself with employees who were engaged in hostilities with them in the lower country [the south] and who do not hesitate to express the most improper and hostile language toward them."[8]

Next, there was the matter of housing. Those twenty-seven board houses were not exactly sufficient for a population of more than two thousand. In other words, the vast majority of the Indians were to suffer the drenching rains of another winter without proper shelter.

Then, the problem of food. Potatoes, a principal staple, had been planted in the spring, but the Indians, accustomed to eating roots, dug up the plants before they had flowered—thus, the end of the potato crop. Without food for the winter, and with transport across the mountains so difficult, a schooner loaded with fifty-five thousand pounds of flour, a ton of potatoes, and other winter stores was sent down in December 1856. It foundered at the mouth of the Siletz, and all was lost.

As noted above, transport of supplies by land was exceedingly toilsome, the trail from Kings Valley barely broken. However, with the bar of the Siletz so dangerous, an attempt was made to bring supplies overland. Meanwhile, snow had made the mountains impassable to pack animals, and so those Indians who still had the strength were obliged to pack the flour—twenty thousand pounds of it—on their backs, the thirty miles from the valley mills over the mountains to the reservation. When a new shipment arrived at Yaquina Bay in April, it was found to be cattle feed. By now, however, the Indians were starving and so had no alternative but to eat it. It made many of them sick, and they concluded that the whites were out to poison them. * Added to these woes were the internecine animosities among the fourteen tribes interned at Siletz. The crux of this hostility lay in the successful conclusion of treaties with some tribes but not with others—some treaties had not yet been ratified—which meant that the treaty tribes received services and goods that the non-treaty tribes did not. The galling irony to the nontreaty tribes—such as the Siuslaw, Alsea, Tillamook, and Ya-quina—was that they had not waged war against the whites, whereas the treaty tribes—such as the Shasta, Coquille, and Rogue—had and, it appeared, were being rewarded for it.

* The reservation was charged twenty dollars a barrel for this "flour" that sold in Portland for eight dollars. It came from the mills of George Abernethy, the former governor—the same mills that had provided "flour" for the volunteers in the Cayuse War. In this case, at least, no distinction was made between Indian and white—both were given cattle fodder.

Of all the tribes engaged in these struggles, the Rogues were the most violent, continually fighting with other tribes as well as with each other. In 1859, the agent alleged that more than one hundred Rogues had been killed by Rogues. They caused other serious problems, for example, their custom of burning all the possessions of the dead—houses, clothes, food stores, implements, everything—and this in a place where everything was in very short supply.

J. Ross Browne called the Rogue chiefs together on his visit to Siletz in the fall of 1857. He told them that, as the Great White Father's heart "was good toward them," it pained him to learn that after all he had done for their benefit, they still appeared to be dissatisfied.[9] The chiefs replied that they were dissatisfied because none of the promises made to them had been kept. Where, they asked, were the houses, mills, horses, nets, doctors, medicines, and guns they had been promised? And where was Table Rock, which both Chief John and Chief George claimed had been excluded from the treaty and to which they were assured they might return? And who had made these promises? All the chiefs concurred: it was Palmer.

There is no doubt that, with the exception of Table Rock, Palmer did make these promises. But they were made out of the exigencies of ending the war and out of his usual optimism. He surely could not have taken pleasure in the fact that his word had proven false. As suggested earlier here, that may have been one of his reasons for seeking the post at Siletz, his desire to see that those promises might be kept, however belatedly. As for Table Rock, the relevant treaties stipulated that Table Rock was a "temporary" reserve from which the Indians might be removed at any time. Table Rock was within Rogue territory, however, and the Indians had lived there for a time, which may have led to their belief that it was a permanent reservation.

Whatever the misunderstandings and empty promises, the condition of the Rogues at Siletz was pitiful. "My heart is sick," Chief John told Browne. "Many of my people have died since they came here; many are still dying. There will soon be none left of us."[10] And indeed, within a few years, the southern Oregon Indians at Siletz would be practically extinct.*

*Chief John, however, prevailed for some time and indeed, more than prevailed, for his obstreperousness was such that he was finally sent to Alcatraz. In 1862, he was allowed to return to Oregon so that, as he told Frances Victor, he "could see again his wife and daughters, who would tend upon him and comb his hair." See Victor, Early Indian Wars, 418.

BROWNE'S REPORT TO WASHINGTON had little effect. Agent David Newcome, arriving in 1860, found most of the Indians "enfeebled and half starved," and Superintendent Rector reported in 1861 that all the buildings were "dilapidated." Then in 1864, the whites' plundering of reservation land began. Oysters were found in great quantities in Yaquina Bay, and for which there were good markets in Portland and San Francisco. Also, the state decided it needed another port and, furthermore, that the land in the region of the bay could be sold to settlers at a profit. Thus were the Indians forced out of a thirty-mile stretch of their reservation.* It may have been the threat of this seizure that compelled William Rector to retire as superintendent. He later complained:

*The state paid the Indians $16,500. These forced sales continued until 1892, by which time the original reservation of almost 1,400,000 acres had been reduced to 47,000 acres. Such seizures call to mind a passage in J. Ross Browne's 1857 report on Northwest Indian affairs: "None of

> I . . . learned that no man could hold that office [the superintendency] and deal honestly with the government and all parties without haveing to take much abuce . . . concequently I made no effort to sustain myself prefering to be relieved rather thern live so boistrous a life and take the abuse consequent for a righteous corse of conduct.[11]

Complaints such as Rector's multiplied. Finally, in an attempt to replace corrupt reservation officials with honest personnel and to generally improve services to the Indians, President Grant handed the reservations over to the military in 1869. Congress, deprived of its powers of patronage, protested and passed legislation prohibiting the use of the military. In another tack altogether, the next policy gave the direction of the reservations to the various religious denominations. Siletz came under the hand of the Methodists, and employees at the reservation were required to be of that persuasion.

Palmer, it will be remembered, was a Quaker. He was born of a family that had been Quakers for some generations, was indentured to a Quaker family in his youth, and for some years had lived in the strongly Quaker community of Indiana's Whitewater Valley. In Oregon, however, Palmer's Quaker associations largely ceased. There was at this time no Quaker community in the state, and an official Quaker meeting was not established until after his death. Lacking an official meeting, Quakers were encouraged to join another Protestant denomination. Though Palmer was reputed to have been a friend of Methodism and though he offered land and lumber to the Episcopalians for a church, he himself joined no church. Not, that is, until 1870 or 1871, when he became a Methodist, shortly before he was appointed agent at Siletz and where, as noted above, employees were required to be of that persuasion.

Palmer's predecessor at Siletz was Ben Simpson, agent from 1863-71. Simpson seemed, in general, to have been pleased with the progress made at the reservation. Palmer thought otherwise. Arriving at Siletz at the end of April 1871, he wrote:

> if we judge of the future by the little progress among these people during the last sixteen years, the prospect is not hopeful. Still there is hope. But I would rather have taken these people precisely in the condition they were when I sent them here nearly sixteen years ago, than now.[12]

Palmer's first task was to see to the planting of the spring crops. But the fields were infested with fern, the workhorses and oxen incapacitated with age and disease, the few agricultural implements broken, and most of the fences down, which left the arable land open to straying cattle.

And not only were the fences down. The sawmill was in such disrepair that it was no longer operational, making it impossible to repair the reservation's dilapidated physical plant, such as the insecure jail. Much-needed new construction was impossible as well: a bridge across the river, a schoolhouse (only six adult Indians knew their ABCs), and a flour mill. The latter would have greatly benefited the reservation, since there was still no road to the valley, and thus the cost of imported flour remained exorbitant.

Then there were the appalling social conditions with which Palmer was faced. Housing consisted of verminous ramshackle hovels lacking windows and any kind of sanitary facility. The Indians' diet of oats, potatoes, and fish was seriously unbalanced. Of the population of one thousand, four-fifths were syphilitic. Finally, prostitution and alcoholism were rampant. But as usual, Palmer was optimistic: "I will not complain of the mistakes of others but try to improve by the mistakes of the past."[13]

Palmer sought to improve conditions at the reservation in a number of areas. He purchased several new teams of workhorses, acquired a thresher, repaired the fencing, and encouraged the Indians to plant family garden plots. For provision of adequate food was the central problem at the reservation. The Indians could live, at least for a while, with disease, but not without food. Because of the inadequate food supply, Palmer was sometimes forced, against his better judgment, to give the Indians permission to work outside the reservation. In general, however, he increased the reservation's agricultural production.

Palmer also made some progress in providing more facilities for sanitation, better housing, and in discouraging the destruction of the property of the dead. Of particular concern to Palmer was the condition of Indian women. He countered the polygamous practices of his charges by simply "divorcing" from the men any additional wives they might have. He also sought to lessen by fines and rewards the heavy toil imposed on the women by their largely idle men. Prostitution and alcoholism were fostered, he believed, by "a class of vicious, degraded vagabonds who have congregated around the reservation," and he made them as unwelcome as he could.[14] Finally, and to regulate and adjudicate in all of these matters, Palmer set up Indian courts, for he had always believed that, insofar as possible, it was desirable for the Indians to rule themselves.

By the end of Palmer's first year at Siletz, there had been some improvement in conditions. But far more than a year would be needed to correct the mistakes of the previous sixteen. Palmer was not to have it. As in the past, white opposition would frustrate his efforts.

In the early summer of 1872, the Reverend John Howard was sent to join the Siletz staff. Howard was not pleased with Palmer's administration, judging that it lacked missionary zeal. After all, and as the Methodists had stated in their official organ, "the tribes were handed over to us for redemption and salvation." This meant much time should be devoted to sermons, public prayer, hymn singing, and the general work of conversion. T. W. Davenport reported that the Methodists wanted "the agency [run] on a . . . revival basis." Although Palmer was "more of a practical Christian than any other Methodist I knew," Davenport observed, he had "never been a shouter." Palmer's own defense in these matters was simple: "It is useless to preach Christian conversion to a starving man—first feed him."[15]

Palmer's refusal to spend more of his already burdened time exhorting the Indians to Methodism was most distressing to certain persons in the church. On 19 September 1872, the *Pacific Christian Advocate* accused Palmer of "little organization and labor looking to direct religious results." Meanwhile, Howard was inciting certain of the Indians against Palmer. Also, Palmer may have believed, with Davenport, that Howard was an "unscrupulous meddler aspiring to the chief place [agent]." In any event, Palmer fired him. The *Advocate* was enraged: "Let no one suppose the church is either careless or powerless in this matter."[16]

Palmer, however, had his defenders, among them the Reverend Josiah Parrish, a much-respected and influential member of the Methodist Conference who had served as an Indian agent when Palmer was superintendent. In the 31 October issue of the *Advocate*, Parrish wrote that Palmer had been entirely justified in dismissing Howard and that he had the fullest confidence in the agent. But despite these assurances, rancor among certain elements of the Methodist community remained.

At about the same time as this dispute—this "sectarian jangle," as Davenport put it—white settlers in the vicinity of Siletz demanded that Palmer disarm the reservation Indians, citing rumors of rebellion. This was a serious matter, for as usual, there was a shortage of food, and guns for hunting were essential. Palmer would have none of it:

> I deem this application for disarming the Indians at this season of the year so unjust and unreasonable as to hardly admit of serious thought. The apprehension of an outbreak has not the least shadow of foundation and it is difficult finding

an excuse for such a conjecture. In my opinion, it is intended as a plea of justification for shooting others of them [a chief had recently been shot by a settler] or
else to strengthen the application for abandoning this
tract as a reservation. *[17]

There was at this time an effort in the legislature to move the Siletz Indians to eastern Oregon and open the entire reservation to settlement.

The demands of the settlers, the disapproval of elements of the Methodist establishment, the lack of funds with which to implement his projects at Siletz, and perhaps his own financial problems* led Palmer to confess to Parrish that he was "disheartened and utterly discouraged in this work." In November, he sent in his resignation. Thus ended for good Palmer's official efforts for the Indians of Oregon.[18]

His old friend, former Governor Gibbs, had been meeting Palmer's most pressing debts and for some time had urged Palmer to resign as agent so that he would be free to look after his interests in Dayton.

PALMER'S LAST YEARS were troubled by illness and financial problems. By 1877, he suffered from "impaired health," and despite occasional rallies, he continued to sicken. His finances suffered a similar decline. In 1876, Sarah Palmer wrote her nephew, Alex Derbyshire, asking if he would sell certain of her securities. "I would advise thee not to do it," Derbyshire replied. "It is bad enough to know how shamefully thy husband spent the funds of thine already, gone to pay his debts which appear to have not freed him from embarrassment."[19] Finally, it is probable that the Palmers were now alone, for in 1875, Alice, the last of their children, married and left the family home.

In short, these last years of the Palmers may not have been their happiest. Although there is vast official correspondence relating to Joel Palmer, there is little material of a personal nature. Few family letters are extant, and though Palmer kept a diary, he rarely wrote of his private life.

Of his wife, Sarah Ann, it is known only that she came of Bucks County Philadelphia stock, was left an orphan at an early age and raised by maiden aunts, married Palmer at age fifteen, received a modest inheritance, returned at least once to Philadelphia, in 1865, and died in 1891. The furniture and books in the Palmers' Dayton house suggest that she grew up in rather cultivated surroundings. Her obituary states that she

was of Quaker ancestry; professed that faith all her life, and lived in accord with it. Though not obtrusive, she had a very kind and generous nature and per-

formed innumerable benefactories for those who needed them in early
Oregon.[20]

Likewise, little is known of the eight Palmer children except for dates of
birth, marriage, and death and, in some cases, occupation and place of residence. It is known, however, that the Palmers sent some, if not most, of their
children to institutions such as Pacific University, Willamette University, and
the Portland Academy.

Despite this decline, Palmer did not entirely withdraw from public life.
One of his interests was the Oregon State Fair. The first fair was held at Glad-
stone in 1861, thereafter in Salem. By the 1870s, it was the major statewide
event of the year. In particular, it was "the favored meeting place of the pioneers," wrote Governor Oswald West, who had grown up in Salem and had
often frequented the fairgrounds. West further commented that:

> For many, attendance meant a long tiresome journey over primitive roads. Yet
> they came, for it was looked upon as a big event. Harvest over, the old wagon
> was made ready for the trip and loaded with camping equipment, food and
> family. The boys usually trailed along on their ponies, leading, perhaps, dad's
> quarter horse which, it was hoped, might bring renown to the family through
> winning some racing event.
>
> As opening day approached, the old campground, shaded by spreading
> oaks, became dotted with hundreds of tents and at night lighted by as many
> camp fires. Each fall . . . here gathered those who had found Oregon in the
> rough, pushed back the brown of wilderness, built homes, schools, churches
> and established a government . . . . Here they renewed friendships, reviewed
> their trips across the plains, talked "hosses," politics and of the future.[21]

Beyond the campgrounds lay the exhibits pavilion, the stock barns, and the
racetrack, all festooned with flags and swagged with evergreens. There was a
great variety of entertainment, the racetrack perhaps the most popular but also
braying bands, balloon ascents, as well as the usual carnival attractions: freak
shows, magicians, strong men, and those booths where one might throw
baseballs at effigies of the heads of national and state politicians. There were,
too, all manner of contests: horseshoes, hog calling, target shooting, dog-
fights, plowing matches, bull races, and joking competitions. In the evening,
fireworks spangled the sky, and the dancing went on till dawn.

Other aspects of the fair, and more instructional in nature, were the exhibits and daily grand parade of animals. The latter consisted of various breeds of
horses, cattle, sheep, and swine—a reminder to the pioneers of the enormous

increase in the diversity and numbers of the state's livestock. When Palmer arrived in 1845, there were practically no sheep, let alone a variety of breeds, and the same was true of cattle, horses, fowl, and swine. To the husbandmen who made up almost the whole of Oregon's population, these advances in the number and kind of farm animals were of the greatest significance.

The exhibits reflected advances in other areas as well. New strains of fruits and vegetables were a cornucopia compared to the wild berries, peas, and boiled wheat of the pioneers' years. Now, too, canned foods were exhibited, almost unknown in early Oregon, due to the dearth of suitable containers. Also, the exhibits of cloth articles—everything from horse cinches to ladies' drawers—were in decided contrast to the buckskin the pioneers had been forced to wear when their clothes wore out. The *Oregonian*, writing of the fair on 2 July 1880, referred to the "half forgotten legends of Grandmother's looms and memories of once buzzing but now silent spinning wheels!"

But the exhibits that reflected change more than any other were those featuring farm machinery. The labor shortage caused by the Civil War had spurred the inventors on, and now, Palmer and those of his generation could look on devices undreamt of when they arrived in Oregon with their simple hoes and crude plowshares. Now, "gorgeous in red paint," as the 2 July *Oregonian* put it, there were mechanical mowers, harrows, reapers, cultivators, separators, and most marvelous of all, steam-driven threshers. Finally, there was an invention that ended that most characteristic of pioneer labors, the toil of cutting fence rails—barbed wire.

The exhibits reflected other changes and advances in agriculture. The clearing of brush- and stumpland had greatly increased with the arrival by 1870 of bands of Chinese laborers. Between 1874 and 1880, sixty thousand acres were made ready for cultivation. Much of this new land was planted in orchards and hops, the soil and climate of the valley highly suitable to each. Now, too, there were dairy farms on the coast exporting butter to California, while in the high country, wheat fields stretched for miles, and sheep and cattle in the thousands grazed. This was all a far cry from the pioneers' kitchen garden and patch of grain.

Then there was the development of manufacturing and industry, also well reflected in the fair's exhibits. From a few crude sawmills and cooperages, entrepreneurs had gone on to produce the necessities of everyday Oregon life: cloth, paper, soap, pottery, leather, furniture, wagons, brushes, and beer. At Coos Bay, they were mining coal—at Oswego, founding iron. There were the gold mines of eastern Oregon, while along the Columbia, thirteen canneries processed thousands of pounds of salmon for export. Indeed, export in general had increased enormously, from about three million dollars a year in the 1850s to eighteen million dollars by the end of the 1870s: wheat, flour, lumber, coal, wool, salmon, potatoes, gold, silver, hides, and dried fruit. In short, Oregon, as the fair revealed, had left behind the subsistence economy of its early years.

Along with these great material advances, there were those appendages, those graces, that the pioneers deemed necessary to a civilized life. Within thirty miles of Palmer's house, there were now four colleges. A walk away from the fairgrounds stood schools of medicine and pharmacy, institutions for the handicapped, as well as the state prison.* This amelioration of the harsh pioneer conditions, this gentling of life, was to be seen in every area. Wallis Nash noted that most of the log cabins had been degraded to a woodshed or piggery and that many farmers lived in substantial, two-story, white houses that might well contain an organ or a piano, engravings on the wall, a shelf of books, and curtains at the window. Calling on one of these men, who could have been Palmer himself, he wrote:

> Think of the change the old gentleman has seen . . . .
> Now, his white farmhouse, with good barn and out-
> buildings, fronts on a well-traveled road, leading past
> many a neighbor's house, and to the church and vil
> lage. The woods on the hill-sides have disappeared,

and the ruled furrows of the wheat-fields have replaced the native grass; the elk and deer which found him food as well as sport have retired shyly away into the far-off fastnesses round Mary's Peak . . . and the fleecy flocks have usurped their place. The thievish Calapooyas and good Klick-i-tats have lost their tribal connections, and their shrunken remnants have been shifted away north to the Indian reserve. As you stand on the hill above his house, and the vision ranges over the gentle outlines of [the] Valley, dotted with farms and lined with fences, it is but the noble forms of the distant mountains that could identify the scene with that which he scanned with wayworn eye as he halted his weary oxen after his six months' journey.[22]

In the towns, too, Nash saw a softening of the early harshness: wooden sidewalks, elm-lined streets, a common hall or public room where townspeople and farmers met for lectures, theatricals, and balls—harp, fiddle, and cornet—the dancers chipping in to pay the cost of candles and the music. There was, Nash estimated, a newspaper for every three or four hundred per-

* It was not until 1883 that the state hospital moved from Portland to Salem. Wallis Nash, an Englishman traveling in Oregon in the 1870s, was informed that most of the inmates were from elsewhere, that is, not Oregon. Nash, *Oregon: There and Back in 1877*, 219.

sons, and the same could be said of the churches. And finally, every town of any size, like Palmer's Dayton, had its academy where students could memorize their Cicero and Caesar.

Another reflection of this passage to an easier, more graceful life was the fact that there was now time as well as inclination for outings, the fair being one of the most popular. But trips to the seashore and mountains were also much favored. Nash wrote:

> During the late summer and autumn, the mountains are the resort of numbers of farmers of the Willamette valley and their families, as well as of the store-keepers from the cities and towns. Packing their stores into one of the long narrow wagons of the country, and not forgetting the rifle, shot-gun, and "fish-pole" the whole family shut up house in the valley and start for the mountains. Very likely they may be four or five days on the road . . . . At night they pitch a thin tent for the females, and the men and boys sleep, rolled in their blankets, round a huge camp-fire.
>
> Arrived in the mountains, they choose some favorite dell, high up, with a cool spring babbling over the rocks at one side, amid a clear sward, upon which the two horses are picketed, in front. The wagon is unpacked, the tent pitched, the stores arranged, and the family disperse; the men to hunt the black-tailed deer, and later on in the season the elk (wapiti) and the black bear. The boys find a lake near by filled with trout, large and small, and perseveringly fish with a clothes' prop, a cord, and a bunch of worms, and catch, not much. The women and children fill huge baskets with the mountains berries, which they boil down into jam for winter use, the black pot being always kept simmering on the cross sticks over the fire.
>
> And so they pass three, four, or five weeks, in the clear sunny mountain air, till the harvest in the valley is ripe.
>
> That this holiday is generally enjoyed may be judged from the fact that one hundred and fifty wagons of campers-out paid toll, as we were told, in one season, at one gate in a pass on the Willamette and Cascade mountains military-wagon road.[23]

Nash's mention of the wagons is a reminder that when Palmer arrived in the Oregon Country there was only one road: the Oregon Trail. Now, there were roads along both sides of the Willamette, up the Columbia and Santiam to the high country, over the Coast Range to both the north and south coasts, and in addition, a network of subsidiary roads connecting major communities throughout the state.

Far more important than these roads, at least in eventual effect, was a new kind of road, one that the promoters of the fair made much of in their attempts to attract visitors. A long, specially constructed platform stood adjacent to the fairgrounds, and at this platform twice daily there arrived from both north and south "the iron horse." For indeed, by now the valley had its railroad, from Portland to Roseburg, and in addition, branch lines were a-building to the valley's other major centers. Of all the wonders of the fair, nothing matched the wonder of the railroad, especially to men like Palmer who remembered the wagon trains and "the empty, awesome face of distance" they had confronted in their oxen-paced, six-month trek across the continent.

The railroad, the accouterments of culture, the products of Oregon's own manufacture, the farm machinery, the vastly augmented agriculture, and at the end of the decade of the 1870s, those two marvelous inventions, the telephone and electric light—all of this was at the fair. Nothing in the state reflected better than the fair how far, in a mere thirty years or so, the people and their place had come, how quickly the past had passed.

IT MAY HAVE BEEN AWARENESS of this rapidity of change that led to the founding of the Oregon Pioneer Association in 1873. Limited to persons who had arrived in Oregon prior to 1853, the society's purpose was to collect and record from living witnesses facts about the pioneer experience in Oregon.

Palmer, one of the founders of the society, spoke at the first reunion at Champoeg in 1873 and was scheduled to speak at a later reunion, but illness prevented him. He did, however, appear at the 1878 reunion at the State Fair campgrounds in Salem. By reason of several curious coincidences, the occasion signified the close of Palmer's life, as well as the era in which he had lived.

The fourteenth of June dawned a sunny day. By 10:30 that morning, the pioneers—the majority having arrived by train—assembled. The program began with a procession and a prayer, followed by speeches, a picnic dinner in the grove at noon, and more speeches. In the evening, a giant campfire was lit at the center of the campground, and people told stories of their early years in Oregon. This was followed by a ball that lasted until five in the morning.

Early on that first day, Hubert Howe Bancroft interviewed Palmer for the Northwest history archive that Bancroft was then amassing. It was a lengthy interview, spanning, in a sense, his life—his birth in Canada, his time as a bound boy in upstate New York, his marriage and removal to the Whitewater Valley of Indiana, his career there as a canal builder and legislator, his captaining of wagon trains in the migrations of 1845 and 1847, and finally, the years in Oregon: his founding of Dayton, the Indian wars, his superintendency, the

Fraser River trading and other business ventures, his achievements in the legislature.

But it was a peculiar interview. At times, Palmer appeared confused, to have lost his way in passing back across the landscape of his life. It may have been for this reason that his old friend, Cris Taylor, was present, for Taylor on occasion was obliged to clarify the general's comments.

Later in the day, Palmer addressed the assembled pioneers, but briefly, for the minutes of the reunion state that he was "quite feeble."[24] And indeed, Palmer would never again address the public, for soon after the reunion, Cris Taylor wrote Bancroft that General Palmer was no longer of sound mind.

On the same day as this, his last public appearance, Palmer's era ended. Earlier in the year, the Bannocks and Paiutes, deprived of their hunting grounds by white settlers, had begun the Bannock-Paiute War. Egan was their war chief. Born a Cayuse—the first tribe with whom Palmer had had dealings—Egan had been captured by the Paiutes as a child and raised by them. On reaching manhood, he, like Palmer, was renowned for his integrity, intelligence, and presence.

For some months, Egan had successfully evaded Gen. O.O. Howard, the commander of the U.S. forces. Howard, now pursuing Egan into the Blue Mountains, offered a thousand-dollar reward to a Umatilla mercenary for Egan's scalp. On 14 June, the day on which the enfeebled Palmer spoke his last, Egan was shot. And on that day, and with his death, the Indian wars of Oregon ended.

The pioneers at the campgrounds obviously knew nothing of Egan's death, and yet in some way, it almost seems they sensed that an era was over. The following afternoon, they appointed a committee to collect Indian "relics" and place them for safekeeping in the society's museum. No act could have made it more clear that the past had now been consigned to history.

It seems a rightness, a kind of poetic justice, that these events had come together, joined in time. For this was the end of white and Indian bloodshed and, in effect, the end, as well, of General Palmer's life—as if now, at last, he were free to leave.

Notes

Prologue

1. Quoted in Stanley Sheldon Spaid's Ph.D. thesis entitled "Joel Palmer and Indian Affairs in Oregon," Eugene: University of Oregon, 1950, 286.

O N E   *From the Blackwater to the Whitewater*

1. Quoted in Barbara Miller Solomon, ed., with Patricia Ann King, *Travels in New England and New York* (Cambridge, Mass: The Belknap Press of Harvard University Press, 1969), 8.
2. Joel Palmer, interview with Hubert Howe Bancroft, Salem, Ore., 1878, copy, MSS 114, Oregon Historical Society, Portland, Ore., 2.
3. Palmer–Bancroft interview, 2.
4. Palmer–Bancroft interview, 3.
5. Palmer–Bancroft interview, 3.
6. A.B. Guthrie, Jr., *The Way West* (New York: William Sloane Associates, 1949), 154, 20.
7. Palmer–Bancroft interview, 17.

T W O   *To Oregon*

1. Joel Palmer, *Journal of Travels over the Rocky Mountains to the Mouth of the Columbia River; Made during the Years 1845 and 1846* (Cincinnati: J.A. and U.P. James, 1847),

reprinted in *Early Western Travels, 1748-1846*, ed. Reuben Gold Thwaites, vol. 30 (Cleveland: Arthur H. Clark Company, 1906), 29, 30.

2. Palmer, *Journal*, 30.

3. Palmer, *Journal*, 34.

4. Palmer, *Journal*, 32, 36.

5. Palmer, *Journal*, 38.

6. Quoted in John Mack Faragher, *Women and Men on the Overland Trail* (New Haven, Conn.: Yale University Press, 1979), 27.

7. Quoted in Fred Lockley, *History of the Columbia River Valley from The Dalles to the Sea*, vol. 1 (Chicago: The S.J. Clarke Publishing Company, 1928), 1069-70, 1071.

8. Palmer, *Journal*, 40.

9. Palmer, *Journal*, 41.

10. Palmer, *Journal*, 41.

11. A.B. Guthrie, Jr., *The Way West* (New York: William Sloane Associates, 1949), 51.

12. Jacob Snyder, "The Diary of Jacob R. Snyder," *Quarterly of the Society of California Pioneers* 8 (1931):230; Quoted in Donna M. Wojcik, *The Brazen Overlanders of 1845* (Portland, Ore.: Donna M. Wojcik, 1976), 118, 58.

13. Palmer, *Journal*, 53-54.

14. Palmer, *Journal*, 258.

15. Quoted in Wojcik, *Brazen Overlanders*, 27.

16. Palmer, *Journal*, 42.

17. Palmer, *Journal*, 43.

18. Palmer, *Journal*, 44; Quoted in Fred Lockley, *Captain Sol. Tetherow: Wagon Train Master* (Fairfield, Wash.: Ye Galleon Press, 1970), 8.

19. John E. Howell, "Diary of an Immigrant of 1845," *Washington Historical Quarterly* 3 (1907):140.

20. James Field, "Crossing the Plains," MSS 520, Oregon Historical Society, 10.

21. Francis Parkman, *The Oregon Trail*, ed. by E.N. Feltskog (Madison: University of Wisconsin Press, 1969), 66.

22. Palmer, *Journal*, 47.

23. Palmer, *Journal*, 47, 48; Howell, "Diary of an Immigrant," 141, 142.

24. Samuel Parker, "Diary, 1845," typescript, Overland Journeys Collection, MSS 1508, Oregon Historical Society, 21 July 1845; Quoted in Wojcik, *Brazen Overlanders*, 54.

25. Field, "Crossing the Plains," 26-27.

26. Palmer, *Journal*, 52.

27. Guthrie, *The Way West*, 76.

28. Sarah J. Cummins, *Autobiography and Reminiscences* (Cleveland: Arthur H. Clark Company, 1914), 24; Kenneth L. Holmes, ed., *Covered Wagon Women*, vol. 1 (Glendale, Calif.: Arthur H. Clark Company, 1983), 42-43.

29. Parker, "Diary," 5 June 1845; W.W. Walter, "Reminiscences of an Old 45er," typescript, MSS 739, Oregon Historical Society, 1; Quoted in Faragher, *Women and Men on the Overland Trail*, 45.

30. Palmer, *Journal*, 55, 56.

31. Palmer, *Journal*, 55; Parkman, *Oregon Trail*, 75-76.

32. Palmer, *Journal*, 54; Quoted in A.J. Allen, *Ten Years in Oregon* (Ithaca, N.Y.: Mack, Andrus, & Co., 1848), 283-84.

33. Palmer, *Journal*, 58.

34. Palmer, *Journal*, 59, 60.

35. Parkman, *Oregon Trail*, 46a-47a.

36. Snyder, "Diary," 225.

37. Betsy Bayley, "Betsy Bayley to Mrs. Lucy P. Griffith," *Letter of 1845*, Overland Journeys Collection, MSS 1508, Oregon Historical Society, 20 September 1849.

38. Wojcik, *Brazen Overlanders*, 215.

39. W.A. Goulder, *Reminiscences of Pioneers* (Boise, Idaho: Timothy Regan, 1909), 113; Lockley, *History of the Columbia River Valley*, 1070-71, 1073.

40. William Barlow, "Reminiscences of Seventy Years," *Oregon Historical Quarterly* 13 (1912):256.

41. Palmer, *Journal*, 60, 116.

42. Field, "Crossing the Plains," 18.

43. Quoted in Wojcik, *Brazen Overlanders*, 113, 116.

44. Parkman, *Oregon Trail*, 88-89.

45. Quoted in Wojcik, *Brazen Overlanders*, 116.

46. Palmer, *Journal*, 71.

47. Cummins, *Autobiography*, 29; William G. Findley, "Diary, 1845-1847," typescript, MSS 494, Oregon Historical Society, 6; Palmer, *Journal*, 74; Guthrie, *The Way West*, 169-70.

48. Palmer, *Journal*, 86.

49. Palmer, *Journal*, 88.

50. Fred Lockley, "Recollections of Benjamin Franklin Bonney," *Oregon Historical Quarterly* 24 (1923):40; Palmer, *Journal*, 89.

51. Overton Johnson and William H. Winter, *Route Across the Rocky Mountains* (Princeton, N.J.: Princeton University Press, 1932), 30; Palmer, *Journal*, 102, 103.

52. Palmer, *Journal*, 124; Barlow, "Reminiscences," 254.

53. Palmer, *Journal*, 105-106.

54. Palmer, *Journal*, 107.

55. Palmer, *Journal*, 109.

56. Palmer, *Journal*, 113.

57. Palmer, *Journal*, 115, 120.

58. Barlow, "Reminiscences," 260.

59. Palmer, *Journal*, 130, 133.

60. Palmer, *Journal*, 136.
61. Palmer, *Journal*, 133-34n.
62. Palmer, *Journal*, 139.
63. Palmer, *Journal*, 145, 147.
64. Barlow, "Reminiscences," 264-65.
65. Palmer, *Journal*, 152.
66. Palmer, *Journal*, 157.

THREE   *Trail's End*

1. Elliott Coues, ed., *The Manuscript Journals of Alexander Henry and of David Thompson*, vol. 2 (New York: Francis P. Harper, 1897), 812, 819-20.
2. Milo Milton Quaife, ed., *Adventures on the Oregon* (Chicago: R.R. Donnelly & Sons, The Lakeside Press, 1923), 254, 255.
3. Robert Carlton Clark, *History of the Willamette Valley, Oregon* (Chicago: S.J. Clarke Publishing Company, 1927), 69.
4. Quoted in Jeff Zucker, Kay Hummel, and Bob Høgfoss, *Oregon Indians: Culture, History & Current Affairs* (Portland, Ore.: Western Imprints, 1983), 61.
5. Paul Kane, *Wanderings of an Artist Among the Indians of North America* (London: Longman, Brown, Green, Longmans, and Roberts, 1859), 196.
6. Quoted in McLoughlin to Hudson's Bay Company, 19 July 1845, in Leslie M. Scott, "Report of Lieutenant Peel on Oregon in 1845-46," *Oregon Historical Quarterly* 29 (1928):76; A.B. Guthrie, Jr., *The Way West* (New York: William Sloane Associates, 1949), 255.
7. Hubert Howe Bancroft, *History of Oregon*, vol. 1 (San Francisco: The History Company, 1886), 168-69. (Note: It is generally believed that Frances Fuller Victor wrote much of Bancroft's *History of Oregon*.)
8. Bancroft, *History of Oregon*, vol. 1, 425, 392, 449.
9. Peter H. Burnett, *An Old California Pioneer* (Oakland, Calif.: Biobooks, 1946), 106, 108.
10. Burnett, *An Old California Pioneer*, 106.
11. E. Ruth Rockwood, ed., "Diary of Rev. George H. Atkinson, D.D., 1847-1858," *Oregon Historical Quarterly* 40 (1939):349.
12. Mrs. S.A. Long, "Mrs. Jesse Applegate," *Oregon Historical Quarterly* 9 (1908):181; Clark, *History of the Willamette*, 390-92.
13. Charles Wilkes, *Narrative of the United States Exploring Expedition*, vol. 4 (Philadelphia: Lea and Blanchard, 1845), 361.
14. Quaife, *Adventures on the Oregon*, 255.
15. William A. Bowen, *The Willamette Valley: Migration and Settlement on the Oregon Frontier* (Seattle: University of Washington Press, 1978), 24; Clark, *History of the Willamette*, 375.

16. Francis Parkman, *The Oregon Trail* (Madison: University of Wisconsin Press, 1969), 7; Burnett, *An Old California Pioneer*, 107, 108; Horace Sumner Lyman, "Biography," MSS 722, Oregon Historical Society; Joseph Schafer, "Documents Relative to Warre and Vavasour's Military Reconnoisance in Oregon, 1845-6," *Oregon Historical Quarterly* 10 (1909): 53; Charles L. Camp, ed., *James Clyman, Frontiersman* (Portland, Ore.: Champoeg Press, 1960), 119.

17. Dorothy O. Johansen, ed., *Robert Newell's Memoranda* (Portland, Ore.: Champoeg Press, 1959), 119.

18. Joel Palmer, *Journal of Travels over the Rocky Mountains to the Mouth of the Columbia River; Made during the Years 1845 and 1846* (Cincinnati: J.A. and U.P. James, 1847), reprinted in *Early Western Travels, 1748-1846*, ed. Reuben Gold Thwaites, vol. 30 (Cleveland: Arthur H. Clark Company, 1906), 158, 159.

19. Palmer, *Journal*, 159.

20. *Transactions of the Seventh Annual Re-union of the Oregon Pioneer Association, 1879* (Salem, Ore.: E.M. Waite, Steam Printer and Bookbinder, 1880) 26-27.

21. Lawrence Clark Powell, "Flumgudgeon Gazette in 1845 Antedated the Spectator," *Oregon Historical Quarterly* 41 (1940):206; *Flumgudgeon Gazette and Bumble Bee Budget*, MSS 1176, Oregon Historical Society, 12.

22. Palmer, *Journal*, 164, 176, 177.

23. Palmer, *Journal*, 180.

24. Palmer, *Journal*, 182.

25. Palmer, *Journal*, 186.

26. Palmer, *Journal*, 201.

27. Palmer, *Journal*, 196, 201, 202.

28. Palmer, *Journal*, 207.

29. Palmer, *Journal*, 208.

30. Palmer, *Journal*, 209.

31. Palmer, *Journal*, 209.

32. Palmer, *Journal*, 223.

33. Palmer's letter is reproduced in Camp, *James Clyman*, 274.

FOUR   *The Cayuse War*

1. Hubert Howe Bancroft, *History of Oregon*, vol. 1 (San Francisco: The History Company, 1886), 623.

2. Bancroft, *History of Oregon*, vol. 1, 623.

3. E. Ruth Rockwood, ed., "Diary of Rev. George H. Atkinson, D.D., 1847-1858," *Oregon Historical Quarterly* 40 (1939):267.

4. Quoted in Bancroft, *History of Oregon*, vol. 1, 592.

5. Quoted in Bancroft, *History of Oregon*, vol. 1, 618-19.

6. Bancroft, *History of Oregon*, vol. 1, 614.

7. Bancroft, *History of Oregon*, vol. 1, 614-15.

8. Walter Carlton Woodward, *The Rise and Early History of Political Parties in Oregon, 1843-1868* (Portland, Ore.: J.K. Gill Company, 1913), 26.

9. *Flumgudgeon Gazette and Bumble Bee Budget*, MSS 1176, Oregon Historical Society.

10. Peter H. Burnett, *An Old California Pioneer* (Oakland, Calif.: Biobooks, 1946), 149; Bancroft, *History of Oregon*, vol. 1, 782.

11. In Burnett, *An Old California Pioneer*, 147-48.

12. Quoted in Robert Carlton Clark, *History of the Willamette Valley, Oregon* (Chicago: S.J. Clarke Publishing Company, 1927), 237.

13. Quoted in Robert H. Ruby and John A. Brown, *The Cayuse Indians: Imperial Tribesmen of Old Oregon* (Norman: University of Oklahoma Press, 1972), 66, 86.

14. Quoted in John Wain, *Samuel Johnson* (New York: Viking Press, 1974), 325.

15. Robert J. Loewenberg, "The Missionary Idea in Oregon: Illustrations from the Life and Times of Methodist Henry Perkins," in *The Western Shore*, ed. Thomas Vaughan (Portland: Oregon Historical Society, 1976), 162-63.

16. Quoted in Archer Butler Hulbert and Dorothy Printup Hulbert, eds., *Marcus Whitman, Crusader*, pt. 2 (Denver: Stewart Commission of Colorado College and Denver Public Library, 1938), 15.

17. Quoted in Hulbert, *Marcus Whitman*, 14.

18. Quoted in Alvin M. Josephy, Jr., *The Nez Perce Indians and the Opening of the Northwest* (New Haven, Conn.: Yale University Press, 1965), 197.

19. Quoted in Josephy, *Nez Perce Indians*, 238.

20. Quoted in Clifford Merrill Drury, *Marcus Whitman, M.D.: Pioneer and Martyr* (Caldwell, Idaho: The Caxton Printers, Ltd., 1937), 458-60.

21. Quoted in Drury, *Marcus Whitman, M.D.* 459.

22. Quoted in Frances Fuller Victor, *The Early Indian Wars of Oregon* (Salem, Ore.: Frank C. Baker, State Printer, 1894), 112-13.

23. Quoted in Bancroft, *History of Oregon*, vol.1, 677.

24. Quoted in Bancroft, *History of Oregon*, vol.1, 410-11n.

25. Victor, *Early Indian Wars*, 157.

26. Joel Palmer, interview with Hubert Howe Bancroft, Salem, Ore., 1878, copy, MSS 114, Oregon Historical Society, 12.

27. Quoted in J. Henry Brown, *Brown's Political History of Oregon* (Portland, Ore.: Lewis & Dryden, 1892), 342.

28. Quoted in Clarence B. Bagley, ed., *Early Catholic Missions in Old Oregon*, vol. 1 (Seattle: Lowman & Hanford Company, 1932), 200.

29. Quoted in Bagley, *Early Catholic Missions*, 202, 203.

30. Fred Lockley, *History of the Columbia River Valley from The Dalles to the Sea* (Chicago: The S.J. Clarke Publishing Company, 1928), 1078.

31. Quoted in Victor, *Early Indian Wars*, 162.

32. Bancroft, *History of Oregon*, vol. 1, 32, 693.

33. Quoted in Bancroft, *History of Oregon*, vol. 1, 694.

34. Brown, *Political History of Oregon*, 329; Sir George Henry Simpson, *Narration of a Journey Around the World*, vol. 1 (London: Henry Colburn, 1847), 164.

35. Victor, *Early Indian Wars*, 123.

36. Victor, *Early Indian Wars*, 123-24.

37. Cornelius Gilliam, "Correspondence 1847-48," MSS 2205, Oregon Historical Society, 25 January 1848, letter to his wife, children, and brethren in the church.

38. Joel Palmer, *Journal of Travels over the Rocky Mountains to the Mouth of the Columbia River; Made during the Years 1845 and 1846* (Cincinnati: J.A. and U.P. James, 1847), reprinted in *Early Western Travels, 1748-1846*, ed. Reuben Gold Thwaites, vol. 30 (Cleveland: Arthur H. Clark Company, 1906), 108.

39. Quoted in Ruby and Brown, *The Cayuse Indians*, 52.

40. Quoted in Ruby and Brown, *The Cayuse Indians*, 26; John K. Townsend, *Narrative of a Journey Across the Rocky Mountains to the Columbia River* (1839), reprinted in *Early Western Travels, 1748-1846*, ed. Reuben Gold Thwaites, vol. 21 (Cleveland: Arthur H. Clark Company, 1905), 350.

41. Ruby and Brown, *The Cayuse Indians*, 37.

42. Quoted in Ruby and Brown, *The Cayuse Indians*, 3, 30, 88, 42-43; Townsend, *Across the Rocky Mountains*, 281.

43. Quoted in Woodward, *Early Political Parties*, 10.

44. Quoted in Brown, *Political History of Oregon*, 352-54.

45. Gilliam, "Correspondence," 25 January 1848.

46. Cornelius Gilliam to William Dunson Stillwell, Military Collection, MSS 1514, Oregon Historical Society; Brown, *Political History of Oregon*, 356; William Dunson Stillwell to Conrade Walker, regarding Cayuse War, 1848, MSS 1514, Oregon Historical Society, 21 January 1915.

47. Victor, *Early Indian Wars*, 163, 164.

48. Stillwell to Walker, 21 January 1915; Brown, *Political History of Oregon*, 357.

49. Gilliam, "Correspondence," 25 January 1848.

50. Stillwell to Walker, 21 January 1915; Quoted in Brown, *Political History of Oregon*, 357.

51. Quoted in Victor, *Early Indian Wars*, 163, 164.

52. Bancroft, *History of Oregon*, vol. 1, 575n.

53. Dorothy O. Johansen, ed., *Robert Newell's Memoranda* (Portland, Ore.: Champoeg Press, 1959), 85; Burnett, *An Old California Pioneer*, 98.

54. Brown, *Political History of Oregon*, 386.

55. Quoted in Bancroft, *History of Oregon*, vol. 1, 705-706n.

56. Quoted in Bancroft, *History of Oregon*, vol. 1, 705-706n.

57. Johansen, *Robert Newell's Memoranda*, 105.

58. Quoted in Brown, *Political History of Oregon*, 149-51.

59. Quoted in Brown, *Political History of Oregon*, 358-60.

60. Joel Palmer to M. Crawford, Special Collection Division, University of Oregon Library, Eugene [Palmer Collection] 10 February 1848.

61. Quoted in Vaughan, Thomas, ed., *High & Mighty: Select Sketches about the Deschutes Country* (Portland: Oregon Historical Society Press, 1981), 19.

62. Johansen, *Robert Newell's Memoranda*, 106.

63. Johansen, *Robert Newell's Memoranda*, 106.

64. Johansen, *Robert Newell's Memoranda*, 106; Victor, *Early Indian Wars*, 169.

65. W.W. Walter, "Reminiscences," MSS 739, Oregon Historical Society, 4.

66. Johansen, *Robert Newell's Memoranda*, 106.

67. Johansen, *Robert Newell's Memoranda*, 106.

68. Johansen, *Robert Newell's Memoranda*, 107.

69. Johansen, *Robert Newell's Memoranda*, 107.

70. Quoted in Victor, *Early Indian Wars*, 171.

71. Quoted in Victor, *Early Indian Wars*, 172.

72. Johansen, *Robert Newell's Memoranda*, 108.

73. Gilliam, "Correspondence," C.R. Shaw letter, 20 February 1848.

74. Berryman Jennings, J.D. Crawford to Berryman Jennings, MSS 1181, Oregon Historical Society, 26 February 1848.

75. Quoted in Victor, *Early Indian Wars*, 112.

76. Quoted in Johansen, *Robert Newell's Memoranda*, 133.

77. Victor, *Early Indian Wars*, 175.

78. Johansen, *Robert Newell's Memoranda*, 121, 133.

79. Palmer–Bancroft interview, 15.

80. A.E. Garrison, MSS 1009, Oregon Historical Society, 47.

81. Johansen, *Robert Newell's Memoranda*, 134.

82. Quoted in Brown, *Political History of Oregon*, 363.

83. Garrison, 47.

84. Walter, "Reminiscences," 5.

85. Bancroft, *History of Oregon*, vol. 1, 717.

86. Johansen, *Robert Newell's Memoranda*, 111; Quoted in Brown, *Political History of Oregon*, 367; Horace Sumner Lyman, "Reminiscences of John T. Cox, of 1846," MSS 722, Oregon Historical Society, 9.

87. Johansen, *Robert Newell's Memoranda*, 111-12.

88. Johansen, *Robert Newell's Memoranda*, 134.

89. Quoted in Brown, *Political History of Oregon*, 391.

90. Quoted in Brown, *Political History of Oregon*, 394-96.

91. Quoted in Brown, *Political History of Oregon*, 393.

92. Quoted in Brown, *Political History of Oregon*, 393-94.

93. Quoted in Brown, *Political History of Oregon*, 391.

94. Quoted in Brown, *Political History of Oregon*, 391.

95. Quoted in Johansen, *Robert Newell's Memoranda*, 135.

96. Quoted in Brown, *Political History of Oregon*, 396.

97. Johansen, *Robert Newell's Memoranda*, 112.

98. Johansen, *Robert Newell's Memoranda*, 113.

99. Quoted in Johansen, *Robert Newell's Memoranda*, 136.

100. Quoted in Johansen, *Robert Newell's Memoranda*, 137.

101. Quoted in Brown, *Political History of Oregon*, 379; Walter, "Reminiscences," 6.

102. Quoted in Brown, *Political History of Oregon*, 379-80.

103. Palmer to Loan Commissioners, Cayuse Indian War Claim Records, Accession number 89-A12, boxes 45-47, Military Department, Oregon State Archives, Salem.

104. Quoted in Victor, *Early Indian Wars*, 201.

105. Joel Palmer to Berryman Jennings, "Letters 1848-68," Palmer Papers, MSS 114, Oregon Historical Society, 1 April 1848.

106. L.H. Goodhue to Joel Palmer, 8 April 1848, Palmer Collection, University of Oregon.

107. Quoted in Brown, *Political History of Oregon*, 404, 385.

108. John Mix Stanley to Robert Newell, Palmer Collection, University of Oregon.

109. Berryman Jennings, MSS 1181, Oregon Historical Society, 4 May 1848.

110. Joel Palmer to Loan Commissioners, May 1848, Cayuse Indian War Claim Records, Military Department, Oregon State Archives, Salem.

111. Quoted in Victor, *Early Indian Wars*, 211; Cris Taylor to Joel Palmer, 2 June 1848, Palmer Collection, University of Oregon.

112. Berryman Jennings, MSS 1181, Oregon Historical Society, 5 June 1848; Quoted in Brown, *Political History of Oregon*, 413.

113. Berryman Jennings to Joel Palmer, Provisional and Territorial Records, Oregon State Archives, 20 June 1848; Quoted in Brown, *Political History of Oregon*, 413; Rockwood, "Diary of Rev. George H. Atkinson," 186; Robert Allen Bennett, *We'll All Go Home in the Spring* (Walla Walla, Wash.: Pioneer Press Books, 1984), 47.

114. Quoted in Brown, *Political History of Oregon*, 408.

115. Bennett, *We'll All Go Home*, 47; *Spectator*, 11 July 1848.

116. Brown, *Political History of Oregon*, 410.

117. Quoted in Brown, *Political History of Oregon*, 393.

118. Victor, *Early Indian Wars*, 217; *Spectator*, 28 January 1848.

FIVE   *Settling In*

1. Fred Lockley, *History of the Columbia River Valley from the Dalles to the Sea*, vol. 1 (Chicago: The S.J. Clarke Publishing Company, 1928), 1079.

2. Peter H. Burnett, *An Old California Pioneer* (Oakland, Calif.: Biobooks, 1946), 153, 154.

3. Burnett, *An Old California Pioneer*, 163.

4. Hubert Howe Bancroft, *History of Oregon*, vol. 2 (San Francisco: The History Company, 1886), 46.

5. Bancroft, *History of Oregon*, vol. 2, 65.

6. Joel Palmer, interview with Hubert Howe Bancroft, Salem, Ore., 1878, copy, MSS 114, Oregon Historical Society, 19-20.

7. Elliott Coues, ed., *The Manuscript Journals of Alexander Henry and of David Thompson*, vol. 2 (New York: Francis P. Harper, 1897), 812.

8. Leslie M. Scott, "John Work's Journey from Fort Vancouver to Umpqua River, and Return, in 1834," *Oregon Historical Quarterly* 24 (1923):246-47.

9. Charles Wilkes, *Narrative of the United States Exploring Expedition*, vol. 4 (Philadelphia: Lea and Blanchard, 1845), 358.

10. Joel Palmer, *Journal of Travels over the Rocky Mountains to the Mouth of the Columbia River; Made during the Years 1845 and 1846* (Cincinnati: J.A. and U.P. James, 1847), reprinted in *Early Western Travels, 1748-1846*, ed. Reuben Gold Thwaites, vol. 30 (Cleveland: Arthur H. Clark Company, 1906), 171.

11. Bancroft, *History of Oregon*, vol. 2, 159.

12. Richard Hofstadter, *The Progressive Historians* (New York: Knopf, 1968), 50, 4.

13. Palmer to Joseph Lane, Joseph Lane Papers, MSS 1146, Oregon Historical Society, 31 December 1852.

SIX   *The Troubles of 1853*

1. Quoted in Robert H. Ruby and John A. Brown, *The Cayuse Indians: Imperial Tribesmen of Old Oregon* (Norman: University of Oklahoma Press, 1972), 63.

2. Quoted in Ruby and Brown, *The Cayuse Indians*, 86.

3. Quoted in Ruby and Brown, *The Cayuse Indians*, 86; quoted in Alvin M. Josephy, Jr., *The Nez Perce Indians and the Opening of the Northwest* (New Haven, Conn.: Yale University Press, 1965), 236; Hubert Howe Bancroft, *History of Oregon*, vol. 1 (San Francisco: The History Company, 1886), 155, 391.

4. Quoted in Robert M. Kvasnicka and Herman J. Viola, *The Commissioners of Indian Affairs, 1824-1977* (Lincoln: University of Nebraska Press, 1979), 26.

5. A.J. Allen, *Ten Years in Oregon* (Ithaca, N.Y.: Mack, Andrus, & Co., 1848), 320.

6. Allen, *Ten Years in Oregon*, 184-85.

7. Charles H. Carey, *General History of Oregon*, vol. 2 (Portland, Ore.: Binfords and Mort, 1971), 526.

8. Quoted in Carey, *General History of Oregon*, vol. 2, 191, 193.

9. Peter H. Burnett, *An Old California Pioneer* (Oakland, Calif.: Biobooks, 1946), 89-90.

10. Bancroft, *History of Oregon*, vol. 1, 278, 280.

11. Allen, *Ten Years in Oregon*, 218.

12. Bancroft, *History of Oregon*, vol. 2, 62.

13. Joseph Lane to William Tolmie, reel 2, Joseph Lane Papers, 17 May 1849, 2; Bancroft, *History of Oregon*, vol. 2, 154.

14. Joseph Lane to Secretary of War, reel 2, Joseph Lane Papers, October 1849, 38.

15. Joseph Lane to Young Chief of the Cayuse, reel 2, Joseph Lane Papers, 25 January 1850, 2; Joseph Lane to Nez Perce Chiefs, reel 2, Joseph Lane Papers, 28 January 1850, 76; Quoted in Ruby and Brown, *The Cayuse Indians*, 154.

16. Frances Fuller Victor, "The First Oregon Cavalry," *Oregon Historical Quarterly* 3 (1902):125.

17. Quoted in Bancroft, *History of Oregon*, vol. 2, 95.

18. Quoted in Bancroft, *History of Oregon*, vol. 2, 95.

19. Frances Fuller Victor, *The Early Indian Wars of Oregon* (Salem, Ore.: Frank C. Baker, State Printer, 1894), 250.

20. Quoted in Frances Fuller Victor, *The River of the West* (Hartford, Conn.: R. W. Bliss & Co., 1870), 495.

21. Edward J. Kowrach, ed., *Journal of a Catholic Bishop on the Oregon Trail* (Fairfield, Wash.: Ye Galleon Press, 1978), 115.

22. Kowrach, *Journal of a Catholic Bishop*, 115.

23. Bancroft, *History of Oregon*, vol. 2, 210; Alban W. Hoopes, *Indian Affairs and Their Administration* (Philadelphia: University of Pennsylvania Press, 1832), 77.

24. Bancroft, *History of Oregon*, vol. 2, 212.

25. Commissioner of Indian Affairs, *Annual Report*, 27 November 1851, 32 Congress, 1st sess., H.Ex.Doc. 32, 274.

26. Quoted in *Statesman*, 4 August 1852.

27. Commissioner of Indian Affairs, *Annual Report*, 27 November 1851, 32 Congress, 1st sess., H.Ex.Doc. 21, 293; Quoted in Kvasnicka and Viola, *Commissioners of Indian Affairs*, 53.

28. Quoted in Stanley Sheldon Spaid, "Joel Palmer and Indian Affairs in Oregon," PH.D. Thesis (Eugene: University of Oregon, 1950), 72; Anson Dart to Luke Lea, reel 11, Oregon Superintendency Records, September 1851, 23.

29. Joseph Lane, "Autobiography," microfilm, Bancroft Library, University of California, Berkeley, P-8 43, 130; Bancroft, *History of Oregon*, vol. 2, 216.

30. Joel Palmer to George Manypenny, reel 3, Oregon Superintendency Records, 27 May 1853, 274.

31. Joel Palmer to George Manypenny, reel 3, Oregon Superintendency Records, 8 July 1853, 291.

32. T. W. Davenport, "Recollections of an Indian Agent—III," *Oregon Historical Quarterly* 8 (1907):236-37.

33. *Oregonian*, 14 May 1853.

34. *Oregonian*, 18 June 1853.

35. Joel Palmer to Josiah Parrish, reel 3, Oregon Superintendency Records, 2 June

1853, 407; Joel Palmer to E.J. Stone, reel 3, Oregon Superintendency Records, 5 June 1853, 429.

36. Joel Palmer to George Manypenny, reel 11, Oregon Superintendency Records, 23 June 1853, 84.

37. Joel Palmer to George Manypenny, reel 11, Oregon Superintendency Records, 23 June 1853, 84.

38. Dorothy and Jack Sutton, eds., *Indian Wars of the Rogue River* (Grants Pass, Ore.: Josephine County Historical Society, 1969), 74.

39. Quoted in Sutton, *Indian Wars*, 74.

40. B.F. Dowell to Frances Victor, H.H. Bancroft microfilm, reel 3, Bancroft Library, University of California, Berkeley, 4 (Oregon Historical Society Microfilm 176).

41. *Statesman*, 23 August 1853.

42. *Statesman*, 30 August 1853.

43. *Statesman*, 6 September 1853.

44. Bancroft, *History of Oregon*, vol. 2, 317.

45. *Statesman*, 13 September 1853, 18 October 1853.

46. *Statesman*, 6 September 1853.

47. Palmer, Joel, 1853 Diary, MSS 114, Oregon Historical Society.

48. Quoted in Albert G. Walling, *History of Southern Oregon* (Portland, Ore.: Printing House of A.G. Walling, 1884), 223.

49. Victor, *Early Indian Wars*, 315; James W. Nesmith, "Reminiscences of the Indian War," *Oregon Historical Quarterly* 7 (1906):218.

50. Victor, *Early Indian Wars*, 219.

51. Bancroft, *History of Oregon*, vol. 2, 319.

52. *Statesman*, 4 October 1853.

53. R.R. Thompson to Palmer, reel 13, Oregon Superintendency Records, 16 August 1853, 42; W.W. Raymond to Joel Palmer, reel 3, Oregon Superintendency Records, 17 October 1853, 356.

54. George Manypenny to Joel Palmer, reel 3, Oregon Superintendency Records, 5 August 1853, 326.

55. Quoted in C.F. Coan, "The Adoption of the Reservation Policy in Pacific Northwest," *Oregon Historical Quarterly* 23 (1922):30.

56. Quoted in Coan, "Adoption of the Reservation Policy," 31.

57. Quoted in Coan, "Adoption of the Reservation Policy," 33.

58. Joel Palmer to Samuel Culver, reel 2, Oregon Superintendency Records, 4 November 1853, 353.

59. S.M. Smith to Joel Palmer, reel 3, Oregon Superintendency Records, 8 November 1853, 386.

60. William Chinook to Joel Palmer, Oregon Superintendency Records, reel 3, 3 November 1853, 484; Robert Hull to Joel Palmer, reel 4, Oregon Superintendency Records, 17 November 1853, 24.

61. Joel Palmer to Robert Hull, reel 4, Oregon Superintendency Records, 20 December 1853, 25.
62. Joel Palmer to George Manypenny, reel 4, Oregon Superintendency Records, 20 December 1853, 17.
63. Quoted in Allen Johnson and Dumas Malone, eds., *Dictionary of American Biography*, vol. 5 (New York: Charles Scribner's Sons, 1930), 136.

SEVEN   *Massacre and Politics*

1. S.M. Smith to Joel Palmer, reel 4, Oregon Superintendency Records, 1 January 1854, 69.
2. *Statesman*, 7 March 1854.
3. S.M. Smith to Joel Palmer, reel 4, Oregon Superintendency Records, 1 January 1854, 69.
4. Quoted in Frances Fuller Victor, *Early Indian Wars of Oregon* (Salem: Frank C. Baker, State Printer, 1894), 324.
5. Quoted in Victor, *Early Indian Wars*, 324.
6. Victor, *Early Indian Wars*, 326.
7. S.M. Smith to Joel Palmer, reel 4, Oregon Superintendency Records, 5 February 1854, 110.
8. Joel Palmer to Joseph Lane, Joseph Lane Papers, MSS 1146, Oregon Historical Society, 26 February 1854.
9. Commissioner of Indian Affairs, *Annual Report*, reel 7, Oregon Superintendency Records, 11 September 1854, 40.
10. Joel Palmer to Orville C. Pratt, reel 4, Oregon Superintendency Records, 9 February 1854, 77.
11. Joel Palmer to Tualatin Band, reel 4, Oregon Superintendency Records, 21 March 1854, 134.
12. Joel Palmer to Joseph Lane, Joseph Lane Papers, 30 March 1854.
13. Quoted in Samuel Culver to Joel Palmer, reel 4, Oregon Superintendency Records, 23 February 1854, 125.
14. Joel Palmer to George Manypenny, Annual Report, reel 7, Oregon Superintendency Records, 11 September 1854, 40.
15. Joel Palmer to George Manypenny, Annual Report, reel 7, Oregon Superintendency Records, 11 September 1854, 40.
16. Joel Palmer to George Manypenny, Annual Report, reel 7, Oregon Superintendency Records, 11 September 1854, 40.
17. Joel Palmer to Joseph Lane, Joseph Lane Papers, 3 March 1854.
18. Joel Palmer to Gen. John Wool, reel 4, Oregon Superintendency Records, 12 May 1854, 203.
19. Joel Palmer to C. Ivess, reel 5, Oregon Superintendency Records, 20 May 1854,

44; Superintendent of Indian Affairs, *Annual Report*, reel 7, 11 September 1854, 40.

20. Samuel Culver to Joel Palmer, reel 4, Oregon Superintendency Records, 1 June 1854, 213.

21. Samuel Culver to Joel Palmer, reel 4, Oregon Superintendency Records, 1 June 1854, 213.

22. Joel Palmer to Josiah Parrish, reel 5, Oregon Superintendency Records, 28 June 1854, 20.

23. Superintendent of Indian Affairs, *Annual Report*, reel 7, 11 September 1854, 40.

24. Superintendent of Indian Affairs, *Annual Report*, reel 7, 11 September 1854, 40.

25. Perit Huntington to Joel Palmer, reel 4, Oregon Superintendency Records, 9 July 1854, 222.

26. Joel Palmer to William Martin, reel 4, Oregon Superintendency Records, 29 July 1854, 236; quoted in Jeff Zucker, Kay Hummel, and Bob Høgfoss, *Oregon Indians: Culture, History & Current Affairs* (Portland, Ore.: Western Imprints, 1983), 82.

27. Joel Palmer to William Martin, reel 4, Oregon Superintendency Records, 29 July 1854, 236.

28. Samuel Culver to Joel Palmer, Superintendency Records, 20 July 1854, 33 Congress, 2d sess., Doc 96, 292.

29. Josiah Parrish to Joel Palmer, Superintendency Records, 10 July 1854, 33 Congress, 2d sess., Doc 95, 286.

30. Josiah Parrish to Joel Palmer, reel 4, Oregon Superintendency Records, 20 July 1854, 247.

31. Roger Atwill to Joel Palmer, reel 5, Oregon Superintendency Records, 12 July 1854, 3.

32. Commissioner of Indian Affairs, *Annual Report*, reel 7, Oregon Superintendency Records, 11 September 1854, 40.

33. Commissioner of Indian Affairs, *Annual Report*, reel 7, Oregon Superintendency Records, 11 September 1854, 40.

34. Commissioner of Indian Affairs, *Annual Report*, reel 7, Oregon Superintendency Records, 11 September 1854, 40.

35. Quoted in Dorothy and Jack Sutton, eds., *Indian Wars of the Rogue River* (Medford, Ore.: Klocker Printery, 1969), 120.

36. Hubert Howe Bancroft, *History of Oregon*, vol. 2 (San Francisco: The History Company, 1886), 348.

37. Commissioner of Indian Affairs, *Annual Report*, reel 7, Oregon Superintendency Records, 11 September 1854, 40.

38. Joel Palmer to Nathan Olney, reel 5, Oregon Superintendency Records, 28 September 1855, 47.

39. Joel Palmer to Nathan Olney, reel 5, Oregon Superintendency Records, 28 September 1854, 47.

40. Charles S. Drew, *An Account of the Origin and Early Prosecution of the Indian War in Oregon* (Fairfield, Wash.: Ye Galleon Press, 1973), 38.

41. Joel Palmer to Joseph Lane, Joseph Lane Papers, 30 December 1854; Rodney Glisan, *Journal of Army Life* (San Francisco: A.L. Bancroft and Company, 1874), 364.

42. Joel Palmer to Nathan Olney, reel 11, Oregon Superintendency Records, 28 September 1854, 173.

43. Joel Palmer to George Manypenny, reel 5, Oregon Superintendency Records, 24 December 1854, 94.

44. Citizens of Camus Valley to Joel Palmer, reel 5, Oregon Superintendency Records, 31 August 1854, 27.

45. Joel Palmer to George Manypenny, reel 5, Oregon Superintendency Records, 12 September 1854, 6; Joel Palmer to Samuel Culver, reel 5, Oregon Superintendency Records, 2 September 1854, 11.

46. Joel Palmer to Joseph Lane, Joseph Lane Papers, MSS 1146, Oregon Historical Society, 26 November 1854.

47. Bancroft, *History of Oregon*, vol. 2, 353; *Oregonian*, 5 May 1855.

48. Joel Palmer to Joseph Lane, Joseph Lane Papers, MSS 1146, Oregon Historical Society, 30 December 1854.

EIGHT *Know Nothings*

1. James Nesmith to Joseph Lane, Joseph Lane Papers, MSS 1146, Oregon Historical Society, 1 January 1855.

2. Joel Palmer to Joseph Lane, Joseph Lane Papers, MSS 1146, Oregon Historical Society, 14 January 1855.

3. Joel Palmer to Joseph Lane, Joseph Lane Papers, MSS 1146, Oregon Historical Society, 30 December 1855.

4. Joel Palmer to Joseph Lane, Joseph Lane Papers, MSS 1146, Oregon Historical Society, 14 January 1855.

5. James Nesmith to Matthew Deady, Matthew Deady Papers, MSS 48, Oregon Historical Society, April 1855.

6. Joel Palmer to Joseph Lane, Joseph Lane Papers, MSS 1146, Oregon Historical Society, 14 January 1855.

7. Joel Palmer to William Martin, Bush Papers, Bush House, Salem, Ore., 7 March 1855.

8. *Statesman*, 14 July 1855.

9. Joel Palmer to G.H. Ambrose, reel 5, Oregon Superintendency Records, 16 March 1855, 155.

10. Joel Palmer to R.B. Metcalf, reel 5, Oregon Superintendency Records, 19 April 1855, 251.

11. Ben Wright to Joel Palmer, reel 5, Oregon Superintendency Records, 6 February 1855, 144.

12.   Ben Wright to Joel Palmer, reel 5, Oregon Superintendency Records, 6 February 1855, 144.

NINE   *Walla Walla*

1.   Joel Palmer to George Manypenny, reel 4, Oregon Superintendency Records, 20 December 1853, 17.
2.   Quoted in Hazard Stevens, *The Life of Isaac Ingalls Stevens*, vol. 2 (Boston: Houghton Mifflin, 1900), 25.
3.   Quoted in Leo Marx, *The Machine in the Garden* (New York: Oxford University Press, 1964), 13.
4.   Joel Palmer to R.R. Thompson, reel 5, Oregon Superintendency Records, 5 April 1855, 171; R.R. Thompson to Joel Palmer, reel 5, Oregon Superintendency Records, 14 April 1855, 171.
5.   Quoted in Stevens, *Isaac Ingalls Stevens*, vol. 2, 29, 30; Joel Palmer to George Manypenny, 9 October 1855, 34 Congress, 1st sess., Doc. 3, 55–60.
6.   Lawrence Kip, *The Indian Council in the Valley of the Walla-Walla* (San Francisco: Whitton, Towne and Company, 1855), 14.
7.   Stevens, *Isaac Ingalls Stevens*, vol. 2, 31.
8.   Stevens, *Isaac Ingalls Stevens*, vol. 2, 34–35.
9.   Kip, *The Indian Council*, 12.
10.   Stevens, *Isaac Ingalls Stevens*, vol. 2, 37.
11.   Quoted in Stevens, *Isaac Ingalls Stevens*, vol. 2, 37.
12.   James Doty, "Journal of Operations," 22 December 1919, MSS 1179, Oregon Historical Society, typescript from the original journal of James Doty as transcribed by William S. Lewis, Eastern Washington State Historical Society, 26.
13.   R.R. Thompson to Joel Palmer, reel 5, Oregon Superintendency Records, 14 April 1855, 196.
14.   Kip, *The Indian Council*, 28; Quoted in Stevens, *Isaac Ingalls Stevens*, vol. 2, 38.
15.   Theodore Winthrop, quoted in Alvin M. Josephy, Jr., *The Nez Perce Indians and the Opening of the Northwest* (New Haven, Conn.: Yale University Press, 1965), 298; Quoted in Stevens, *Isaac Ingalls Stevens*, vol. 2, 38.
16.   Quoted in Kent D. Richards, *Isaac I. Stevens: Young Man in a Hurry* (Provo, Utah: Brigham Young University Press, 1979), 217; Quoted in Stevens, *Isaac Ingalls Stevens*, vol. 2, 36, 40.
17.   Isaac Ingalls Stevens, *A True Copy of the Record of the Official Proceedings at the Council in the Walla Walla Valley 1855*, Isaac Ingalls Stevens, ed. Darrell Scott (Fairfield, Wash.: Ye Galleon Press, 1985), 35.
18.   Stevens, *A True Copy of the Record*, 37.
19.   Kip, *The Indian Council*, 18; Quoted in Stevens, *Isaac Ingalls Stevens*, 58.

20. Allen P. Slickpoo, Sr., *Noon, Nee-me-poo (We, the Nez Perces)*, vol. 1 (n.p.: Nez Perce Tribe of Idaho, 1973), 89.

21. Slickpoo, *Noon, Nee-me-poo*, vol. 1, 92.

22. Slickpoo, *Noon, Nee-me-poo*, vol. 1, 101, 99, 102.

23. Slickpoo, *Noon, Nee-me-poo*, vol. 1, 103.

24. Slickpoo, *Noon, Nee-me-poo*, vol. 1, 104, 106, 107, 123.

25. Slickpoo, *Noon, Nee-me-poo*, vol. 1, 102.

26. Slickpoo, *Noon, Nee-me-poo*, vol. 1, 123, 125, 106.

27. Slickpoo, *Noon, Nee-me-poo*, vol. 1, 116, 119.

28. Slickpoo, *Noon, Nee-me-poo*, vol. 1, 120-21.

29. Slickpoo, *Noon, Nee-me-poo*, vol. 1, 119; Walla Walla and Cayuse tribes to Governor Stevens, reel 14, Oregon Superintendency Records, February 1856, 43.

30. Kip, *The Indian Council*, 19.

31. Isaac Stevens to Andrew Bolon, quoted in Richards, *Isaac I. Stevens*, 212; Kip, *The Indian Council*, 20, 21.

32. Slickpoo, *Noon, Nee-me-poo*, vol. 1, 122.

33. Quoted in Stevens, *Isaac Ingalls Stevens*, vol. 2, 54.

34. Quoted in Richards, *Isaac I. Stevens*, 222; Kip, *The Indian Council*, 27.

35. Slickpoo, *Noon, Nee-me-poo*, vol. 1, 130, 133, 134.

36. Stevens, *A True Copy of the Record*, 6.

37. Quoted in Josephy, *The Nez Perce Indians*, 331; Kip, *The Indian Council*, 28.

38. Quoted in Clifford Merrill Drury, *Chief Lawyer of the Nez Perce Indians, 1796-1876* (Glendale, Calif.: Arthur H. Clark Company, 1979), 133.

39. Slickpoo, *Noon, Nee-me-poo*, vol. 1, 139; Joel Palmer to George Manypenny, 9 October 1855, 34 Congress, 1st sess., Doc. 3, 55.

40. Quoted in Robert Ignatius Burns, S.J., *The Jesuits and the Indian Wars of the Northwest* (New Haven, Conn.: Yale University Press, 1966), 79.

41. Quoted in Stevens, *Isaac Ingalls Stevens*, vol. 2, 61; Stevens, *A True Copy of the Record*, 18.

42. Slickpoo, *Noon, Nee-me-poo*, vol. 1, 102.

TEN   *War*

1. Joel Palmer to George Manypenny, reel 5, Oregon Superintendency Records, 9 July 1855, 230, 32, 37.

2. G.H. Ambrose to Joel Palmer, reel 13, Oregon Superintendency Records, 25 July 1855, 68.

3. Rodney Glisan, *Journal of Army Life* (San Francisco: A.L. Bancroft and Company, 1874), 244-45.

4. Quoted in Albert G. Walling, *History of Southern Oregon* (Portland, Ore.: Printing

House of A.G. Walling, 1884), 238, 239.

5. Walling, *History of Southern Oregon*, 239.

6. Frances Fuller Victor, *The Early Indian Wars of Oregon* (Salem, Ore.: Frank C. Baker, State Printer, 1894), 238.

7. Victor, *Early Indian Wars*, 342.

8. G.H. Ambrose to Joel Palmer, reel 5, Oregon Superintendency Records, 10 September 1855, 305.

9. Joel Palmer to George Manypenny, 9 October 1855, 34 Congress, 1st sess., Doc. 3, 57.

10. Walling, *History of Southern Oregon*, 243.

ELEVEN   *The Fires of Autumn*

1. Joel Palmer to George Manypenny, 9 October 1855, 34 Congress, 1st sess., Doc. 3, 60.

2. Albert G. Walling, *History of Southern Oregon* (Portland, Ore.: Printing House of A.G. Walling, 1884), 243.

3. G.H. Ambrose to Joel Palmer, 11 October 1855, 34 Congress, 1st sess., Doc. 3, 66.

4. Frank K. Walsh, *Indian Battles Along the Rogue River, 1855-56* (Grants Pass, Ore.: Te-cum-tom Publications, 1972), 1; quoted in Dorothy and Jack Sutton, eds., *Indian Wars of the Rogue River* (Grants Pass, Ore.: Josephine County Historical Society, 1969), 143-44.

5. Quoted in Sutton, *Indian Wars*, 148-49.

6. Rodney Glisan, *Journal of Army Life* (San Francisco: A.L. Bancroft and Company, 1874), 259.

7. Joel Palmer to George Manypenny, 19 October 1855, 34 Congress, 1st sess., 75; Joel Palmer to G.H. Ambrose, 13 October 1855, letter book D in Stanley Sheldon Spaid's PH.D. Thesis "Joel Palmer and Indian Affairs in Oregon" (Eugene: University of Oregon, 1950), 316.

8. Sutton, *Indian Wars*, 149.

9. Quoted in Sutton, *Indian Wars*, 172.

10. G.H. Ambrose to Matthew Deady, Matthew Deady Papers, MSS 48, Oregon Historical Society, 15 October 1855.

11. Walling, *History of Southern Oregon*, 237.

12. Samuel Culver to Joel Palmer, 20 July 1855, 33 Congress, 2d sess., 292.

13. Walling, *History of Southern Oregon*, 250; Frances Fuller Victor, *The Early Indian Wars of Oregon* (Salem, Ore.: Frank C. Baker, State Printer, 1894), 351.

14. Martin P. Schmitt, ed., *General George Crook: His Autobiography* (Norman: University of Oklahoma Press, 1946), 26-27.

15. Harvey Robbins, "Journal of Rogue River War, 1855," *Oregon Historical Quarterly* 34 (1933):347.

16. Cyrenius Mulkey, "Eighty-one Years of Frontier Life," MSS 981, Oregon Historical Society, 68.

17. Mulkey, "Eighty-one Years of Frontier Life," 68.

18. Sutton, *Indian Wars*, 162; Walling, *History of Southern Oregon*, 253; Schmitt, *Crook: His Autobiography*, 26.

19. Mulkey, "Eighty-one Years of Frontier Life," 69-70.

20. Quoted in Hubert Howe Bancroft, *History of Oregon*, vol. 2 (San Francisco: The History Company, 1886), 222n.

21. *Statesman*, 18 October 1853.

22. Lafayette Grover, MSS 1069, Oregon Historical Society; Philip H. Sheridan, *Indian Fighting in the Fifties in Oregon and Washington Territories* (Fairfield, Wash.: Ye Galleon Press, 1987), 79.

23. Mulkey, "Eighty-one Years of Frontier Life," 72.

24. Quoted in Sutton, *Indian Wars*, 178.

25. Robbins, "Journal of Rogue River War," 353.

26. Robbins, "Journal of Rogue River War," 256, 353.

27. Walling, *History of Southern Oregon*, 256.

28. Edward Geary to Joel Palmer, reel 5, Oregon Superintendency Records, 21 October 1855, 326.

29. Edward Geary to Joel Palmer, reel 5, Oregon Superintendency Records, 21 October 1855, 326.

30. Victor, *Early Indian Wars*, 429.

31. Quoted in Victor, *Early Indian Wars*, 430-31; Robert Ignatius Burns, S.J., *The Jesuits and the Indian Wars of the Northwest* (New Haven, Conn.: Yale University Press, 1966), 129.

32. Joel Palmer to Gen. John Wool, 21 November 1855, 34 Congress, 3d sess., 114.

33. G.H. Ambrose to Joel Palmer, 20 October 1855, 34 Congress, 1st sess., Exec.Doc. 93, no. 17, 88; Joel Palmer to G.H. Ambrose, reel 13, Oregon Superintendency Records, 6 November 1855.

34. Joel Palmer to George Manypenny, 12 November 1855, 34 Congress, 1st sess., Exec.Doc. 93, no. 15, 83.

35. Joel Palmer to George Manypenny, 12 November 1855, 34 Congress, 1st sess., Exec.Doc. 93, no. 15, 83.

36. Joel Palmer to Joseph Jeffers, reel 5, Oregon Superintendency Records, 24 November 1855, 408.

37. G.H. Ambrose to Joel Palmer, 22 November 1855, 30 November 1855, 34 Congress, 1st sess., Exec.Doc. 93, nos. 39, 40, 117, 188; G.H. Ambrose to Joel Palmer, 2 December 1855, 34 Congress, 1st sess., Exec.Doc. 93, no. 41, 120.

38. Joel Palmer to Courtney M. Walker, reel 5, Oregon Superintendency Records, 21

November 1855, 391; Nathaniel Ford to Joel Palmer, reel 13, Oregon Superintendency Records, 18 December 1855, 122.

39. Joel Palmer to Gen. John Wool, 1 December 1855, 34 Congress, 1st sess., Exec. Doc. 93, no. 3, 23-24.

40. Joel Palmer to Gen. John Wool, 1 December 1855, 34 Congress, 1st sess., Exec. Doc. 93, no. 3, 23-24.

41. Joel Palmer to George Manypenny, 9 January 1856, 34 Congress, 1st sess., Exec. Doc. 93, no. 33, 108.

42. Bancroft, *History of Oregon*, vol. 2, 413; Journal of the House of Representatives of the Territory of Oregon, 7th regular sess., Salem, Ore., 17.

43. Walls, Florence, "The Letters of Asahel Bush to Matthew P. Deady, 1851-1863" (Portland, Ore.: Reed College B.A. Thesis, 1941), Asahel Bush to Matthew Deady, 30 September 1855, 120.

44. *Statesman*, 25 December 1855.

45. *Statesman*, 25 December 1855.

46. *Statesman*, 25 December 1855.

47. *Statesman*, 1 January 1856.

48. *Statesman*, 1 January 1856.

49. *Statesman*, 1 January 1856.

50. *Statesman*, 1 January 1856.

51. *Statesman*, 1 January 1856.

52. *Oregonian*, 29 December 1855.

T W E L V E *The General and the Politicians*

1. *Oregonian*, 19 January 1856; *Statesman*, 15 January 1856.

2. *Oregonian*, 19 January 1856.

3. *Statesman*, 15 January 1856.

4. *Statesman*, 15 January 1856.

5. Quoted in Allen Johnson and Dumas Malone, eds., *Dictionary of American Biography*, vol. 20 (New York: Charles Scribner's Sons, 1930), 514; Will J. Trimble, "A Soldier of the Oregon Frontier," *Oregon Historical Quarterly* 8 (1907):45.

6. Gen. John Wool to Col. George Wright, 29 January 1856, 34 Congress, 1st sess., Senate, 463.

7. Gen. John Wool to Lt.-Col. L. Thomas, 19 January 1856, 34 Congress, 1st sess., H. Exec. Doc. 93, 34; Gen. John Wool to Lt.-Col. L. Thomas, 20 March 1856, 34 Congress, 1st sess., H. Exec. Doc. 93, 50.

8. Joel Palmer to Gen. John Wool, 1 December 1855, 34 Congress, 1st sess., H. Exec. Doc. 93, no. 3, 23.

9. Joel Palmer to George Manypenny, 8 January 1856, 34 Congress, 1st sess., H.Exec.Doc. 93, no. 26, 99; George Manypenny to Joel Palmer, reel 14, Oregon Superintendency Records, 17 January 1856, 82.

10. Joel Palmer to *Statesman*, reel 6, Oregon Superintendency Records, 15 January 1856, 15.

11. *Statesman*, 5 February 1856.

THIRTEEN   *Winter on the Rogue and Columbia*

1. *Oregonian*, 5 January 1856.

2. Albert G. Walling, *History of Southern Oregon* (Portland, Ore.: Printing House of A.G. Walling, 1884), 259; G.H. Ambrose to Joel Palmer, reel 14, Oregon Superintendency Records, 4 January 1856, 39; Dorothy and Jack Sutton, eds., *Indian Wars of the Rogue River* (Grants Pass, Ore.: Josephine County Historical Society, 1969), 183.

3. Sutton, *Indian Wars*, 187; *Statesman*, 12 January 1856.

4. Sutton, *Indian Wars*, 188.

5. Father E.C. Chirouse to Father Mesplie, reel 6, Oregon Superintendency Records, 15 January 1856, 27; R.R. Thompson to Joel Palmer, reel 14, Oregon Superintendency Records, 19 December 1855, 36; R.R. Thompson to Joel Palmer, reel 14, Oregon Superintendency Records, 20 January 1856, 50.

6. Walla Walla and Cayuse Indians to Governor Isaac Stevens, reel 14, Oregon Superintendency Records, February 1856, 43.

7. Joel Palmer to George Manypenny, 8 January 1856, 34 Congress, 1st sess., H.Exec.Doc. 93, no. 26, 99.

8. Quoted in Alvin M. Josephy, Jr., *The Nez Perce Indians and the Opening of the Northwest* (New Haven, Conn.: Yale University Press, 1965), 359; Frances Fuller Victor, *The Early Indian Wars of Oregon* (Salem, Ore.: Frank C. Baker, State Printer, 1894), 447n.

9. Walla Walla and Cayuse Indians to Governor Isaac Stevens, February 1856; Joel Palmer to Gen. John Wool, Oregon Superintendency Records, 27 January 1856, Message and Documents, 1856–57, Part 1, 34 Congress, 3d sess., H.Exec.Doc. 1, no. 75, 744.

10. Joseph Jeffers to Joel Palmer, reel 14, Oregon Superintendency Records, 7 February 1856, 46.

11. Berryman Jennings to Joel Palmer, reel 14, Oregon Superintendency Records, 5 March 1856, 88.

12. G.H. Ambrose to Joel Palmer, reel 14, Oregon Superintendency Records, 29 February 1856, 95.

1 3.   *Statesman*, 4 March 1856.

1 4.   Hubert Howe Bancroft, *History of Oregon*, vol. 2 (San Francisco: The History Company, 1886), 406.

1 5.   G.H. Ambrose to Joel Palmer, reel 14, Oregon Superintendency Records, 18 February 1856, 98.

1 6.   R.W. Dunbar to Joseph Lane, 15 February 1856, Lane Collection, Lilly Library, Indiana University, Bloomington.

1 7.   Berryman Jennings to Joel Palmer, reel 14, Oregon Superintendency Records, 5 March 1856, 88; Joseph Jeffers to Joel Palmer, reel 14, Oregon Superintendency Records, 22 January 1856, 24.

1 8.   Joel Palmer to George Manypenny, reel 6, Oregon Superintendency Records, 11 February 1856, 33.

1 9.   Joseph Lane autobiography, Joseph Lane Papers, microfilm, OHS MSS 1146 130; Joel Palmer to George Manypenny, reel 6, Oregon Superintendency Records, 5 March 1856, 61; Joel Palmer to George Manypenny, reel 6, Oregon Superintendency Records, 11 February 1856, 33.

F O U R T E E N   *Victory and Defeat*

1.   Rodney Glisan, *Journal of Army Life* (San Francisco: A.L. Bancroft and Company, 1874), 364.

2.   Dorothy and Jack Sutton, eds., *Indian Wars of the Rogue River* (Grants Pass, Ore.: Josephine County Historical Society, 1969), 206; *Harper's Magazine* 13 (September 1856):524.

3.   Joel Palmer to George Manypenny, 8 March 1856, Message and Documents, 1856–57, Part 1, 34 Congress, 3d sess., House, 750.

4.   John Boyd to Joel Palmer, reel 14, Oregon Superintendency Records, 19 March 1856, 141.

5.   Palmer diary, MSS 114, Oregon Historical Society, 5.

6.   Joel Palmer to George Manypenny, reel 6, Oregon Superintendency Records, 11 April 1856, 109.

7.   Joel Palmer to Captain Rinearson, reel 6, Oregon Superintendency Records, 3 April 1856, 99.

8.   Joel Palmer to W.W. Raymond, reel 6, Oregon Superintendency Records, March 1856, 98.

9.   Joel Palmer to Gen. John Wool, 13 April 1856, 34 Congress, 1st sess., H.Exec.Doc. 188, 13.

1 0.   Joel Palmer to A.D. Babcock, reel 6, Oregon Superintendency Records, 22 April 1856, 124.

11. Joel Palmer to R.R. Thompson, reel 6, Oregon Superintendency Records, 21 April 1856, 122.

12. R.R. Thompson to Joel Palmer, reel 14, Oregon Superintendency Records, 13 April 1856, 162.

13. Gen. John Wool to Joel Palmer, reel 14, Oregon Superintendency Records, 27 April 1856, 174; Joel Palmer to Gen. John Wool, 27 April 1856, 34 Congress, 1st sess., H.Exec.Doc. 118, 14.

14. R.B. Metcalf to Joseph Lane, 21 April 1856, copy, Lane Collection, Lilly Library, Indiana University, Bloomington.

15. Joel Palmer to W.W. Raymond, reel 6, Oregon Superintendency Records, 13 May 1856, 140.

16. Joel Palmer to R.B. Metcalf, reel 6, Oregon Superintendency Records, 13 May 1856, 139.

17. Albert G. Walling, *History of Southern Oregon* (Portland, Ore.: Printing House of A.G. Walling, 1884), 265, 266.

18. Walling, *History of Southern Oregon*, 269.

19. R.W. Dunbar to Joseph Lane, Joseph Lane Papers, microfilm, MSS 1146, Oregon Historical Society, 15 May 1856.

20. Joel Palmer to Nathan Olney, reel 6, Oregon Superintendency Records, 19 May 1856, 151.

21. G.H. Ambrose to Joel Palmer, reel 14, Oregon Superintendency Records, 18 May 1856, 216; Quoted in *Statesman*, 20 May 1856.

22. Quoted in Frances Fuller Victor, *The Early Indian Wars of Oregon* (Salem, Ore.: Frank C. Baker, State Printer, 1894), 407.

23. Walling, *History of Southern Oregon*, 280.

24. Quoted in Victor, *Early Indian Wars*, 409.

25. *Statesman*, 17 June 1856.

26. Palmer diary, 11.

27. Edwin Drew to Joel Palmer, reel 14, Oregon Superintendency Records, 19 May 1856, 234.

28. Stephen Dain to Joel Palmer, reel 14, Oregon Superintendency Records, 6 June 1856, 283.

29. Aseph Hinch to Joel Palmer, reel 14, Oregon Superintendency Records, 16 June 1856, 245.

30. Palmer diary, 11; Walling, *History of Southern Oregon*, 283.

31. Palmer diary, 11; Joel Palmer to George Manypenny, reel 6, Oregon Superintendency Records, 3 July 1856, 763.

32. Quoted in Sutton, *Indian Wars*, 256.

33. *Statesman*, 22 July 1856.

34. Glisan, *Journal of Army Life*, 349.

35. *Statesman*, 28 June 1856.

36. *Oregonian*, 28 June 1856.

37. Joel Palmer to George Manypenny, 23 June 1856, Message and Documents, 34 Congress, 3d sess., H.Exec.Doc. 1, no. 91, 762; *Statesman*, 12 August 1856.

38. Joel Palmer to George Manypenny, reel 6, Oregon Superintendency Records, 24 June 1856, 164.

39. Joel Palmer to Dr. Stell, reel 6, Oregon Superintendency Records, 1 July 1856, 176.

40. Joel Palmer to Captain Rinearson, reel 6, Oregon Superintendency Records, 13 July 1856, 186; Joel Palmer to R.B. Metcalf, reel 6, Oregon Superintendency Records, 31 July 1856, 198.

41. Joel Palmer to Edwin Drew, reel 6, Oregon Superintendency Records, 15 August 1856, 206.

42. Absalom Hedges to George Manypenny, reel 6, Oregon Superintendency Records, 21 August 1856, 209; Absalom Hedges to George Manypenny, reel 6, Oregon Superintendency Records, 8 November 1856, 248.

43. Palmer diary, 31 March 1857.

44. In Joseph Drew to Matthew Deady, Matthew Deady Papers, MSS 48, Oregon Historical Society, 21 April 1857.

FIFTEEN *Last Years*

1. Stanley Sheldon Spaid, "Life of General Joel Palmer," *Oregon Historical Quarterly* 55 (1954):315.

2. Spaid, "Life of General Joel Palmer," 324.

3. T.W. Davenport, "Recollections of an Indian Agent—III," *Oregon Historical Quarterly* 8 (1907):237.

4. Quoted in Dorothy and Jack Sutton, eds., *Indian Wars of the Rogue River* (Grants Pass, Ore.: Josephine County Historical Society, 1969), 262.

5. *Overland Monthly*, October 1871, 344-53 and November 1871, 425-33, San Francisco.

6. Davenport, "Recollections—III," 18, 110.

7. J. Ross Browne, report, 35 Congress, 1st sess., H.Exec.Doc. 39, 40.

8. Philip Sheridan to Capt. C.C. Augur, 35 Congress, 1st sess., H.Exec.Doc. 112, no. 1, 17.

9. J. Ross Browne, report, 35 Congress, 1st sess., H.Exec.Doc. 39, 44.

10. J. Ross Browne, report, 35 Congress, 1st sess., H.Exec.Doc. 39, 45.

11. Quoted in William Eugene Kent, *The Siletz Indian Reservation, 1855-1900* (Newport, Ore.: Lincoln County Historical Society, 1977), 41; Quoted in Fred Lock-

ley, *History of the Columbia River Valley from The Dalles to the Sea* (Chicago: The S.J. Clarke Publishing Company, 1928), 1085.

12. Joel Palmer to W.W. Raymond, W.W. Raymond Papers. MSS 555, Oregon Historical Society, 10 August 1871, 2.

13. Joel Palmer to W.W. Raymond, W.W. Raymond Papers, 10 August 1871, 2.

14. Joel Palmer to Matthew Deady, Matthew Deady Papers, MSS 48, Oregon Historical Society, 3 August 1871.

15. *Pacific Christian Advocate*, 19 September 1872; Davenport, "Recollections—III," 241, 239; Joel Palmer to Josiah Parrish (Siletz), reel 27, Oregon Superintendency Records, 14 November 1872.

16. Davenport, "Recollections—III," 241; *Pacific Christian Advocate*, 17 October 1872.

17. Davenport, "Recollections—III," 241; Joel Palmer to Thomas Odeneal, superintendent of Indian affairs, reel 27, Oregon Superintendency Records, 31 December 1872.

18. Joel Palmer to Josiah Parrish, reel 27, Oregon Superintendency Records, 14 November 1872.

19. Alex Derbyshire to Sarah Palmer, Palmer Papers, MSS 114, Oregon Historical Society, 14 September 1876.

20. Palmer family papers, vertical file, Oregon Historical Society.

21. Oswald West, "Famous Horses and Horsemen of the Pioneer Period," *Oregon Historical Quarterly* 46 (1945):148.

22. Wallis Nash, *Two Years in Oregon* (New York: D. Appleton and Company, 1882), 199-200.

23. Wallis Nash, *Oregon: There and Back in 1877* (London: Macmillan and Co., 1878), 122-24.

24. *Transactions of the Sixth Annual Re-union of the Oregon Pioneer Association, 1878* (Salem, Ore.: E.M. Waite, Steam Printer and Bookbinder, 1879), 4.

Sources

BOOKS

Allen, A.J. *Ten Years in Oregon*. Ithaca, N.Y.: Mack, Andrus, & Co., 1848.

Bagley, B. *Early Catholic Missions in Old Oregon*. Seattle: Lowman and Hanford, 1932.

Bancroft, Hubert Howe. *History of Oregon*, vols. 1 & 2. San Francisco: The History Company, 1886.

Beckham, Stephen Dow. *The Indians of Western Oregon: This Land Was Theirs*. Coos Bay, Ore.: Arago Books, 1977.

Beckham, Stephen Dow. *Requiem for a People: The Rogue Indians and the Frontiersmen*. Norman: University of Oklahoma Press, 1971.

Bennett, Robert Allen. *We'll All Go Home in the Spring*. Walla Walla, Wash.: Pioneer Press Books, 1984.

Bowen, William A. *The Willamette Valley: Migration and Settlement on the Oregon Frontier*. Seattle: University of Washington Press, 1978.

Brown, J. Henry. *Brown's Political History of Oregon*. Portland, Ore.: Lewis & Dryden, 1892.

Burnett, Peter. *An Old California Pioneer*. Oakland, Calif.: Biobooks, 1946.

Burns, Robert Ignatius, s.j. *The Jesuits and the Indian Wars of the Northwest.* New Haven, Conn.: Yale University Press, 1966.

Camp, Charles L., ed. *James Clyman, Frontiersman.* Portland, Ore.: Champoeg Press, 1960.

Carey, Charles H. *General History of Oregon*, vol. 2. Portland, Ore.: Binfords and Mort, 1971.

Clark, Malcolm, Jr., ed. *Pharisee Among Philistines*, vols. 1 & 2. Portland: Oregon Historical Society, 1975.

Clark, Robert Carlton. *History of the Willamette Valley, Oregon.* Chicago: The S.J. Clarke Publishing Company, 1927.

Corning, Howard McKinley, ed. *Dictionary of Oregon History.* Portland, Ore.: Binford and Mort, 1956.

Coues, Elliott, ed. *The Manuscript Journals of Alexander Henry and of David Thompson*, vol. 2. New York: Francis P. Harper, 1897.

Cummins, Sarah J. *Autobiography and Reminiscences.* Cleveland: Arthur H. Clark Company, 1914.

Drew, Charles S. *An Account of the Origin and Early Prosecution of the Indian War in Oregon.* Fairfield, Wash.: Ye Galleon Press, 1973.

Drury, Clifford Merrill. *Chief Lawyer of the Nez Perce Indians, 1796-1876.* Glendale, Calif.: Arthur H. Clark Company, 1979.

———. *Marcus Whitman, M.D.: Pioneer and Martyr.* Caldwell, Idaho: The Caxton Printers, Ltd., 1937.

Faragher, John Mack. *Women and Men on the Overland Trail.* New Haven, Conn.: Yale University Press, 1979.

Fitzgerald, Frances. *Fire in the Lake.* New York: Random House, 1973.

Glisan, Rodney. *Journal of Army Life.* San Francisco: A.L. Bancroft and Company, 1874.

Goulder, W.A. *Reminiscences of a Pioneer.* Boise, Idaho: Timothy Regan, 1909.

Guthrie, A.B., Jr. *The Way West*. New York: William Sloane Associates, 1949.

Hendrickson, James E. *Joe Lane of Oregon: Machine Politics and the Sectional Crisis, 1849-1861*. New Haven: Yale University Press, 1967.

Hofstadter, Richard. *The Progressive Historians*. New York: Alfred A. Knopf, 1968.

Holmes, Kenneth L., ed. *Covered Wagon Women*, vol. 1. Glendale, Calif.: Arthur H. Clark Company, 1983.

Hoopes, Alban W. *Indian Affairs and Their Administration*. London: University of Pennsylvania Press and Oxford University Press, 1932.

Hulbert, Archer Butler, and Dorothy Printup Hulbert, eds. *Marcus Whitman, Crusader*. Denver: Stewart Commission of Colorado College and Denver Public Library, 1938.

Hutton, Paul Andrew, ed. *Soldiers West: Biographies from the Military Routine*. Lincoln: University of Nebraska Press, 1987.

Johansen, Dorothy O., ed. *Robert Newell's Memoranda*. Portland, Ore.: Champoeg Press, 1959.

Johnson, Allen, and Dumas Malone, eds. *Dictionary of American Biography*, vol. 5. New York: Charles Scribner's Sons, 1930.

Johnson, Overton, and William H. Winter. *Route Across the Rocky Mountains*. Princeton, N.J.: Princeton University Press, 1932.

Josephy, Alvin M., Jr. *The Nez Perce Indians and the Opening of the Northwest*. New Haven, Conn.: Yale University Press, 1965.

Kane, Paul. *Wanderings of an Artist Among the Indians of North America*. London: Longman, Brown, Green, Longmans and Roberts, 1859.

Kent, William Eugene. *The Siletz Indian Reservation, 1855-1900*. Newport, Ore.: Lincoln County Historical Society, 1977.

Kip, Lawrence. *The Indian Council in the Valley of the Walla-Walla*. San Francisco: Whitton, Towne and Company, 1855.

Kowrach, Edward J., ed. *Journal of a Catholic Bishop on the Oregon Trail*. Fairfield, Wash.: Ye Galleon Press, 1978.

Kvasnicka, Robert M., and Herman J. Viola. *The Commissioners of Indian Affairs, 1824-1977*. Lincoln: University of Nebraska Press, 1979.

Lockley, Fred. *Captain Sol. Tetherow: Wagon Train Master*. Fairfield, Wash.: Ye Galleon Press, 1970.

Lockley, Fred. *History of the Columbia River Valley from The Dalles to the Sea*. Chicago: The S.J. Clarke Publishing Company, 1928.

Loewenberg, Robert J. "The Missionary Idea in Oregon: Illustrations from the Life and Times of Methodist Henry Perkins." In *The Western Shore*. Edited by Thomas Vaughan. Portland: Oregon Historical Society Press, 1976.

Mackey, Harold. *The Kalapuyahs*. Salem, Ore.: Mission Mill Museum Association, 1974.

Marx, Leo. *The Machine in the Garden*. New York: Oxford University Press, 1964.

Nash, Wallis. *Oregon: There and Back in 1877*. London: Macmillan and Company, 1878.

Nash, Wallis. *Two Years in Oregon*. New York: D. Appleton and Company, 1882.

Palmer, Joel. *Journal of Travels over the Rocky Mountains to the Mouth of the Columbia River; Made During the Years 1845 and 1846*. Cincinnati: J.A. and U.P. James, 1847. Reprinted in Reuben Gold Thwaites, ed., *Early Western Travels, 1748-1846*, vol. 30. Cleveland: Arthur H. Clark Company, 1906.

Parkman, Francis. *The Oregon Trail*. Edited by E.N. Feltskog. Madison: University of Wisconsin Press, 1969.

Quaife, Milo Milton, ed. *Adventures on the Oregon*. Chicago: R.R. Donnelly & Sons, The Lakeside Press, 1923.

Richards, Kent D. *Isaac I. Stevens: Young Man in a Hurry*. Provo, Utah: Brigham Young University Press, 1979.

Ross, Alexander. *The Fur Hunters of the Far West*. Chicago: The Lakeside Press, 1924.

Ruby, Robert H., and John A. Brown. *The Cayuse Indians: Imperial Tribesmen of Old Oregon*. Norman: University of Oklahoma Press, 1972.

Schmitt, Martin P., ed. *General George Crook: His Autobiography*. Norman: University of Oklahoma Press, 1946.

Sheridan, Philip H. *Indian Fighting in the Fifties in Oregon and Washington Territories*. Fairfield, Wash.: Ye Galleon Press, 1987.

Simpson, Sir George Henry. *Narration of a Journey Around the World*, vol. 1. London: Henry Colburn, 1847.

Slickpoo, Allen P., Sr. *Noon, Nee-me-poo (We, The Nez Perces)*. Lapwai: Nez Perce Tribe of Idaho, 1973.

Snowden, Clinton A. *History of Washington*. New York: Century History Company, 1909-11.

Solomon, Barbara Miller, ed., with Patricia Ann King. *Travels in New England and New York*. Cambridge, Mass: The Belknap Press of Harvard University Press, 1969.

Stevens, Hazard. *The Life of Isaac Ingalls Stevens*. Boston: Houghton Mifflin, 1900.

Stevens, Isaac Ingalls. *A True Copy of the Record of the Official Proceedings at the Council in the Walla Walla Valley 1855, Isaac Ingalls Stevens*, ed. by Darrell Scott. Fairfield, Wash.: Ye Galleon Press, 1985.

Sutton, Dorothy, and Jack Sutton, eds. *Indian Wars of the Rogue River*. Grants Pass, Ore.: Josephine County Historical Society, 1969.

Townsend, John K. *Narrative of a Journey Across the Rocky Mountains to the Columbia River*. Philadelphia: H. Perlans, 1839. Reprinted in Reuben Gold Thwaites, ed. *Early Western Travels, 1748-1846*, vol. 21. Cleveland: Arthur H. Clark Company, 1905.

Transactions of the Seventh Annual Re-union of the Oregon Pioneer Association, 1879. Salem, Ore., 1880.

Transactions of the Sixth Annual Re-union of the Oregon Pioneer Association, 1878. Salem, Ore., 1879.

Victor, Frances Fuller. *The Early Indian Wars of Oregon*. Salem, Ore.: Frank C. Baker, State Printer, 1894.

Victor, Frances Fuller. *The River of the West*. Hartford, Conn.: R. W. Bliss & Co., 1870.

Wain, John. *Samuel Johnson*. New York: Viking Press, 1974.

Walling, Albert G. *History of Southern Oregon*. Portland, Ore.: Printing House of A.G. Walling, 1884.

Walsh, Frank K. *Indian Battles Along the Rogue River, 1855-56*. Grants Pass, Ore.: Tecum-tom Publications, 1972.

Wilkes, Charles. *Narrative of the United States Exploring Expedition*, vol. 4. Philadelphia: Lea and Blanchard, 1845.

Wojcik, Donna M. *The Brazen Overlanders of 1845*. Portland, Ore.: Donna M. Wojcik, 1976.

Woodward, Walter Carlton. *The Rise and Early History of Political Parties in Oregon, 1843-1868*. Portland, Ore.: J.K. Gill Company, 1913.

Zucker, Jeff, Kay Hummel, and Bob Høgfoss. *Oregon Indians: Culture, History & Current Affairs*. Portland, Ore.: Western Imprints, 1983.

ARTICLES

Barlow, William. "Reminiscences of Seventy Years." *Oregon Historical Quarterly* 13 (1912).

Coan, C.F. "The Adoption of the Reservation Policy in Pacific Northwest." *Oregon Historical Quarterly* 23 (1922).

Colvig, William M. "Indian Wars of Southern Oregon." *Oregon Historical Quarterly* 4 (1903).

Davenport, T.W. "Recollections of an Indian Agent—III." *Oregon Historical Quarterly* 8 (1907).

Harper's Magazine, 13 (September 1856), New York.

Howell, John E. "Diary of an Immigrant of 1845." *Washington Historical Quarterly*, 3 (April 1907).

Lockley, Fred. "Recollections of Benjamin Franklin Bonney." *Oregon Historical Quarterly* 24 (March 1923).

Long, Mrs. S.A. "Mrs. Jesse Applegate." *Oregon Historical Quarterly* 9 (1908).

Nesmith, James W. "Reminiscences of the Indian War," *Oregon Historical Quarterly* 7 (1906).

Overland Monthly, October and November 1871, San Francisco.

Powell, Lawrence Clark. "Flumgudgeon Gazette in 1845 Antedated the Spectator." *Oregon Historical Quarterly* 41 (June 1940).

Robbins, Harvey. "Journal of Rogue River War, 1855." *Oregon Historical Quarterly* 34 (1933).

Rockwood, E. Ruth, ed. "Diary of Rev. George H. Atkinson, D.D., 1847-1858." *Oregon Historical Quarterly* 40 (September and December 1939).

Schafer, Joseph, ed. "Documents Relative to Warre and Vavasour's Military Reconnoissance in Oregon, 1845-6." *Oregon Historical Quarterly* 10 (1909).

Scott, Leslie M. "John Work's Journey from Fort Vancouver to Umpqua River, and Return, in 1834." *Oregon Historical Quarterly* 24 (1923).

Scott, Leslie M. "Report of Lieutenant Peel on Oregon in 1845-46." *Oregon Historical Quarterly* 29 (March 1928).

Snyder, Jacob. "The Diary of Jacob R. Snyder." *Quarterly of the Society of California Pioneers* (December 1931).

Spaid, Stanley Sheldon. "Life of General Joel Palmer." *Oregon Historical Quarterly* 55 (1954).

West, Oswald. "Famous Horses and Horsemen of the Pioneer Period." *Oregon Historical Quarterly* 46 (1945).

MANUSCRIPTS

Bayley, Betsey. "Letter of 1845." Overland Journeys Collection, MSS 1508, Oregon Historical Society (OHS).

Cayuse Indian War Claim Records, Accession number 89-A12, boxes 45-47, Military Department, Oregon State Archives, Salem.

Deady, Matthew. Matthew Deady Papers. MSS 48, OHS.

Doty, James. "Journal of Operations." MSS 1179, OHS, typescript from the original journal of James Doty as transcribed by William S. Lewis, Eastern Washington State Historical Society.

Field, James. "Crossing the Plains." MSS 520, OHS.

Findley, William G. "Diary, 1845-1847." MSS 494, OHS.

Flumgudgeon Gazette and Bumble Bee Budget. MSS 1176, OHS.

Garrison, A.E. MSS 1009, OHS.

Gilliam, Col. Cornelius. "Correspondence 1847-48." MSS 2205, OHS.

Grover, Lafayette. MSS 1069. OHS.

Jennings, Berryman. MSS 1181, OHS.

Lane, Joseph. Jospeh Lane Collection. Lilly Library, Indiana University, Bloomington.

——. Joseph Lane Papers. MSS 1146, OHS.

—— "Autobiography." Bancroft Library, University of California, Berkeley, P-8 43, microfilm.

Lehman, Florence Walls. "The Letters of Asahel Bush to Matthew P. Deady, 1851-1863." Portland, Reed College B.A. thesis, 1941.

Lyman, Horace Sumner. "Autobiography." MSS 722, OHS.

——. "Reminiscences of John T. Cox, of 1846." MSS 722, OHS.

Mulkey, Cyrenius. "Eighty-one Years of Frontier Life." MSS 981, OHS.

Palmer, General Joel. Palmer Papers. MSS 114, OHS. Includes interview with Hubert Howe Bancroft, Salem, Ore., 1878, copy; "Letters 1848-68"; and Palmer Diary. Palmer family papers, vertical file, Oregon Historical Society.

—— Correspondence. Special Collection Division [Palmer Collection], University of Oregon, Eugene.

Parker, Samuel. "Diary, 1845." Overland Journeys Collection, MSS 1508, OHS.

Raymond, W. W. W. W. Raymond Papers. MSS 555, OHS.

Spaid, Stanley Sheldon. "Joel Palmer and Indian Affairs in Oregon." Eugene, University of Oregon PH.D. thesis, 1950.

Stillwell, William Dunson. Military Collection, MSS 1514, OHS.

Walter, W. W. "Reminiscences of an Old 45er." MSS 739, OHS.

Index

337

338

Colophon

Design & Production
by OREGON HISTORICAL SOCIETY PRESS

Typesetting
In Bembo text type
by THE TYPEWORKS, Point Roberts, Washington

Printing & Binding
On 60 lb. Booktext Natural
by BOOKCRAFTERS, Chelsea, Michigan

Cover Color Separation
by SPECTRUM WEST, Beaverton, Oregon

Frontis Portrait
by KAREN BEYERS, Portland, Oregon

Maps
by MICHELE BORIS LYTLE, Portland, Oregon